P9-ARV-369

DEBATING DEMOCRACY

Joseph Pasztor

DEBATING DEMOCRACY

A Reader in American Politics

Fourth Edition

Bruce Miroff

STATE UNIVERSITY OF NEW YORK–ALBANY

Raymond Seidelman

SARAH LAWRENCE COLLEGE

Todd Swanstrom

SAINT LOUIS UNIVERSITY

Houghton Mifflin Company   Boston   New York

To our parents: Martin and Sophie Miroff, Herb and Thelma Seidelman, and Beatrice and Glenn Swanstrom

Editor-in-Chief: Jean L. Woy
Sponsoring Editor: Katherine Meisenheimer
Editorial Associate: Tonya Lobato
Project Editor: Jane Lee
Editorial Assistant: Talia Kingsbury
Associate Production/Design Coordinator: Christine Gervais
Manufacturing Manager: Florence Cadran
Marketing Manager: Nicola Poser

Cover Image: Copyright © Rommel/Masterfile. Capitol Building, Washington, DC, USA.

Text credits appear on p. 377.

Copyright © 2003 by Houghton Mifflin Company. All rights reserved.

No part of this work may be reproduced or transmitted in any form or by any means, electronic and mechanical, including photocopying and recording, or by any information storage and retrieval system without the prior written permission of the copyright owner unless such copying is expressly permitted by federal copyright law. With the exception of nonprofit transcription in Braille, Houghton Mifflin is not authorized to grant permission for further uses of copyrighted selections reprinted in this text without the permission of their owners. Permission must be obtained from the individual copyright owners as identified herein. Address requests for permission to make copies of Houghton Mifflin material to College Permissions, Houghton Mifflin Company, 222 Berkeley Street, Boston, MA 02116-3764.

Printed in the U.S.A.

Library of Congress Control Number: 2001099561

ISBN: 0-618-25108-1

23456789-CRS-06 05 04 03

However unwillingly a person who has a strong opinion may admit the possibility that his opinion may be false, he ought to be moved by the consideration that, however true it may be, if it is not fully, frequently, and fearlessly discussed, it will be held as a dead dogma, not as a living truth.

John Stuart Mill, *On Liberty* (1859)

C O N T E N T S

Wе have been very pleased by readers' and reviewers' enthusiastic reactions to the first three editions of *Debating Democracy*. They warmly endorsed our belief in the need for a reader for courses in American politics that makes democracy its unifying theme. Of course, Americans agree in the abstract about democracy, but in practice we often disagree about democracy's meaning and implications. To explore these crucial disagreements, the fourth edition is constructed around a series of debates about democracy in America. Two recent events that have critical implications for American democracy—the disputed presidential contest of 2000 and the terrorist strikes of September 11, 2001—provide a special focus for this edition.

Special Features of *Debating Democracy*

Debating Democracy is different from other readers in American politics. The selections in our reader are organized around a common theme. All the chapters address the meaning and improvement of American democracy. Thus, reading through the selections has a cumulative effect, helping students to think more clearly and deeply about democracy.

Our experience as teachers of introductory courses in American politics suggests that debate-type readers can leave students confused, wondering how to respond to a bewildering array of different arguments. Many students conclude that political debates are just a matter of opinion, that there is no cumulative knowledge generated by debating the issues. To prevent such confusion, we provide an Introduction, highly praised by reviewers of the first three editions, that gives students a framework for evaluating democratic debates. This framework is designed to help students develop their own political philosophies and critical abilities for analyzing political issues. In the end, we believe, engaging students in these democratic debates will help them to understand that democracy is a complex and contested idea and that although there is no One Truth, the search for democratic truths is well worth the effort.

In order to engage students in the search for democratic truths, we have included lively and clearly written selections from political leaders, journalists, and scholars. In each case we have chosen two contrasting views on a controversial topic. To help students in evaluating the selections, we introduce each debate with a short essay that places the issue in a meaningful context and alerts the reader to be on the lookout for contrasting values and hidden assumptions.

Debating Democracy seeks to generate further debate. After each set of selections we include questions that can be used by readers to analyze the issues or by teachers to spark class discussions. We end with suggested readings and web sites that students can use to pursue the topic further.

Each chapter in the book can be used as the basis for a structured in-class debate. Our own introductory lecture courses have discussion sections of ten to twenty students led by teaching assistants. The TA divides the class in two and assigns each group one side in the debate. The students are asked to meet outside of class and prepare their arguments based on the readings. A session of the discussion section is then devoted to a formal debate. We do two or three of these structured debates in the course of a semester. Students enjoy these debates and often report that this is the high point of the course for them.

Following the formal debates, each student is required to write a short paper setting out the arguments of her or his side and rebutting the arguments of the other side. We are convinced that this exercise helps students to achieve what is often an important goal in introductory American politics courses: improving writing skills. Requiring students to take a stand on a political issue and develop a coherent argument for their position in a thematic essay is an effective way, we believe, to teach writing.

Structure of *Debating Democracy*

Debating Democracy has been structured to fit with almost all introductory texts in American politics. We cover topics usually covered in an introductory text, but we have also included debates on civil society, political economy, and local democracy because we believe these are important subjects for understanding American democracy.

The editors of this book make no claim to being impartial observers of democratic debates. We support the extension of democratic decision making into broader spheres of the economy and society with greater emphasis on equality and community. Our participatory democratic inclinations are evident in our textbook, *The Democratic Debate: An Introduction to American Politics,* Third Edition (Houghton Mifflin, 2002).

Although we make no claim to impartiality, we have made every effort in the chapters that follow to select the strongest arguments on both sides of the issues. The reader can be used with any textbook in American government, no matter what the political inclinations of the professor. The reader can also stand by itself as an introduction to the critical issues facing American democracy at the beginning of the twenty-first century.

New to the Fourth Edition

The fourth edition contains fourteen new selections, about 40 percent of the book. Three of the new chapters concern the profound issues for American democracy raised by two extraordinary events that have occurred since we produced the previous edition: the presidential election of 2000 and the terrorist attacks of September 11, 2001.

There are five new chapters:

Chapter 4   Civil Society: Does America Face A Crisis in Civic Engagement?

Chapter 8   Public Opinion: The American People After September 11

Chapter 10 Political Parties and Elections: The 2000 Presidential Election and U.S. Democracy

Chapter 12 Local Democracy: Is Suburban Sprawl the Realization or Violation of Democratic Values?

Chapter 18 U.S. Foreign Policy: What Should It Be After September 11?

In addition, there are two new debates in existing chapters:

Chapter 9   The New Media and the Internet: Corporate Wasteland or Democratic Frontier?

Chapter 14 The Presidency: How Much Difference Does the Individual Make?

Many of the essays in the seven new chapters have been written by leading figures in political science (Robert Putnam, William Galston, Fred Greenstein, Stephen Skowronek, Benjamin Barber), law (Cass Sunstein, Lani Guinier), and journalism (David Brooks, Bill Moyers, Charles Krauthammer). While incorporating previously published materials, the new essays by Robert McChesney, Todd Swanstrom, and Stephen Skowronek have been expressly prepared for this book.

Acknowledgments

We are grateful to all of those who helped us to carry forward our original hopes for *Debating Democracy*. At SUNY, Albany, skillful research assistance was supplied by Molly Flynn, Paul Goggi, Timothy Gordinier, Christopher Latimer, Liu Runyu, Jordan Wishy, Christopher Witko, and Fred Wood. The folks at Houghton Mifflin—especially Tonya Lobato, Jane Lee, Katherine Meisenheimer, and Jean Woy—brought just the right blend of professional expertise and good cheer to the project.

The outside reviewers selected by Houghton Mifflin, whose names are listed in the following paragraphs, were of more than usual help. Their incisive suggestions led us to change some selections, add new subjects, and improve our pedagogical framework.

Six scholars provided helpful criticisms of the draft manuscript for the first edition: John L. Anderson, University of Nebraska at Kearney; Edmond Costantini, University of California at Davis; William R. Lund, University of Idaho; David J. Olson, University of Washington; Marvin L. Overby, University of Mississippi; and Gregory G. Rocha, University of Texas at El Paso.

The following individuals gave us valuable feedback in response to the first and second editions: Stephen C. Baker, Jacksonville University; Jennifer Disney, John Jay College of Criminal Justice; Dana K. Glencross, Oklahoma City Community College; Thomas Hensley, Kent State University; William J. Hughes, Southern Oregon University; Fredrick Paul Lee, Winona State University; Suzanne Marilley, Capital University; Noelle Norton, University of San Diego; Paula L. O'Loughlin, University of Minnesota at Morris; Larry Schwab, John Carroll University; Dennis Shea, State University of New York College at Oneonta; Kevin Smith, University of Nebraska, Lincoln; Linda O. Valenty, San Jose State University; Kenneth F. Warren, St. Louis University; and Stephen Wiener, University of California at Santa Barbara.

We are grateful to the following reviewers of the third edition who gave us valuable suggestions for this revision: Scott Adler, University of Colorado at Boulder; Matthew H. Bosworth, Winona State University; Thomas P. Dolan, Columbus State University; Keith Rollin Eakins, University of Central Oklahoma; Philip Meeks, Creighton University; Stuart W. Schulman, Drake University; James R. Simmons, University of Wisconsin–Oshkosh; Donna J. Swarthout, Montana State University; Robert C. Turner, Skidmore College; and Bruce Wallin, Northeastern University.

Finally, we continue to depend on the love, the support, and especially the patience of our families: Melinda, Nick, and Anna; Fay, Eva, and Rosa; Katie, Jessica, Madeleine, and Eleanore.

B. M.

R. S.

T. S.

DEBATING DEMOCRACY

How to Read
This Book

When we think of democratic debates, we often think of the debates that take place every four years between or among the leading candidates for president. Beginning with the 1960 Kennedy-Nixon debate, these nationally televised events have often been a crucial part of presidential campaigns. Presidential debates, however, are very different from the debates about the key issues facing American democracy that we have gathered together in this volume. A good way to understand this difference is to examine the first debate in the 2000 presidential campaign between Al Gore and George W. Bush.

A skilled debater with many decades of experience in federal goverment, Gore was widely expected to outshine the relatively inexperienced Bush, a man known for his lack of foreign policy experience and verbal gaffes. Indeed, immediately after the debate most commentators thought that Gore had won. Bush did do better than many people expected, showing, for example, that he could talk knowledgeably about foreign policy. But Gore frequently scored debater's points by using his knowledge of such complex issues as taxes and prescription drug plans. Gore came across as clearly more informed.

Within a few days, however, public opinion polls showed that Bush had in fact won with the voters. Most pundits had mistakenly judged the outcome like a college debate, deciding who had been most persuasive using facts and

1

logic. But the average voter was not primarily interested in who was the better debater but in who had the best character, temperament, and leadership qualities to be president.

Gore came across as a know-it-all who, instead of explaining his positions, lectured to the audience in a condescending manner. He appeared anxious to show off his knowledge and frequently broke the rules by interrupting Bush and the moderator, Jim Lehrer. Bush was more folksy and relaxed. Instead of explaining complex issues, Bush spent more time stressing his principles, criticizing those who "rely upon polls and focus groups." This meant that Bush often spoke in generalities, such as "End the bickering in Washington" or "Empower people in their own lives," but he nevertheless came across as more authentic than Gore. Bush's performance was reminiscent of Ronald Reagan's in his 1980 debates with Jimmy Carter. In those, too, commentators thought that Carter had prevailed, but Reagan's folksy charm won the day with the voters.

In presidential debates, the candidates frequently attack their opponents. In an issues debate, this is considered a logical fallacy (called the *ad hominem* fallacy, literally addressing the man instead of the issue). Because the issue in presidential debates is choosing a president, attacking your opponent's judgment or character is relevant. On this dimension, Bush clearly outshone Gore. In probably the most memorable exchange or the debate, Bush responded to Gore's attack on his tax cut as biased toward the rich by going on the attack. "Look, this is a man, he's got great numbers. He talks about numbers. I'm beginning to think not only did he invent the Internet, but he invented the calculator. It's fuzzy math. It's scaring—trying to scare people in the voting booth."

Instead of trying to persuade voters to change their positions on the issues, presidential candidates generally try to convince the voters that they are closest to the positions most voters already hold. Thoroughly briefed by pollsters about what the voters want to hear, each candidate, without appearing unprincipled, tries to mold his views to the undecided voters—especially the undecided voters in key states where the electoral votes are still up for grabs. Thus, Bush downplayed his views on abortion and Gore kept repeating his support for the middle class.

The debates we have gathered together in *Debating Democracy* are far different from presidential debates. In this book, each chapter addresses a central issue in American democracy and the debaters focus exclusively on the issue. The personality or background of the debaters is irrelevant. In the real world no debate is perfectly free and fair, if only because one side has more resources to make itself heard. Nevertheless, we can approximate the conditions of a free and fair debate, as we have attempted to do in the pages that follow. We present arguments by authors who are experts on the issues. They concentrate on the issue at hand, not on their image. Each gets equal time. For the most part, they avoid begging (avoiding) the question, mudslinging, or manipulating stereotypes. The contest is decided not by who has the most money or who projects the best image but by who has the best arguments using logical reasoning and facts.

Political debates are not just methods for acquiring information in elections; they are the heart of a democratic system. In a true democracy, debates do not just concern who will be elected to office every few years; they address the issues of everyday life, and they occur every day, extending from television studios to dinner tables, from shop floors to classrooms. Even though political debates can become heated because they involve our most deeply held beliefs, democracies do not deny anyone the right to disagree. In a democracy we recognize that no one has a monopoly on the truth. Debates are not tangential to democracy; they are central to its meaning. "Agreeing to disagree" is the essence of democracy.

Debate as the Lifeblood of Democracy

Debate as dialogue, not demagoguery, is the lifeblood of democracy. Democracy is the one form of government that requires leaders to give reasons for their decisions and defend them in public. Some theorists argue that free and fair deliberation, or debate, is not only a good method for arriving at democratic decisions but is also the essence of democracy itself.[1]

Debate is crucial to a democracy not just because it leads to better decisions but because it helps to create better citizens. Democratic debate requires that we be open-minded, that we listen to both sides. This process of listening attentively to different sides and examining their assumptions helps us to clarify and critically examine our own political values. As the nineteenth-century British political philosopher John Stuart Mill wrote:

> So essential is this discipline [attending equally and impartially to both sides] to a real understanding of moral and human subjects that, if opponents of all-important truths do not exist, it is indispensable to imagine them and supply them with the strongest arguments which the most skillful devil's advocate can conjure up.[2]

According to Mill, if we are not challenged in our beliefs, they become dead dogmas instead of living truths. (Consider what happened to communist ideologies in Eastern Europe, where they were never tested in public debate.) Once we have honed our skills analyzing political debates, we are less vulnerable to being manipulated by demagogues. By hearing the rhetoric and manipulation in others' speech, we are better able to purge it from our own.[3] Instead of basing our beliefs on unconscious prejudices or ethnocentric values, we consciously and freely choose our political beliefs.

In order for a debate to be truly democratic it must be free and fair. In a free and fair debate the only power exerted is the power of reason. We are moved to adopt a position not by force but by the persuasiveness of the argument. In a democratic debate proponents argue for their positions not by appealing to this or that private interest but by appealing to the public interest, the values and aspirations we share as a democratic people. Democracy is not simply a process for adding up the individual preferences that citizens bring with them to the issues to see which side wins. In a democratic debate people are required to frame their arguments in terms of the public interest.[4] And as citizens deliberate about the public interest through debates, they are changed.[5]

In this book we have gathered two contrasting arguments on a range of the most pressing issues facing democracy in the United States. The reader's task is to compare the two positions and decide which argument is most persuasive. After reading the selections, readers may feel frustrated seeing that opponents can adopt diametrically opposed stands on the same issue depending on their point of view. It may seem as if political positions on the issues are simply based on personal values, as if political judgments are simply a matter of opinion. Being able to understand divergent viewpoints other than our own, however, is the beginning of political toleration and insight. There is no One Truth on political issues that can be handed to us on a platter by experts. Nevertheless, making public choices is *not* simply a matter of opinion. There are fundamental political values that Americans subscribe to and that we struggle to achieve in our political decisions. Political stands are not just a matter of opinion, because some decisions will promote the democratic public interest better than others.

The purpose of this introduction is to give you, the reader, tools for evaluating democratic debates. The agreements and disagreements in American politics are not random; they exhibit patterns, and understanding these patterns can help orient you in the debates. In the pages that follow we draw a preliminary map of the territory of democratic debates in the United States to guide the reader in negotiating this difficult terrain. Your goal should not be just to take a stand on this or that issue but to clarify your own values and chart your own path in pursuit of the public interest of American democracy.

Democratic Debates: Conflict Within Consensus

In order for a true debate to occur, there have to be both consensus and conflict. If there were no consensus, or agreement, on basic values or standards of evaluation, the debaters would talk past each other, like two people speaking foreign tongues. Without some common standard of evaluation, there would be no way to settle the debate. But, if there were no fundamental disagreements, no conflict, the debate would be trivial and boring. Factual disagreements are not enough. Consider a debate between two political scientists about this question: How many people voted in the last election? The debate might be informative, but few people would care about the outcome because it does not engage deeply held values or beliefs. Factual disputes are important, but they rarely decide important political debates. Democratic debates are interesting and important when they engage us in struggles over the meaning and application of our basic values.

Judging a political debate is tricky. Political reasoning is different from economic reasoning or individual rational decision making. Political debates are rarely settled by toting up the costs and benefits of alternative courses of action and choosing the one that maximizes benefits over costs. It is not that costs and benefits do not matter; rather, what we see as benefits or costs depends on how we frame the issue. In political debates each side tries to get the audience to see the issue its way, to frame the issue in language that reinforces its position. On the issue of abortion, for example, is your position best described as pro-choice or pro-life? Should programs to help minorities be characterized as affirmative action or reverse discrimination? Clearly, the terms we use to describe a political position make a difference. Each term casts light on the issue in a different way, highlighting different values that are at stake in the controversy. The terms used to describe the abortion issue, for example, emphasize either the right of an unborn fetus or the right of a woman to control her body.

As these examples illustrate, in political debates the outcome frequently hinges on the standard of evaluation itself, on what values and principles will be applied to the decision at hand. In political debates the issue is always what is good for the community as a whole, the public interest, not just some segment of the community. The selections that follow are all examples of debates over the meaning of the public interest in American democracy. In the United States, political debates, with the notable exception of slavery, have been characterized by consensus on basic democratic principles *combined with* conflicts over how best to realize those principles in practice.

As conflicts within a consensus, democratic debates in this country go back to its founding and the original debate over the U.S. Constitution more than two hundred years ago. Americans worship the Constitution as an almost divinely inspired document that embodies the highest ideals of democracy. Yet throughout history Americans have disagreed vehemently on what the Constitution means. This is not surprising. The Constitution was born as much in conflict and compromise as in consensus. In the words of former Supreme Court Justice William J. Brennan Jr., the framers "hid their differences in cloaks of generality."[6] The general language of the Constitution left many conflicts over specifics to later generations. The Constitution, for example, gave the federal government the power to provide for the "general welfare," but we have been debating ever since about what this should include. Thus, the Constitution is both a source of consensus, by embodying our ideals, and a source of conflict, by failing to specify exactly how those ideals should be applied in practice.[7]

Three Sources of Conflict

Behind the words of the Constitution lie three ideals that supposedly animate our system of government: *democracy, freedom,* and *equality.* Americans agree that we should have a government of, by, and for the people (as President Lincoln so eloquently put it), a government that treats everybody equally, and a government that achieves the maximum level of freedom consistent with an or-dered society. These ideals seem simple, but they are not. While Americans are united in their aspirations, they are divided in their visions of how to achieve those aspirations.[8] Democracy, freedom, and equality are what political theorists call "essentially contested concepts."[9]

I. Democracy

Democracy comes from the Greek words *demos,* meaning "the people," and *kratein,* meaning "to rule." Hence, democracy means, simply, "rule by the people." Americans agree that democracy is the best form of government. They disagree, however, on what this means.

Elite (Limited) Democracy   For some, democracy is basically a method for making decisions. According to this minimalist definition of democracy, a decision is democratic if it is made according to the criterion of majority rule. Of course, there are other requirements of democratic decision making, such as open nominations for office and free speech, but once the basic conditions have been met, the resulting decision is by definition democratic.

Following this limited definition, the most important characteristic of a democracy is free and fair elections for choosing government officials. Democracy basically means the ability of citizens to choose their leaders.[10] Elites compete for the votes to win office, but once in office, they have substantial autonomy to rule as they see fit. According to this view, ultimate power rests in the hands of the people at election time, but between elections they cede decision-making authority to elites who have the expertise and experience to make the right decisions in a technologically complex and dangerous world. We call this school of democracy *elite democracy.*[11]

Elite democrats favor a minimal definition of democracy not because it is ideal but because it is the only type of democracy that is achievable in large modern nation-states. Thus, as you will see in the selection by John Mueller in Chapter 2, elite democrats question many of the precepts of participatory democracy as myths. By contrast, Paul Rogat Loeb maintains that active citizens who sacrifice for the common good are possible, even in our flawed democratic system.

Popular (Expansive) Democracy   Opponents of elite democrats adopt a more demanding definition of democracy. They argue that we cannot call a decision democratic just because it came out of a democratic process. Democratic decisions must also respect certain values such as tolerance, a respect for individual freedom, and the attainment of a basic level of social and economic equality. If the majority rules in such a way as to violate people's rights or policies result in tremendous inequalities of wealth, the system cannot be called democratic. For this group, democracy means more than a political system with free and fair elections; it means an economy and society that reflect a democratic desire for equality and respect for differences.

For adherents of an expansive definition of democracy, democracy means more than going to the polls every few years; it means citizens participating in the institutions of society, including corporations, unions, and neighborhood associations. In Chapter 5, Samuel Bowles and Richard Edwards represent this position, calling for expanding democratic decision making into the economy. Countering the view of elite democrats that people are not interested in or capable of governing effectively, those who advocate a more participatory system argue that in an atmosphere of toleration, respect, and rough equality, citizens are capable of governing themselves fairly and effectively. We call those who advocate a more participatory conception of democracy *popular democrats.*[12]

II. Freedom

Most of us have a basic intuitive idea of freedom: to be free means being able to do what we want, without someone telling us what to do. Any time we are forced to do something against our will by somebody else, our freedom is reduced. Freedom seems like an exceedingly simple idea. Once again, however, we find that there is plenty of room for disagreement.

Negative (Freedom From)   The central issue for freedom is deciding where to draw the line between the power of the group and the freedom of the individual. In other words, how far should government power extend, for any time the government imposes a tax or passes a law, it limits someone's freedom? In a justly famous essay, *On Liberty,* John Stuart Mill argues that the only justification for government power over individuals is self-protection: "[T]he only purpose for which power can be rightfully exercised over any member of a civilized community, against his will, is to prevent harm to others."[13] In other words, your freedom to swing your arm ends where my nose begins.

Under Mill's view, the purpose of government is to maximize individual freedom. Freedom is understood negatively, as freedom from external constraints. Since government actions always reduce individual freedom, their only justification is to counter other restrictions on our freedom, as when the government passes laws against robbery or assault. Clearly, this view places severe limits on what democracies can legitimately do, even under the principle of majority rule. If the majority passes laws that restrict someone's freedom, without those laws being justified by the principle of self-protection, then it is no longer a true democracy because the laws violate a basic democratic value.

Positive (Freedom To)   In contrast to the negative conception of freedom— freedom *from*—there is an equally compelling positive definition of freedom— freedom *to.*[14] The positive conception of freedom recognizes that in order to be free, to exercise meaningful choice, we need to possess certain resources and have certain capacities. Education, for example, increases our freedom because it increases our ability to imagine alternatives and find solutions to problems. Freedom, therefore, is not simply the absence of external coercion but freedom to get an education, travel to foreign countries, or receive expert medical care.

A positive conception of freedom justifies an expanded role for government and for citizens acting together in other ways. When government taxes us, it reduces negative freedom, but when it uses the money to build a highway or a public library, it gives us a greater positive freedom to do things we previously were unable to do. Under the positive conception of freedom, the scope of freedom is increased when the capacity of individuals to act is enhanced by government action, such as protecting the right of workers to join a union (thus giving workers the ability to bargain over wages and working conditions) or requiring buildings to be handicapped accessible (thus giving the handicapped access to places they were previously excluded from).[15]

Whether one subscribes to a positive or a negative conception of freedom will make a big difference in one's political philosophy. The negative conception of freedom is conducive to limited government and highlights the more acquisitive and competitive side of human nature. Under this view, the expansion of power in one part of society necessarily leads to a reduction of freedom in some other part of society. The selection by Milton Friedman on political economy in Chapter 5 is based on a negative conception of freedom. Friedman warns that too much government leads to coercion and a reduction in individual freedom, which is maximized by free competition in the marketplace. The positive conception of freedom emphasizes the more cooperative side of human beings. According to this conception, government as a form of social cooperation can actually expand the realm of freedom by bringing more and more matters of social importance under human control.

III. Equality

Like democracy and freedom, equality seems an exceedingly simple idea. Equality marches forward under banners that read, "Treat everybody equally" or "Treat like cases alike." These are not working definitions, however, but political rhetoric that hides serious ambiguities in the concept of equality. In truth, how we apply the idea of equality depends on how we envision it in a broader context.

Process Orientation   For some people, equality is basically generated by a fair process. So long as competition is fair—everybody has an equal opportunity to succeed—then the results are fair, even if the resulting distribution is highly unequal. Inequalities that reflect differences among people in intelligence, talent, ambition, or strength are said to be legitimate. Inequalities that result from biases in the rules of competition are unjustified and should be eliminated.

The process orientation toward equality is best reflected in free market theory. According to market theory, the distribution of income and wealth is fair if it is the result of a process of voluntary contracting among responsible adults. As long as the requirements for a free market are met (perfect competition, free flow of information, no coercion or manipulation, and so on), no one exerts power over the market and market outcomes are just and fair. Market theorists, like Milton Friedman, stress equal opportunity, not equal results. The role of government, in this view, is to serve as a neutral umpire, enforcing the rules and treating everyone alike.[16]

Results Orientation   Opponents argue that if the government treats everybody equally, the results will still be highly unequal because people start the race from very different positions. Some have a head start in the race, while others enter with serious handicaps. To ignore these differences is to perpetuate inequalities. Treating unequals equally is, in effect, unequal. The French writer Anatole France discussed what he called "the majestic egalitarianism of the law, which forbids rich and poor alike to sleep under bridges, to beg in the streets, and to steal bread."[17] Even though the law formally treats everyone alike, it is clear that only certain people will suffer the consequences.

Those who take a results orientation toward equality don't deny the importance of equal opportunity but argue that equal opportunity means the ability of everyone to participate equally in the decisions that affect their lives. These democrats charge that their opponents elevate the individual over the community and privileged elites over ordinary citizens, as if the wagon train could make it to the promised land only if some of the weak and frail were left behind alongside the trail. Those who support a results orientation argue that it is possible for everyone to make it together.

Those who support a results orientation do not believe in a strict leveling of society but argue that certain resources are necessary for people to participate fully in society and realize their potential. In other words, government cannot just stand aside and watch people compete; it must establish the conditions for community and equal participation. At a minimum, many would argue, adequate nutrition, good education, safety, and decent health care are necessary for a fulfilling life.

American Ideologies: Patterns in Political Stands

With two contrasting positions on each of the three issues just discussed— democracy, equality, and freedom—there are eight possible combinations of issue positions. Stands on the three issues are not random, however; they correlate in ways that generate distinct patterns characteristic of American political ideologies.

One of the clearest ideological distinctions in American politics is between those who favor markets and those who favor government. As Charles Lindblom has noted, "Aside from the difference between despotic and libertarian governments, the greatest distinction between one government and another is in the degree to which market replaces government or government replaces market."[18] A central issue in American politics is where to draw the line between the public and private sectors. If you believe that the market is basically free and fair, then you will support only a limited role for government. Generally, those who favor the market subscribe to a negative conception of freedom and a process orientation toward equality. This position corresponds to what we call *free market conservatism.* If, however, you believe that markets are penetrated by relations of power and are prone to discrimination, then you will support an expanded role for political participation and democratic government. Those who advocate an increased role for government generally subscribe to a positive conception of freedom and favor a results orientation toward equality. These views correspond to what is commonly called *liberalism.*

Usually, we think of social conservatives as adhering to a more elite view of democracy and social liberals as being more inclined toward popular democracy. In the 1960s, for example, *left-wing populists* supported maximum feasible participation by poor people to solve poverty and advocated democratic control of corporations. In recent years, however, because they support a large role for the federal government in Washington, D.C., liberals have been accused by conservatives of being, in effect, elitist. A *right-wing populist* movement has arisen that combines popular democratic appeals with a negative conception of individual freedom and a process approach to equality, opposing the redistribution of wealth through government. To add to the complexity, however, right-wing populists do not always favor limiting the role of government. The *religious right* generally wants the government to interfere less in the economy but more in society—exerting more democratic control over moral issues, such as abortion and pornography.

Although distinct patterns appear in American politics on the issues of democracy, freedom, and equality, they are not fixed in stone. It is possible to mix and match different positions in putting together your own political philosophy. In developing your own political philosophy, you will need to address a fundamental question: what are human beings capable of; that is, what is your conception of human nature?

Human Nature: The Big Debate

Throughout history political philosophers have debated different conceptions of human nature. Human nature is the clay out of which all political systems must be constructed. The nature of this clay, its elasticity or hardness, its ability to assume different shapes and hold them, largely determines what we can and cannot do in politics. Since the original debate over the U.S. Constitution, Americans have disagreed about human nature and therefore about politics.

The Private View   Many argue that Americans are quintessentially individualistic, well suited to the marketplace and private pursuits but not well suited to democratic citizenship. The framers of the Constitution, the Federalists, argued that the common people were self-interested and passionate creatures who should not be entrusted with all of the reins of government. Thus, as you will see in Chapter 1, James Madison argues in "Federalist No. 10" that the greatest danger in a democracy is the tyranny of the majority, especially the taking away of the property of wealthy elites by the majority of common people. Madison recommended various checks on majority rule that would guarantee the rights of minorities and give elites substantial autonomy to rule in the public interest.

This view of human nature is reflected in contemporary debates. In the United States the debate shifts from human nature to the nature of Americans as a people and whether we are different from other people. According to the theory of exceptionalism, Americans are more individualistic and self-interested than other people.[19] As a nation of immigrants, we fled feudal systems and traditional cultures in search of greater freedom and assimilated into an American value system that stressed upward mobility through individual effort. The pursuit of fortune in the marketplace is the special genius of Americans. Whether this is good or bad depends on your view of markets and governments.

The Social View　During the debate over the Constitution in the 1780s, a group of dissenters, the Anti-federalists, argued that the Constitution placed too many limits on citizen participation. (We have included a selection by the Anti-federalist Brutus in Chapter 1.) The Anti-federalists argued that the common people could overcome or check their selfish inclinations through democratic participation and education in civic virtue. As much power as possible, therefore, should be placed in the hands of the people at the grassroots level. The main threat to democracy, Anti-federalists believed, came not from the tyranny of the majority but from power-hungry elites. The best way to protect against elite tyranny was to have the people participate directly in deciding important issues. The Anti-federalists founded the tradition of popular (expansive) democracy that is still alive in the United States.

Even today, when Americans seem caught up in acquisitive pursuits and politics seems so mean-spirited, some observers argue that there are important sources of social commitment in American culture. An influential book by Robert Bellah and colleagues, *Habits of the Heart,* argues that Americans are attached to powerful civic traditions that pull us out of our individualistic orientations. These civic traditions are rooted in religion and republicanism, both of which emphasize commitments to public service. Indeed, Americans exhibit lively commitments to grassroots participation and public service.

Conclusion: A Guide to Critical Thinking

Everyone has a political philosophy. Whether we recognize it or not, we bring certain assumptions about democracy, freedom, equality, and human nature to political debates. The goal is not to give up these assumptions but to convert them from unconscious prejudices into carefully chosen elements of a political philosophy. A good way to develop a thoughtful political philosophy is to analyze political debates like those included here. Clever debaters, for example, will appear as if they are supporting equality in general, but in order to make their argument work, they must adopt one conception of equality over another. Readers must get behind the rhetoric and evaluate these assumptions, as well as the logic and evidence of the argument itself.

As a guide to critical thinking, we suggest that readers keep in mind five questions and evaluate the evidence that supports their answers. (Some questions may not apply to some selections.)

1. What is the author's concept of democracy, elite (limited) or popular (expansive)?
2. What is the author's concept of freedom, negative (freedom from) or positive (freedom to)?
3. What is the author's concept of equality—process or results?
4. How would you classify each author's ideology?
5. What concept of human nature, individualist or social, lies behind the author's argument?

In conclusion, it often may seem as if Americans disagree so much (Republicans versus Democrats, conservatives versus liberals, populists versus elitists) that our society will fly apart in conflict. But there is one thing that finally does unite us: the belief that open and public debate is the best, in fact the only, democratic way to settle our differences.

NOTES

1. See Jon Elster, ed., *Deliberative Democracy* (New York: Cambridge University Press, 1998). The German political theorist Jürgen Habermas has spent many years developing a theory of the ideal speech situation as the foundation of democracy. See especially his *The Theory of Communicative Action,* 2 vols. (Boston: Beacon Press, 1984–1987).

2. John Stuart Mill, *On Liberty,* ed. and with an introduction by Currin V. Shields (Indianapolis, Ind.: Bobbs-Merrill, 1956), p. 46.

3. See Stephen L. Esquith, *Intimacy and Spectacle: Liberal Theory as Political Education* (Ithaca, N.Y.: Cornell University Press, 1994).

4. Amy Gutmann and Dennis Thompson call this the principle of reciprocity—that in a democratic debate citizens appeal to reasons that can be mutually acceptable to other citizens. See *Democracy and Disagreement* (Cambridge, Mass.: Harvard University Press, 1996).

5. Joshua Cohen, "Deliberation and Democratic Legitimacy," in *The Good Polity: Normative Analysis of the State* (Oxford: Basil Blackwell, 1989), p. 29.

6. Justice William J. Brennan Jr., "Federal Judges Properly and Inevitably Make Law Through 'Loose' Constitutional Construction," in *Debating American Government,* ed. Peter Woll (2d ed.; Glenview, Ill.: Scott, Foresman, 1988), p. 338.

7. It is neither possible nor desirable for a constitution to specify every application. If it did, it would be a rigid constitution that would be incapable of adapting to new conditions.

8. The following discussion of the sources of democratic disagreements in the United States draws heavily on Deborah A. Stone, *Political Paradox: The Art of Political Decision Making* (New York: Norton, 1997); and Frances Moore Lappé, *Rediscovering America's Values* (New York: Ballantine Books, 1989).

9. For an insightful discussion of essentially contested concepts, see William E. Connolly, *The Terms of Political Discourse* (2d ed.; Princeton, N.J.: Princeton University Press, 1983).

10. For the most famous definition of democracy along these lines, see Joseph A. Schumpeter, *Capitalism, Socialism, and Democracy* (3d ed.; New York: Harper, 1950), p. 269.

11. For elaboration on the concepts of elite and popular democracy, see Bruce Miroff, Raymond Seidelman, and Todd Swanstrom, *The Democratic Debate: An Introduction to American Politics* (3d ed.; Boston: Houghton Mifflin, 2002).

12. Robert A. Dahl is the most influential contemporary political scientist who has written on the ideas of elite and popular democracy. Dahl began his career by defending a version of elite democratic theory in *A Preface to Democratic Theory* (Chicago: University of Chicago Press, 1956) and *Who Governs? Democracy and Power in an American City* (New Haven, Conn.: Yale University Press, 1961). In later works, Dahl shifted dramatically to a more popular democratic position. See *A Preface to Economic Democracy* (Berkeley and Los Angeles: University of California Press, 1985); *Democracy and Its Critics* (New Haven, Conn.: Yale University Press, 1989); and *How Democratic Is the American Constitution?* (New Haven: Yale University Press, 2001).

13. Mill, *On Liberty*, p. 13.

14. The classic statement on positive and negative freedom is Isaiah Berlin's "Two Concepts of Liberty," in *Four Essays on Liberty* (New York: Oxford University Press, 1969), pp. 118–172.

15. For an eloquent defense of a positive conception of freedom, see President Franklin D. Roosevelt's speech to Congress on "An Economic Bill of Rights," in *Documents of American History*, ed. Henry Steele Commager (New York: Appleton-Century-Crofts, 1963), Vol. 2, pp. 483–485.

16. One of the best statements of a process orientation toward equality is Robert Nozick, *Anarchy, State, and Utopia* (New York: Basic Books, 1974).

17. *The Oxford Dictionary of Quotations* (3d ed.; Oxford: Oxford University Press, 1979), p. 217.

18. Charles Lindblom, *Politics and Markets: The World's Political-Economic Systems* (New York: Basic Books, 1977), p. ix.

19. For an influential statement on American exceptionalism, see Louis Hartz, *The Liberal Tradition in American Thought* (New York: Harcourt, Brace, 1955).

1

The Founding: Debating the Constitution

Although Americans relish political controversy in the present, we project onto the distant past of our nation's origins a more dignified political consensus. The founders of our republic—Washington, Adams, Jefferson, Hamilton, Madison—are cast in stone monuments and treated as political saints. Their ideas are invoked as hallowed truths that should inspire us. Seldom are these ideas treated as arguments that we should ponder and debate.

In fact, consensus was not the hallmark of the era in which the American republic was founded. Passionate political controversies raged during the American Revolution and its aftermath. These controversies ranged over the most basic issues of political life. The most profound was the debate over the ratification of the Constitution. The supporters of the Constitution, known as Federalists, and its opponents, known as Anti-federalists, disagreed over what kind of a republic Americans should have. Although their debate took place over two hundred years ago, it still illuminates the core dilemmas of our democratic society.

The readings that follow highlight some of the fundamental issues debated by Federalists and Anti-federalists. They pit the greatest thinker among the Federalists, James Madison, against a New York Anti-federalist who used the pseudonym Brutus in an argument over the appropriate scale of democratic political life. (Scholars are not absolutely certain who Brutus was; the most likely candidate is Robert Yates, a New York judge. The pseudonym, by recalling the Roman republican who killed the tyrant Julius Caesar, evokes the threat allegedly posed by the Constitution to republican liberty.)

In his classic essay "Federalist No. 10," Madison favors the large, national republic established by the Constitution over small republics (state governments). In small republics, Madison warns, selfish factions can attain majority status and will use their power over the government to oppress minorities (such as the wealthy or those who hold unorthodox religious beliefs). Small republics thus allow the worst qualities in human nature to prevail: they allow irrational passion to overwhelm reasoned deliberation and injustice to supplant the public good.

The large republic created by the new Constitution, Madison prophesies, will be more rational and more just. Elected in large districts, representatives will likely be the most-distinguished and patriotic citizens, and they will "refine and enlarge the public views" by filtering out the most selfish and shortsighted popular impulses. There will also be a greater diversity of factions in the large republic, making it unlikely that a majority can come together except on the basis of the common good. In Madison's essay, the chief threat to republican liberty comes, ironically, from the people themselves. His solution is to create a large republic in which the people will be divided into so many different interest groups that they can do little harm, while a small number of decision makers at the top take care of the common needs.

Brutus's essay (the first in a series that he wrote) takes issue with Madison on every count. He predicts that the large republic established by the Constitution will be run by aristocratic rulers who will eagerly expand their powers and oppress the common people. The greater distance from voters that Madison thinks will promote deliberation and public spirit in representatives will instead, Brutus argues, foster corruption and self-seeking in them. The diversity of the large republic is also, for Brutus, an unwelcome development since it will increase selfish factionalism, conflict, and stalemate.

Whereas Madison sees small republics as scenes of turbulence and misery, Brutus portrays them in a favorable light. In the smaller political scale of a state, the people will share common economic and social characteristics. Electoral districts will be smaller, so voters will personally know and trust their representatives and these representatives in turn will mirror their constituents' values and sentiments. Rather than breeding tyrannical majorities, small republics, as Brutus depicts them, educate law-abiding and virtuous citizens. In sum, Brutus rests his political hopes on the mass of ordinary people in the small republic, whose political impulses Madison fears, while directing his criticisms against a national elite, to whom Madison looks for wise political rule.

Anti-federalist fears that the Constitution would create an oppressive government, fatal to republican liberty, strike us today as grossly exaggerated. Yet in at least one respect these fears were fortunate—they helped produce the Bill of Rights. Initially, Federalists such as Madison and his collaborator on *The Federalist Papers,* Alexander Hamilton, claimed that a national bill of rights was both unnecessary and undesirable. By establishing a national government that possessed only enumerated, limited powers, they insisted, the Constitution had not granted any authority to invade the liberties and rights of the people; but if a list of particular rights was nonetheless appended to the Constitution, it might imply that the government *could* invade rights that had not been listed. These arguments were brushed aside by the Anti-federalists, who continued to argue that without specific guarantees the liberties for which Americans had fought in the Revolution might be usurped by a government of their own creation. To conciliate the Anti-federalists and win greater public support for the new Constitution, Madison dropped his objections and took the lead in pushing for the Bill of Rights in the first Congress.

Although Federalists and Anti-federalists could ultimately find common ground in the Bill of Rights, the philosophical and political differences between them remained profound. Their disagreements began the American debate between elite democracy and popular democracy. Nowhere is this more evident than in the contrast between Madison's reliance on a deliberative elite and Brutus's regard for the capacities of ordinary citizens. But it can also be seen in the difference between Madison's belief that liberty will inevitably produce inequality of property and Brutus's belief that in a small republic large-scale inequalities can be avoided.

The Federalists and Anti-federalists debated basic questions about democracy, and their disagreements still echo in our politics today. Thinking about the issues in their debate can help to clarify your own perspective toward democracy in the United States. Do you believe, with Madison, that it is only at the national level that selfish majorities can be blocked and government policies can be framed by deliberative and public-spirited representatives? Do you believe, with Brutus, that we should prefer state and local governments in order to promote greater civic participation and to enhance the trust between representatives and their constituents? Even more fundamentally, do you agree with Madison that ordinary citizens are too uninformed and self-seeking to be trusted with great political influence and that decisions are best left to elected representatives who can "refine and enlarge" what the people think? Or do you agree with Brutus that elites pose the greater danger to democracy and that democracy flourishes only when conditions are established that encourage ordinary citizens to involve themselves in the search for the public good?

Federalist No. 10

JAMES MADISON

Among the numerous advantages promised by a well-constructed Union, none deserves to be more accurately developed than its tendency to break and control the violence of faction.[1] The friend of popular governments never finds himself so much alarmed for their character and fate as when he contemplates their propensity to this dangerous vice. He will not fail, therefore, to set a due value on any plan which, without violating the principles to which he is attached, provides a proper cure for it. The instability, injustice, and confusion introduced into the public councils have, in truth, been the mortal diseases under which popular governments have everywhere perished, as they continue to be the favorite and fruitful topics from which the adversaries to liberty derive their most specious declamations. The valuable improvements made by the American constitutions on the popular models, both ancient and modern, cannot certainly be too much admired; but it would be an unwarrantable partiality to contend that they have as effectually obviated the danger on this side, as was wished and expected. Complaints are everywhere heard from our most considerate and virtuous citizens, equally the friends of public and private faith and of public and personal liberty, that our governments are too unstable, that the public good is disregarded in the conflicts of rival parties, and that measures are too often decided, not according to the rules of justice and the rights of the minor party, but by the superior force of an interested and overbearing majority. However anxiously we may wish that these complaints had no foundation, the evidence of known facts will not permit us to deny that they are in some degree true. It will be found, indeed, on a candid review of our situation, that some of the distresses under which we labor have been erroneously charged on the operation of our governments; but it will be found, at the same time, that other causes will not alone account for many of our heaviest misfortunes; and, particularly, for that prevailing and increasing distrust of public engagements and alarm for private rights which are echoed from one end of the continent to the other. These must be chiefly, if not wholly, effects of the unsteadiness and injustice with which a factious spirit has tainted our public administration.

---

1. In modern terms, both interest groups and political parties are examples of Madison's factions. Note that by the definition Madison offers later, no faction can legitimately claim to represent the public interest.

By a faction I understand a number of citizens, whether amounting to a majority or minority of the whole, who are united and actuated by some common impulse of passion, or of interest, adverse to the rights of other citizens, or to the permanent and aggregate interests of the community.

There are two methods of curing the mischiefs of faction: the one, by removing its causes; the other, by controlling its effects.

There are again two methods of removing the causes of faction: the one, by destroying the liberty which is essential to its existence; the other, by giving to every citizen the same opinions, the same passions, and the same interests.

It could never be more truly said than of the first remedy that it was worse than the disease. Liberty is to faction what air is to fire, an aliment without which it instantly expires. But it could not be a less folly to abolish liberty, which is essential to political life, because it nourishes faction than it would be to wish the annihilation of air, which is essential to animal life, because it imparts to fire its destructive agency.

The second expedient is as impracticable as the first would be unwise. As long as the reason of man continues fallible, and he is at liberty to exercise it, different opinions will be formed. As long as the connection subsists between his reason and his self-love, his opinions and his passions will have a reciprocal influence on each other; and the former will be objects to which the latter will attach themselves. The diversity in the faculties of men, from which the rights of property originate, is not less an insuperable obstacle to a uniformity of interests. The protection of these faculties is the first object of government. From the protection of different and unequal faculties of acquiring property, the possession of different degrees and kinds of property immediately results; and from the influence of these on the sentiments and views of the respective proprietors ensues a division of the society into different interests and parties.

The latent causes of faction are thus sown in the nature of man; and we see them everywhere brought into different degrees of activity, according to the different circumstances of civil society. A zeal for different opinions concerning religion, concerning government, and many other points, as well of speculation as of practice; an attachment to different leaders ambitiously contending for pre-eminence and power; or to persons of other descriptions whose fortunes have been interesting to the human passions, have, in turn, divided mankind into parties, inflamed them with mutual animosity, and rendered them much more disposed to vex and oppress each other than to co-operate for their common good. So strong is this propensity of mankind to fall into mutual animosities that where no substantial occasion presents itself the most frivolous and fanciful distinctions have been sufficient to kindle their unfriendly passions and excite their most violent conflicts. But the most common and durable source of factions has been the various and unequal distribution of property. Those who hold and those who are without property have ever formed distinct interests in society. Those who are creditors, and those who are debtors, fall under a like discrimination. A landed interest, a manufacturing interest, a mercantile interest, a moneyed interest, with many lesser interests, grow up of necessity in civilized nations, and divide them into different classes, actuated by different sentiments and views. The regulation of these various and interfering interests forms the principal task of modern legislation and involves the spirit of party and faction in the necessary and ordinary operations of government.

No man is allowed to be a judge in his own cause, because his interest would certainly bias his judgment, and, not improbably, corrupt his integrity. With equal, nay with greater reason, a body of men are unfit to be both judges and parties at the same time; yet what are many of the most important acts of legislation but so many judicial determinations, not indeed concerning the rights of single persons, but concerning the rights of large bodies of citizens? And what are the different classes of legislators but advocates and parties to the causes which they determine? Is a law proposed concerning private debts? It is a question to which the creditors are parties on one side and the debtors on the other. Justice ought to hold the balance between them. Yet the parties are, and must be, themselves the judges; and the most numerous party, or in other words, the most powerful faction must be expected to prevail. Shall domestic manufacturers be encouraged, and in what degree, by restrictions on foreign manufacturers? are questions which would be differently decided by the landed and the manufacturing classes, and probably by neither with a sole regard to justice and the public good. The apportionment of taxes on the various descriptions of property is an act which seems to require the most exact impartiality; yet there is, perhaps, no legislative act in which greater opportunity and temptation are given to a predominant party to trample on the rules of justice. Every shilling with which they overburden the inferior number is a shilling saved to their own pockets.

It is in vain to say that enlightened statesmen will be able to adjust these clashing interests and render them all subservient to the public good. Enlightened statesmen will not always be at the helm. Nor, in many cases, can such an adjustment be made at all without taking into view indirect and remote considerations, which will rarely prevail over the immediate interest which one party may find in disregarding the rights of another or the good of the whole.

The inference to which we are brought is that the *causes* of faction cannot be removed and that relief is only to be sought in the means of controlling its *effects*.

If a faction consists of less than a majority, relief is supplied by the republican principle, which enables the majority to defeat its sinister views by regular vote. It may clog the administration, it may convulse the society; but it will be unable to execute and mask its violence under the forms of the Constitution. When a majority is included in a faction, the form of popular government, on the other hand, enables it to sacrifice to its ruling passion or interest both the public good and the rights of other citizens. To secure the public good and private rights against the danger of such a faction, and at the same time to preserve the spirit and the form of popular government, is then the great object to which our inquiries are directed. Let me add that it is the great desideratum by which alone this form of government can be rescued from the opprobrium under which it has so long labored and be recommended to the esteem and adoption of mankind.

By what means is this object attainable? Evidently by one of two only. Either the existence of the same passion or interest in a majority at the same time must be prevented, or the majority, having such coexistent passion of interest, must be rendered, by their number and local situation, unable to concert and carry into effect schemes of oppression. If the impulse and the opportunity be suffered to coincide, we well know that neither moral nor religious motives can be relied on as an adequate control. They are not found to be such on the injustice and violence of individuals, and lose their efficacy in proportion to the number combined together, that is, in proportion as their efficacy becomes needful.

From this view of the subject it may be concluded that a pure democracy, by which I mean a society consisting of a small number of citizens, who assemble and administer the government in person, can admit of no cure for the mischiefs of faction. A common passion or interest will, in almost every case, be felt by a majority of the whole; a communication and concert results from the form of government itself; and there is nothing to check the inducements to sacrifice the weaker party or an obnoxious individual. Hence it is that such democracies have ever been spectacles of turbulence and contention; have ever been found incompatible with personal security or the rights of property; and have in general been as short in their lives as they have been violent in their deaths. Theoretic politicians, who have patronized this species of government, have erroneously supposed that by reducing mankind to a perfect equality in their political rights, they would at the same time be perfectly equalized and assimilated in their possessions, their opinions, and their passions.

A republic, by which I mean a government in which the scheme of representation takes place, opens a different prospect and promises the cure for which we are seeking. Let us examine the points in which it varies from pure democracy, and we shall comprehend both the nature of the cure and the efficacy which it must derive from the Union.

The two great points of difference between a democracy and a republic are: first, the delegation of the government, in the latter, to a small number of citizens elected by the rest; secondly, the greater number of citizens and greater sphere of country over which the latter may be extended.

The effect of the first difference is, on the one hand, to refine and enlarge the public views by passing them through the medium of a chosen body of citizens, whose wisdom may best discern the true interest of their country and whose patriotism and love of justice will be least likely to sacrifice it to temporary or partial considerations. Under such a regulation it may well happen that the public voice, pronounced by the representatives

of the people, will be more consonant to the public good than if pronounced by the people themselves, convened for the purpose. On the other
hand, the effect may be inverted. Men of factious tempers, of local prejudices, or of sinister designs, may, by intrigue, by corruption, or by other
means, first obtain the suffrages, and then betray the interests of the people. The question resulting is, whether small or extensive republics are most
favorable to the election of proper guardians of the public weal; and it is
clearly decided in favor of the latter by two obvious considerations.

In the first place it is to be remarked that however small the republic
may be the representatives must be raised to a certain number in order to
guard against the cabals of a few; and that however large it may be they
must be limited to a certain number in order to guard against the confusion
of a multitude. Hence, the number of representatives in the two cases not
being in proportion to that of the constituents, and being proportionally
greatest in the small republic, it follows that if the proportion of fit characters be not less in the large than in the small republic, the former will present a greater option, and consequently a greater probability of a fit choice.

In the next place, as each representative will be chosen by a greater
number of citizens in the large than in the small republic, it will be more
difficult for unworthy candidates to practise with success the vicious arts by
which elections are too often carried; and the suffrages of the people being
more free, will be more likely to center on men who possess the most attractive merit and the most diffusive and established characters.

It must be confessed that in this, as in most other cases, there is a mean,
on both sides of which inconveniencies will be found to lie. By enlarging
too much the number of electors, you render the representative too little
acquainted with all their local circumstances and lesser interests; as by reducing it too much, you render him unduly attached to these, and too little
fit to comprehend and pursue great and national objects. The federal Constitution forms a happy combination in this respect; the great and aggregate
interests being referred to the national, the local and particular to the State
legislatures.

The other point of difference is the greater number of citizens and extent of territory which may be brought within the compass of republican
than of democratic government; and it is this circumstance principally
which renders factious combinations less to be dreaded in the former than
in the latter. The smaller the society, the fewer probably will be the distinct
parties and interests composing it; the fewer the distinct parties and interests, the more frequently will a majority be found of the same party; and
the smaller the number of individuals composing a majority, and the
smaller the compass within which they are placed, the more easily will they
concert and execute their plans of oppression. Extend the sphere and you
take in a greater variety of parties and interests; you make it less probable
that a majority of the whole will have a common motive to invade the
rights of other citizens; or if such a common motive exists, it will be more
difficult for all who feel it to discover their own strength and to act in

unison with each other. Besides other impediments, it may be remarked that, where there is a consciousness of unjust or dishonorable purposes, communication is always checked by distrust in proportion to the number whose concurrence is necessary.

Hence, it clearly appears that the same advantage which a republic has over a democracy in controlling the effects of faction is enjoyed by a large over a small republic—is enjoyed by the Union over the States composing it. Does this advantage consist in the substitution of representatives whose enlightened views and virtuous sentiments render them superior to local prejudices and to schemes of injustice? It will not be denied that the representation of the Union will be most likely to possess these requisite endowments. Does it consist in the greater security afforded by a greater variety of parties, against the event of any one party being able to outnumber and oppress the rest? In an equal degree does the increased variety of parties comprised within the Union increase this security. Does it, in fine, consist in the greater obstacles opposed to the concert and accomplishment of the secret wishes of an unjust and interested majority? Here again the extent of the Union gives it the most palpable advantage.

The influence of factious leaders may kindle a flame within their particular States but will be unable to spread a general conflagration through the other States. A religious sect may degenerate into a political faction in a part of the Confederacy; but the variety of sects dispersed over the entire face of it must secure the national councils against any danger from that source. A rage for paper money, for an abolition of debts, for an equal division of property, or for any other improper or wicked project, will be less apt to pervade the whole body of the Union than a particular member of it, in the same proportion as such a malady is more likely to taint a particular county or district than an entire State.[2]

In the extent and proper structure of the Union, therefore, we behold a republican remedy for the diseases most incident to republican government. And according to the degree of pleasure and pride we feel in being republicans ought to be our zeal in cherishing the spirit and supporting the character of federalists.   PUBLIUS

---

2. The examples of factional objectives (for example, paper money's benefiting debtors at the expense of creditors) that Madison cites are drawn from the economic conflicts that pervaded the states in the 1780s. The movement for a new national constitution aimed to put an end to the possibility that radical factional goals might be achieved in the states.

Anti-federalist Paper 18 October 1787

BRUTUS

To the Citizens of the State of New-York.

Perhaps this country never saw so critical a period in their political concerns. We have felt the feebleness of the ties by which these United-States are held together, and the want of sufficient energy in our present confederation, to manage, in some instances, our general concerns. Various expedients have been proposed to remedy these evils, but none have succeeded. At length a Convention of the states has been assembled, they have formed a constitution which will now, probably, be submitted to the people to ratify or reject, who are the fountain of all power, to whom alone it of right belongs to make or unmake constitutions, or forms of government, at their pleasure. The most important question that was ever proposed to your decision, or to the decision of any people under heaven, is before you, and you are to decide upon it by men of your own election, chosen specially for this purpose. If the constitution, offered to your acceptance, be a wise one, calculated to preserve the invaluable blessings of liberty, to secure the inestimable rights of mankind, and promote human happiness, then, if you accept it, you will lay a lasting foundation of happiness for millions yet unborn; generations to come will rise up and call you blessed. . . . But if, on the other hand, this form of government contains principles that will lead to the subversion of liberty—if it tends to establish a despotism, or, what is worse, a tyrannic aristocracy; then, if you adopt it, this only remaining asylum for liberty will be shut up, and posterity will execrate your memory. . . .

With these few introductory remarks, I shall proceed to a consideration of this constitution:

The first question that presents itself on the subject is, whether a confederated government be the best for the United States or not. Or in other words, whether the thirteen United States should be reduced to one great republic, governed by one legislature, and under the direction of one executive and judicial; or whether they should continue thirteen confederated republics, under the direction and control of a supreme federal head for certain defined national purposes only?

This enquiry is important, because, although the government reported by the convention does not go to a perfect and entire consolidation,[1] yet it

---

1. The Anti-federalists charged that the proposed Constitution aimed not at federalism (a division of powers between the national government and the state governments) but at consolidation (the centralization of all powers in the national government).

approaches so near to it, that it must, if executed, certainly and infallibly terminate in it.

This government is to possess absolute and uncontrolable power, legislative, executive and judicial, with respect to every object to which it extends, for by the last clause of section 8th, article 1st, it is declared "that the Congress shall have power to make all laws which shall be necessary and proper for carrying into execution the foregoing powers, and all other powers vested by this constitution, in the government of the United States; or in any department or office thereof." And by the 6th article, it is declared "that this constitution, and the laws of the United States, which shall be made in pursuance thereof, and the treaties made, or which shall be made, under the authority of the United States, shall be the supreme law of the land; and the judges in every state shall be bound thereby, any thing in the constitution, or law of any state to the contrary notwithstanding." It appears from these articles that there is no need of any intervention of the state governments, between the Congress and the people, to execute any one power vested in the general government, and that the constitution and laws of every state are nullified and declared void, so far as they are or shall be inconsistent with this constitution, or the laws made in pursuance of it, or with treaties made under the authority of the United States.—The government then, so far as it extends, is a complete one, and not a confederation. It is as much one complete government as that of New-York or Massachusetts, has as absolute and perfect powers to make and execute all laws, to appoint officers, institute courts, declare offences, and annex penalties, with respect to every object to which it extends, as any other in the world. So far therefore as its powers reach, all ideas of confederation are given up and lost. It is true this government is limited to certain objects, or to speak more properly, some small degree of power is still left to the states, but a little attention to the powers vested in the general government, will convince every candid man, that if it is capable of being executed, all that is reserved for the individual states must very soon be annihilated, except so far as they are barely necessary to the organization of the general government. The powers of the general legislature extend to every case that is of the least importance—there is nothing valuable to human nature, nothing dear to freemen, but what is within its power. It has authority to make laws which will affect the lives, the liberty, and property of every man in the United States; nor can the constitution or laws of any state, in any way prevent or impede the full and complete execution of every power given. The legislative power is competent to lay taxes, duties, imposts, and excises—there is no limitation to this power, unless it be said that the clause which directs the use to which those taxes, and duties shall be applied, may be said to be a limitation: but this is no restriction of the power at all, for by this clause they are to be applied to pay the debts and provide for the common defence and general welfare of the United States; but the legislature have authority to contract debts at their discretion; they are the sole judges of what is necessary to provide for the common defence, and they only are to determine what is for the general welfare; this power therefore is neither more nor less, than a power to lay and collect taxes, imposts, and excises, at their pleasure; not only [is] the power to lay taxes unlimited, as to the amount they may require, but it is perfect and absolute to raise them in any mode they please. No state legislature, or any power in the state governments, have any more to do in carrying this into effect, than the authority of one state has to do with that of another. In the business therefore of laying and collecting taxes, the idea of confederation is totally lost, and that of one entire republic is embraced. . . .

Let us now proceed to enquire, as I at first proposed, whether it be best the thirteen United States should be reduced to one great republic, or not? It is here taken for granted, that all agree in this, that whatever government we adopt, it ought to be a free one; that it should be so framed as to secure the liberty of the citizens of America, and such an one as to admit of a full, fair, and equal representation of the people. The question then will be, whether a government thus constituted, and founded on such principles, is practicable, and can be exercised over the whole United States, reduced into one state?

If respect is to be paid to the opinion of the greatest and wisest men who have ever thought or wrote on the science of government, we shall be constrained to conclude, that a free republic cannot succeed over a country of such immense extent, containing such a number of inhabitants, and these encreasing in such rapid progression as that of the whole United States. Among the many illustrious authorities which might be produced to this point, I shall content myself with quoting only two. The one is the baron de Montesquieu, spirit of laws, chap. xvi. vol. I [book VIII].[2] "It is natural to a republic to have only a small territory, otherwise it cannot long subsist. In a large republic there are men of large fortunes, and consequently of less moderation; there are trusts too great to be placed in any single subject; he has interest of his own; he soon begins to think that he may be happy, great and glorious, by oppressing his fellow citizens; and that he may raise himself to grandeur on the ruins of his country. In a large republic, the public good is sacrificed to a thousand views; it is subordinate to exceptions, and depends on accidents. In a small one, the interest of the public is easier perceived, better understood, and more within the reach of every citizen; abuses are of less extent, and of course are less protected." Of the same opinion is the marquis Beccaria.[3]

History furnishes no example of a free republic, any thing like the extent of the United States. The Grecian republics were of small extent; so also was that of the Romans. Both of these, it is true, in process of time, extended their conquests over large territories of country; and the con-

2. Baron Charles de Montesquieu was an eighteenth-century French political theorist whose ideas were highly influential in the era of the American Revolution and the Constitution.
3. Cesare Beccaria was an eighteenth-century Italian legal philosopher.

sequence was, that their governments were changed from that of free governments to those of the most tyrannical that ever existed in the world.

Not only the opinion of the greatest men, and the experience of mankind, are against the idea of an extensive republic, but a variety of reasons may be drawn from the reason and nature of things, against it. In every government, the will of the sovereign is the law. In despotic governments, the supreme authority being lodged in one, his will is law, and can be as easily expressed to a large extensive territory as to a small one. In a pure democracy the people are the sovereign, and their will is declared by themselves; for this purpose they must all come together to deliberate, and decide. This kind of government cannot be exercised, therefore, over a country of any considerable extent; it must be confined to a single city, or at least limited to such bounds as that the people can conveniently assemble, be able to debate, understand the subject submitted to them, and declare their opinion concerning it.

In a free republic, although all laws are derived from the consent of the people, yet the people do not declare their consent by themselves in person, but by representatives, chosen by them, who are supposed to know the minds of their constituents, and to be possessed of integrity to declare this mind.

In every free government, the people must give their assent to the laws by which they are governed. This is the true criterion between a free government and an arbitrary one. The former are ruled by the will of the whole, expressed in any manner they may agree upon; the latter by the will of one, or a few. If the people are to give their assent to the laws, by persons chosen and appointed by them, the manner of the choice and the number chosen, must be such, as to possess, be disposed, and consequently qualified to declare the sentiments of the people; for if they do not know, or are not disposed to speak the sentiments of the people, the people do not govern, but the sovereignty is in a few. Now, in a large extended country, it is impossible to have a representation, possessing the sentiments, and of integrity, to declare the minds of the people, without having it so numerous and unwieldly, as to be subject in great measure to the inconveniency of a democratic government.

The territory of the United States is of vast extent; it now contains near three millions of souls, and is capable of containing much more than ten times that number. Is it practicable for a country, so large and so numerous as they will soon become, to elect a representation, that will speak their sentiments, without their becoming so numerous as to be incapable of transacting public business? It certainly is not.

In a republic, the manners, sentiments, and interests of the people should be similar. If this be not the case, there will be a constant clashing of opinions; and the representatives of one part will be continually striving against those of the other. This will retard the operations of government, and prevent such conclusions as will promote the public good. If we apply this remark to the condition of the United States, we shall be convinced that it forbids that we should be one government. The United States includes a variety of climates. The productions of the different parts of the union are very variant, and their interests, of consequence, diverse. Their manners and habits differ as much as their climates and productions; and their sentiments are by no means coincident. The laws and customs of the several states are, in many respects, very diverse, and in some opposite; each would be in favor of its own interests and customs, and, of consequence, a legislature, formed of representatives from the respective parts, would not only be too numerous to act with any care or decision, but would be composed of such heterogenous and discordant principles, as would constantly be contending with each other.

The laws cannot be executed in a republic, of an extent equal to that of the United States, with promptitude.

The magistrates in every government must be supported in the execution of the laws, either by an armed force, maintained at the public expence for that purpose; or by the people turning out to aid the magistrate upon his command, in case of resistance.

In despotic governments, as well as in all the monarchies of Europe, standing armies are kept up to execute the commands of the prince or the magistrate, and are employed for this purpose when occasion requires: But they have always proved the destruction of liberty, and [are] abhorrent to the spirit of a free republic. In England, where they depend upon the parliament for their annual support, they have always been complained of as oppressive and unconstitutional, and are seldom employed in executing of the laws; never except on extraordinary occasions, and then under the direction of a civil magistrate.

A free republic will never keep a standing army to execute its laws. It must depend upon the support of its citizens. But when a government is to receive its support from the aid of the citizens, it must be so constructed as to have the confidence, respect, and affection of the people. Men who, upon the call of the magistrate, offer themselves to execute the laws, are influenced to do it either by affection to the government, or from fear; where a standing army is at hand to punish offenders, every man is actuated by the latter principle, and therefore, when the magistrate calls, will obey: but, where this is not the case, the government must rest for its support upon the confidence and respect which the people have for their government and laws. The body of the people being attached, the government will always be sufficient to support and execute its laws, and to operate upon the fears of any faction which may be opposed to it, not only to prevent an opposition to the execution of the laws themselves, but also to compel the most of them to aid the magistrate; but the people will not be likely to have such confidence in their rulers, in a republic so extensive as the United States, as necessary for these purposes. The confidence which the people have in their rulers, in a free republic, arises from their knowing them, from their being responsible to them for their conduct, and from the power they have of displacing them when they misbehave: but in a republic of the extent of this continent, the people in general would be acquainted with very few of their rulers: the people at large would know little of their proceedings, and it would be extremely difficult to change them. . . . The consequence will be, they will have no confidence in their legislature, suspect them of ambitious views, be jealous of every measure they adopt, and will not support the laws they pass. Hence the government will be nerveless and inefficient, and no way will be left to render it otherwise, but by establishing an armed force to execute the laws at the point of the bayonet—a government of all others the most to be dreaded.

In a republic of such vast extent as the United-States, the legislature cannot attend to the various concerns and wants of its different parts. It cannot be sufficiently numerous to be acquainted with the local condition and wants of the different districts, and if it could, it is impossible it should have sufficient time to attend to and provide for all the variety of cases of this nature, that would be continually arising.

In so extensive a republic, the great officers of government would soon become above the control of the people, and abuse their power to the purpose of aggrandizing themselves, and oppressing them. The trust committed to the executive offices, in a country of the extent of the United-States, must be various and of magnitude. The command of all the troops and navy of the republic, the appointment of officers, the power of pardoning offences, the collecting of all the public revenues, and the power of expending them, with a number of other powers, must be lodged and exercised in every state, in the hands of a few. When these are attended with great honor and emolument, as they always will be in large states, so as greatly to interest men to pursue them, and to be proper objects for ambitious and designing men, such men will be ever restless in their pursuit after them. They will use the power, when they have acquired it, to the purposes of gratifying their own interest and ambition, and it is scarcely possible, in a very large republic, to call them to account for their misconduct, or to prevent their abuse of power.

These are some of the reasons by which it appears, that a free republic cannot long subsist over a country of the great extent of these states. If then this new constitution is calculated to consolidate the thirteen states into one, as it evidently is, it ought not to be adopted. . . .

■ **DISCUSSION QUESTIONS**

1. How do the Federalists and the Anti-federalists view human nature? Why does Madison think individuals are "much more disposed to vex and oppress each other than to co-operate for their common good"? Why is

Brutus more hopeful that, under the proper political circumstances, citizens will cooperate for their common good? Whose perspective on human nature do you find more persuasive?

2. How do the Federalists and the Anti-federalists view participation by ordinary citizens at the local level? Why does Madison feel that "pure democracy" leads to disaster? Why does Brutus have a more positive view of politics within local communities? Do you think a "face-to-face" politics of ordinary citizens fosters individual growth and public spirit or produces ignorant decisions and unfairness to minorities?

3. How do the Federalists and the Anti-federalists view the role of elected representatives? Why does Madison want representatives to deliberate at a distance from the demands of their constituents? Why does Brutus want representatives to be closely tied to their constituents' ideas and interests? Do you think, like Madison, that representatives should be trustees who do what they think is best for the country, or do you believe, like Brutus, that representatives should be delegates who follow the expressed wishes of their constituents?

4. In what ways is the debate between Madison and Brutus reflected in today's political debates? In what ways have the arguments changed? Do contemporary defenders of a large policy role for the federal government share Madison's fundamental assumptions? Do contemporary critics of the federal government share Brutus's fundamental assumptions?

SUGGESTED READINGS AND INTERNET RESOURCES

The best source on the debate between the Federalists and the Anti-federalists is the original texts themselves. For inexpensive editions, see Clinton Rossiter, ed., *The Federalist Papers* (New York: Mentor Books, 1999); and Ralph Ketcham, ed., *The Anti-Federalist Papers* (New York: Mentor Books, 1996). On the political ideas of the founding era, see Gordon S. Wood, *The Creation of the American Republic, 1776–1787* (Chapel Hill: University of North Carolina Press, 1998); and Jack N. Rakove, *Original Meanings: Politics and Ideas in the Making of the Constitution* (New York: Knopf, 1996). In *If Men Were Angels: James Madison and the Heartless Empire of Reason* (Lawrence: University Press of Kansas, 1995), Richard K. Matthews provides a provocative interpretation of the great Federalist's political theory. Instructive commentaries on the political philosophy of the Anti-federalists are Herbert J. Storing, *What the Anti-Federalists Were For* (Chicago: University of Chicago Press, 1981) and Saul Cornell, *The Other Founders: Anti-Federalism and the Dissenting Tradition in America, 1788–1828* (Chapel Hill: University of North Carolina Press, 1999).

Emory Law School
www.law.emory.edu/FEDERAL
This searchable index of information on the Constitution and *The Federalist Papers* requires a forms-capable browser.

The Founders' Constitution
press-pubs.uchicago.edu/founders/
This site presents over 3,200 pages of documents containing the Founders' ideas and arguments about the U.S. Constitution.

2

Democracy: Overrated or Undervalued?

Almost everybody in America believes in democracy. When Americans are asked by interviewers about basic questions of majority rule, equality of opportunity, or individual freedom, more than 95 percent profess a belief in democratic values. As our introduction to this book suggests, however, once we probe a bit deeper into what Americans think democracy means, we find that they are not at all of one mind about how far democracy should extend into political, social, and economic life. Elite democrats believe that democracy is a valuable method for selecting those who will govern us, but they are skeptical about the political capacities and interests of ordinary citizens and want important decisions left to those with experience and expertise. Popular democrats distrust elites as potentially self-serving and believe that under the right circumstances ordinary citizens are both capable of and entitled to a significant share in deciding public matters.

The debate over democracy began at the time of the nation's founding and has continued to this day. In the previous chapter, we saw Federalists and Anti-federalists arguing about whether the American experiment in self-government should rest on elite democracy or popular democracy. To James Madison, only a national republic manned by a deliberative elite, who could filter out the irrational passions of the public, could sustain the American experiment. In the eyes of Brutus, this national republic would breed an oppressive aristocracy, who would crush popular democracy, which must be rooted in law-abiding and virtuous citizens and flourish at the local and state levels.

Although the Federalists prevailed in the original American debate over democracy, securing the ratification of the Constitution, nineteenth-century America looked more like the Anti-federalists' (and Thomas Jefferson's) vision of democracy than the Federalists'. For most of the century, political and economic life was small scale and decentralized, with the federal government in Washington, D.C., exercising only limited powers. Nineteenth-century America witnessed the establishment of the most democratic society the world had contained since the Golden Era of democracy in ancient Athens. Levels of political involvement and rates of voting among ordinary citizens were remarkably high—much higher, in fact, than they would be a century later. To be sure, this was a white man's democracy; Native Americans, African Americans, and women paid a high price for white men's freedoms, and the latter two groups had to launch long and painful struggles for democratic inclusion that would not achieve much success until the twentieth century.

The transformation of the United States between the Civil War and World War I from a largely agrarian and decentralized society into an urbanized and industrialized nation called into question the popular democratic assumptions held by the heirs of the Anti-federalists and Jefferson. Could ordinary citizens obtain, understand, and act on the increasingly complex information that characterized modern American society? America's premier journalist, Walter Lippmann, argued in the 1920s that ordinary citizens viewed the world through stereotypes, simplistic pictures that distorted reality, and that effective government for the industrial age required a greater emphasis on trained, dispassionate experts. Agreeing with Lippmann that the American public had been eclipsed by forces that seemed beyond its control, America's premier philosopher, John Dewey, warned of the elitist tendencies of Lippmann's experts. Dewey sought to revive popular democracy in face-to-face communities where ordinary citizens, informed by the latest findings of social science, would participate in public affairs.

In the 1950s (like the 1920s, a decade of apparent public apathy), Lippmann's argument received reinforcement from the empirical surveys conducted by political scientists. Most Americans, these surveys suggested, were not very interested in political life, did not know much about public affairs, and did not participate at very high levels in politics. Prevailing American conceptions about democracy would have to be modified, many political scientists now argued, to reflect what Robert Dahl called "citizenship without politics." But a minority of political scientists began in the 1960s to object, on both theoretical and empirical grounds, to this redefinition of democracy, claiming that the new perspective was less democratic realism than it was democratic elitism. These critics found support among the emerging political movements that would mark the 1960s as a decade of popular democratic upsurge. Students for a Democratic Society (SDS), the most important organization of the '60s New Left, gave the period its political watchword: *participatory democracy.*

Our selections in this chapter, excerpted from books published in 1999, are two of the latest versions of America's enduring debate over democracy. John Mueller attacks what he considers to be the romantic and unrealistic conception of democracy put forward by popular democrats. All that is required for democracy, Mueller contends, is a political system that eschews violence and that allows citizens to criticize, pressure, and remove those in power. Democracy, he suggests, will always consist of a messy, unequal conflict for advantage among special interests. What it will never achieve, he argues, are the misty ideals of popular democrats: political equality, participation, and an enlightened citizenry. Holding democracy to these standards only fosters cynicism. Mueller's analysis updates the classic elite democratic perspective of Madison, Lippmann, and Dahl.

Paul Rogat Loeb represents the popular democratic perspective of the Anti-federalists, Jefferson, Dewey, and SDS. He ascribes the widespread cynicism about politics in the 1990s not to the romantic ideals of popular democrats but to the skeptical views of public involvement broadcast by the dominant forces in American society. "We've all but forgotten," he writes, "that public participation is the very soul of democratic citizenship, and how much it can enrich our lives." In our selection, Loeb tells the story of Pete Knutson (one of many stories in his book), a commercial fisherman who organized his fellow fishermen, environmentalists, and Native Americans to defeat an initiative by large industries that would have destroyed salmon spawning grounds. Loeb argues that active citizenship is required both to fulfill our responsibility to take care of the common good and to grow as individuals in psychological and spiritual depth.

Evaluating the debate between Mueller and Loeb should help to clarify your own conception of democracy. Do you believe, with Mueller, that Americans have many more interesting things to do than spend their time on political pursuits? Or do you believe, with Loeb, that political involvement is necessary for a sense of freedom and personal dignity? Do you believe, with Mueller, that self-interest and inequality will always characterize democracy and that attempts to reduce their influence through political and economic reforms will inevitably fail? Or do you believe, with Loeb, that politics can also reflect our more social impulses and can redress political and economic injustices? Above all, do you agree with Mueller that acceptance of elite democracy is the only realistic perspective, or do you agree with Loeb that the abandonment of popular democracy is a surrender to cynicism?

Democracy's Romantic Myths

JOHN MUELLER

T here is a famous Norman Rockwell painting that purports to portray democracy in action. It depicts a New England town meeting in which a workingman has risen in a contentious situation to present his point of view. His rustic commonsense, it appears, has cut through the indecisiveness and bickering to provide a consensual solution to the problem at hand, and the others in the picture are looking up at him admiringly.

As it happens, that misty-eyed, idealized snapshot has almost nothing to do with democracy in actual practice. Democracy is not a process in which one shining idea conquers all as erstwhile contenders fall into blissful consensus. Rather, it is an extremely disorderly muddle in which clashing ideas and interests (all of them "special") do unkempt and unequal, if peaceful, battle and in which ideas are often reduced to slogans, data to distorted fragments, evidence to gestures, and arguments to poses. Speculation is rampant, caricature is routine, and posturing is de rigueur. If one idea wins out, it is likely to be severely compromised in the process, and no one goes away entirely reconciled or happy. And there is rarely a sense of completion or finality or permanence: in a democracy, as Tod Lindberg points out, "the fat lady never sings." It's a mess, and the only saving grace is that other methods for reaching decisions are even worse.

. . . I develop an approach to democracy that contrasts substantially with the romantic Rockwell ideal. It stresses petition and lobbying—the chaotic and distinctly nonconsensual combat of "special interests"—as the dominant and central characteristic of democracy and it suggests that while elections are useful and often valuable in a democracy, they may not be absolutely necessary. I also argue that democracy in practice is not about equality, but rather about the freedom to become politically unequal, and that it functions not so much by rule by the majority as by minority rule with majority acquiescence. . . .

. . . I also contrast democracy with other governmental forms. Although the advantage is only comparative, democracy seems to do better at generating effective governments, choosing leaders, addressing minority concerns, creating a livable society, and functioning effectively with real, flawed human beings. . . .

In defining democracy, it is particularly important, I think, to separate the essential institution itself from the operating devices that are commonly associated with it—mechanisms like written constitutions, the separation of powers or "checks and balances" (including an independent judiciary), and even elections. Any definition of democracy is inadequate, I think, if it can logically be taken to suggest that Britain (which has neither a written constitution nor separation of powers) is not a democracy or that Switzerland did not become one until 1971 (when women were finally given the vote). . . .

In my view, democracy is characterized by government that is necessarily and routinely responsive—although this responsiveness is not always even, fair, or equal. It comes into effect when the people effectively agree not to use violence to replace the leadership, and the leadership effectively leaves them free to criticize, to pressure, to organize, and to try to dislodge it by any other means. This approach can be used to set up a sort of sliding scale of governmental forms. An *authoritarian* government may effectively and sometimes intentionally allow a degree of opposition—a limited amount of press disagreement, for example, or the freedom to complain privately, something sometimes known as the freedom of conversation. But it will not tolerate organized attempts to replace it, even if they are peaceful. A *totalitarian* government does not allow even those limited freedoms. On the other end of the scale is *anarchy:* a condition which holds when a government "allows" the use of violence to try to overthrow it—presumably mainly out of weakness or ineffectiveness.

Authoritarian and even totalitarian governments can sometimes be responsive as well, of course. But their responsiveness depends on the will and the mindset of the leadership. By contrast, democracy is *routinely, necessarily* responsive: because people are free to develop and use peaceful methods to criticize, pressure, and replace the leadership, the leaders must pay attention to their critics and petitioners.

It seems to me that the formal and informal institutional mechanisms variously applied in democracies to facilitate this core consideration are secondary—though this does not mean that all institutions are equally fair or efficient. One can embellish this central democratic relationship with concerns about ethos, way of life, social culture, shared goals, economic correlates, common purposes, customs, preferred policy outcomes, norms, patriotism, shared traditions, and the like. These issues are interesting, but . . . they don't seem to be essential or necessary to the functioning of democracy. . . .

Apathy

. . . One of the great, neglected aspects of free speech is the freedom not to listen. As Hubert Humphrey reportedly put it, "The right to be heard doesn't automatically include the right to be taken seriously."[1] It is no easy task to

---

1. Hubert Humphrey was a Democratic senator from Minnesota and served as vice president under President Lyndon B. Johnson.

persuade free people to agree with one's point of view, but as any experienced demagogue is likely to point out with some exasperation, what is most difficult of all is to get them to pay attention at all. People, particularly those in a free, open society, are regularly barraged by shysters and schemers, by people with new angles and neglected remedies, with purveyors of panaceas and palliatives. Very few are successful—and even those who do succeed, including Adolf Hitler, owe their success as much to luck as to skill.

. . . [Such] apathy helps importantly with the problem that is usually called the tyranny of the majority. It is not difficult to find a place where the majority harbors a considerable hatred for a minority—indeed, it may be difficult to find one where this is not the case. Polls in the United States regularly have found plenty of people who would cheerfully restrict not only the undeserving rich, but also homosexuals, atheists, accused Communists, Nazi paraders, flag burners, and people who like to shout unpleasant words and perpetrate unconventional messages. But it is not easy to get this majority to do anything about it—after all, that would require a certain amount of work.

Because of apathy, therefore, people, sometimes despite their political predispositions, are effectively tolerant. For democracies the danger is not so much that agile demagogues will play on hatreds and weaknesses to fabricate a vindictive mob-like tyranny of the majority: the perversions of the French Revolution have proved unusual. More to be feared, it seems, is the tyranny of a few who obtain bland acquiescence from the uninterested, and essentially unaffected, many. . . .

The Quest for Political Equality

. . . The notion that all men are created equal suggests that people are *born* equal—that is, that none should necessarily be denied political opportunity merely because of their hereditary entrance into the wrong social or economic class or because they do not adhere to the visions or dictates of a particular ideological group. The notion does not, however, suggest that people must necessarily be equal in their impact on the political system, but this damaging extrapolation is often made by reformers, at least as a goal to be quested after.

An extensive study on the issue of equality by a team of political scientists finds, none too surprisingly, that people in a real democracy like the United States differ in the degree to which they affect the political system. Political effectiveness, the study concludes, depends on three varying factors: resources, especially time, money, and skills; psychological engagement with politics; and "access to networks through which individuals can be recruited to political life." The variance of effectiveness, the authors then conclude, poses a "threat to the democratic principle of equal protection of interests." Another analyst, reviewing their findings, makes a similar observation: "liberal democracies fail to live up to the norm of equal responsiveness to the interests of each citizen."

But instead of seeking to reform the system or the people who make it up, we may want instead to abandon, or at least substantially to modify, the principle and the norm. They clearly express a romantic perspective about democracy, a perspective which has now been fully and repeatedly disconfirmed in practice. Democracies are responsive and attentive to the interests of the citizenry—at least when compared to other forms of government—but they are nowhere near equally responsive to the interests of each citizen.

Related is the perennial clamor against "special interests." As the futile struggle for campaign finance reform in the United States suggests, people who want or need to influence public policy are very likely to find ways to do so no matter how clever the laws that seek to restrict them. As Gil Troy observes, "for all the pious hopes, the goal of the Watergate-era reforms—to remove the influence of money from presidential elections—was, in hard and inescapable fact, ridiculous." (He also notes that the entire cost of the 1996 election campaigns was about 25 percent of what Procter & Gamble routinely spends every year to market its products.) A rare voice of realism amid all the sanctimonious, politically correct bluster from politicians about campaign finance reform in the United States in the 1990s was that of Senator Robert Bennett of Utah: "rich people will always have influence in politics, and the solution is not to create barriers that cause the rich people to spend even more money to hire lawyers and consultants to find ways around the law to get the same results."

In the end, "special interests" can be effectively reined in only by abandoning democracy itself, because their activities are absolutely vital to the form. Indeed, it is quite incredible that two prominent Washington reporters merely deem it "simplistic" to argue that "people with common interests should not attempt to sway government policy." In a democracy the free, competitive play of "special interests" is fundamental. To reform this out of existence would be uncomprehending and profoundly anti-democratic.

Most of the agitation against political inequality is focused on the special privileges business is presumed to enjoy. For example, concern is voiced that the attention of public officials can be differently arrested: "a phone call from the CEO of a major employer in the district may carry considerably more weight than one from an unknown constituent." It is possible, of course, that the unweighty and unknown constituent has just come up with a plan which will achieve permanent worldwide bliss in the course of the next six months, but, since there are only twenty-four hours in a day, public officials (like the rest of us) are forced to ration their time, and they are probably correct to assume, as a first approximation at least, that the concerns of a major employer are likely to be of wider relevance to more people than are those of the hapless lone constituent.

But if the CEO's access advantage to a time-pressured politician is somehow reprehensible and must be reformed, what about other inequalities—that is, why focus only on economic ones? A telephone call from a big-time political columnist like David Broder of the *Washington Post* is likely to get the politician's attention even faster than that of the CEO. Should the influential David Broder hold off on his next column until the rest of us deserving unknowns have had a chance to put in our two cents in the same forum? Inequalities like these are simply and unavoidably endemic to the whole political system as, indeed, they are to life itself. It may be possible to reduce this inequality, but it is difficult to imagine a reform that could possibly raise the political impact of the average factory worker—or even of the average business executive—remotely to equal that enjoyed by Broder. . . .

The Quest for Participation

Democratic theorists, idealists, and image-makers maintain that "democratic states require . . . participation in order to flourish," or that "a politically active citizenry is a requisite of any theory of democracy," or that "democracy was built on the principle that political participation was not only the privilege of every man, but a necessity in ensuring the efficiency and prosperity of the democratic system," or that "high levels of electoral participation are essential for guaranteeing that government represents the public as a whole," or that "to make a democracy that works, we need citizens who are engaged."

But we now have over two hundred years of experience with living, breathing, messy democracy, and truly significant participation has almost never been achieved anywhere. Since democracy exists, *it simply can't be true* that wide participation is a notable requirement, requisite, guarantee, need, or necessity for it to prosper or work. Routinely, huge numbers of citizens even—in fact, especially—in "mature" democracies simply decline to participate, and the trend in participation seems to be, if anything, mostly downward. In the United States, nearly half of those eligible fail to vote even in high-visibility elections and only a few percent ever actively participate in politics. The final winner of a recent election for the mayor of Rochester, N.Y., received only about 6 percent of the vote of the total electorate. (However, he is a very popular choice: if everybody had voted, he would almost certainly have achieved the same victory.) Switzerland is Europe's oldest democracy, and it also boasts the continent's lowest voter turnout.

Statistics like these frequently inspire a great deal of concern—after all, it is argued, "political participation" is one of the "basic democratic ideals." But it may be more useful to reshape democratic theories and ideals to take notice of the elemental fact that democracy works even though it often fails to inspire very much in the way of participation from its citizenry.

And it might also be asked, why, exactly, is it so important for citizens to participate? Most analyses suggest that nonvoters do not differ all that much from voters in their policy concerns, though there are some (controversial) suggestions that leftist parties might do a bit better in some countries if everyone were forced to vote. However, once in office, responsible leftist and rightist parties both face the same constraining conditions and, despite their ideologies and campaign promises, often do not differ all that much from each other in their policies—frequently to the disillusionment and disgust of their supporters who may come to feel they have been conned.

Some hold voting to be important because "of the problem of legitimacy." The idea is that "as fewer and fewer citizens participate in elections, the extent to which government truly rests on the consent of the governed may be called into question"; moreover the "quality of the link between elites and citizens" will erode. Actually, such callings into question seem to happen mostly when a candidate, like Bill Clinton in 1992, gets less than half of the recorded *vote*—and these are principally inspired by partisan maneuvering by the losers to undercut any claim that the winner has a mandate. And in local elections, the often exceedingly low turnout and participation levels rarely even cause much notice: I have yet to hear anyone suggest that the mayor of Rochester is illegitimate or "unlinked" because hardly anybody managed to make it to the polls when he was elected.

Moreover, it really seems to strain credulity to suggest that "if people feel distant from the electoral process, they can take no pride in the successes of the government." *No* pride? It seems that even nonvoters celebrated victory in the Gulf War. Or that nonvoters "avoid responsibility for the problems facing the nation." But nonvoters seem to have no more difficulty than voters in routinely (and sometimes even correctly) blaming the politicians for whatever is wrong. And it is simply too glib to conclude that "if you don't vote, you don't count." If that were true, women would never have gotten the vote, slavery would still exist, and there would never have been prison reform or legislation aiding the homeless.

There are also claims that low turnout levels "contribute to the problem of an unrepresentative policy agenda." But it is difficult to understand what this could possibly mean—or, better, what a "representative policy agenda" would look like. Agendas are set by people actively trying to pursue their interests; they are not out there somewhere in the miasma waiting for us objectively to snap them up. As Steven Rosenstone and John Mark Hansen argue, "political participation is the product of strategic interactions of citizens and leaders." People "participate when politicians, political parties, interest groups, and activists persuade them to get involved." Thus, there will not be an "ideal" or even "normal" degree of participation. Rather, participation will increase when "salient issues reach the public agenda . . . when governments approach crucial decisions . . . when competitive election campaigns stimulate, when social movements inspire."

Hundreds of years of experience, then, suggest that the pursuit of participation for the sake of participation is rather quixotic. Instead, applying a philosophical observation attributed to impresario Sol Hurok, perhaps we should accept the fact that "if people don't want to come, nothing will stop them." Moreover, discontent and cynicism about the system itself (and consequently perhaps nonvoting) are increased when alarmists passionately lament that many people, as they have throughout democratic eternity, freely decide to pursue interests they find more pressing than politics, or manage to come up with more interesting things to do on election day than to go through the often inconsequential ritual of voting. (Sometimes, actually, nonvoters, by the very act of not voting, may be indicating their concerns and preferences more eloquently than those who actually do vote.)

The Quest for an Enlightened Citizenry

"If a nation expects to be ignorant and free," Thomas Jefferson once said, "it expects what never was and never will be." Pretty much ever since those memorable words were issued, the United States has managed to be both, and with considerable alacrity.

Fortunately for America, eternal vigilance has not proven to be the price of democracy—it can come quite a bit cheaper. In ideal democracies, James Bryce once suggested, "the average citizen will give close and constant attention to public affairs, recognizing that this is his interest as well as his duty"—but not in real ones.[2] And Horace Mann's ringing prediction that "with universal suffrage, there must be universal elevation of character, intellectual and moral, or there will be universal mismanagement and calamity" has proven untrue.[3]

Nonetheless, democratic idealists continue to insist that "democracies require responsibility." Or they contend that democracy "relies on informed popular judgment and political vigilance." Or they persist in defining democracy "as a political system in which people actively attend to what is significant." One would think it would be obvious by now that democracy works despite the fact that it often fails to inspire or require very much in the way of responsibility and knowledge from its citizenry. Democracy does feed on the bandying about of information, but that is going to happen pretty much automatically when people are free to ferret it out and to exchange it. Democracy clearly does not require that people generally be well informed, responsible, or actively attentive.

Recent surveys find that around half the American people haven't the foggiest idea which party controls the Senate or what the first ten amendments of the Constitution are called or what the Fifth Amendment does or who their congressional representative or senators are. Moreover, this lack of knowledge has generally increased (particularly when education is controlled for) since the 1940s. A month after the Republican victory in the 1994 election that propelled the vocal and energetic Newt Gingrich into the speakership of the House of Representatives and into the media stratosphere, a national poll found that 50 percent hadn't heard enough about

---

2. James Bryce was a British writer who published a classic study, *The American Commonwealth,* in the late nineteenth century.
3. Horace Mann was a nineteenth-century educational reformer.

Gingrich even to have an opinion about him. Four months later, after endless publicity over Gingrich's varying fortunes and after *Time* magazine had designated him its "Man of the Year," that number had not changed (so much for the power of the press). In a poll conducted two years later, half were still unable to indicate who the speaker was. Meanwhile, less than 20 percent guessed correctly that over the preceding twenty years air pollution and the number of the elderly living in poverty had declined, and most people were of the wildly distorted impression that foreign aid comprised a larger share of the federal budget than Medicare.

One recent analysis observes that "for the last 200 years the United States has survived as a stable democracy, despite continued evidence of an uninformed public." It also notes that "in theory, a democracy requires knowledgeable citizens." Although it then labels the contradictory condition "the paradox of modern democracy," it seems, rather, that it is the theory that should be called into question, not the reality.

Moreover, it may not be entirely clear why one should expect people to spend a lot of time worrying about politics when democratic capitalism not only leaves them free to choose other ways to get their kicks, but in its seemingly infinite quest for variety is constantly developing seductive distractions. Democratic theorists and idealists may be intensely interested in government and its processes, but it verges on the arrogant, even the self-righteous, to suggest that other people are somehow inadequate or derelict unless they share the same curious passion. Many studies have determined that it is the politically interested who are the most politically active. It is also doubtless true that those most interested in unidentified flying objects are the ones most likely to join UFO clubs. UFO enthusiasts, however, get no special credit by political theorists for servicing their particular obsession, while politics junkies are lauded because they seem to be fulfilling a higher, theory-sanctified function.

In the end, the insistence that terrible things will happen unless the citizenry becomes addicted to C-SPAN can inspire cynicism about the process when it is observed that the Beverly Hillbillies (or whatever) enjoy vastly higher ratings.

The Active Citizen

PAUL ROGAT LOEB

I n the personal realm, most Americans are thoughtful, caring, generous. We try to do our best by family and friends. At times we'll even stop to help another driver stranded with a roadside breakdown, or give some spare change to a stranger. But increasingly, a wall now separates each of us from the world outside, and from others who've likewise taken refuge in their own private sanctuaries. We've all but forgotten that public participation is the very soul of democratic citizenship, and how much it can enrich our lives.

However, the reason for our wholesale retreat from social involvement is not, I believe, that most of us feel all is well with the world. I live in Seattle, a city with a seemingly unstoppable economy. Yet every time I go downtown I see men and women with signs saying "I'll work for food," or "Homeless vet. Please help." Their suffering diminishes me as a human being. I also travel extensively, doing research and giving lectures throughout the country. Except in the wealthiest of enclaves, people everywhere say, "Things are hard here." America's economic boom has passed many of us by. We struggle to live on meager paychecks. We worry about layoffs, random violence, the rising cost of health care, and the miseducation of our kids. Too stretched to save, uncertain about Social Security, many of us wonder just how we'll survive when we get old. We feel overwhelmed, we say, and helpless to change things.

Even those of us who are economically comfortable seem stressed. We spend hours commuting on crowded freeways, and hours more at jobs whose demands never end. We complain that we don't have enough time left for families and friends. We worry about the kind of world we'll pass on to our grandchildren. Then we also shrug and say there's nothing we can do.

To be sure, the issues we now face are complex—perhaps more so than in the past. How can we comprehend the moral implications of a world in which Nike pays Michael Jordan more to appear in its ads than it pays all the workers at its Indonesian shoe factories combined? Today the five hundred richest people on the planet control more wealth than the bottom three billion, half of the human population. Is it possible even to grasp the process that led to this most extraordinary imbalance? More important, how do we even begin to redress it?

Yet what leaves too many of us sitting on the sidelines is not only a lack of understanding of the complexities of our world. It's not only an absence of readily apparent ways to begin or resume public involvement. Certainly we need to decide for ourselves whether particular causes are wise or foolish—be they the politics of campaign finance reform, attempts to address the growing gap between rich and poor, or efforts to safeguard water, air, and wilderness. We need to identify and connect with worthy groups that take on these issues, whether locally or globally. But first we need to believe that our individual involvement is worthwhile, that what we might do in the public sphere will not be in vain.

This means we face a challenge that is as much psychological as political. As the Ethiopian proverb says, "He who conceals his disease cannot be cured." We need to understand our cultural diseases of callousness, shortsightedness, and denial, and learn what it will take to heal our society and heal our souls. How did so many of us become convinced that we can do nothing to affect our common future? And how have some other Americans managed to remove the cataracts from their vision and work power-fully for change?

When we do take a stand, we grow psychologically and spiritually. Pete Knutson is one of my oldest friends. During his twenty-five years as a com-mercial fisherman in Washington and Alaska, he's been forced, time and again, to respond to the steady degradation of salmon spawning grounds. "You'd have a hard time spawning, too, if you had a bulldozer in your bed-room," he says, explaining the destruction of once-rich salmon habitat by commercial development and timber industry clear-cutting. Pete could have simply accepted this degradation as fate, focusing on getting a maxi-mum share of the dwindling fish populations. Instead, he's gradually built an alliance between Washington State fishermen, environmentalists, and Native American tribes, persuading them to work collectively to demand that the habitat be preserved and restored.

The cooperation Pete created didn't come easy: Washington's fisher-men were historically individualistic and politically mistrustful, more in-clined, in Pete's judgment, "to grumble or blame the Indians than to act." Now, with their new allies, they began to push for cleaner spawning streams, preservation of the Endangered Species Act, and an increased flow of water over major regional dams to help boost salmon runs. But large in-dustrial interests, such as the aluminum companies, feared that these mea-sures would raise their electricity costs or restrict their opportunities for development. So a few years ago they bankrolled a statewide initiative to regulate fishing nets in a way that would eliminate small family fishing operations.

"I think we may be toast," said Pete, when Initiative 640 first surfaced. In an Orwellian twist, its backers even presented the initiative as environ-mentally friendly, to mislead casual voters. It was called "Save Our Sealife," although fishermen soon rechristened it "Save Our Smelters." At first, those opposing 640 thought they had no chance of success: They were outspent, outstaffed, outgunned. Similar initiatives had already passed in Florida, Louisiana, and Texas, backed by similar industrial interests. I remember Pete sitting in a Seattle tavern with two fisherman friends, laughing bitterly and saying, "The three of us are going to take on the aluminum companies? We're going to beat Reynolds and Kaiser?"

But they refused to give up. Instead, Pete and his coworkers systemati-cally enlisted the region's major environmental groups to campaign against the initiative. They worked with the media to explain the larger issues at stake. And they focused public attention on the measure's powerful finan-cial backers, and their interest in its outcome. On election night, November 1995, Initiative 640 was defeated throughout the state. White fishermen, Native American activists, and Friends of the Earth staffers threw their arms around each other in victory. "I'm really proud of you, Dad," Pete's twelve-year-old son kept repeating. Pete was stunned.

"Everyone felt it was hopeless," Pete said, looking back. "But if we were going to lose, I wanted at least to put up a good fight. And we won because of all the earlier work we'd done, year after year, to build up our environmental relationships, get some credibility, and show that we weren't just in it for ourselves."

We often think of social involvement as noble but impractical. Yet as Pete's story attests, it can serve enlightened self-interest and the interests of others simultaneously, while giving us a sense of connection and purpose nearly impossible to find in purely private life. "It takes energy to act," said Pete. "But it's more draining to bury your anger, convince yourself you're powerless, and swallow whatever's handed to you. The times I've compromised my integrity and accepted something I shouldn't, the ghosts of my choices have haunted me. When you get involved in something meaningful, you make your life count. What you do makes a difference. It blows my mind that we beat 640 starting out with just a small group of people who felt it was wrong to tell lies."

In fighting to save the environment and his economic livelihood, Pete strengthened his own soul. How the rest of us might achieve something similar is not always clear. We often don't know where to start. Most of us would like to see people treated more justly, to have the earth accorded the respect it deserves, and to feel less pressure in our lives. But we find it hard to imagine having much of a role in this process. We mistrust our own ability to make a difference. The magnitude of the issues at hand, coupled with this sense of powerlessness, has led far too many of us to conclude that social involvement isn't worth the cost.

Such resignation isn't an innate response, or the creation of some inevitable fate. Rather, it's what psychologists call learned helplessness. Society has systematically taught us to ignore the ills we see, and leave them to others to handle. Understandably, we find it unsettling even to think about crises as huge and profound in their implications as the extinction of species, depletion of the ozone layer, and destruction of the rainforests. Or the desperate poverty that blights entire neighborhoods in our nation's largest cities. We're led to believe that if we can't solve every one of these kinds of problems, we shouldn't bother to become socially active at all. We're also taught to doubt our voice—to feel we lack either the time to properly learn and articulate the issues we care about, or the standing to speak out and be heard. To get socially involved, we believe, requires almost saintlike judgment, confidence, and character—a standard we can never meet. Whatever impulses toward involvement we might have, they're dampened by a culture that demeans idealism, enshrines cynicism, and makes us feel naive for caring about our fellow human beings or the planet we inhabit. . . .

Learned Helplessness

America's prevailing culture of cynicism insists that nothing we do can matter. It teaches us not to get involved in shaping the world we'll pass on to our children. It encourages us to leave such important decisions to others—whether they be corporate and government leaders, or social activists whose lifestyles seem impossibly selfless or foreign. Sadly, and ironically, in a country born of a democratic political revolution, to be American today is to be apolitical. Civic withdrawal has become our norm. To challenge this requires courage. It also requires creating a renewed definition of ourselves as citizens—something closer to the nation of active stakeholders that leaders like Thomas Jefferson had in mind.

The importance of citizens' direct participation in a democracy was expressed thousands of years ago, by the ancient Greeks. In fact, they used the word "idiot" for people incapable of involving themselves in civic life. Now, the very word "political" has become so debased in our culture that we use it to describe either trivial office power plays or the inherently corrupt world of elected leaders. We've lost sight of its original roots in the Greek notion of the polis: the democratic sphere in which citizens, acting in concert, determine the character and direction of their society. "All persons alike," wrote Aristotle, should share "in the government to the utmost." . . .

Bowling Alone

Creating any kind of activist community is harder when the civic associations and institutions that might once have offered a foundation have themselves eroded. In a much-discussed article, "Bowling Alone," (see Chapter 4) the Harvard political theorist Robert Putnam observes that during the past thirty years Americans have steadily reduced their participation not only in voting, but also in traditional forms of community involvement, such as the PTA, the League of Women Voters, unions, mainstream churches, the Boy Scouts and Campfire Girls, and service clubs like the Lions and Kiwanis. We've squandered the "social capital" that allows people to work together effectively to pursue shared objectives. As a strangely poignant example of this trend, Putnam notes that local bowling leagues have seen a 40 percent decline in membership since 1980. During the same period, however, the number of individuals who actually bowl has risen until it now exceeds the number who vote in congressional elections. These trends bode ill for American democracy, Putnam argues, because the more socially isolated our citizens become, the fewer chances they have for the kinds of civic conversations that fuel involvement in crucial public concerns.

Putnam's critics, like *Atlantic Monthly* writer Nicholas Lemann, have argued that citizens are still just as likely to get involved in community social networks, but that as America's population shifts toward the suburbs, the networks have changed form. Youth soccer leagues, in which parents participate on the weekends, are booming, he says. So are Internet discussion groups and self-help associations like Alcoholics Anonymous. Organizations from NOW and the Sierra Club to the NRA and the Christian Coalition have taken the place of the old political machines.[1]

---

1. NOW is an acronym for the National Organization for Women; NRA is an acronym for the National Rifle Association.

Such examples notwithstanding, I remain convinced by Putnam's basic proposition, that civic involvement has dropped off significantly. In a follow-up article, Putnam examines a number of possible causes for the decline, including suburbanization, the increased numbers of women in the workforce, and the general demands of modern life. While most of these factors seem to play some role, they don't account for the fact that the decline cuts across cities and suburbs, the married and the single, working men, working women, and stay-at-home moms. The key change during the past fifty years, Putnam concludes, is the steadily increasing influence of television. Regardless of background or current circumstances, the more people watch TV, he finds, the less they involve themselves in civic activities of any kind, and the more mistrusting and pessimistic they become about human nature. As their sense of connectedness and common purpose erodes, they find it easy to scapegoat others, to view the world in prejudicial and unforgiving terms, and to believe that ordinary citizens can do nothing to shape the history of our time. This is all the more troubling given that extensive TV watching now begins in early childhood, taking up as much time among average kids aged nine to fourteen as all other discretionary activities combined. For many adults, TV has gradually replaced nearly every social activity outside the home.

It worries me that so many of us now sit alone for hours on end, passive spectators, paying more attention to the strangers on the screen than to the real people next door. What are the consequences for ourselves and our society? The greatest misfortune, in my view, is that by focusing so much on stories scripted by others, we forfeit the opportunity to create our own.

Fishing Together

Whatever the reasons for our declining civic involvement, we need to rebuild local communities even as we work to expand their vision. Pete Knutson took this approach in working with his fellow fishermen: First he helped create a cohesive community; then he involved its members in larger public issues. Pete, the son of a plainspoken Lutheran minister, grew up in the hardscrabble mill town of Everett, Washington. He had a Barry Goldwater poster on his wall, "because Goldwater spoke his mind."[2] At first Pete supported the Vietnam War, and even got a jingoistic letter published on the *Everett Herald*'s youth page. His views changed as friends who'd enlisted came back, feeling betrayed, and told him, "Don't believe anything the military tells you. They always lie." Before long, Pete was organizing an antiwar moratorium at his high school; then he went off to Stanford, and became the only draft-age man to testify before Congress. He even got his

---

2. Barry Goldwater, a founder of modern American conservatism and a senator from Arizona, was the Republican candidate for president in 1964.

fifteen minutes of fame on the national news, after Strom Thurmond stormed out when Pete had the audacity to ask a Senate committee, "If you're so eager to fight this war, why don't you pick up an M16 and lead the first wave?"

Pete began fishing to work his way through school. Soon, fishing became a way of life, as he bought his own boat, with borrowed money, to support his wife and two young sons. Because he knew his fellow fishermen were powerless in isolation, he helped build the Puget Sound Gillnetters' Association, which enabled members to market fish jointly, lobby on laws that affected them, and gain leverage against the giant canneries. "I felt we had to trust each other," he says. "If we didn't, we had no chance." The association became a base through which fishermen gradually became conversant with large ecological issues, such as the destruction of salmon habitat, upon whose outcome their livelihoods depended.

Pete worked steadily to bridge the gap between fishermen and the generally more middle-class environmentalists. That was no easy task, given long-standing mutual mistrust fed by class divides and stereotypes. Yet a coalition did in fact emerge, and the fishermen brought a powerful blue-collar presence to issues like the Endangered Species Act and habitat protection. When President Clinton visited Seattle for a Pacific Rim trade conference, a parade of fishing boats joined with Greenpeace activists to challenge his environmental timidity. Both Pete's ethical stand and pride in craft were evoked by the bumper sticker on his truck: "Jesus Was a Gillnetter."

This hard-won and unexpected alliance proved critical when Initiative 640 threatened to shut down the gillnetters' operations by banning the nets they used. The fishermen held joint press conferences with the now-supportive environmental groups, picketed a pleasure-boat company that was a prime initial backer of the initiative, and generally refused to succumb quietly to their opponents' well-financed campaign. They survived because Pete, along with a few others, had helped change their vision from one of enlightened self-interest to a more complex and sustainable ethic, best summed up when he spoke of nurturing the salmon habitat "so my kids can fish, too, and everyone's children can inherit a healthy planet." First the fishermen learned to work together, then to reach beyond their own ranks. Building their association's internal cohesion made it easier for them to tackle difficult issues later on. . . .

The Fullness of Time

However we promote social change, we do so in time: We link past, present, and future in our attempts to create a better world. Some historical eras, however, seem more pregnant with possibility than others. . . .

The 1960s were marked by a . . . sense of urgency and creative ferment. Ordinary people worldwide challenged entrenched institutions and policies. They talked of realizing a more humane and generous future. These

movements then collapsed because of powerful opposition, their participants' exhaustion, and some dangerous moments of arrogance. But for a
time, people unleashed powerful dreams.

Our lives today are hardly stagnant. We have access to a world of food,
music, sights, sounds, and healing traditions. We can log onto Websites
from Bangkok and Reykjavik to Nairobi and Calcutta. As technology
changes by leaps and bounds, it alters our lives and the earth at an almost
incomprehensible pace. So does the relentless global economy. Change
happens so fast we can barely keep up.

But politically, we often feel powerless, incapable of moving forward.
We may have witnessed citizens fighting for democracy in the streets of
Prague, Berlin, and Moscow, Tiananmen Square and Soweto, Manila, and
Jakarta. But we saw them from a distance on TV. People risked their lives to
have a say in their common future, but the lessons seemed remote from our
world. They didn't apply to us. Not here, and certainly not now.

It's tempting to gaze back longingly toward the most dramatic periods
of history, while disdaining our own era as unheroic and meaningless.
"People seem so stuck these days," says Ginny Nicarthy. "But things looked
pretty grim in the late 1950s too, when I first got involved. A dozen of us
would picket the bomb shelters or stores that were racist in their hiring, and
people would yell at us, tell us to 'Go back to Russia,' 'Go back to your
kitchen, where you belong.' There were no clear reasons to believe that we
could change things, but somehow we did. We leaped forward, started the
ball rolling, and built enough political mass that it kept going. Maybe we
need to do that again."

Seeding the ground for the next round of highly visible social progress
will take work. Yet major gains for human dignity are possible, even in
seemingly resistant times. Indeed, our efforts may be even more critical
now than in periods when the whole world seems to be watching.

The Turnings of History

Historical contexts can change shape suddenly and dramatically. As Václav
Havel wrote before the epochal Eastern European revolutions, "Hope is not
prognostication."[3] Richard Flacks remembers visiting Berkeley in September
1964 and hearing members of the activist student group SDS complain that
their fellow students were almost terminally apathetic, uncaring, and passive. They said that nothing they could try would work. A few weeks later,
the free speech movement erupted.

We can never predict when a historical mood will suddenly shift and
new hopes and possibilities emerge. But we do know that this shift won't

---

3. Václav Havel, a prominent playwright and a dissident during communist rule in
Czechoslovakia, is now president of the Czech Republic.

occur unless someone takes action. Recall the struggle of Susan B. Anthony. She labored her entire life for women's suffrage, then died fourteen years before it was achieved. Thirty years ago, few would have thought that the Soviet bloc would crumble, thanks in part to the persistence of individuals from Havel to Lech Walesa and Andrei Sakharov, who voiced prophetic truths despite all costs. Few would have thought that South Africa would become a democracy, with Nelson Mandela its president. Few would have imagined that women throughout the world would begin to insist on shaping their own destiny. Major victories for human dignity rarely come easily or quickly. But they do come.

"When nothing seems to help," said the early twentieth-century reformer Jacob Riis, "I go and look at a stonecutter hammering away at his rock perhaps a hundred times without as much as a crack showing in it. Yet at the hundred and first blow it will split in two, and I know it was not that blow that did it—but all that had gone before." . . .

Faith and Hope

Even if the past holds no guarantees for the future, we can still take heart from previous examples of courage and vision. We can draw hope from those who came before us, to whom we owe so much. We can remember that history unfolds in ways we can never predict, but that again and again bring astounding transformations, often against the longest of odds. Our strength can come, as I've suggested, from a radical stubbornness, from savoring the richness of our journey, and from the victories we win and the lives that we change. We can draw on the community we build.

More than anything, activists religious and secular keep going because participation is essential to their dignity, to their very identity, to the person they see in the mirror. To stay silent, they say, would be self-betrayal, a violation of their soul. Plainly stated, it would feel cheap and tacky. "That's why we were put here on this earth," they stress again and again. "What better thing can you do with your life?" "There'll be nobody like you ever again," says veteran environmentalist David Brower. "Make the most of every molecule you've got, as long as you've got a second to go. That's your charge."

This means responding to the ills of our time with what Rabbi Abraham Heschel once called "a persistent effort to be worthy of the name human." A technical editor who chaired her local Amnesty International chapter felt demeaned just by knowing about incidents of torture. To do something about it helped her recover her spirit. "When you stand in front of the Creator," says Carol McNulty, "you want to say, 'I tried to make a difference.' It isn't going to be what kind of car I had or how big a house. I'd like to think I tried."

Being true to oneself in this fashion doesn't eradicate human destructiveness. We need to live, as Albert Camus suggests, with a "double memory—a memory of the best and the worst."[4] We can't deny the cynicism and callousness of which humans are capable. We also can't deny the courage and compassion that offer us hope. It's our choice which characteristics we'll steer our lives by. . . .

DISCUSSION QUESTIONS

1. What are the most important differences between the elite democratic perspective and the popular democratic perspective? In your view, which side has the stronger case?

2. Mueller argues that "'special interests' can be effectively reined in only by abandoning democracy itself." Do you agree?

3. Mueller believes that there is no greater intrinsic value in being a "politics junky" than in pursuing any other interest or hobby, while Loeb sees public involvement as essential for personal growth. Is there anything distinctive about political participation that makes it especially worthy of our time and commitments?

4. Are most Americans too preoccupied with their private affairs to pay much attention to public ones, or can they be taught to see critical links between their own needs and interests and the shared pursuit of public goods?

SUGGESTED READINGS AND INTERNET RESOURCES

The classic work on the meaning, practices, and dilemmas of American democracy remains Alexis de Tocqueville, *Democracy in America,* Vols. 1 and 2 (New York: Vintage Books, 1990). Two provocative histories of American democracy are Robert H. Wiebe, *Self-Rule: A Cultural History of American Democracy* (Chicago: University of Chicago Press, 1995) and Michael Schudson, *The Good Citizen; A History of American Civic Life* (Cambridge, Mass.: Harvard University Press, 1999). Perhaps the greatest work of modern political science in the elite democratic vein is Robert A. Dahl, *Who Governs? Democracy and Power in an American City* (New Haven, Conn.: Yale University Press, 1961). For a fascinating study of the 1960s experiment with participatory democracy, see James Miller, *"Democracy Is in the Streets": From Port Huron to the Siege of Chicago* (Cambridge, Mass.: Harvard University Press, 1994). A prominent attempt to develop the theory of participatory democracy is Benjamin Barber, *Strong Democracy: Participatory Politics for a New Age* (Berkeley and Los Angeles: University of California Press, 1984).

---

4. Albert Camus was a French philosopher and novelist who won the Nobel Prize for Literature.

Center for Democracy and Citizenship
www.hhh.umn.edu/centers/cdc
The Center for Democracy and Citizenship, located at the University of
Minnesota's Hubert H. Humphrey Institute of Public Affairs, offers information
about various citizenship projects as well as information about the center's own
publications; it provides links to other sites on citizenship.

Institute for the Study of Civic Values
www.iscv.org
A nonprofit organization in Philadelphia, its web site provides classic articles
and lectures on American democratic values as well as information on civic
values projects.

}

The New Federalism: Does It Create Laboratories of Democracy or a Race to the Bottom?[1]

American politics often takes a peculiar form: instead of debating *what* policy should be enacted, people argue about *where* the policy decision should be made—at the federal, state, or local level. One side will proclaim its adherence to "states' rights" or "community control," while the other side touts the need for the federal government to guarantee fairness and equal protection of the laws. Often the two sides are sincere in their defense of different levels of democracy. As you might suspect, however, the debate is not just about ideals but about who will win and who will lose. This is because where decisions are made strongly affects who wins and who loses. This peculiar quality of the "game" of politics in the United States is determined by a system we call *federalism*.

Federalism is a system of government that divides power between a central government and state and local governments. As a concept of government, federalism was born in compromise during the struggle over the U.S. Constitution. Some of the framers of the Constitution favored a unitary system in which all significant powers would be placed in the hands of a central government. Realizing that such a system would never be approved by the

---

1. Both phrases, "laboratories of democracy" and "race to the bottom," were coined by Louis Brandeis, U.S. Supreme Court justice from 1916 to 1939.

voters, the framers compromised on a system that divided power between the two levels of government. As we saw in Chapter 1, the opponents of the Constitution, the Anti-federalists, still feared that too much power had been given to the federal government at the expense of the states.

The ratification of the Constitution in 1789 did not settle the federalism issue, primarily because the language in the original Constitution is exceedingly vague. The framers were themselves divided, so they left it up to future genera-tions to settle the issue. The biggest crisis of federalism occurred over slavery. In 1861, the southern states decided they had the right to secede from the United States if they did not agree with the policies of the federal government. The issue was settled in a bloody civil war: states do *not* have the right to secede unilaterally from the union; they have to work out their differences within the federal system.

Until Franklin Roosevelt's New Deal of the 1930s, the federal government was remarkably uninvolved in a wide range of domestic policy functions that we now take for granted. The halting response of states and localities to the Great Depression changed all that. Roosevelt swiftly moved the federal government into a whole range of functions, including social security, welfare, and regulation of the economy, that had previously been considered off limits. For the most part, however, Washington did not take over these functions but instead funded new programs with grants that were administered by state and local governments under varied federal rules. In the 1960s, under President Lyndon Johnson's leadership, the system of intergovernmental grants expanded tremendously.

Richard Nixon's election in 1968 began a period of reaction against the expanded powers of the federal government that has continued to this day. For the most part, Nixon did not try to roll back the functions of the federal government but instead deregulated the federal grant system and gave more power over grants to states and localities. The election of Ronald Reagan inaugu-rated a more radical phase of this new federalism in which efforts were made to return to the system that had existed before the New Deal when the federal gov-ernment left many domestic policy functions to the states. Although confidence in all levels of government has fallen since the 1960s, the drop in confidence has been most severe for the federal government. A 1995 CBS/*New York Times* poll found that 48 percent of the respondents felt that the federal government had "too much power," whereas only 6 percent felt that the states had too much.

The 1994 Republican takeover of Congress accelerated the trend toward devolution of federal powers to the states. In 1996, Congress passed, and Presi-dent Bill Clinton signed, the Personal Responsibility and Work Opportunity Act, which converted welfare from a federal entitlement for individuals to a block grant to states, leaving them significant freedom to set their own eligibility criteria and conditions for aid.

The Supreme Court is also moving in the direction of restricting federal power. In 1995, the Court ruled for the first time in sixty years that Congress had exceeded its authority under the Interstate Commerce Clause of the Constitution and declared the federal Gun-Free School Zone Act of 1990 unconstitutional

(*U.S.* v. *Lopez*). In a series of cases decided in 1999, 2000, and 2001, the Supreme Court made it more difficult for the federal government to enforce uniform national standards by giving states immunity against lawsuits alleging violation of federal laws in such areas as labor rights, violence against women, and discrimination on the basis of age or disability. As a former governor, President George W. Bush has promised to nominate justices who will support states' rights.

Those who favor devolution, however, have not completely carried the day. President Clinton pushed modest but popular extensions of federal responsibility in such areas as day care and education and appointed justices more supportive of federal power. In *Bush* v. *Gore* (2000), the conservative majority on the Supreme Court abandoned states' rights and overturned the order of the Florida Supreme Court to proceed with a statewide hand recount of the votes. The Court's decision effectively handed the presidency to Bush. The September 11 terrorist attacks greatly strengthened the case for expanded federal responsibilities, especially in law enforcement, public health, and airline safety. Finally, the 2002 Enron bankruptcy and scandal renewed calls for the federal government to more closely regulate corporations and ensure that accurate information is available to stockholders about the financial condition of companies.

In their essay "Beyond the Beltway," William Eggers and John O'Leary identify themselves with the "devolution revolution" sweeping the country at the grassroots. They stress that the purpose of devolution is not just to make the existing government programs work more efficiently but to raise the question of whether certain functions should be the responsibility of government at all. Such decisions, they maintain, are better left with those governments that are closest to the grassroots, where citizens can see immediately the costs as well as the benefits of government programs. Shrink the federal government, Eggers and O'Leary say, and grassroots organizations will flourish, becoming "laboratories of democracy." In place of the "one-size-fits-all" approach of the federal government, local organizations can fine tune their policies to suit local conditions. Moreover, argue Eggers and O'Leary in a section not reprinted here, the expanded powers of the federal government violate the U.S. Constitution, which in the Tenth Amendment reserves all powers not specifically given to the federal government "to the States respectively, or to the people."

John Donahue, the author of "The Devil in Devolution," argues that the words of the Constitution are much more ambiguous about the division of power between the federal government and the states than Eggers and O'Leary admit. Moreover, Donahue argues, it is up to each generation to adapt the federal system to the needs of the time. Donahue is critical of the recent trend toward devolution. Whereas Eggers and O'Leary base their argument primarily on what we call in the Introduction negative freedom—getting the government out of individual's lives—Donahue stresses positive freedom, or the idea that by acting together, we can accomplish things we cannot accomplish separately. Donahue argues that when each state acts separately, those things that we all share, what he calls the "commons," can be damaged. For example, states may pursue economic development knowing that much of the pollution produced by it will drift to other states. Donahue admits that federal bureaucracy may be wasteful, but he says the gains from decentralization have been greatly exaggerated. Moreover, the "courtship of capital" by individual states results in greater inequality. Instead of devolution resulting in "laboratories of democracy," Donahue suggests, the more likely result will be a "race to the bottom."

The contemporary debate on federalism reverberates with the same issues and arguments that have been made since the country's founding. It is unlikely that this debate will ever be completely settled. It seems as though each generation is doomed to decide anew the proper balance between Washington, D.C., and the states and localities. Even though there is no one neat answer, this does not mean there is not a better answer for our time. It is up to the reader to decide which position will best serve the core values of American democracy.

An intriguing aspect of this debate is that both sides argue that their position is reinforced by modern technology. The reader will have to sort this out. Do you think that new technologies make it easier for decision making to be decentralized, or do they increase the interdependencies in society, thus requiring more central coordination? Note that in the debate the two sides stress different values. Eggers and O'Leary emphasize individual freedom and local democracy, whereas Donahue puts more stress on national values and equality. In this debate are we forced to choose among competing values, or is there some way to slip between the horns of the dilemmas of devolution and serve all values?

Beyond the Beltway

WILLIAM D. EGGERS
AND JOHN O'LEARY

Our swollen federal government is in large measure incompatible with the demands of a modern society. In today's Information Age, there is little rationale for the federal government to control as much as it does. Large, centralized bureaucracies—whether that be IBM headquarters, the Kremlin, or Washington, D.C.—aren't well suited to an age of rapid technological change. In business, companies are decentralizing, empowering workers, and establishing autonomous business units. (It's not just trendy, it's an economic necessity.) In politics, economic reality is relegating central planning to the dustbin of history.

Washington, D.C., is becoming increasingly irrelevant. Explain authors Alvin and Heidi Toffler:

> It is not possible for a society to de-massify economic activity, communications and many other crucial processes without also, sooner

or later, being compelled to decentralize government decision-making as well. There is no possibility of restoring sense, order, and management "efficiency" to many governments without a substantial devolution of central power.

In today's rapidly changing world, the performance of the federal government looks worse and worse. There is a reason for this. As technology advances, decentralized decision making becomes more efficient in more and more cases. The problems of centralized decision making are inherent to *any* central authority, whether corporate or governmental, and are based on the relationship between knowledge, decision-making power, and technology.

As technology advances, productivity increasingly depends on knowledge. And, as communications technology advances, *general* knowledge—the kind that can be written down—becomes widely accessible. But *specific* knowledge—the kind that requires firsthand experience and that is difficult to communicate—is as difficult to obtain today as it has ever been. Other things being equal, *specific* knowledge—the kind that is dispersed throughout society—is growing in importance relative to *general* knowledge. Thus, as technology advances, it makes less and less sense to bottle up decision-making authority in a distant, centralized bureaucracy. Dictating the "one best way" from Washington, whether in education, welfare, or crime fighting, makes less and less sense. In particular cases, there may be a compelling reason for maintaining centralized control, such as the need for a coordinated national defense. But as a general principle, for efficiency's sake we should be increasingly devolving power *away* from centralized bureaucracies.

More than simply efficiency is at stake, however. We need to return to our roots as a self-governing people. Democracy is not a spectator sport. In a healthy democracy, citizens are actively involved in their own governance—and not simply on election day. Americans need to reconnect with the political process. Numerous functions now handled (and mishandled) by the federal government should be transferred back to the states and, wherever possible, to communities and individuals. Radical devolution brings government closer to home.

The Revolt Against Washington

In 1992, a highly respected economist wrote, "The federal government should eliminate most of its programs in education, housing, highways, social services, economic development, and job training."

These radical sentiments come from Alice Rivlin, then a Brookings Institution scholar and currently President Clinton's director of the Office of Management and Budget. Writing as an independent scholar, Rivlin called for a massive, radical devolution of federal programs to states.

Devolution is not a partisan issue. It is a recognition that centralized control and centralized decision making carries unacceptably high costs, both in terms of efficiency and democratic accountability. It is not a question of Democratic dictates from Washington versus Republican dictates. Following the election of 1994, Republican governors seem ready to oppose federal usurpation even when orchestrated by their fellow party members. "My priority is for Texans to be running Texas," says Texas Governor George W. Bush. "We're pretty good at what we do in Texas, and we like to be left alone by the federal government as much as possible." It's time to end the unequal partnership and the whole idea of one-size-fits-all national prescriptions. The American people have said it's time to move power *and responsibility* out of Washington—for good.

Devolution would restore clearer lines of responsibility between state and federal tasks. By bringing government closer to home, citizens could once again understand what each level of government does and hold the appropriate officials accountable at election time. Radical devolution will make much of what goes on inside the Beltway redundant or unnecessary. "You have to get rid of a lot of those vested interests in Washington," says Mayor [Stephen] Goldsmith [of Indianapolis]. "There are tens of thousands of people there whose only job in life is to control what I do."

The Department of Education, for example, spends about $15 billion a year on 150 different elementary and secondary programs. Since the department was created in 1979, Washington has become fond of imposing top-down solutions on local schools. Ohio Governor George Voinovich says his state's school superintendents spend nearly half their time filling out federal forms to get money that makes up only 5 to 6 percent of their school budgets.

. . . Joann Wysocki, [a] first-grade teacher from the Los Angeles Unified School District, . . . told us that the federal government was providing money for school days lost due to the 1994 earthquake. The rules required a special form, so every teacher had to copy *by hand* the attendance register. Photocopies were not acceptable. That's the rule. Wysocki doesn't like to jump through hoops for money from Washington, "That 'federal money' is our money to begin with, on the local level," she says. "Please don't insult anyone's intelligence saying anything else. The money comes back to us with strings attached. Why should the money go in the first place? Let it stay!"

Former Education Secretary William J. Bennett concurs: "We really do not need a Department of Education. We were educating our kids better before we had a Department of Education. Why do we have to pass the dollars from the states and locales to Washington and back out again?"

Sending housing, welfare, and social service programs to the states, as Rivlin proposes, would mean that Health and Human Services (HHS) and the Department of Housing and Urban Development (HUD) can also be dramatically downsized or eliminated. Even [former] Housing Secretary Henry Cisneros has admitted that much of what HUD does is expendable. "Many aspects of this department are simply indefensible," said Cisneros. "Change is necessary."

As for the Environmental Protection Agency (EPA), state environmental agencies are better positioned to know the problems of their states. "We don't need an EPA in Washington, D.C.," says [Arizona] Governor [Fife] Symington. "We have a Department of Environmental Quality in Arizona that is better at dealing with environmental problems in our state. You don't need an EPA in Washington with a command-and-control structure dictating environmental policies to the states." Though we believe the EPA's powers should be greatly curtailed, we're not as radical as Governor Symington in this regard. There are certain cross-border pollution issues that may require some form of federal involvement.

No More Federal Santa Claus

For radical devolution to become a reality will require a fundamental change in mind-set not only in Washington, but also among state and local politicians. Since the beginning of the Great Society, state and local officials have come to see the federal government as a kind of Santa Claus, doling out money for all sorts of programs. Many mayors and governors became professional beggars at the Capitol's steps. Programs that would never be funded with local tax dollars become "vital" so long as they are paid for with "federal" dollars.

Even more than states, big cities turned to Washington for help. Today, most cities are addicted to federal funds. Local politicians fear the loss of federal funds, but where do they imagine this money comes from in the first place? France, perhaps? Jersey City Mayor Bret Schundler, one of the few big-city mayors to oppose the crime bill, did so because he recognized that all "federal money" comes from people living in one of the 50 states to begin with. Says Schundler:

> Clinton wants to shift the burden of policing to the federal gov-
> ernment and increase taxes. After he takes his big cut, he'll give us a
> portion of the money back for local policing. What a bonehead idea.
> The solution is not to shift taxes and make us pay more. The solution is
> reducing the cost of local policing.

Washington doesn't add any value to the tax dollars it receives and then sends back down to cities and states; in fact, the federal bureaucracy subtracts value as it takes its cut before sending money back to local governments.

Less federal money flowing out of Washington should mean less money flowing into Washington from the residents of cities and states. Keeping the money closer to home will also mean more flexibility, control, and accountability. "We understand this is going to mean less dollars from Washington," says New Jersey Governor Christine Todd Whitman, "but if you relieve us of some of the most onerous mandates, we will live with that." State and local officials need to stop judging the worth of joint federal/state programs merely in terms of whether they are funded by "federal dollars." "We as Governors need to begin to ask a new question about programs," says Utah Governor Mike Leavitt. "Instead of asking is this a funded program, we should ask, should there be a federal role?"

In the transportation arena, for example, the federal government could get out of highway and airport funding by forgoing the gasoline tax and letting states raise construction money themselves—whether through a state gasoline tax, by raising landing fees or highway tolls, or by securing private debt. This approach would allow states to avoid a host of federal mandates—including the 55-mile-per-hour speed limit, the Davis Bacon Act, and the minimum drinking age—that accompany acceptance of federal highway funds.

Local Money for Local Problems

In many areas the ultimate goal of policy must be to transfer as much power, authority, and responsibility as possible from government to individuals and local communities. Once citizens see the true cost of local programs now being financed from Washington, they may not think they're worth the tax dollars spent on them.

Consider, for example, the uproar that ensued in Manhattan Beach, California, (where one of us lives) after the city council voted to spend money expanding a parking garage that residents felt would benefit only merchants. A front-page story in *The Beach Reporter* noted that "three dozen residents . . . bombarded the Manhattan Beach City Council on Tuesday. . . ." Another story noted:

> [M]any residents complained that they were continually having to come down to City Hall to protect their interests. District 4 Councilmember Bob Pinzler told the residents that they should continue voicing their opinions and concerns. "You have to keep coming down here to protect your interests," Pinzler said, "because the special interest groups are here all the time."

This is democracy at its local, messy best, with vigilant residents watching over elected officials spending their tax dollars. Chances are no one in Manhattan Beach even knew that the federal government spent $2.5 million of tax money to build a parking garage in Burlington, Iowa. That little item didn't make the front page of *The Beach Reporter,* and no Manhattan Beach residents drove the 3,000-odd miles to Washington, D.C., to testify before a congressional committee. At the federal level, organized interests have an enormous advantage. Former Education Secretary William Bennett estimates that 285 education lobbying groups have offices within walking distance of the Department of Education headquarters. The average Manhattan Beach parent doesn't have a prayer.

The parking garage story illustrates the phenomenon known as "bill averaging." Imagine going out to dinner by yourself. When ordering, you'll closely watch the cost of each menu selection because you'll be paying the entire bill. Even if you were going out to dinner with one or two friends, you still wouldn't spend outrageously because you'd still be footing a good portion of the bill.

Now imagine that you are going out to dinner with 75 strangers, and that the bill is to be divided evenly. If you are like most people, you are going to order liberally, enjoy an extra drink, maybe even dessert and coffee. And why not? Your order will only affect your bill a minuscule amount; besides, you can bet that everyone else will be ordering big. The only way to get your "fair share" is to order lobster and Lowenbrau.

The federal government is like going to dinner with 250 million strangers. Rather than everyone paying his own way, a complex tangle of cross-subsidies obscures everyone's actual bill.

It's time to ask for separate checks. The good folks of Burlington, Iowa, got a new parking garage because Uncle Sam took about one penny from every Manhattan Beach resident—and every other American. Because local taxpayers don't feel the bite, local officials love to spend "federal dollars." Would Altoonans have approved Altoona, Pennsylvania's multimillion dollar moving sidewalk if Altoonan taxes were going to pay for it? Unlikely. But since the folks in Burlington, Iowa, and Manhattan Beach, California, are footing the bill, the Altoonans are happy to be carried along.

The Devil in Devolution

JOHN D. DONAHUE

The shift in government's center of gravity away from Washington and toward the states—a transition propelled by both popular sentiment and budget imperatives, and blessed by leaders in both major parties—reflects an uncommon pause in an endless American argument over the balance between nation and state.

This moment of consensus in favor of letting Washington fade while the states take the lead is badly timed. The public sector's current trajectory—the devolution of welfare and other programs, legislative and judicial action circumscribing Washington's authority, and the federal government's retreat to a domestic role largely defined by writing checks to entitlement claimants, creditors, and state and local governments—would make sense if economic and cultural ties reaching across state lines were *weakening* over time. But state borders are becoming more, not less, permeable.

From a vantage point three-fifths of the way between James Madison's day and our own, Woodrow Wilson wrote that the "common interests of a nation brought together in thought and interest and action by the telegraph and the telephone, as well as by the rushing mails which every express train carries, have a scope and variety, an infinite multiplication and intricate interlacing, of which a simpler day can have had no conception." Issues in which other states' citizens have no stakes, and hence no valid claim to a voice, are becoming rarer still in an age of air freight, interlinked computers, nonstop currency trading, and site-shopping global corporations. Our current enchantment with devolution will be seen one day as oddly discordant with our era's challenges.

The concept of "the commons" can help to cast in a sharper light the perils of fragmented decision-making on issues of national consequence. In a much-noted 1968 article in *Science,* biologist Garrett Hardin invoked the parable of a herdsman pondering how many cattle to graze on the village commons. Self-interest will lead the herdsman to increase the size of his herd even if the commons is already overburdened, since he alone benefits from raising an extra animal, but shares the consequent damage to the common pasture. As each farmer follows the same logic, overgrazing wrecks the commons.

Where the nation as a whole is a commons, whether as an economic reality or as a political ideal, and states take action that ignores or narrowly exploits that fact, the frequent result is the kind of "tragedy" that Hardin's metaphor predicts: Collective value is squandered in the name of a constricted definition of gain. States win advantages that seem worthwhile only because other states bear much of the costs. America's most urgent public challenges—shoring up the economic underpinnings of an imperiled middle-class culture; developing and deploying productive workplace skills; orchestrating Americans' engagement with increasingly global capital—involve the stewardship of common interests. The fragmentation of authority makes success less likely. The phenomenon is by no means limited to contemporary economic issues, and a smattering of examples from other times and other policy agendas illustrate the theme.

Environmental Regulation

Antipollution law is perhaps the most obvious application of the "commons" metaphor to policy-making in a federal system. If a state maintains a lax regime of environmental laws it spares its own citizens, businesses, and government agencies from economic burdens. The "benefits" of environmental recklessness, in other words, are collected instate. Part of the pollution consequently dumped into the air or water, however, drifts away to do its damage elsewhere in the nation. If states held all authority over environmental rule-making, the predictable result would be feeble regulations against any kinds of pollution where in-state costs and benefits of control are seriously out of balance. Even in states whose citizens valued the environment—even if the citizens of *all* states were willing to accept substantial economic costs in the name of cleaner air and water—constituents and representatives would calculate that their sacrifice could not on its own stem the tide and reluctantly settle for weaker rules than they would otherwise prefer.

A state contemplating tough antipollution rules might calculate that its citizens will pay for environmental improvements that will be enjoyed, in part, by others. Even worse, by imposing higher costs on business than do other states, it risks repelling investment, and thus losing jobs and tax revenues to states with weak environmental laws. Congress explicitly invoked the specter of a "race for the bottom"—competitive loosening of environmental laws in order to lure business—to justify federal standards that would "preclude efforts on the part of states to compete with each other in trying to attract new plants." In a series of legislative changes starting in the early 1970s, the major choices about how aggressively to act against pollution were moved to the federal government. While aspects of enforcement remained state responsibilities—introducing another level of complications that continues to plague environmental policy—the trade-off between environmental and economic values moved much closer to a single national standard.

National regulation in a diverse economy does have a downside. States differ in their environmental problems, and in the priorities of their citizens. Requiring all states to accept the same balance between environmental and economic values imposes some real costs and generates real political friction. Yet even if the tilt toward national authority is, on balance, the correct approach to environmental regulation, there is reason to doubt we got all the details right. Moreover, logic suggests that the federal role should be stronger for forms of pollution that readily cross state borders, and weaker for pollution that stays put. But federal authority is actually weaker under the Clean Air Act and the Clean Water Act than under the "Superfund" law covering hazardous waste. Toxic-waste sites are undeniably nasty things. But most of them are situated within a single state, and stay there.

Governmental Efficiency

There is an alluring a priori case for predicting that public-sector efficiency will increase as responsibilities flow to lower levels of government. Yet this *potential* advantage largely fails to pan out; there is little evidence of a significant or systematic state efficiency edge. The states share with Washington the basic operational handicaps of the public sector.

The devolution debate, moreover, is almost wholly irrelevant to the debt service and middle-class entitlements causing most of the strain on citizens' tolerance for taxation. It is safe to assert that the ascendancy of the states will have, at best, a limited impact on the cost of American government. This is not an argument based on ideology, or economic theory, or learned predictions about comparative administrative behavior. It is a matter of arithmetic. In 1996 total public spending came to about $2.3 trillion. State and local activities, funded by state and local taxes, *already* accounted for about one-third of this total. Another one-third consisted of check-writing programs like Social Security and Medicare. National defense (12 percent of the total), interest on the national debt (10 percent), and federal grants to state and local governments (another 10 percent) accounted for most of the remaining third of the public sector. All other federal domestic undertakings, taken together, claimed between 4 and 5 percent of total government spending. Suppose every last thing the federal government does, aside from running defense and foreign affairs and writing checks (to entitlement claimants, debt holders, and state and local governments) were transferred to the states—national parks and museums, air-traffic control, the FBI, the border patrol, the Centers for Disease Control, the National Weather Service, student loans, the space program, and all the rest. Suppose, then, that the states proved able to do *everything* that the federal government used to do a full 10 percent more efficiently. The cost of government would fall by a little under one-half of one percent.

Beyond the low ceiling on cost savings—and more pertinent to the hidden issue of the *quality* of government—is the similarity between most federal agencies and most state agencies on the core characteristics of scale, complexity, and administration by legislative statute and formal rules. It is rare that economic or managerial imperatives will call for the reassignment of authority away from central government, but then stop at the states. State boundaries have been drawn by a capricious history, and only occasionally (and then by accident) does a state constitute the most logical economic unit for either making policy or delivering services. The coalition between the state-sovereignty constitutionalists and the efficient-scale decentralizers is based on a misunderstanding, and will break down as soon as it begins to succeed.

More promising strategies for improving the efficiency with which public purposes are pursued usually involve going *beyond* devolution to the states. The array of options includes privatization, to enlist private-sector efficiency advantages in the service of public goals; vouchers, to assign purchasing power while letting individuals choose how to deploy it; and the empowerment (through authority and resources) of levels of government smaller than the state, including cities, towns, and school districts. None of these strategies is without its risks and limits, but together they form a far richer menu of reform possibilities than the simple switch from federal to state bureaucracy.

Devolution is often, though misleadingly, cast as a way station toward such fundamental reforms. Its popularity among those convinced of American government's shortcomings, and committed to repairing them, diverts reformist energy that could be put to better use. State governments are only slightly, if any, less bureaucratic than Washington, and no less jealous of power or resistant to change. Power dislodged from federal bureaus is likely to stick at the state level instead of diffusing further. The characteristic pattern of American intergovernmental relations is rivalry between state and local officials, and Washington more often acts as local government's shield against state hegemony than as the common oppressor of cities and states. The ascendancy of the states is thus unlikely either to liberate local governments or to unleash fundamental reform in how government operates.

Rising Inequality

It is by no means certain that America will prove able to reverse growing economic inequality and the erosion of the middle class, no matter how we structure our politics. Devolution, however, will worsen the odds. Shared prosperity, amid the maelstrom of economic change tearing away at the industrial underpinnings of middle-class culture, is an artifact of policy. Policies to shore up the middle class include work-based antipoverty efforts that become both more important and more expensive as unskilled jobs evaporate; relentless investments in education and job training; measures to strengthen employees' leverage in the workplace; and a more progressive tilt in the overall burden of taxation. The individual states—each scrambling to lure mobile capital, fearful of losing businesses and well-off residents to lower-tax rivals, anxious to minimize their burden of needy citizens—will find such policies nearly impossible to sustain. As Washington sheds responsibilities and interstate rivalry intensifies, only a small-government agenda becomes realistic. But even for principled small-government conservatives, devolution is likely to prove less satisfying than many expect. Since it has been justified in terms of improving, not shrinking, government, the ascendancy of the states represents no conclusion to the debate over the public sector's proper size and scope.

Like the run-up in federal debt in the 1980s and early 1990s, devolution short-circuits (rather than settles) deliberation over government's purpose by making activism impossible—for a time. America's federal system is sufficiently resilient that unless citizens are convinced of small government's merits, the tilt toward the states that suppress public-sector ambition will eventually be reversed, though only after an unpredictable price has been paid. The conservative intellectual Herbert Storing has argued that a strategy of crippling the activist impulse through devolution, instead of discrediting it through reasoned appeal, was "not only contrary to the best conservative tradition but also hopelessly unrealistic." By attempting to enthrone the states as the sole locus of legitimate government, conservatives muffle their own voices in the conversation over the country's future.

By the standards of those who credit any diagnosis of what ails America *other than* "big government," shifting authority to competing states is likely to solve minor problems while causing, or perpetuating, far graver ills. As states gain a greater share of governmental duties but prove reluctant or unable to tax mobile firms or well-off individuals, the burden of funding the public sector will tilt even more heavily toward middle-class taxpayers. Their resentment of government can be expected to intensify. Efforts to use state laws or regulations to strengthen employees' leverage in the workplace will often be rendered unworkable by interstate competition for business. America's largest source of fiscal imbalance—the unsustainability of middle-class entitlement programs as the baby boom generation ages—will be untouched by devolution, feeding cynicism about the imperviousness to solution of America's public problems. And the fragmentation of taxing and spending authority puts in peril the education and training agenda that defines our single most promising tactic for shoring up the middle class.

The global marketplace both gives new fuel to America's culture of opportunity *and* allows the range of economic conditions experienced within this erstwhile middle-class country to reflect, with less and less filtering, the whole planet's disparate array of fates. A middle-class national economy, within a world of economic extremes, is a precious but unnatural thing. The policies that sustain shared prosperity will be difficult, perhaps impossible, to pursue if America's center of gravity in economic policy-making continues its precipitous shift toward the separate states. Federal officials, as a class, are certainly no wiser, more farsighted, or defter at implementation than their state counterparts. But our country as a whole remains much less subject to the flight of wealth and the influx of need than are its constituent states. Policies to shrink the underclass and solidify the middle class are thus far more sustainable at the federal level.

Fixing the federal government is an intimidating proposition in the late 1990s. The trajectory of fiscal and political trends suggests that devolution will remain the focus of politicians' promises and citizens' hopes for some time to come. But the inherent limits of a fragmented approach to national adaptation will eventually inspire America to reappraise the ascendancy of the states. Not too far into the new century we will again collect the resolve to confront together our common fate. And we will once more take up, in the two-century tradition of Americans before us, the echoing challenge of George Washington's 1796 farewell address: "Is there a doubt whether a common government can embrace so large a sphere? Let experience solve it."

▮ DISCUSSION QUESTIONS

1. Think of a policy issue that you are interested in. Which level of government do you think is the most appropriate one to make decisions on this issue? Why?

2. Which level of government do you think is the most democratic—federal, state, or local? Can privileged elites more easily dominate at the local level or at the national level?

3. Many people argue that justice should be the same no matter where you live and that therefore the federal government should establish minimal standards of justice on certain issues. Do you agree or disagree? Do you think the federal government should guarantee every American medical care or a minimum income?

4. One of the problems with decentralizing decision making is that some local governments have much larger tax resources than others. Many inner cities, for example, are very poor. How would Eggers and O'Leary respond to this problem? What can be done about it?

5. Do you think that marriage law (divorce, child custody, and so on) should be decided by the federal government or the states? What about educational policy? Should the federal government establish national standards in education?

SUGGESTED READINGS AND INTERNET RESOURCES

In *From New Federalism to Devolution* (Washington, D.C.: Brookings Institution Press, 1998), Timothy Conlan argues that Nixon and Reagan actually had very different approaches to federalism. Jeffrey M. Berry, Kent E. Portney, and Ken Thomson in *The Rebirth of American Democracy* (Washington, D.C.: Brookings Institution Press, 1993) present evidence that decentralizing power all the way to neighborhood governments makes sense. Grant McConnell, in *Private Power and American Democracy* (New York: Vintage Books, 1966) argues, in contrast, that decentralization of power leads to tyranny by elites. Probably the best book on the possibilities and limits of state economic development efforts is Paul Brace, *State Government and Economic Performance* (Baltimore, Md.: Johns Hopkins University Press, 1993). For an interesting change of pace, read Ernest Callenbach's *Ecotopia* (New York: Bantam Books, 1975), an entertaining novel about environmentalists who take over part of the Northwest and secede from the United States.

James Madison Institute
www.jamesmadison.org
The James Madison Institute is a public policy research organization dedicated to promoting economic freedom, limited government, federalism, the rule of law, and individual liberty coupled with individual responsibility. The site includes a list of current books and policy studies.

Center for the Study of Federalism
www.temple.edu/federalism
This is the web site of a research and educational institute dedicated to the
scholarly study of federal principles, institutions, and processes. The center
seeks to increase and disseminate knowledge about federal systems around the
world. The site includes links to publications, including abstracts of articles in
the center's journal, *Publius.*

National Council of State Governments
www.csg.org
The web site of the National Council of State Governments has information on
state governments and state-level public policies.

U.S. Federalism Site
www.min.net/~kala/fed
In addition to descriptions of the issues and overviews of major contemporary
debates, the U.S. Federalism Site links to essential documents, key legal
decisions, and sites where debates are currently under way as part of the
unfolding debate on federalism.

4

Civil Society: Does America Face a Crisis in Civic Engagement?

In his magisterial *Democracy in America,* first published in 1835, the French political theorist Alexis de Tocqueville emphasized how important voluntary associations were to the health of American democracy. "Americans of all ages, all conditions, and dispositions, constantly form associations," wrote Tocqueville. Associations come in a thousand different types, he noted, "religious, moral, serious, futile, extensive or restricted, enormous or diminutive. . . . Wherever at the head of some new undertaking, you see the Government in France, or a man of rank in England, in the United States you will be sure to find an association."

The idea that associations are crucial to democracy is known as the theory of civil society. All voluntary associations that are neither part of government nor part of private, profit-making activities are included in civil society. These associations range all the way from the huge American Association of Retired Persons and the Red Cross to the local neighborhood association or even bridge club. Many of the associations of civil society are incorporated as nonprofits and therefore enjoy certain tax privileges. They can have large payrolls and raise large amounts of money through charitable contributions and government grants. Others are informally organized and often come and go with great rapidity.

Associations, both political and nonpolitical, are thought to perform important functions for democracy. First, they provide what are called "mediating institutions" between powerful public and private corporations on the one

hand and isolated individuals on the other. By joining together, people can protect themselves from being dominated or repressed by large bureaucratic organizations. Voluntary associations also provide important services that the public
and private sectors do not perform or perform poorly. Churches, a very
important part of civil society in the United States, take care of the homeless
and provide hospice care for the dying. In fact, the government now provides
many social services through grants to nonprofits, recognizing that nonprofits
may be more sensitive to the needs of particular populations and may be able
to leverage volunteers to extend the reach of government funds.

Perhaps the most important function assigned to associations in American
democracy is lifting citizens out of extreme individualism and educating them
into more public-spirited commitments. Tocqueville called this "self interest
rightly understood." What he meant by this is that by participating in voluntary
associations citizens begin to identify their own individual well-being with the
well-being of the group. Eventually, people attach these local public commitments to the nation as a whole. In the body of thought known as *republicanism*
(not to be confused with the Republican Party), this is known as educating
citizens into "civic virtue."

Periodically, throughout our history, Americans have become anxious
about our tendency to become excessively individualistic and materialistic. In
1985 a much-discussed book, *Habits of the Heart,* examined the problem of
excessive individualism and explored its antidotes in religion, politics, and work.
Many people argued that Americans had become too preoccupied with their
rights and were ignoring their responsibilities. Led by the sociologist Amitai
Etzioni, they formed themselves, in classically American fashion, into an association, the Communitarian Network. In 1991, they issued the Communitarian
Platform, a manifesto that stressed that our democratic rights ultimately
depend on strong communities rooted in moral values.

The collapse of communism in 1989 stimulated interest in civil society. As
the fledgling democracies in Eastern Europe and the former Soviet Union tried
to sink roots, it became clear that the soil of democracy was thin. Under
totalitarian communist governments people were discouraged from forming
independent associations that could challenge the authority of the Communist
Party. The new democracies lacked a rich association life that could give citizens
experience in self-government and pull them out of parochial mindsets. Democracy did better in nations that had formed strong associations. The democratic revolution in Poland was led by Solidarity, which gained its strength
from defiant trade unions and the Catholic Church.

In 1995, an article in an obscure academic journal entitled "Bowling Alone"
riveted the public's attention on the condition of civil society. Written by
Harvard University professor Robert Putnam, the title was based on the fact that
Americans were bowling more than ever but increasingly they were doing it
alone instead of in bowling leagues. In the article, Putnam documented the
decline of civic engagement, including voting, as well as more general
membership in associations. To organize his findings, Putnam utilized the
concept of social capital. This concept refers to the network, norms, and trust

that enable people to accomplish together what they cannot accomplish alone. Like financial or physical capital, social capital enables us to become more productive. Social capital does not just improve the functioning of democracy; it also can produce better schools, faster economic growth, and lower crime (for example, community watch programs, where neighbors watch each other's homes, reduce crime). By forcefully raising the question of whether the store of social capital in American society dangerously depleted, "Bowling Alone" became the subject of innumerable editorials and Putnam was invited more than once to discuss his theory at the White House.

The selection by Putnam that follows is from the book he published on the subject five years after the article. In the book Putnam analyzes an enormous amount of data on the condition of civil society. All the indicators point in the same direction—civic participation is declining, and Americans are simply not joining groups as much as they did in earlier periods. While older Americans are still quite civic-minded, those born after 1964, the Baby Boomers and Generation Xers, are much less involved. The decline of social capital, Putnam warns, could have dire consequences for American democracy. The political skills of citizens could atrophy, and they could lose trust in politicians and become alienated from politics. The result could be a political system that is less able to represent the various parts of society in decision making and less able to solve problems.

The article by William Galston and Peter Levine of the National Commission on Civic Renewal questions both the factual basis of Putnam's analysis and his interpretation of the facts. Many commentators have argued, as Galston and Levine do, that Putnam exaggerates the decline of social capital in the United States. Compared to other nations, Americans are still joiners. Instead of withdrawing from associations, Galston and Levine suggest, Americans may be simply shifting their activities from national and formal political organizations to more local and voluntary activities. They argue that we cannot simply equate membership in civic associations with a healthier democracy. Instead of voluntary associations being a steppingstone to political involvement, they may serve as a retreat from a political system that is viewed as immoral and untrustworthy.

In the selections that follow, we focus on the questions of whether there has been a decline in civil society and if there is, what this means. In his book Putnam extensively analyzes the question of the causes of the alleged decline of civil society. He cites a number of culprits, including work pressures and suburban sprawl, but attributes the most explanatory power to the privatization of leisure, particularly increased television viewing. Those who came of age when television became the dominant form of entertainment, his data show, have much less interest and involvement in civic affairs. In contrast, what Putnam calls the "long civic generation," those born between 1910 and 1940, have sustained impressive levels of civic engagement.

The debate over the causes of the decline in civil society has taken many different forms. One wing of the debate has been a dispute between conservatives and liberals. Conservatives argue that big government in the form of the welfare state has taken over many of the functions of voluntary associations, causing them to shrivel up and in many cases die. Welfare laws allegedly treat everyone the same and do not recognize the importance of community self-help and charity that builds on moral relationships. President George W. Bush's faith-based initiative is an effort to transform the relationship between government and churches, the most important voluntary associations in America. Bush wants to contract with churches to deliver social welfare services, such as drug counseling and job training. This is known as "charitable choice." Liberals are concerned that this will violate the separation of church and state, with public funds being used by churches to proselytize. Conservatives are concerned that public funding will force churches to give up their distinctive religious and spiritual commitments.

Instead of focusing on government, liberals frequently argue that the private economy is the main cause of the decline of civil society. Consumption and the accumulation of wealth, stimulated by advertising and economic booms (as occurred in the 1990s), have crowded out civic voluntarism and political activism. Americans are working longer hours than ever and have less free time to devote to civic affairs. Increasingly, Americans have substituted writing a check for being involved in face-to-face associations. Political scientist Theda Skocpol argues that, far from being harmful to voluntary groups, federal social policies have strengthened them. The American Legion played a major role in passing the 1944 GI Bill, which gave returning veterans free college tuition, and this bill, in turn, helped the American Legion to grow. More recently, former President Bill Clinton pushed passage of the AmeriCorps, which rewards young Americans for participating in voluntary activities by giving them a voucher at the end of their tour of duty that can be used to pay for education.

Although most analysts agree that a strong civil society is necessary for a strong democracy, there is much less agreement about how to go about building a stronger civil society. Civic commitments often grow not by deliberate actions but by accidents of history. The terrorist attacks of September 11, 2001, are an excellent case in point. Americans really seemed to unite together in the wake of the attacks. New Yorkers, widely known for ignoring each other, engaged in widespread acts of heroism and bravery to aid strangers. People volunteered to help out with the dangerous work of cleaning up and carting away the rubble. Voluntary contributions poured in from around the country to help the victims of terror. Roughly a quarter of all Americans reported giving blood immediately following the attacks. People's trust in government soared. Whether the surge in civic commitments following 9/11 will be long lasting or short lived remains to be seen.

Bowling Alone: The Collapse and Revival of American Community

ROBERT D. PUTNAM

I n recent years social scientists have framed concerns about the changing character of American society in terms of the concept of "social capital." By analogy with notions of physical capital and human capital—tools and training that enhance individual productivity—the core idea of social capital theory is that social networks have value. Just as a screwdriver (physical capital) or a college education (human capital) can increase productivity (both individual and collective), so too social contacts affect the productivity of individuals and groups.

Whereas physical capital refers to physical objects and human capital refers to properties of individuals, social capital refers to connections among individuals—social networks and the norms of reciprocity and trustworthiness that arise from them. In that sense social capital is closely related to what some have called "civic virtue." The difference is that "social capital" calls attention to the fact that civic virtue is most powerful when embedded in a dense network of reciprocal social relations. A society of many virtuous but isolated individuals is not necessarily rich in social capital. . . .

American society, like the continent on which we live, is massive and polymorphous, and our civic engagement historically has come in many sizes and shapes. A few of us still share plowing chores with neighbors, while many more pitch in to wire classrooms to the Internet. Some of us run for Congress, and others join self-help groups. Some of us hang out at the local bar association and others at the local bar. Some of us attend mass once a day, while others struggle to remember to send holiday greetings once a year. The forms of our social capital—the ways in which we connect with friends and neighbors and strangers—are varied.

So our review of trends in social capital and civic engagement ranges widely across various sectors of this complex society. . . . The dominant theme is simple: For the first two-thirds of the twentieth century a powerful tide bore Americans into ever deeper engagement in the life of their communities, but a few decades ago—silently, without warning—that tide reversed and we were overtaken by a treacherous rip current. Without at first noticing, we have been pulled apart from one another and from our communities over the last third of the century. . . .

Political Participation

. . . We begin with the most common act of democratic citizenship—voting. In 1960, 62.8 percent of voting-age Americans went to the polls to choose between John F. Kennedy and Richard M. Nixon. In 1996, after decades of slippage, 48.9 percent of voting-age Americans chose among Bill Clinton, Bob Dole, and Ross Perot, very nearly the lowest turnout in the twentieth century. Participation in presidential elections has declined by roughly a quarter over the last thirty-six years. Turnout in off-year and local elections is down by roughly this same amount. . . .

Voting is by a substantial margin the most common form of political activity, and it embodies the most fundamental democratic principle of equality. Not to vote is to withdraw from the political community. . . . On the other hand, in some important respects voting is not a typical mode of political participation. Based on their exhaustive assessment of different forms of participation in American politics, political scientists Sidney Verba, Kay Schlozman, and Henry Brady conclude that "it is incomplete and misleading to understand citizen participation solely through the vote. . . . Compared with those who engage in various other political acts, voters report a different mix of gratification and a different bundle of issue concerns as being behind their activity. . . . [V]oting is sui generis." Declining electoral participation is merely the most visible symptom of a broader disengagement from community life.[1] Like a fever, electoral abstention is even more important as a sign of deeper trouble in the body politic than as a malady itself. It is not just from the voting booth that Americans are increasingly AWOL.

Political knowledge and interest in public affairs are critical preconditions for more active forms of involvement. If you don't know the rules of the game and the players and don't care about the outcome, you're unlikely to try playing yourself. Encouragingly, Americans in the aggregate at century's end are about as likely to know, for example, which party controls the House of Representatives or who their senators are as were their grandparents a half century ago. On the other hand, we are much better educated than our grandparents, and since civics knowledge is boosted by formal education, it is surprising that civics knowledge has not improved accordingly. The average college graduate today knows little more about public affairs than did the average high school graduate in the 1940s.[2]

Roughly every other month from 1974 to 1998 Roper pollsters asked Americans, "Have you recently been taking a good deal of interest in current events and what's happening in the world today, some interest, or not very much interest?" Popular interest in current events naturally tends to rise and fall with what's in the news, so this chart of attention to public affairs looks like the sawtooth traces left by an errant seismograph. Beneath these choppy waves, however, the tide of the public's interest in current events gradually ebbed by roughly 20 percent over this quarter century. . . .

Scandals and war can still rouse out attention, but generally speaking, fewer Americans follow public affairs now than did a quarter century ago.

Even more worrying are intergenerational differences in political knowledge and interest. Like the decline in voting turnout, to which it is linked, the slow slump in interest in politics and current events is due to the replacement of an older generation that was relatively interested in public affairs by a younger generation that is relatively uninterested. Among both young and old, of course, curiosity about public affairs continues to fluctuate in response to daily headlines, but the base level of interest is gradually fading, as an older generation of news and politics junkies passes slowly from the scene. The fact that the decline is generation-specific, rather than nationwide, argues against the view that public affairs have simply become boring in some objective sense.

The post-baby boom generations—roughly speaking, men and women who were born after 1964 and thus came of age in the 1980s and 1990s—are substantially less knowledgeable about public affairs, despite the proliferation of sources of information. Even in the midst of national election campaigns in the 1980s and 1990s, for example, these young people were about a third less likely than their elders to know, for instance, which political party controlled the House of Representatives.[3]

Today's generation gap in political knowledge does not reflect some permanent tendency for the young to be less well informed than their elders but is instead a recent development. From the earliest opinion polls in the 1940s to the mid-1970s, younger people were at least as well informed as their elders were, but that is no longer the case. This news and information gap, affecting not just politics, but even things like airline crashes, terrorism, and financial news, first opened up with the boomers in the 1970s and widened considerably with the advent of the X generation. Daily newspaper readership among people under thirty-five dropped from two-thirds in 1965 to one-third in 1990, at the same time that TV news viewership in this same age group fell from 52 percent to 41 percent. Today's under-thirties pay less attention to the news and know less about current events than their elders do today or than people their age did two or three decades ago.[4]

. . . Voting and following politics are relatively undemanding forms of participation. In fact, they are not, strictly speaking, forms of social capital at all, because they can be done utterly alone. As we have seen, these measures show some thinning of the ranks of political spectators, particularly at the end of the stadium where the younger generation sits. But most of the fans are still in their seats, following the action and chatting about the antics of the star players. How about the grassroots gladiators who volunteer to work for political parties, posting signs, attending campaign rallies, and the like? What is the evidence on trends in partisan participation?

On the positive side of the ledger, one might argue, party organizations themselves are as strong as ever at both state and local levels. Over the last thirty to forty years these organizations have become bigger, richer, and more professional. During presidential campaigns from the late 1950s to the late 1970s, more and more voters reported being contacted by one or both of the major political parties. After a slump from 1980 to 1992, this measure of party vitality soared nearly to an all-time high in 1996, as GOTV ("Get out the vote") activities blossomed.[5]

Party finances, too, skyrocketed in the 1970s and 1980s. Between 1976 and 1986, for example, the Democrats' intake rose at more than twice the rate of inflation, while the Republicans' rose at more than four times the rate of inflation. More money meant more staff, more polling, more advertising, better candidate recruitment and training, and more party outreach. The number of political organizations, partisan and nonpartisan, with regular paid staff has exploded over the last two decades. . . .

Yet viewed by the "consumers" in the political marketplace, this picture of vigorous health seems a bizarre parody. The rate of party identification—the voter's sense of commitment to her own team—fell from more than 75 percent around 1960 to less than 65 percent in the late 1990s. Despite a partial recovery in the late 1980s, at century's end party "brand loyalty" remained well below the levels of the 1950s and early 1960s. What is more, this form of political engagement is significantly lower in more recent cohorts, so that as older, more partisan voters depart from the electorate to be replaced by younger independents, the net attachment to the parties may continue to decline.[6] Again, the Grim Reaper is silently at work, lowering political involvement.

Beyond party identification, at the grassroots level attending a campaign meeting or volunteering to work for a political party has become much rarer over the last thirty years. From the 1950s to the 1960s growing numbers of Americans worked for a political party during election campaigns, ringing doorbells, stuffing envelopes, and the like. Since 1968, however, that form of political engagement has plunged, reaching an all-time low for a presidential election year in 1996. Attendance at political meetings and campaign rallies has followed a similar trajectory over the last half century—up from the 1950s to the 1960s, instability in the 1970s, and general decline since the 1980s. . . .[7] In short, while the parties themselves are better financed and more professionally staffed than ever, fewer and fewer Americans participate in partisan political activities.

How can we reconcile these two conflicting pictures—organizational health, as seen from the parties, and organizational decay, as seen from the voters' side? . . . On reflection, . . . the contrast between increasing party organizational vitality and declining voter involvement is perfectly intelligible. Since their "consumers" are tuning out from politics, parties have to work harder and spend much more, competing furiously to woo votes, workers, and donations, and to do that they need a (paid) organizational infrastructure. Party-as-organization and party-in-government have become stronger, even as the public has grown less attached to the parties.[8] If we think of politics as an industry, we might delight in its new "labor-saving efficiency," but if we think of politics as democratic deliberation, to leave people out is to miss the whole point of the exercise. . . .

So far we have been considering political participation from the important but limited perspective of partisan and electoral activities. For most Americans, however, national election campaigns occupy only a small part of their time and attention. What about trends in political participation outside the context of national elections, especially at the local level? . . . The answer is simple: *The frequency of virtually every form of community involvement measured in . . . Roper polls* [from 1973 through 1994] *declined significantly, from the most common—petition signing—to the least common—running for office.* Americans are playing virtually every aspect of the civic game less frequently today than we did two decades ago.

Consider first the new evidence on trends in partisan and campaign activities. . . . In round numbers, Americans were roughly half as likely to work for a political party or attend a political rally or speech in the 1990s as in the 1970s. Barely two decades ago election campaigns were for millions of Americans an occasion for active participation in national deliberation. Campaigning was something we did, not something we merely witnessed. Now for almost all Americans, an election campaign is something that happens around us, a grating element in the background noise of everyday life, a fleeting image on a TV screen. Strikingly, the dropout rate from these campaign activities (about 50 percent) is even greater than the dropout rate in the voting booth itself (25 percent). . . .

That Americans in recent years have deserted party politics is perhaps not astonishing news, for antiparty sentiments had become a commonplace of punditry even before Ross Perot rode the antiparty bandwagon to national prominence in 1992. But how about communal forms of activity, like attending local meetings, serving local organizations, and taking part in "good government" activities? Here the new evidence is startling, for involvement in these everyday forms of community life has dwindled as rapidly as has partisan and electoral participation. The pattern is broadly similar to that for campaign activities—a slump in the late 1970s, a pause in the early 1980s, and then a renewed and intensified decline from the late 1980s into the 1990s. . . .

Like battlefield casualties dryly reported from someone else's distant war, these unadorned numbers scarcely convey the decimation of American community life they represent. In round numbers every single percentage-point drop represents two million fewer Americans involved in some aspect of community life every year. So, the numbers imply, we now have sixteen million fewer participants in public meetings about local affairs, eight million fewer committee members, eight million fewer local organizational leaders, and three million fewer men and women organized to work for better government than we would have had if Americans had stayed as involved in community affairs as we were in the mid-1970s. . . .

Let's sum up what we've learned about trends in political participation. On the positive side of the ledger, Americans today score about as well on a civics test as our parents and grandparents did, though our self-congratulation should be restrained, since we have on average four more years of formal schooling than they had.[9] Moreover, at election time we are no less likely than they were to talk politics or express interest in the campaign. On the other hand, since the mid-1960s, the weight of the evidence suggests, despite the rapid rise in levels of education Americans have become perhaps 10–15 percent less likely to voice our views publicly by running for office or writing Congress or the local newspaper, 15–20 percent less interested in politics and public affairs, roughly 25 percent less likely to vote, roughly 35 percent less likely to attend public meetings, both partisan and nonpartisan, and roughly 40 percent less engaged in party politics and indeed in political and civic organizations of all sorts. We remain, in short, reasonably well-informed spectators of public affairs, but many fewer of us actually partake in the game. . . .

So What?

By virtually every conceivable measure, social capital has eroded steadily and sometimes dramatically over the past two generations. The quantitative evidence is overwhelming, yet most Americans did not need to see charts and graphs to know that something bad has been happening in their communities and in their country. Americans have had a growing sense at some visceral level of disintegrating social bonds. It is perhaps no coincidence that on the eve of the millennium the market for civic nostalgia was hotter than the market for blue-chip stocks. For example, newscaster Tom Brokaw's book profiling the heroic World War II generation got mixed reviews from critics yet was a runaway best-seller. In Los Angeles there was an on-again, off-again movement to rename the LAX airport after the actor Jimmy Stewart, a military hero in real life who brought civic heroes Jefferson Smith and George Bailey to the silver screen. American nostalgia in the late twentieth century is no run-of-the-mill, rosy-red remembrance of things past. It is an attempt to recapture a time when public-spiritedness really did carry more value and when communities really did "work." As we buy books and rename airports, we seem to be saying that at a profound level civic virtue and social capital do matter.

Are we right? Does social capital have salutary effects on individuals, communities, or even entire nations? Yes, an impressive and growing body of research suggests that civic connections help make us healthy, wealthy, and wise. Living without social capital is not easy, whether one is a villager in southern Italy or a poor person in the American inner city or a well-heeled entrepreneur in a high-tech industrial district. . . .

The playwright Oscar Wilde is said to have mused, "The trouble with socialism is that it would take too many evenings."[10] Fair enough, but how many evenings does liberal democracy take? That democratic self-government re-quires an actively engaged citizenry has been a truism for centuries. (Not until the middle of the twentieth century did some political theorists begin to assert that good citizenship requires simply choosing among competing teams of politicians at the ballot box, as one might choose among compet-ing brands of toothpaste.)[11] [Here] I consider both the conventional claim that the health of American democracy requires citizens to perform our *public* duties and the more expansive and controversial claim that the health of our *public* institutions depends, at least in part, on widespread participation in *private* voluntary groups—those networks of civic engagement that em-body social capital.

The ideal of participatory democracy has deep roots in American politi-cal philosophy. With our experiment in democracy still in its infancy, Thomas Jefferson proposed amending the Constitution to facilitate grass-roots democracy. In an 1816 letter he suggested that "counties be divided into wards of such size that every citizen can attend, when called on, and act in person." The ward governments would have been charged with everything from running schools to caring for the poor to operating police and military forces to maintaining public roads. Jefferson believed that "making every citizen an acting member of the government, and in the of-fices nearest and most interesting to him, will attach him by his strongest feelings to the independence of his country, and its republican constitu-tion."[12]

Visiting American shores a decade later, Alexis de Tocqueville struck a similar note, suggesting that even in the absence of Jeffersonian ward gov-ernments, Americans' local civic activity served as the handmaiden of their national democratic community: "It is difficult to draw a man out of his own circle to interest him in the destiny of the state," Tocqueville observed, "because he does not clearly understand what influence the destiny of the state can have upon his own lot. But if it is proposed to make a road cross the end of his estate, he will see at a glance that there is a connection be-tween the small public affair and his greatest private affairs; and he will dis-cover, without its being shown to him, the close tie that unites private to general interest." . . .[13]

Echoing Tocqueville's observations, many contemporary students of democracy have come to celebrate "mediating" or "intermediary" associa-tions, be they self-consciously or only indirectly political, as fundamental to maintaining a vibrant democracy.[14] Voluntary associations and the social networks of civil society that we have been calling "social capital" con-tribute to democracy in two different ways: they have "external" effects on the larger polity, and they have "internal" effects on participants them-selves.

Externally, voluntary associations, from churches and professional soci-eties to Elks clubs and reading groups, allow individuals to express their in-terests and demands on government and to protect themselves from abuses of power by their political leaders. Political information flows through social networks, and in these networks public life is discussed. As so often, Tocqueville saw this point clearly: "When some view is represented by an association, it must take clearer and more precise shape. It counts its supporters and involves them in its cause; these supporters get to know one another, and numbers increase zeal. An association unites the energies of divergent minds and vigorously directs them toward a clearly indicated goal." . . .[15]

Internally, associations and less formal networks of civic engagement instill in their members habits of cooperation and public-spiritedness, as well as the practical skills necessary to partake in public life. Tocqueville observed that "feelings and ideas are renewed, the heart enlarged, and the understanding developed only by the reciprocal action of men one upon another."[16] Prophylactically, community bonds keep individuals from falling prey to extremist groups that target isolated and untethered individuals. Studies of political psychology over the last forty years have suggested that "people divorced from community, occupation, and association are first and foremost among the supporters of extremism."[17]

More positively, voluntary associations are places where social and civic skills are learned—"schools for democracy." . . . The most systematic study of civic skills in contemporary America suggests that for working-class Americans voluntary associations and churches offer the best opportunities for civic skill building, and even for professionals such groups are second only to the workplace as sites for civic learning. Two-thirds or more of the members of religious, literary, youth, and fraternal/service organizations exercised such civic skills as giving a presentation or running a meeting.[18] Churches, in particular, are one of the few vital institutions left in which low-income, minority, and disadvantaged citizens of all races can learn politically relevant skills and be recruited into political action.[19] The implication is vitally important to anyone who values egalitarian democracy: without such institutions, the class bias in American politics would be much greater.[20]

Just as associations inculcate democratic habits, they also serve as forums for thoughtful deliberation over vital public issues. Political theorists have lately renewed their attention to the promise and pitfalls of "deliberative democracy."[21] Some argue that voluntary associations best enhance deliberation when they are microcosms of the nation, economically, ethnically, and religiously.[22] Others argue that even homogeneous organizations can enhance deliberative democracy by making our public interactions more inclusive. When minority groups, for example, push for nondiscrimination regulations and mandatory inclusion of ethnic interests in school curricula and on government boards, they are in effect widening the circle of participants.[23]

Voluntary associations may serve not only as forums for deliberation, but also as occasions for learning civic virtues, such as active participation in public life.[24] A follow-up study of high school seniors found that regardless of the students' social class, academic background, and self-esteem, those who took part in voluntary associations in school were far more likely than nonparticipants to vote, take part in political campaigns, and discuss public issues two years after graduating.[25] Another civic virtue is trustworthiness. Much research suggests that when people have repeated interactions, they are far less likely to shirk or cheat.[26] A third civic virtue acquired through social connectedness is reciprocity. . . . The more people are involved in networks of civic engagement (from club meetings to church picnics to informal get-togethers with friends), the more likely they are to display concern for the generalized other—to volunteer, give blood, contribute to charity, and so on. To political theorists, reciprocity has another meaning as well—the willingness of opposing sides in a democratic debate to agree on the ground rules for seeking mutual accommodation after sufficient discussion, even (or especially) when they don't agree on what is to be done.[27] Regular connections with my fellow citizens don't *ensure* that I will be able to put myself in their shoes, but social isolation virtually guarantees that I will not. . . .

Voluntary groups are not a panacea for what ails our democracy. And the absence of social capital—norms, trust, networks of association—does not eliminate politics. But without social capital we are more likely to have politics of a certain type. American democracy evolved historically in an environment unusually rich in social capital, and many of our institutions and practices—such as the unusual degree of decentralization in our governmental processes, compared with that of other industrialized countries—represent adaptations to such a setting. Like a plant overtaken by climatic change, our political practices would have to change if social capital were permanently diminished. How might the American polity function in a setting of much lower social capital and civic engagement?

A politics without face-to-face socializing and organizing might take the form of a Perot-style electronic town hall, a kind of plebiscitary democracy. Many opinions would be heard, but only as a muddle of disembodied voices, neither engaging with one another nor offering much guidance to decision makers. TV-based politics is to political action as watching *ER* is to saving someone in distress. Just as one cannot restart a heart with one's remote control, one cannot jump-start republican citizenship without direct, face-to-face participation. Citizenship is not a spectator sport. . . .

NOTES

1. Sidney Verba, Kay Lehman Schlozman, and Henry E. Brady, *Voice and Equality: Civic Voluntarism in American Politics* (Cambridge, Mass.: Harvard University Press, 1995), 23–24 *et passim*. On the decline in turnout, see Richard A. Brody, "The Puzzle of Political Participation in America," in *The New American Political System,* ed. Anthony King (Washington, D.C.: American Enterprise Institute for Public Policy Research, 1978); Raymond E. Wolfinger and Steven J. Rosenstone, *Who Votes?* (New Haven, Conn.: Yale University Press, 1980); Ruy Teixeira, *The Disappearing American Voter* (Washington, D.C.: Brookings Institution, 1992); Steven J. Rosenstone and John

Mark Hansen, *Mobilization, Participation, and Democracy in America* (New York: Macmillan, 1993); and Warren E. Miller and J. Merrill Shanks, *The New American Voter* (Cambridge, Mass.: Harvard University Press, 1996).

2. Verba, Schlozman, Brady, *Voice and Equality,* 362 *et passim,* and Michael X. Delli Carpini and Scott Keeter, *What Americans Know About Politics and Why It Matters* (New Haven, Conn.: Yale University Press, 1996), 116–134, 196–199.

3. When political interest in the DDB Needham Life Style surveys and interest in current events in the Roper surveys are each regressed on year of birth and year of survey, the regression coefficient for year of birth is quite high, while the coefficient for year of survey is virtually insignificant. In other words, the trends are entirely attributable to intercohort, not intracohort, change. On this methodology, see Glenn Firebaugh, "Methods for Estimating Cohort Replacement Effects," in *Sociological Methodology 1989,* ed. C. C. Clogg (Oxford: Basil Blackwell, 1989), 243–62; Stephen Earl Bennett, "Young Americans' Indifference to Media Coverage of Public Affairs," *PS: Political Science & Politics* 31 (September 1998):540, 539, reports that "individuals between 18 and 29 years of age are less likely than those over 30 to read, listen to, or watch political news stories, and less likely to pay close attention to media coverage of public affairs." See also Delli Carpini and Keeter, *What Americans Know About Politics,* 170.

4. Times Mirror Center for the People and the Press, "The Age of Indifference" (Washington, D.C.: Times Mirror Center, June 28, 1990). Delli Carpini and Keeter, *What Americans Know About Politics,* 172, confirm that "the knowledge gap . . . is driven more by generational than life cycle processes."

5. Joseph A. Schlesinger, "The New American Political Party," *American Political Science Review* 79 (December 1985):1152–1169; Larry Sabato, *The Party's Just Begun* (Glenview, Ill.: Scott, Foresman, 1988); John H. Aldrich, *Why Parties?* (Chicago: University of Chicago Press, 1995), esp. 15, 260. Author's analysis of National Election Studies, 1952–96.

6. On declining party identification, see Miller and Shanks, *The New American Voter,* ch. 7; Rosenstone and Hansen, *Mobilization, Participation, and Democracy,* ch. 5; and Russell J. Dalton, "Parties without Partisans: The Decline of Party Identifications Among Democratic Publics," (Irvine: University of California at Irvine, 1998). Independents are much less attentive to politics and public affairs and much less likely to participate. See Angus Campbell, Philip E. Converse, Warren E. Miller, and Donald E. Stokes, *The American Voter* (New York: John Wiley & Sons, 1960), and Miller and Shanks, *The New American Voter.*

7. Participation has declined in presidential election years more than in midterm years. Roughly half of the decline in presidential year activities and virtually all of the downward trend in midterm activities is due to generational replacement. Two other forms of campaign involvement are also measured in the National Election Studies: 1) displaying one's political preferences, by wearing a button, putting a campaign sticker on one's car, or putting up a sign at one's house; and 2) making a campaign contribution. Both show irregular changes, due in part perhaps to changes in question wording.

8. John Aldrich and Richard G. Niemi, "The Sixth American Party System: Electoral Change, 1952–1992," in *Broken Contract: Changing Relationships Between Americans and Their Government,* ed. Stephen C. Craig (Boulder, Colo.: Westview Press, 1995), 87–109.

9. In 1947 the median American adult had completed nine years of formal schooling; in 1998 that figure was about thirteen. According to the Census Bureau, the fraction of adults who had completed high school rose from 31 percent in 1947 to 82 percent in 1998.

10. Though this bon mot is widely attributed to Wilde, I have been unable to confirm that attribution.

11. Joseph Schumpeter, *Capitalism, Socialism, and Democracy* (London: Harper and Brothers, 1942).

12. Jefferson to Kercheval, July 12, 1816, in Merrill Peterson, ed., *Writings* (New York: Library of America, 1984), 1227, quoted in James P. Young, *Reconsidering American Liberalism* (Boulder, Colo.: Westview Press, 1996), 86.

13. Alexis de Tocqueville, *Democracy in America,* ed. J. P. Mayer, trans. George Lawrence (Garden City, N.Y.: Doubleday, 1969), 511.

14. See, for example, Peter L. Berger and Richard John Neuhaus, *To Empower People: From State to Civil Society* (Washington, D.C.: AEI Press, 1977; 1996).

15. Tocqueville, *Democracy in America,* 190.

16. Tocqueville, *Democracy in America,* 515.

17. William Kornhauser, *The Politics of Mass Society* (Glencoe, Ill.: Free Press, 1959), 73.

18. Verba, Schlozman, Brady, *Voice and Equality,* 378.

19. Frederick C. Harris, "Religious Institutions and African American Political Mobilization," in Paul Peterson, ed., *Classifying by Race* (Princeton, N.J.: Princeton University Press, 1995), 299. The evidence suggests that churches organized congregationally, such as Protestant denominations, tend to provide more opportunities for parishioners to build civic skills than do hierarchically organized churches, including Catholic and evangelical denominations. Protestants are three times as likely as Catholics to report opportunities to exercise civic skills. Verba, Schlozman, Brady, *Voice and Equality,* 321–322, 329.

20. Verba, Schlozman, Brady, *Voice and Equality,* 385.

21. Jon Elster, ed., *Deliberative Democracy* (Cambridge, UK: Cambridge University Press, 1998); Amy Gutmann and Dennis Thompson, *Democracy and Disagreement* (Cambridge, Mass.: Harvard University Press, 1996); J. Bohman, *Public Deliberation* (Cambridge, Mass.: MIT Press, 1996); C. Nino, *The Constitution of Deliberative Democracy* (New Haven, Conn.: Yale University Press, 1996).

22. Amy Gutmann, "Freedom of Association: An Introductory Essay," in Amy Gutmann, ed., *Freedom of Association* (Princeton, N.J.: Princeton University Press, 1998), 25.

23. See, for example, Will Kymlicka, "Ethnic Associations and Democratic Citizenship," in Gutmann, *Freedom of Association,* 177–213.

24. See Michael Walzer, "The Civil Society Argument," in Ronald Beiner, ed., *Theorizing Citizenship* (Albany: State University of New York Press, 1995).

25. Michael Hanks, "Youth, Voluntary Associations, and Political Socialization," *Social Forces* 60 (1981): 211–223.

26. David Sally, "Conversation and Cooperation in Social Dilemmas: A Meta-Analysis of Experiments from 1958 to 1992," *Rationality and Society* 7, no. 1 (1995): 58–92.

27. Gutmann and Thompson, *Democracy and Disagreement,* 52–53.

America's Civic Condition: A Glance at the Evidence

WILLIAM A. GALSTON AND
PETER LEVINE

T he publication of Robert Putnam's "Bowling Alone" in 1995 sparked a vigorous but often murky debate about America's civic condition. Some of the confusion arose from the inconclusiveness of the available data and some from a failure to draw certain basic distinctions.

It is not always recognized that civic health may be measured along several dimensions: participation in electoral politics, political and social trust, voluntary sector activity, and attitudes and conduct bearing on the moral condition of society, to name but a few. No one doubts that many forms of participation in official political institutions and activities have declined in recent decades or that Americans are less inclined to express trust in political leaders—and in one another. It is equally clear that in overwhelming numbers, Americans believe that their society is morally weaker than it once was. Whether they are right to believe this is a different, and more difficult, question. But the fact that they do has contributed to the surprising public salience of what might have remained an abstruse scholarly debate.

When we turn our attention to the voluntary sector, matters become less clear. Here again, some basic distinctions prove useful. Voluntary sector activities include formal organizational membership, volunteering, charitable giving, and informal socializing. Evidence suggests that trends in these areas may be diverging. Moreover, civic trends have not been linear during the past generation. Some declines that began in the 1970s—in aggregate group membership, volunteering, and philanthropy—appear to have halted and even reversed themselves in the late 1980s and early 1990s.

Group Membership

Judged against other industrialized nations, American civil society remains comparatively strong (though its relative standing may have fallen in recent decades). According to the 1990–91 World Values Survey, 82 percent of Americans belong to at least one voluntary association, a rate exceeded only in Iceland, Sweden, and the Netherlands. Furthermore, Americans belong to (and volunteer for) almost all types of groups at above-average rates. Only unions are relatively weak in the United States.

Existing methods for determining and comparing rates of group membership are far from perfect. For example, surveys have not typically asked people how many associations they belong to. Instead, they have asked whether people belong to various types of groups, and answers to these questions have been aggregated to produce a total number of memberships. This aggregate figure is misleading because anyone may belong to several groups of a particular type. Over time, Americans' memberships may have concentrated within certain categories, creating an illusion of decline.

Critics have identified two additional problems with established survey instruments. First, they point out that since strictly comparable poll questions have been asked only since the 1970s, it is hard to know whether aggregate group membership has declined since earlier decades. Second, they argue that existing surveys are unlikely to have captured all recent changes in U.S. associational life—for example, the proliferation of faith-based informal "small groups" that Robert Wuthnow has so painstakingly documented.

Still, there is no evidence that the average rate of membership has increased in the last quarter century. This is a surprise, because in the past rising levels of education have been linked with increased associational activity. It appears that two trends over the past quarter century have roughly counterbalanced each other: the proportion of high school and college graduates in the population has grown larger, but civic participation at every educational level has declined. People with high school diplomas but no college education have become about 32 percent less likely to join any associations, while there has been an increase in the proportion of people who belong to no organizations at all.

Trends among racial and ethnic groups reflect their distinctive history and condition. To take just one example, African Americans have traditionally combined formal political acts, such as registering people to vote, with group membership and protest tactics. Overall, there has been little decline in these forms of civic engagement since the "activist" 1960s, but African Americans have typically shifted their attention from civil rights struggles to quality-of-life issues in local communities. And as Frederick C. Harris has noted, African Americans without much formal education have, like their white counterparts, largely dropped out of community-oriented activities as well as formal political life.

Another way to break down aggregate measures of civil society is to look at types of organizations. Most categories have seen little change since 1972, when the General Social Survey first asked relevant poll questions. For instance, religious associations, sports leagues, and youth organizations have had stable membership levels. However, millions of people have left labor unions and fraternal societies such as the Elks and Masons, and similar numbers have joined professional associations. Membership in school service groups has substantially increased, perhaps because of recent efforts to link community service and learning. Finally, as Everett C. Ladd has pointed out, there has been a huge shift from mainline Protestant denominations to evangelical churches.

Not All Groups Are Created Equal

These changes may prove significant for the future of democracy in America. Throughout American history, voluntary associations have been valued because they are thought to build civic virtue, foster trust, encourage cooperation, and promote political participation. But on closer inspection, it turns out that not all associations promote democratic health in the same way or to the same extent.

Unions, for instance, are important sources of solidarity among working people. They have core functions that attract members, but they also offer social activities, information, and mutual assistance. They also offer a measure of political power to workers, thereby increasing pluralism and encouraging participation. Members of union households are 8 percent more likely than other people to vote. Though John Brehm and Wendy Rahn have found that union membership is a relatively weak predictor of overall associational membership, Eric Uslaner's research shows that unionized workers join more voluntary organizations and make more charitable contributions than other people do. The dramatic decline in union membership over the past 40 years has been exacerbated by factors—automation, international competition, the relocation of factories to nonunion states, and changes in federal labor law enforcement—that do not directly affect other associations.

Fraternal organizations and women's auxiliaries have suffered deep losses in membership since 1974. As Theda Skocpol has demonstrated, these groups traditionally had deep roots in their communities, and they offered men and women of different classes an opportunity to talk and cooperate more or less as equals—something that professional associations, which have grown in recent decades, do not do. The important question is what (if anything) will replace the cross-class local organizations that flourished through most of American history.

Church-affiliated groups are the backbone of civil society in America, involving almost half the population (compared with just 13 percent in the average industrialized democracy). Religious associations offer ways for people to give money, receive aid, hold meetings, recruit members for other associations, and learn about public issues. As Sidney Verba, Kay Lehman Schlozman, and Henry E. Brady have found, they are especially valuable for people with little income or education, who tend not to join other groups. Polls show that membership in such groups correlates with voting, volunteering, charity, and political activity.

Evangelical denominations are no exception. The experience, values, and personal networks that they develop transfer easily to politics. They have little hierarchy, and they demand intense participation from their members. For example, as part of their church activities, Baptists are much more likely to plan meetings and make presentations than are Catholics. The growth of evangelical denominations has introduced many people, especially lower-income people, to the political process and given them powerful tools for mutual aid.

Even as fundamentalist denominations encourage the faithful to rely on one another, however, there is evidence that they promote distrust of outsiders. This practice, ironically, helps voter turnout, because a fervent dislike for others motivates people to vote. The broader point, however, is that increased mutual reliance and trust within groups is not necessarily correlated with increased trust among groups.

Mailing-list associations, from the National Rifle Association to the Children's Defense Fund, have grown since 1970. Members of these groups contribute dues to support professional staff; but they do not donate much time or effort. Presumably, writing a check improves one's skills, knowledge, and interpersonal trust much less than attending a meeting or organizing a grass-roots movement.

But mailing-list organizations must not be stereotyped. The Sierra Club, for instance, has been described as a group whose members merely write checks and read newsletters. But as George Pettinico has noted, in one May weekend, the Los Angeles chapter alone organized 39 events, from classes to camping excursions, that were cooperative and participatory.

The controversy over contemporary national check-writing organizations raises broader historical and political issues about the relationship between top-down and bottom-up activities. Theda Skocpol argues that classic voluntary associations such as the PTA and the American Legion succeeded in creating both effective national lobbying arms and vital chapters or affiliates at the state and local levels, with close communication between the various tiers. It should also be said that even pure mailing-list organizations can be effective political actors, thereby freeing members to perform other civic tasks.

Still, a large shift from grass-roots groups to national membership organizations would be grounds for concern. In general, today's associations offer relatively few opportunities for local leadership and deliberation. The past 25 years have seen a marked decline in the share of people who belong to committees and serve as officers of local groups, a trend that parallels declines in such forms of local political activity as attending school board meetings and participating in political parties.

Associational Life and Healthy Democracy

Recent scholarship suggests complex links between associational activities and key political variables such as political participation, social trust, and confidence in government. Controlling for education and income, members of church groups, neighborhood associations, and sports leagues are especially likely to follow politics and vote—a correlation that supports the hypothesis that political participation is significantly more attractive for individuals who belong to social networks. It's not hard to see why. Making a meaningful decision at the polls requires a big investment of time and attention. Because members of voluntary groups have many opportunities to discuss politics, they can easily acquire information, and they are sometimes persuaded to vote by each other or by local politicians and activists who gravitate to organizations. By urging fellow members to support particular candidates or causes, citizens can multiply their political power.

Most studies find that associational membership is also linked to trust in other people. But researchers differ on the strength of the relationship and on the direction of the causal arrow between the two. A recent poll of Philadelphians by the Pew Research Center for the People and the Press showed no strong direct link between trust and participation in voluntary activities. However, Philadelphians who believed that they could "make a difference" tended to be trusting; they were also especially likely to volunteer.

Interpersonal trust and confidence in government tend to go together. Some research suggests that disenchantment with official institutions is an important cause of wariness toward other people. When political leaders let us down, we draw negative conclusions about human nature in general. The reverse is presumably true as well: wariness toward other people (stemming from crime, family dysfunction, and other sources) may affect our confidence in politicians.

Yet trust in government has fallen more precipitously than interpersonal trust. Much of the decline took place in 1963–75, an era defined largely by Vietnam and Watergate. And perhaps, to a significant extent, the decline was justified. But there now exists, at least at the extremes, evidence of paranoia rather than healthy distrust. According to a recent study by the University of Virginia's Post-Modernity Project, a fifth of Americans believe that the governing elite is "involved in a conspiracy." Widespread fear of major public institutions not only creates generalized distrust thereby discouraging group membership—but may also cause people to favor exclusive and inward-looking organizations. As noted by Warren E. Miller and J. Merrill Shanks, excessive cynicism about politics and government may well discourage voting and other forms of political participation. A presumption that politicians are unworthy keeps many honorable people out of the field. And a belief in conspiracies prevents citizens from making critical distinctions among leaders, organizations, and ideologies.

A Refuge from Politics?

The evidence now available does not permit firm conclusions about the overall condition of associational life in America. But it does seem that voluntary activities are on balance healthier than are formal political institutions and processes. Indeed, citizens, particularly the youngest, seem to be shifting their preferred civic involvement from official politics to the voluntary sector. If so, the classic Tocquevillian thesis would have to be modified: local civic life, far from acting as a school for wider political involvement, may increasingly serve as a refuge from (and alternative to) it. The consequences for the future of our democracy could be significant.

DISCUSSION QUESTIONS

1. How many voluntary organizations do you belong to? Are they mainly political or civic? What is the main reason you do not join more?

2. Is it better if people trust the government more, or is it better to be skeptical of the government and constantly question its actions?

3. Do you think young people today are less civically involved than their parents? Does society today make it more difficult to get involved than, say, thirty years ago? Do young people today use voluntary commitments as a substitute for political participation, as Galston and Levine suggest?

4. Advertising stimulates us to consume more and earn more money. In your opinion, would advertisements that tried to make civic involvements sexy or cool be effective? What is the best way to stimulate greater civic participation?

5. What effect did the terrorist attacks have on your attitudes toward government and civic voluntarism? Are you concerned that the surge in patriotism that followed the attacks of 9/11 will result in the loss of civil liberties or in unjustified use of military force abroad?

SUGGESTED READINGS AND INTERNET RESOURCES

Robert Putnam's *Bowling Alone: The Collapse and Revival of American Community* (New York: Simon and Schuster, 2000) is an excellent starting point to enter the debate on the condition of American civil society. The most extensive factual critique of Putnam's thesis is Everett Carll Ladd's *The Ladd Report* (New York: Free Press, 1999). An influential early statement of the thesis that big government is responsible for the decline of civil society is Peter L. Berger and Richard John Neuhaus, *To Empower People: The Role of Mediating Structures in Public Policy* (Washington, D.C.: American Enterprise Institute for Public Policy Research, 1977). An excellent collection of articles from both ends of the political spectrum is E. J. Dionne Jr., *Community Works: The Revival of Civil Society in America* (Washington, D.C.: Brookings Institution Press, 1998). One of the best collection of scholarly articles on civil society is Theda Skocpol and

Morris P. Fiorina, eds., *Civic Engagement in American Democracy* (Washington, D.C.: Brookings Institution Press, 1999).

Civil Society International
www.civilsoc.org
This is the web site of an organization dedicated to strengthening civic organizations and democratic institutions all over the globe.

Center for Civil Society Studies
www.jhu.edu/~ccss
Housed at the Johns Hopkins University Institute for Policy Studies, this web site reports on research designed to help philanthropies and nonprofits carry out their missions.

Informal Education Encyclopedia/Forum
www.infed.org/thinkers/putnam.htm
This site provides background on Putnam and a bibliography that gives hyper-links to his works as well as to other publications examining the civil society debate.

5

Political Economy: How Democratic Is the Free Market Economy?

At first glance, democratic politics and free market economics seem to go together. The liberty to speak, to practice any religion or none at all, and to participate in politics has often come to be associated with the right to make as much money as we can, to succeed or fail according to our own merits in a free marketplace. Free enterprise seems as unintimidating as a yard sale or a bazaar, with many buyers and sellers, colorful haggling, and a variety of products from which to choose. In contrast, big, intrusive government, with its taxes, police, laws, and bureaucracy, appears to present the greatest threat to all these rights. The equation of democracy with free market capitalism seems, especially since the demise of communism, the best and now the only economic game in town. After all, aren't the most prosperous countries in the world also the most free? And even if there are sometimes problems, what would be an alternative to what we have?

At closer inspection, though, the marriage between democracy and contemporary capitalism continues to be a contentious one everywhere. In Singapore and China, for instance, the rise of the market economy has hardly led to political freedom. And in America, free enterprise capitalism and political democracy may exist at the same time, but their relationship is hardly cozy. Everywhere, free market capitalism seems to generate enormous wealth, but also wrenching instability. *Political economy* is the study of the relationship between the two in the very different countries around the globe. The two essays that follow ask what the roles of government, citizens, corporations, workers, and consumers actually *are* in America and also what they *should* be so as to best serve the public interest.

Perhaps the most important debate in political economy concerns the relationship among democracy, equality, and economic efficiency. Aristotle wrote that democracy couldn't tolerate extremes of wealth and poverty; large inequalities destroyed the spirit of self-sacrifice and fellowship necessary in a democracy. Politics became less the search for the common good than the single-minded pursuit of material interests by rich and poor alike. While the wealthy fell into luxury and decadence, the poor would sink into ignorance and envy.

For those who believe that economic equality and social equality are important for democratic politics, recent trends in our political economy are indeed ominous. Despite impressive economic growth, the U.S. economic system at the beginning of the millenium features high levels of income and wealth inequality. The income and wealth gap has widened continually at the expense of what was once a very large and politically predominant middle class. While the economy has produced new jobs and vast new wealth, workers in the most rapidly expanding areas (home health aides, orderlies, restaurant workers) are paid very low wages and are largely deprived of health and pension benefits. In the late 1990s, nearly half the national income went to just 20 percent of the population. Most U.S. wage earners have been facing increased insecurity, as waves of corporate mergers, downsizing, outsourcing, and other "innovations" make companies leaner but also meaner. Is the free market really free? If it produces such results, can democracy survive such new extremes?

Many corporations and individuals as well as ordinary Americans defend such inequalities by pointing to the efficiency, growth, and technological innovation that they say are consequences of the free enterprise system. They argue that it is healthier to divide a very large economic pie unequally than to have no pie to divide at all; they go on to say that many of the new changes represent necessary and inevitable adjustments to the realities of the new global economy. The market, its many defenders claim, also preserves liberty by allowing each individual to compete fairly and consumers to choose among a wide range of new products. Free market economies are said to be meritocracies, rewarding the industrious with wealth and punishing the lazy with hardship. In George Gilder's words: "A successful economy depends on the proliferation of the rich, on creating a large class of risk-taking men who are willing to shun the easy channels of a comfortable life in order to create new enterprise, win huge profits, and invest them again."

The two essays that follow not only offer opposing views about the meanings of American democracy and capitalism; they also differ about the meaning of freedom, individual liberty, and equality. They disagree profoundly about what role government actually does play in relationship to the U.S. market economy as well as about what role it should play.

The first essay is excerpted from *Capitalism and Freedom,* by Nobel Prize winner Milton Friedman. It was originally written in 1962 and has since been reissued in many editions. Friedman describes himself as a "classic liberal" and tries to restore the original doctrine's political and moral meanings. Classic liberals like Friedman advocate maximum individual freedom in the face of government's tendency to tyrannize. The market economy, Friedman argues, "remov[es] the organization of economic activity from the control of political authority," thereby "eliminat[ing] this source of coercive power." Since liberty is synonymous with democracy, Friedman argues that government has only two legitimate roles. It must defend the national territory and act as an umpire, deciding the rules of the market "game" and interpreting them as necessary when free individuals compete with one another.

In the second essay, Samuel Bowles and Richard Edwards deny Friedman's claim that market capitalism and small government go together. They argue that "the growth of government is not something that happened in *opposition* to capitalism" but something that happened "*because* of capitalism." Bowles and Edwards go on to claim that a capitalist market economy is hardly a meritocracy; political power and economic power are linked and establish biased rules. Unlike Friedman, they say that the marketplace concentrates both kinds of power. Hierarchical corporations determine the investments and life circumstances for workers and communities and severely limit the meaning and scope of democratic government and citizenship themselves. For Bowles and Edwards, growing economic inequality spells the effective denial of liberty to the many. Corporate power often buys undue political influence, whether through campaign contributions or corporate ownership of the mass media.

The authors of both essays base their arguments on a defense of democracy. While reading them, ask the following questions: How would Friedman have defended himself against the charge that the market economy produces corporations that exercise unchecked and undemocratic power? What would Bowles and Edwards say to Friedman's charge that government often poses a threat to individual freedom and choice and thus to democratic liberty? How do both essays deal with voters and citizens and their potential role in controlling the production and distribution of economic resources? How would our political economy change if each author had his way? How would it stay the same?

Capitalism and Freedom

MILTON FRIEDMAN

Introduction

The free man will ask neither what his country can do for him nor what he can do for his country.[1] He will ask rather "What can I and my compatriots do through government" to help us discharge our individual responsibilities, to achieve our several goals and purposes, and above all, to protect our freedom? And he will accompany this question with another: How can we keep the government we create from becoming a Frankenstein that will destroy the very freedom we establish it to protect? Freedom is a rare and delicate plant. Our minds tell us, and history confirms, that the great threat to freedom is the concentration of power. Government is necessary to preserve our freedom, it is an instrument through which we can exercise our freedom; yet by concentrating power in political hands, it is also a threat to freedom. Even though the men who wield this power initially be of good will and even though they be not corrupted by the power they exercise, the power will both attract and form men of a different stamp.

How can we benefit from the promise of government while avoiding the threat to freedom? Two broad principles embodied in our Constitution give an answer that has preserved our freedom so far, though they have been violated repeatedly in practice while proclaimed as precept.

First, the scope of government must be limited. Its major function must be to protect our freedom both from the enemies outside our gates and from our fellow-citizens: to preserve law and order, to enforce private contracts, to foster competitive markets. Beyond this major function, government may enable us at times to accomplish jointly what we would find it more difficult or expensive to accomplish severally. However, any such use of government is fraught with danger. We should not and cannot avoid using government in this way. But there should be a clear and large balance of advantages before we do. By relying primarily on voluntary co-operation and private enterprise, in both economic and other activities, we can insure that the private sector is a check on the powers of the governmental sector and an effective protection of freedom of speech, of religion, and of thought.

---

1. Friedman is referring to John F. Kennedy's 1961 inaugural address.

The second broad principle is that government power must be dispersed. If government is to exercise power, better in the county than in the state, better in the state than in Washington. If I do not like what my local community does, be it in sewage disposal, or zoning, or schools, I can move to another local community, and though few may take this step, the mere possibility acts as a check. If I do not like what my state does, I can move to another. If I do not like what Washington imposes, I have few alternatives in this world of jealous nations. . . .

Government can never duplicate the variety and diversity of individual action. At any moment in time, by imposing uniform standards in housing, or nutrition, or clothing, government could undoubtedly improve the level of living of many individuals; by imposing uniform standards in schooling, road construction, or sanitation, central government could undoubtedly improve the level of performance in many local areas and perhaps even on the average of all communities. But in the process, government would replace progress by stagnation, it would substitute uniform mediocrity for the variety essential for that experimentation which can bring tomorrow's laggards above today's mean. . . .

The Relation Between Economic Freedom and Political Freedom

It is widely believed that politics and economics are separate and largely unconnected; that individual freedom is a political problem and material welfare an economic problem; and that any kind of political arrangements can be combined with any kind of economic arrangements. . . . The thesis of this chapter is . . . that there is an intimate connection between economics and politics, that only certain combinations of political and economic arrangements are possible, and that in particular, a society which is socialist cannot also be democratic, in the sense of guaranteeing individual freedom.

Economic arrangements play a dual role in the promotion of a free society. On the one hand, freedom in economic arrangements is itself a component of freedom broadly understood, so economic freedom is an end in itself. In the second place, economic freedom is also an indispensable means toward the achievement of political freedom.

The first of these roles of economic freedom needs special emphasis because intellectuals in particular have a strong bias against regarding this aspect of freedom as important. They tend to express contempt for what they regard as material aspects of life, and to regard their own pursuit of allegedly higher values as on a different plane of significance and as deserving of special attention. For most citizens of the country, however, if not for the intellectual, the direct importance of economic freedom is at least comparable in significance to the indirect importance of economic freedom as a means to political freedom. . . .

Viewed as a means to the end of political freedom, economic arrangements are important because of their effect on the concentration or dispersion of power. The kind of economic organization that provides economic freedom directly, namely, competitive capitalism, also promotes political freedom because it separates economic power from political power and in this way enables the one to offset the other.

Historical evidence speaks with a single voice on the relation between political freedom and a free market. I know of no example in time or place of a society that has been marked by a large measure of political freedom, and that has not also used something comparable to a free market to organize the bulk of economic activity.

Because we live in a largely free society, we tend to forget how limited is the span of time and the part of the globe for which there has ever been anything like political freedom: the typical state of mankind is tyranny, servitude, and misery. The nineteenth century and early twentieth century in the Western world stand out as striking exceptions to the general trend of historical development. Political freedom in this instance clearly came along with the free market and the development of capitalist institutions. So also did political freedom in the golden age of Greece and in the early days of the Roman era.

History suggests only that capitalism is a necessary condition for political freedom. Clearly it is not a sufficient condition. Fascist Italy and Fascist Spain, Germany at various times in the last seventy years, Japan before World Wars I and II, tzarist Russia in the decades before World War I— are all societies that cannot conceivably be described as politically free. Yet, in each, private enterprise was the dominant form of economic organization. It is therefore clearly possible to have economic arrangements that are fundamentally capitalist and political arrangements that are not free.

Even in those societies, the citizenry had a good deal more freedom than citizens of a modern totalitarian state.[2] . . . Even in Russia under the Tzars, it was possible for some citizens, under some circumstances, to change their jobs without getting permission from political authority because capitalism and the existence of private property provided some check to the centralized power of the state. . . .

Historical evidence by itself can never be convincing. Perhaps it was sheer coincidence that the expansion of freedom occurred at the same time as the development of capitalist and market institutions. Why should there be a connection? What are the logical links between economic and political freedom? In discussing these questions we shall consider first the market as a direct component of freedom, and then the indirect relation between market arrangements and political freedom. A by-product will be an outline of the ideal economic arrangements for a free society.

---

2. A totalitarian state is a political order in which state power is held by a single political party, with no political rights accorded to individuals. Friedman here is referring to the former Soviet Union and to other communist countries.

As liberals, we take freedom of the individual, or perhaps the family, as our ultimate goal in judging social arrangements. Freedom as a value in this sense has to do with the interrelations among people; it has no meaning whatsoever to a Robinson Crusoe on an isolated island. . . . Robinson Crusoe on his island is subject to "constraint," he has limited "power," and he has only a limited number of alternatives, but there is no problem of freedom in the sense that is relevant to our discussion. Similarly, in a society freedom has nothing to say about what an individual does with his freedom; it is not an all-embracing ethic. Indeed, a major aim of the liberal is to leave the ethical problem for the individual to wrestle with. The "really" important ethical problems are those that face an individual in a free society—what he should do with his freedom. There are thus two sets of values that a liberal will emphasize—the values that are relevant to relations among people, which is the context in which he assigns first priority to freedom; and the values that are relevant to the individual in the exercise of his freedom, which is the realm of individual ethics and philosophy.

The liberal conceives of men as imperfect beings. He regards the problem of social organization to be as much a negative problem of preventing "bad" people from doing harm as of enabling "good" people to do good; and, of course, "bad" and "good" people may be the same people, depending on who is judging them.

The basic problem of social organization is how to co-ordinate the economic activities of large numbers of people. Even in relatively backward societies, extensive division of labor and specialization of function is required to make effective use of available resources. In advanced societies, the scale on which co-ordination is needed, to take full advantage of the opportunities offered by modern science and technology, is enormously greater. Literally millions of people are involved in providing one another with their daily bread, let alone with their yearly automobiles. The challenge to the believer in liberty is to reconcile this widespread interdependence with individual freedom.

Fundamentally, there are only two ways of co-ordinating the economic activities of millions. One is central direction involving the use of coercion—the technique of the army and of the modern totalitarian state. The other is voluntary co-operation of individuals—the technique of the market place.

The possibility of co-ordination through voluntary co-operation rests on the elementary—yet frequently denied—proposition that both parties to an economic transaction benefit from it, *provided the transaction is bilaterally voluntary and informed.*

Exchange can therefore bring about co-ordination without coercion. A working model of a society organized through voluntary exchange is a *free private enterprise exchange economy*—what we have been calling competitive capitalism.

In its simplest form, such a society consists of a number of independent households—a collection of Robinson Crusoes, as it were. Each household uses the resources it controls to produce goods and services that it exchanges for goods and services produced by other households, on terms mutually acceptable to the two parties to the bargain. It is thereby enabled to satisfy its wants indirectly by producing goods and services for others, rather than directly by producing goods for its own immediate use. The incentive for adopting this indirect route is, of course, the increased product made possible by division of labor and specialization of function. Since the household always has the alternative of producing directly for itself, it need not enter into any exchange unless it benefits from it. Hence, no exchange will take place unless both parties do benefit from it. Co-operation is thereby achieved without coercion.

Specialization of function and division of labor would not go far if the ultimate productive unit were the household. In a modern society, we have gone much further. We have introduced enterprises which are intermediaries between individuals in their capacities as suppliers of service and as purchasers of goods. And similarly, specialization of function and division of labor could not go very far if we had to continue to rely on the barter of product for product. In consequence, money has been introduced as a means of facilitating exchange, and of enabling the acts of purchase and of sale to be separated into two parts.

Despite the important role of enterprises and of money in our actual economy, and despite the numerous and complex problems they raise, the central characteristic of the market technique of achieving co-ordination is fully displayed in the simple exchange economy that contains neither enterprises nor money. As in that simple model, so in the complex enterprise and money-exchange economy, co-operation is strictly individual and voluntary *provided:* (*a*) that enterprises are private, so that the ultimate contracting parties are individuals and (*b*) that individuals are effectively free to enter or not to enter into any particular exchange, so that every transaction is strictly voluntary. . . .

So long as effective freedom of exchange is maintained, the central feature of the market organization of economic activity is that it prevents one person from interfering with another in respect of most of his activities. The consumer is protected from coercion by the seller because of the presence of other sellers with whom he can deal. The seller is protected from coercion by the consumer because of other consumers to whom he can sell. The employee is protected from coercion by the employer because of other employers for whom he can work, and so on. And the market does this impersonally and without centralized authority.

Indeed, a major source of objection to a free economy is precisely that it does this task so well. It gives people what they want instead of what a particular group thinks they ought to want. Underlying most arguments against the free market is a lack of belief in freedom itself.

The existence of a free market does not of course eliminate the need for government. On the contrary, government is essential both as a forum for determining the "rules of the game" and as an umpire to interpret and enforce the rules decided on. What the market does is to reduce greatly the range of issues that must be decided through political means, and thereby to minimize the extent to which government need participate directly in the game. The characteristic feature of action through political channels is that it tends to require or enforce substantial conformity. The great advantage of the market, on the other hand, is that it permits wide diversity. It is, in political terms, a system of proportional representation. Each man can vote, as it were, for the color of tie he wants and get it; he does not have to see what color the majority wants and then, if he is in the minority, submit.

It is this feature of the market that we refer to when we say that the market provides economic freedom. But this characteristic also has implications that go far beyond the narrowly economic. Political freedom means the absence of coercion of a man by his fellow men. The fundamental threat to freedom is power to coerce, be it in the hands of a monarch, a dictator, an oligarchy, or a momentary majority. The preservation of freedom requires the elimination of such concentration of power to the fullest possible extent and the dispersal and distribution of whatever power cannot be eliminated—a system of checks and balances. By removing the organization of economic activity from the control of political authority, the market eliminates this source of coercive power. It enables economic strength to be a check to political power rather than a reinforcement.

Economic power can be widely dispersed. There is no law of conservation which forces the growth of new centers of economic strength to be at the expense of existing centers. Political power, on the other hand, is more difficult to decentralize. There can be numerous small independent governments. But it is far more difficult to maintain numerous equipotent small centers of political power in a single large government than it is to have numerous centers of economic strength in a single large economy. There can be many millionaires in one large economy. But can there be more than one really outstanding leader, one person on whom the energies and enthusiasms of his countrymen are centered? If the central government gains power, it is likely to be at the expense of local governments. There seems to be something like a fixed total of political power to be distributed. Consequently, if economic power is joined to political power, concentration seems almost inevitable. On the other hand, if economic power is kept in separate hands from political power, it can serve as a check and a counter to political power. . . .

In a capitalist society, it is only necessary to convince a few wealthy people to get funds to launch any idea, however strange, and there are many such persons, many independent foci of support. And, indeed, it is not even necessary to persuade people or financial institutions with available funds of the soundness of the ideas to be propagated. It is only necessary to persuade them that the propagation can be financially successful; that the newspaper or magazine or book or other venture will be profitable. The competitive publisher, for example, cannot afford to publish only writing with which he personally agrees; his touchstone must be the likelihood that the market will be large enough to yield a satisfactory return on his investment. . . .

The Role of Government in a Free Society

. . . From this standpoint, the role of the market is that it permits unanimity without conformity. . . . On the other hand, the characteristic feature of action through explicitly political channels is that it tends to require or to enforce substantial conformity. . . . The typical issue must be decided "yes" or "no"; at most, provision can be made for a fairly limited number of alternatives. . . .

The use of political channels, while inevitable, tends to strain the social cohesion essential for a stable society. The strain is least if agreement for joint action need be reached only on a limited range of issues on which people in any event have common views. Every extension of the range of issues for which explicit agreement is sought strains further the delicate threads that hold society together. If it goes so far as to touch an issue on which men feel deeply yet differently, it may well disrupt the society. Fundamental differences in basic values can seldom if ever be resolved at the ballot box; ultimately they can only be decided, though not resolved, by conflict. The religious and civil wars of history are a bloody testament to this judgment.

The widespread use of the market reduces the strain on the social fabric by rendering conformity unnecessary with respect to any activities it encompasses. The wider the range of activities covered by the market, the fewer are the issues on which explicitly political decisions are required and hence on which it is necessary to achieve agreement. In turn, the fewer the issues on which agreement is necessary, the greater is the likelihood of getting agreement while maintaining a free society. . . .

Government as Rule-Maker and Umpire

. . . Just as a good game requires acceptance by the players both of the rules and of the umpire to interpret and enforce them, so a good society requires that its members agree on the general conditions that will govern relations among them, on some means of arbitrating different interpretations of these conditions, and on some device for enforcing compliance with the generally accepted rules. . . . In both games and society also, no set of rules can prevail unless most participants most of the time conform to them without external sanctions; unless that is, there is a broad underlying social consensus. But we cannot rely on custom or on this consensus alone to interpret and to enforce the rules; we need an umpire. These then are the basic roles of government in a free society: to provide a means whereby we can modify the rules, to mediate differences among us on the meaning of the rules, and to enforce compliance with the rules on the part of those few who would otherwise not play the game.

The need for government in these respects arises because absolute freedom is impossible. However attractive anarchy may be as a philosophy, it is not feasible in a world of imperfect men. Men's freedoms can conflict, and when they do, one man's freedom must be limited to preserve another's— as a Supreme Court Justice once put it, "My freedom to move my fist must be limited by the proximity of your chin.". . .

Action Through Government on Grounds of Technical Monopoly and Neighborhood Effects

The role of government . . . is to do something that the market cannot do for itself, namely, to determine, arbitrate, and enforce the rules of the game. We may also want to do through government some things that might conceivably be done through the market but that technical or similar conditions render it difficult to do in that way. These all reduce to cases in which strictly voluntary exchange is either exceedingly costly or practically impossible. There are two general classes of such cases: monopoly and similar market imperfections, and neighborhood effects.

Exchange is truly voluntary only when nearly equivalent alternatives exist. Monopoly implies the absence of alternatives and thereby inhibits effective freedom of exchange. In practice, monopoly frequently, if not generally, arises from government support or from collusive agreements among individuals. With respect to these, the problem is either to avoid governmental fostering of monopoly or to stimulate the effective enforcement of rules such as those embodied in our anti-trust laws. However, monopoly may also arise because it is technically efficient to have a single producer or enterprise. I venture to suggest that such cases are more limited than is supposed but they unquestionably do arise. . . .

A second general class of cases in which strictly voluntary exchange is impossible arises when actions of individuals have effects on other individuals for which it is not feasible to charge or recompense them. This is the problem of "neighborhood effects." An obvious example is the pollution of a stream. The man who pollutes a stream is in effect forcing others to exchange good water for bad. These others might be willing to make the exchange at a price. But it is not feasible for them, acting individually, to avoid the exchange or to enforce appropriate compensation. . . .

Parks are an interesting example because they illustrate the difference between cases that can and cases that cannot be justified by neighborhood effects, and because almost everyone at first sight regards the conduct of National Parks as obviously a valid function of government. In fact, however, neighborhood effects may justify a city park; they do not justify a national park, like Yellowstone National Park or the Grand Canyon. What is the fundamental difference between the two? For the city park, it is extremely difficult to identify the people who benefit from it and to charge them for the benefits which they receive. If there is a park in the middle of the city, the houses on all sides get the benefit of the open space, and people who walk through it or by it also benefit. To maintain toll collectors at the gates or to impose annual charges per window overlooking the park would be very expensive and difficult. The entrances to a national park like Yellowstone, on the other hand, are few; most of the people who come stay for a considerable period of time and it is perfectly feasible to set up toll gates and collect admission charges. This is indeed now done, though the charges do not cover the whole costs. If the public wants this kind of an activity enough to pay for it, private enterprises will have every incentive to provide such parks. And, of course, there are many private enterprises of this nature now in existence. I cannot myself conjure up any neighborhood effects or important monopoly effects that would justify governmental activity in this area.

Considerations like those I have treated under the heading of neighborhood effects have been used to rationalize almost every conceivable intervention. In many instances, however, this rationalization is special pleading rather than a legitimate application of the concept of neighborhood effects. Neighborhood effects cut both ways. They can be a reason for limiting the activities of government as well as for expanding them. . . .

Action Through Government on Paternalistic Grounds

Freedom is a tenable objective only for responsible individuals. We do not believe in freedom for madmen or children. The necessity of drawing a line between responsible individuals and others is inescapable, yet it means that there is an essential ambiguity in our ultimate objective of freedom. Paternalism is inescapable for those whom we designate as not responsible.

The clearest case, perhaps, is that of madmen. We are willing neither to permit them freedom nor to shoot them. It would be nice if we could rely on voluntary activities of individuals to house and care for the madmen. But I think we cannot rule out the possibility that such charitable activities will be inadequate, if only because of the neighborhood effect involved in the fact that I benefit if another man contributes to the care of the insane. For this reason, we may be willing to arrange for their care through government.

Children offer a more difficult case. The ultimate operative unit in our society is the family, not the individual. Yet the acceptance of the family as the unit rests in considerable part on expediency rather than principle. We believe that parents are generally best able to protect their children and to provide for their development into responsible individuals for whom freedom is appropriate. But we do not believe in the freedom of parents to do what they will with other people. The children are responsible individuals in embryo, and a believer in freedom believes in protecting their ultimate rights.

To put this in a different and what may seem a more callous way, children are at one and the same time consumer goods and potentially responsible members of society. The freedom of individuals to use their economic resources as they want includes the freedom to use them to have children—to buy, as it were, the services of children as a particular form of consumption. But once this choice is exercised, the children have a value in and of themselves and have a freedom of their own that is not simply an extension of the freedom of the parents.

The paternalistic ground for governmental activity is in many ways the most troublesome to a liberal; for it involves the acceptance of a principle—that some shall decide for others—which he finds objectionable in most applications and which he rightly regards as a hallmark of his chief intellectual opponents, the proponents of collectivism in one or another of its guises, whether it be communism, socialism, or a welfare state. Yet there is no use pretending that problems are simpler than in fact they are. There is no avoiding the need for some measure of paternalism. . . .

Conclusion

A government which maintained law and order, defined property rights, served as a means whereby we could modify property rights and other rules of the economic game, adjudicated disputes about the interpretation of the rules, enforced contracts, promoted competition, provided a monetary framework, engaged in activities to counter technical monopolies and to overcome neighborhood effects widely regarded as sufficiently important to justify government intervention, and which supplemented private charity and the private family in protecting the irresponsible, whether madman or child—such a government would clearly have important functions to perform. The consistent liberal is not an anarchist. . . .

Is it an accident that so many of the governmental reforms of recent decades have gone awry, that the bright hopes have turned to ashes? Is it simply because the programs are faulty in detail?

I believe the answer is clearly in the negative. The central defect of these measures is that they seek through government to force people to act against their own immediate interests in order to promote a supposedly general interest. They seek to resolve what is supposedly a conflict of interest, or a difference in view about interests, not by establishing a framework that will eliminate the conflict, or by persuading people to have different interests, but by forcing people to act against their own interest. They substitute the values of outsiders for the values of participants; either some telling others what is good for them, or the government taking from some to benefit others. These measures are therefore countered by one of the strongest and most creative forces known to man—the attempt by millions of individuals to promote their own interests, to live their lives by their own values. This is the major reason why the measures have so often had the opposite of the effects intended. It is also one of the major strengths of a free society and explains why governmental regulation does not strangle it.

The Market Erodes Democratic Government

SAMUEL BOWLES AND
RICHARD EDWARDS

Government and the Economy

The Expansion of Government Economic Activity

Over the past half-century, the economic importance of the government has grown. There is no single adequate measure by which its growth could be gauged, in part because not all government activities are equally important from an economic standpoint. For this reason, measures of the size of the government—its total expenditures, total employment, or other measures—can capture only roughly the economic impact of the government. But there is little doubt that the growth has been substantial. Though the economic importance of the government has grown in the United States, it is still considerably less than in most other advanced capitalist economies. . . .

The reasons for this growth in the economic importance of the government are much debated. Some see it as a triumph by the ordinary citizen over the self-serving interests of business. Others see it as a carefully orchestrated strategy of business to provide itself with ever-greater opportunities for profit. Still others see it as a triumph of the bureaucratic mentality, which thinks that if there is a problem, there must be or should be some government office to deal with it.

But there is a more persuasive explanation. The survival and workability of capitalism as a system required the government to grow. The ceaseless search for extra profits and the ensuing social, technical, and other changes . . . created conditions that provoked demands for a more economically involved government. These demands, as we will see, have come as often from businesspeople as from workers, as often from the Chamber of Commerce as from the AFL-CIO, as often from Republicans as from Democrats.[1] The growth of government is not something that happened in *opposition* to capitalism, but rather something that happened in very large measure *because* of capitalism. . . .

---

1. The AFL-CIO is the American Federation of Labor–Congress of Industrial Organizations, the largest confederation of labor unions in the United States.

Economic Concentration   Much of the growth of governmental economic activity can be explained by the growth of large corporations and
the decline of small competitive producers. The enormous power of modern
corporations has allowed its owners to engage more effectively in lobbying
and in the formation of public opinion. Partly for this reason, big business
has become more confident that it can put the government to work to raise
its profits. The government involvement in the nuclear power industry and
in the production of military goods are good examples of this. Corporate
leaders have also supported the expansion of government regulation in
those many cases in which they wanted protection from competitive pressures that might lower profits. Examples include regulation of the quality of
meat and other food, and milk price supports. Consumers and workers have
also supported an expansion of the economic activities of the government,
in part to protect themselves from the power of giant corporations. . . .

International Expansion   The increasing international involvement of
the large corporations and of the U.S. economy generally contributed to the
development of a worldwide conception of "U.S. interests." As corporations
expanded from national to international businesses, they changed from
wanting the government to impose tariffs to keep out goods made abroad
to insisting that the government protect "American" (their) investments
around the world. They promoted an increasingly expensive military system to defend these interests. The preparation for war and the payment for
past wars have accounted for much of the economic expansion of the
government. Capitalism did not invent war, but the degree of international
economic interdependence and rivalry produced by the expansion of capitalism did make *world* wars more likely. After World War II, high levels of
military expenditure became a permanent feature of the U.S. economy. . . .

Economic Instability   The increasing instability of the economy, marked
by periods of severe unemployment and dramatized by the Great Depression of the 1930s, has provided another impetus for the growing economic
importance of the government. The stabilization of the economy was a
major objective of the businessmen who promoted the formation of the
Federal Reserve System in 1913 and the Securities and Exchange Commission in 1935.[2] Much more important was the inability of the economy to
revive from the Great Depression without the stimulus of massive World
War II military expenditures. During the depressed 1930s, political instability and radical political movements spread as people came face-to-
face with the failure of the capitalist system to provide for even a minimal
livelihood. . . .

---

2. The Federal Reserve System (the Fed) is composed of twelve Federal Reserve Banks. It facili-
tates exchanges of cash, checks, and credit; it regulates member banks; and it controls the nation's money supply and interest rates through the Federal Reserve Board. The Securities and
Exchange Commission is the federal agency empowered to regulate stock markets.

Income Support   During the Great Depression, large majorities of Americans became convinced that those unable to make a living should be supported, at least at some minimal level, by the government. Government programs to support poor people replaced informal support systems and private charity, both because people who fell on hard times could no longer count on their families or neighbors to tide them over and because private charity (church and private philanthropy) did not have the funds necessary to do the job. When most Americans were self-employed and families and neighborhoods formed tight communities, the families and communities provided much of the support for the handicapped, the elderly, and others unable to work or unable to find work. But as families and communities became less tightly woven, this system of support began to leave increasing numbers of people with little place to turn for help during hard times.

More recently, unemployment has inflicted a form of economic hardship for which even hard work is no remedy, and it has greatly increased the need for income supports. During the Great Depression, for instance, sources of private charity were simply overrun with people needing help. Only the government could provide income support on the scale needed.

Ironically, workers' constant moving around in search of work played a major part in undermining the ability (or perhaps the inclination) of families and neighborhoods to take care of those who did not find paying work. Equally important was that the capitalist accumulation process spelled the doom of the family farm and the small family business. For earlier generations, going home to the family farm or business had been a way of making it through a period of unemployment, but now there was no family farm or business to go home to. . . .

Public Safety   Many groups have demanded that government regulate the conflict between profitability and public safety. While competition pushed firms to develop technology in the most profitable directions, advances in these developments have not always benefited society. The pharmaceutical industry dramatizes the danger of leaving economic decision making solely up to the profitability criterion—drugs dangerous to people's health may be very profitable. For example, drugs that earn big profits for drug companies may have effects that are complicated, long delayed, and potentially lethal for individual consumers. The chemical industry illustrates another conflict between profits and public safety. Some production processes, developed because they are highly profitable, may ultimately inflict brain damage, sterility, and cancer on workers; their effects often become known only after many years of exposure. . . .

Environmental Protection   Many people pressed government to protect the natural environment from capitalist development. Our natural surroundings—our land, fresh water, air, and oceans—were not only being used, they were being used up. Part of the reason was that no one was charged a price for using most of these things. In many cases, the most profitable way of disposing of wastes—even very hazardous ones—was simply to throw them away, using our natural environment as a free dumping ground. . . .

Discrimination   Over the last three decades people have come to realize that the unrestricted exercise of rights in private property and in capital goods often results in racial and sexual discrimination against both customers and workers. The lunch counter sit-ins that began the civil rights movement of the 1960s posed the issue sharply—the right of owners of the restaurants and lunch counters to do what they pleased with their property, including the exclusion of black customers, versus the rights of black people to be treated equally in public places. Since 1964 the U.S. Civil Rights Commission has brought suits against companies, unions, and, other institutions, seeking to force them to eliminate discriminatory practices.

Many of these seven sources of expanded government economic activity may be understood as responses to particular aspects of the accumulation process of the capitalist economy. The growth of the government is as much a part of the capitalist economic growth process as is the growth of investment or the growth of technology.

But if government has had to grow to repair the problems and hardships caused by capitalist development, it does not follow that this has been an adequate response. It is quite debatable whether people are today more secure economically than they were a hundred years ago, or less susceptible to environmental or natural disaster, or less likely to encounter health hazards in their workplace or in their food, or better protected from the unaccountable power of the giant corporations. It seems highly unlikely, in fact, that bigger government programs have managed to keep pace with the escalating challenges posed by the pattern of capitalist economic growth. . . .

The Limits of Democratic Control of the Capitalist Economy

[Yet] can the government really control the economy? . . . Can the citizens of a democratic government control the economy? . . . The ability of the voters—even large majorities of them—to alter the course of economic events in our economy is quite limited as long as the economy remains capitalist . . . .

Our economy may be considered to be like a game in which there are two different sets of rules. One set of rules—the rules of the capitalist economy—confers power and privilege on those who own the capital . . . used in production, particularly on the owners and managers of the largest corporations. The other set of rules—the rules of the democratic government—confers substantial power on the electorate, that is, on the great majority of adult citizens. Thus our social system gives rise to two types of power: the *power of capital* and the *power of citizenry*.[3] . . . The basic idea of democratic

---

3. The power of capital is the ability of corporations in a capitalist system to influence public policies or otherwise to create conditions favorable to the interests of investors. The power of citizenry is the ability of citizens to influence governmental policy or otherwise to create conditions favorable to their interests in a democracy.

government—that government leaders will be selected by the principle of voting, with each person having one vote, after an open competition among competing candidates and ideas—is very different from the rules that govern the capitalist economy.

The heads of a corporation—the management—are not elected by the people who work there, nor by the community in which the firm is located. In fact, they are not elected at all in the sense that we usually use the word *election,* for they are selected by those who own the corporation, with each owner having as many votes as the number of shares of stock he or she owns. Similarly, freedom of speech and other civil liberties are very limited in the workplace. The majority of businesses place restrictions on workers' freedom to post information concerning unions, for example. . . .

Those powers are often at loggerheads, as when the citizens want to restrict the power of capital to sell dangerous or environmentally destructive products. In most of these conflicts, capitalists have immense and often overwhelming advantages, despite the fact that the owners of businesses (and particularly large businesses) are greatly outnumbered. There are three sources of their power—one obvious, the others not so obvious.

One reason capitalists have great political power is that economic resources can often be translated directly into political power. This happens when businesses or wealthy individuals contribute to political campaigns; advertise to alter public opinion; hire lawyers, expert witnesses and others to influence the detailed drafting and implementation of legislation; and otherwise apply their economic resources to the political system. Corporate control of economic resources implies substantial corporate political influence over government officials.

There is a second, more indirect reason for the disproportionate political power of business leaders. It is that mass communications are run by businesses: capitalists in this industry own the TV stations, newspapers, publishing houses, and other capital goods used in production. Even "public" radio and TV depend heavily on corporate contributions. Freedom of speech and of the press (which includes TV and radio) guarantees that people can say, and journalists can write, whatever they please. On the other hand, the private ownership of . . . the TV industry, for example, guarantees that what is broadcast is in the end controlled by capitalists either by the owners of the station or by owners of the major corporations that buy the advertising for the programs. These are people who understandably have little interest in seeing the idea of citizen power applied in ways that limit the freedom or profits of those who own the capital goods used in production, whether in the TV industry or elsewhere.

There is a third way in which money brings power—capitalists control investment, and so they determine the fate of the economy. . . . If profits are low, businesspeople will complain of a bad *investment climate.* They will not invest, or they will choose to invest in some other country. The result will be unemployment, economic stagnation, and perhaps a decline in living standards of the majority of the people, who will lose no time expressing their disappointment on election day.

Since capitalists control investment and hence hold one of the keys to a healthy economy, political leaders often must do what capitalists want, in order to create the right investment climate. They know that in the end it is capitalists who make the decisions on whether to invest and where to invest. Business thus holds a kind of blackmail over democratically elected political leaders.

This form of blackmail is called a *capital strike,* because it involves capital going on strike.[4] When workers strike they refuse to do their part in the economy—they do not work. When capitalists strike they also refuse to do their part—they do not invest. But here the similarity ends. When workers strike they must organize themselves so that they all strike together. A single worker cannot go on strike (that is called quitting). By contrast, when capital goes on strike, no coordination is needed. . . . Each corporation routinely studies the economic and other conditions relevant to its decision to invest. If they do not like what they see, they will simply not invest or will invest elsewhere. *Nobody* organizes a capital strike. It happens through the independent decisions of corporate leaders. If things look bad to a large number of corporations, the effect of their combined withholding of investment will be large enough to alter the course of the economy.

Capital strike severely limits what citizen power can accomplish when citizen power conflicts with the power of capital. An example may make this clear. Unemployed workers may get unemployment insurance checks for 26 weeks. Let us imagine that the voters of a particular state—we will call it Wisconsin—decide they want to provide more generous unemployment benefits, so the checks will keep coming in as long as the worker is unemployed. These payments are to be financed by a heavy tax on the profits of firms that pollute the environment on the "polluter pays principle." . . . Because a majority of the citizens support the idea, the government of the state of Wisconsin enacts the needed taxes and other programs and enforces them. So far, so good.

Now imagine that you are the chief executive officer of General Motors, or of General Electric, or of any other corporation that employs large numbers of workers in Wisconsin. Assume you are considering investing in Wisconsin (say, opening a new plant). Not only will you worry about the taxes, you will wonder how much power you will have over your employees and how hard they will work if they know they have permanent unemployment insurance, should you fire them.

You may ask yourself what the citizenry will vote for next. You obviously will think twice before investing in Wisconsin, not necessarily because you do not like the new laws personally, but because your profit rate, both before and after taxes, will most likely be lower in Wisconsin as a re-

---

4. In particular, it involves decisions by capitalists to reduce or end their investments as the result of a "negative" business climate.

sult of the new laws. And if your profit rate is lower, your company's stocks will sell for less on the stock market, leading the stockholders to complain, or even to look for a new chief executive officer. You will probably put your new plant someplace else, perhaps in a state that actively advertises its favorable investment climate.

Quite independently, other businesspeople will, no doubt, come to the same conclusion. Some may even close plants or offices in Wisconsin and move elsewhere. The result will be increasing unemployment and lower incomes for the people of Wisconsin.

The hard times may bring on a state financial crisis. As unemployment increases, state expenditures on unemployment insurance will rise, as will other costs of maintaining minimum living standards. As income falls, the state's tax revenues will decline. Rising costs and falling revenues create a soaring deficit in the state budget.

But the problems have just begun. In order to spend more money than the taxes are currently bringing in, the state government will be forced to raise taxes again or to borrow more from the banks and from others with money to lend. Because of the declining state of the Wisconsin economy the banks will be unsure that their loans will be paid back promptly or even at all. If they agree to lend the money, they will do so only at high interest rates. If the loans are granted, the problem will be put off, but it will return with greater intensity when the high interest charges must be paid, in addition to the other demands on state revenues. The resulting vicious cycle is called a *state fiscal crisis*.

There are two likely outcomes. First, with repayment increasingly uncertain, the banks may refuse further loans until the state government changes its policy. If the state government is on the verge of bankruptcy—which means breaking contracts with state employees and not paying wages or bills—the banks' advice may be quite persuasive. Second, the sovereign citizens of Wisconsin may decide to elect a new government, in order to revoke the laws.[5] In either case the new laws will be repealed.

Our example was for a single state. But what is true for one state is true for all states, and more important, it is also true for the nation as a whole. . . . General Motors and General Electric do not have to locate in the United States at all.

Let's go back over our Wisconsin example. Were the citizens' voting rights or civil liberties violated? No. Did capitalists collude and deliberately undermine citizen power? No, they acted independently and in competition with each other. Did they use lobbyists to influence the government officials or campaign contributions to influence elections? Maybe they did, but they did not need to.

---

5. Sovereignty is the ability and right to make a decision; democratic government confers it on citizens.

Did the citizens exercise control over the economy? That is a much harder question. The capitalist economy certainly imposed limits on what they could do. The citizens could vote for any policy they wanted, but they could not force businesses to invest in Wisconsin, and that severely limited what citizens could get.

Henry Ford, who was famous for his cheap, single-design, no-frills Model T, once said, "You can have any color car you want as long as it's black." In many respects, the voters of our hypothetical state of Wisconsin had a similar choice.

Where did they go wrong? The example could have turned out very differently.

One course the citizens of Wisconsin could have followed would have been to limit their expectations; they could have instructed their government to concentrate only on those programs that would benefit citizens, but would at the same time *increase* the profit rate in the state, or at least not lower it. In other words, they might have accepted from the outset that they were not "sovereign" in economic matters, and made the best of a less-than-ideal situation.

Thus, for example, they might have concentrated on eliminating those forms of pollution that reduce profits in the recreation business and lower property values. They might have designed programs to give economic security to the elderly, but not to current workers. They might have tried to increase equality of opportunity by giving all children more business-oriented schooling. And they might have voted to finance these programs by taxes that did not fall on profits. If they had done this, many Wisconsin citizens would have benefited, and the losers might not have been in position to disrupt the program. Specifically, capitalists might have looked favorably, or at worst indifferently, on these events and might not have brought about the economic decline of the state by leaving.

Again, this is just a hypothetical example, but it is similar to what actually happened in Wisconsin. Wisconsin was a leader early in this century in trying out programs to make the most of citizen power while operating within the confines of the capitalist economy. The federal government and other state and local governments now engage in many beneficial economic activities that also fit this description. Making the best of the limits of the capitalist economy is most fully developed in some European nations such as Sweden and Austria, where social democratic governments have been in power over much of the post–World War II period. However beneficial, these programs are severely limited, since many of the ways to improve living standards and the quality of life sooner or later also threaten the rate of profit or the idea of profits.

There is a second course that Wisconsin citizens could have followed which, if not likely, is at least conceivable. When General Motors and General Electric decided to close their operations in Wisconsin, the plants could have been bought by the communities in which they are located, by those who work in them, or by the state government. When a business leaves a community, what it takes, usually, is its money. Most of the plant, the machines, and the workers stay. There is no reason the workers could not continue working at their old jobs if they could find a way to purchase the firm. They could do this as part of a community-owned enterprise, a worker-owned firm, or some other organization.

What can we conclude from this example? That citizen power is severely limited in its ability to alter fundamental economic events, unless citizens are willing to change the rules that govern the workings of the capitalist economy. Thus a democratic *government* is not the same thing as a democratic *society,* for in a democratic *society* decision making in the economy, as well as in the government, would be accountable to the majority.

DISCUSSION QUESTIONS

1. In recent years, most Americans seem to have turned against "big government," yet huge majorities support social security and increased spending on education and environmental and consumer regulation. How would the authors of each essay deal with this apparent contradiction?

2. Friedman stresses the point that the market economy is made up of *voluntary exchanges.* No one is forced to buy a particular product or work for a particular company. What would Bowles and Edwards say about Friedman's argument?

3. There is a substantial amount of income inequality in the United States. As long as all citizens still maintain equal political rights, is such inequality necessarily harmful to democracy? How much inequality is a threat to democratic society and why? How much inequality is justified?

4. Friedman argues that the free market promotes individual liberty. Yet many citizens in democratic countries use their liberty to support government programs that limit and regulate the scope and power of the marketplace. How might Friedman have responded to this reality?

SUGGESTED READINGS AND INTERNET RESOURCES

How democratic is the U.S. capitalist system? What is and what should be the function of government and democratic citizens in creating and distributing economic resources? How efficient and how equal is our political economy, and how is each term defined? Two good introductions to these questions are Frances Moore Lappé, *Rediscovering America's Values* (New York: Ballantine Books, 1989); and Charles Lindblom, *The Market System* (New Haven, Conn.:

Yale University Press, 2001). James Galbraith, *Created Unequal: The Crisis in American Pay* (New York: Century Fund, 1999); and Barry Bluestone and Bennett Harrison, *Growing Prosperity* (Boston: Houghton Mifflin, 2000) both make compelling cases against growing economic inequalities. For a mainstream vision of a new, healthy, globalized economy, see Thomas Friedman, *The Lexus and the Olive Tree* (New York: Anchor Books, 2000). A brilliant treatment of how wealth inequality translates into political inequality is William Domhoff, *Who Rules America? Power and Politics in the Year 2000* (Mountain View, Calif.: Mayfield Publishing, 1999).

The Policy Action Network
www.movingideas.org
This is the best site for extensive data and analyses of current economic policy issues and for study of income and wealth trends. Click onto the internal links to the Economic Policy Institute or Center for Budget and Policy Priorities for analysis of current issues, or use the topic search engine. This site is sponsored by *The American Prospect,* a liberal opinion magazine.

The Heritage Foundation
www.heritage.org
This site contains economic news and policy prescriptions from the premier ultraright think tank, as well as good links to other conservative foundations and public policy lobbies.

The Left Business Observer
www.leftbusinessobserver.com
A spirited, iconoclastic newsletter by corporate critic Doug Henwood, this web site has interesting statistics and many links to unconventional left and right web sites.

The Cato Institute
www.cato.org
Here are speeches, research, and opinion from the leading libertarian think tank in the United States. This site provides economic data and opinion supportive of privatization of now-public functions, from social security to environmental protection and education.

6

Civil Liberties: Does the First Amendment Permit Religious Expression in Public Institutions?

The opening words of the First Amendment to the United States Constitution read: "Congress shall make no law respecting an establishment of religion, or prohibiting the free exercise thereof." These words establish a constitutional guarantee of freedom of religion in the United States; they protect religion from government interference and government from religious domination. But like many of the phrases in the Constitution, the language quoted is hardly free of ambiguity. If government and religion are to be kept separate, how strict should the separation be? Is there no place for religious expression in America's public institutions?

One common way to debate these questions is to focus on the intentions of the men who drafted and ratified the First Amendment. Those who champion a strict separation of religion and government tend to emphasize the views of James Madison, the principal drafter of the Bill of Rights, and his close friend Thomas Jefferson, whose famous words interpreted the First Amendment as "building a wall of separation between Church and State." Aiming to safeguard religious minorities from an intolerant majority and to protect religious conscience itself from the coercive powers of the state, Madison and Jefferson believed, according to Isaac Kramnick and R. Laurence Moore, in a "Godless Constitution." Opponents of this view deny that the founding generation meant to keep religious expression out of public life. The First Amendment, they argue, was designed to block Congress from establishing an official *national* religion or telling individuals which religious doctrine they must accept. But the states were still free to favor particular churches, as many of them continued to do, and the federal government was still allowed to sponsor nondenominational expressions of religious devotion, such as national days of prayer or the provision of chaplains for the armed forces.

In the last half-century, the Supreme Court has generally sided with the champions of strict separation. Although a narrow 5 to 4 majority ruled in the landmark *Everson* case (1947) that a subsidy paid by the state of New Jersey for the bus fares of children attending parochial schools was constitutional, the Court allowed this practice only because it did not breach Jefferson's "wall of separation." Following the same doctrine of strict separation, a larger majority ruled in *Engel* v. *Vitale* (1962) that a brief nondenominational prayer recommended by the Board of Regents for students in New York's public schools ("Almighty god, we acknowledge our dependence upon Thee, and we beg Thy blessings upon us, our parents, our teachers, and our country") was unconstitutional. Only in recent years, with the formation of a new Court majority appointed by Republican presidents, has the Court become somewhat more favorable to religious expressions in public institutions. For example, in *Lynch* v. *Donnelly* (1984) the Court approved of a nativity scene (crèche) erected by the city of Pawtucket, Rhode Island, during the Christmas season, but only because it was accompanied by a Christmas tree, Santa's house, colored lights, and other symbols that reflected the city's secular purpose (attracting shoppers to downtown stores).

The Court's insistence on a wall of separation between church and state, particularly its ban on prayer in the schools, has evoked dismay and anger from many Americans, who are a more religious people than are the citizens of any other modern democratic nation. Surveys repeatedly show that about 90 percent of the population describe themselves as religious; about 80 percent of Americans believe that God still works miracles and that they will be called before Him on Judgment Day. Citing the religious faith of the majority, supporters of various constitutional amendments have proposed language that would repudiate the Court's decisions and allow prayer in the schools and other forms of religious expression in public institutions. None of these amendments have been successful so far.

Controversy over the place of religion in public life has continued to mushroom in the last few decades. The most outspoken proponents for breaking down the strict separation between religion and politics have been the leaders of the religious right. Conservative Christian organizations, such as the Reverend Jerry Falwell's Moral Majority and the Reverend Pat Robertson's Christian Coalition, were an important force in the political successes of the Republican Party in the 1980s and 1990s. But it is a mistake to equate support for religious expression in politics exclusively with conservatives. There are numerous writers and political activists who agree with the Supreme Court on such matters as school prayer yet believe that treating religion as purely private denies the positive role it can play in political life. Some political moderates, such as Yale law professor Stephen Carter, complain that "in our sensible zeal to keep religion from dominating our politics, we have created a political and legal culture that presses the religiously faithful to be other than themselves, to act publicly, and sometimes privately as well, as though their faith does not matter to them." Overshadowed by the religious right have been the many faith-based groups that participate in causes usually identified with the political left: unionization, antipoverty programs, environmentalism, opposition to the use of American armed force abroad.

A strong sign that support for religious expression in public life is growing is the frequency of statements of faith by candidates for the presidency. In 1976, it was regarded as somewhat unusual when Democratic candidate Jimmy Carter discussed his convictions as a "born-again" Christian. In 2000, the nominees of both parties, Vice President Al Gore and Texas governor George W. Bush, assumed that few would object and many would applaud when they highlighted the centrality of their religious beliefs to their political philosophies. As president, Bush has pushed for legislation that will funnel federal dollars to faith-based institutions that provide social services to the needy.

Stephen Monsma, author of our first selection, argues that the strict separation between church and state currently enforced by the Supreme Court has actually created a bias against religious expression in our public life. He advocates a new perspective on the relationship between church and state that he calls "positive neutrality": government must be neutral in the sense that it does not favor any particular religion or even religion over nonreligion, but it should be positive in recognizing and providing a place in public institutions for the diverse (and healthy) expressions of Americans' religious values. Applying this doctrine to the controversial issues of church-state relations considered by the Supreme Court, Monsma suggests that the Court should permit silent prayer in the schools and allow teachers to consider religious as well as secular philosophies.

Marvin Frankel, author of our second selection, defends strict separation between church and state and agrees with the thrust of Supreme Court decisions on this subject. He believes that the religious expressions prohibited by the Court, such as prayers in schools, are irrelevant to the health and functioning of religion in the United States. It is opportunistic politicians and representatives of intolerance, he charges, who have fanned the flames of controversy over the Court's decisions for their own purposes. The anecdotes that Frankel relates suggest that religious expression in public institutions will coerce those whose beliefs differ from the majority—precisely what the First Amendment was designed to preclude.

Monsma's perspective suggests that we consider religious expression as a form of positive freedom, with government playing a supportive but neutral role. Frankel insists that both individual conscience and organized religion should be viewed in light of negative freedom, with government taking a hands-off approach. How strict do you think the separation of church and state should be? Is the "wall of separation" image a proper constitutional guide, or does it create a bias against religion in public life and public institutions? Should religion be allowed to mix with politics so long as no particular religions are favored and nonbelievers are protected? Or will the mixture inevitably advantage the dominant religious groups and ostracize those holding unconventional faiths or viewpoints? Would allowing silent prayers in the schools reenforce the religious and moral values of children, or are such vehicles of religious expression better left to the home and the place of worship?

Positive Neutrality: Letting Religious Freedom Ring

STEPHEN V. MONSMA

I t was a cloudy January day when I visited the U.S. military cemetery near Florence, Italy, and walked among the row upon row of stone monuments marking the graves of over 4,000 U.S. citizens who were killed in World War II. It was an impressive, moving experience, but as I walked among the graves and reflected on the sacrifice that many had made, it also struck me that the military had handled a sensitive church-state issue more appropriately than is often done. If ever one's religious faith comes to the fore, it is in the presence of the ultimate fact of death. Thus, cemeteries are typically filled with religious symbolism. However, this was a government cemetery I was visiting: built and, even today, maintained by U.S. tax dollars. Is it appropriate—is it a constitutionally permitted breach in the wall of separation between church and state—for the government to purchase, erect, and maintain overtly religious symbols? (Remember the Christmas displays that have failed or barely managed to pass constitutional muster.) In addition, most of the men and women killed were Christians (defining "Christian" very broadly), but some, of course, were Jews. If religious symbolism is to be permitted, should it be distinctively Christian?

One solution to this situation—and one on which the Supreme Court and U.S. society have insisted in some parallel settings—would have been to ban all religious symbols and to develop a stone monument for the graves that is purely secular. A supposed neutrality among all religions and between religion and nonreligion would have been maintained. Another solution, one some have favored in parallel settings, would have been to provide Christian crosses for all, and if a family objected, its loved one would be buried off to the side and the family could purchase a marker of its choosing. Happily, the military has chosen another course of action. Thus, the cemetery is filled with the most common, powerful symbol of Christianity: the cross, which symbolizes the sacrificial death of Jesus Christ. However, scattered throughout the cemetery, one also sees powerful symbols of the ancient Jewish faith—Stars of David—marking the graves of Jewish Americans who had made the ultimate sacrifice. In following this practice, the military, no doubt unwittingly, has moved in the direction of adopting a solution to this church-state issue that is in keeping with structural pluralism, an approach that I have termed *positive neutrality*.[1]

Under positive neutrality, government is *neutral* in that it does not recognize or favor any one religion or religious group over any other, nor does it favor or recognize religious groups or religion as a whole over secular groups or secular philosophies and mind-sets as a whole. It is evenhanded. Government takes a position of *positive* neutrality by recognizing that in practice, neutrality is often not achieved by government simply failing to do something. Positive neutrality insists that genuine religious freedom is not a negative freedom: it does not spontaneously spring into being in the absence of governmental regulations or programs. Sometimes government will have to take certain positive steps if it is to be truly neutral in the sense of assuring equal freedoms and equal opportunities for all religious persons and groups and for religious and irreligious persons and groups alike.

Thus, in the example of the military cemetery, government is neutral in that neither Christian nor Jewish religious symbols are uniformly placed onto the graves of all those who were killed in action. It is following positive neutrality in that neutrality is not gained by stripping the governmentally owned and operated cemetery of all religious symbols, but by the active, positive use of religious symbols corresponding to the religious faiths of the fallen men and women. Religion is recognized and given its due. If positive neutrality were to be more fully followed in this example, the military ought—especially in today's United States—to develop appropriate Islamic and secular symbols so that the graves of those of the Muslim faith or of no religious faith could also have their graves appropriately marked. Such an approach would break up the uniformity of rows and columns of crosses interspersed with a few Stars of David, but structural pluralism accepts and even celebrates pluralism over uniformity and diversity over conformity, even when things appear a bit messy as a result. . . .

Pluralism and a New Mind-Set

The current mind-set dominant within the Supreme Court and among the leaders of popular U.S. culture tends to see religion—at least in its particularistic manifestations, as distinct from religion-in-general—as having only a private, personal relevance and lacking a real social or political impact. In

---

1. Structural pluralism is Monsma's term for the positive contributions that diverse associations—especially religious ones—make to the functioning of a democratic society.

fact, it views religion, when wedded to issues of social and political import, as a divisive, intolerant, and dangerous force.

Pluralism, in contrast, leads to a quite different perspective with which to approach church-state issues. This mind-set colors everything else, and thus is crucial in setting the context from which the more specific, concrete standard of positive neutrality emerges. Two features of this mind-set are especially important: a positive outlook on the contributions of religion in U.S. society and an unwavering commitment to full freedom of religion.

The first feature of pluralism's mind-set regarding religion and society is its perception that it is natural, healthy, and proper for the people of the United States to adhere to a great variety of faith communities and to join a wide range of churches and other religious associations, and for some to adhere to no religious faith at all. This is seen as an appropriate consequence of a free society. Structural pluralism welcomes religion in its various manifestations and in its various activities as a legitimate, contributing, integral part of U.S. society, including its political aspects. Not merely religion-in-general but also particularistic religion, whose adherents take it as an authoritative force in their lives, is respected and accepted as a part of the life of the U.S. polity. Moreover, it is not merely the individual in his or her religious dimension that pluralism accepts and honors; it is the religious structures of society—faith communities and religious associations—that are accepted and honored *as religious structures*. Catholic parochial schools, inner-city church-sponsored homeless shelters, Jewish senior citizen centers, evangelical Protestant colleges, Mormon nursing homes, Nation of Islam mosques, and those who identify with and have a close attachment to New Age thinking: all these and more are accepted and respected—including their politically relevant aspects. In dealing with them, the pluralist creatively seeks to develop political processes and public policies that will not merely tolerate faith communities and associations and their individual members, but will integrate them fully—as religious structures and persons—into the life of the body politic.

This is an enormously important shift from the mind-set that is prevalent today. . . . That mind-set sees religion largely in individual, not structural, terms, and sees particularistic religion as a force that is largely irrelevant to the realm of politics and public policies and thus with little to contribute. Religious individuals should, of course, be tolerated, and their freedom of religion should not be denied, but their religious beliefs are seen as essentially private beliefs, relevant to individuals' personal lives but irrelevant to the affairs of state. Even worse, religious diversity is seen as socially divisive, and thus a danger when allowed into the political realm. Thus, erecting a wall of separation between religion and the state does no harm to religion and benefits the body politic. Religious structures—as religious structures—must be kept out of the political realm, or, at the most, allowed in in a carefully circumscribed, limited manner. This is held to be especially true of particularistic religious groups such as conservative Protestantism, Roman Catholicism, and Mormonism. Religious structures and individuals with potentially important religiously motivated political goals and insights are thereby finessed and squeezed onto the sidelines. Structural pluralism objects to this, seeing it as a form of religious intolerance and discrimination.

A second basic feature marking the mind-set fostered by pluralism is a commitment to full religious freedom for all faith communities and religious associations—and for persons and structures of no faith as well. Its goal is simple: full, complete freedom of religion. Pluralism has an expansive view of this freedom. It extends to believers in all religious traditions; the wide diversity of Christian religious associations and communities should have full religious freedom, but so also should native American religions, Islam, New Age beliefs, Hinduism, and more. Similarly, persons of no religious faith should have their freedom respected and guaranteed as fully as do persons of deeply held faith. In addition, religious freedom should extend not only to the development and practice of a religious structure's core religious beliefs, but also to the development and practice of the other three roles of religious associations and communities . . . : molding their members' behavior and attitudes, providing an array of services, and influencing the policy-making process. These roles define the appropriate sphere of religion, and pluralism says that if religious associations and faith communities are to be truly, fully free, their freedom of action in their sphere must be assured. Also, religious freedom should extend to the religious beliefs and practices of churches, synagogues, and other such religious associations, but should also include the beliefs and activities of religiously based agencies such as schools, child-care centers, and other service or advocacy associations. A Jewish counseling center should have as full protection for its freedom to act on the basis of its distinctive Jewish character and beliefs as a synagogue. Pluralism insists that the tent of religious freedom be broad enough to encompass all these forms. Otherwise, the freedom of religious structures and their members will be thwarted.

It is important to note that pluralism also recognizes that religious associations and faith communities have certain obligations to other religious associations and faith communities, to the state, and to the rest of society. Full religious freedom does not mean that religious structures can do whatever they want, wherever and whenever they want to. . . .

Current U.S. thinking does not hesitate to proclaim and protect full religious freedom as long as it is kept on the level of private, individual belief. Thus, a privatized religion is granted full religious freedom, but when religion moves from individual to corporate manifestations, from religion-in-general to particularistic religion, from beliefs to practice, or from a private, personal faith to one with social and political dimensions, trouble often arises. For example, the U.S. public and the U.S. legal system are fully comfortable with individual native Americans following their traditional religion in the quiet of their communities, but when that religion begins to move from individual observances to a tribal or area-wide movement, from beliefs to practices such as the use of peyote, and from private beliefs to social implications (such as questioning white society's continued use of traditionally sacred lands), doubts, fears, and challenges quickly surface.

Structural pluralism has a broader, more inclusive, more expansive view of freedom of religion.

Conventional U.S. thinking on church and state tends to see pluralism's twin goals of full religious freedom and full involvement of a wide variety of religious structures in the polity as posing an unresolvable dilemma. To the conventional mind-set, religious freedom implies governmental neutrality toward religion and neutrality implies church-state separation. After all, if government accedes to one religion's demands for certain public policies, financially supports one religious group's drug rehabilitation center, or places the symbol of one religious group in front of city hall at the time of its major religious holiday, is not the state favoring and supporting that religion, thereby compromising the religious freedom of all other religious groups and of nonbelievers? On the other hand, structural pluralism argues that by discouraging religiously based groups from influencing public policy debates, by refusing assistance to religiously based social service agencies when it is being given to all others, and by ignoring the civic contributions of religious but not secular groups, freedom of religion is also being violated. In either case, it appears impossible to have full religious freedom. Either religious freedom is violated by denying religion equal access to or equal recognition in the public realm, or it is violated by favoring one religion over another or religion over secularism.

Structural, normative pluralism and the principle of positive neutrality, which it spawns, show this dilemma to be apparent, not real. There is another way that avoids being impaled on either horn of the dilemma and does not follow an unprincipled, messy middle ground. Religious structures can be given their full due, without favoring one religion over another or religion over secularism. However, to find this new way, old categories and assumptions must be laid aside and replaced by fresh ones. . . .

Religion in the Public Schools

Some of the Supreme Court's most difficult decisions have dealt with the question of whether and in what form religion may be brought into the public schools. This issue has been extremely controversial, and Supreme Court decisions ruling against certain religious exercises in the public schools have aroused intense opposition from large segments of the public. Congressional majorities and Presidents Ronald Reagan and George Bush have paid at least lip service to proposals that organized prayer—contrary to what the Supreme Court has ruled—should be allowed in the public schools.

Intense feelings over Supreme Court decisions regarding religion in the public schools have probably been aroused, first, by the central role of the public schools in the lives of students and their families. With compulsory attendance laws, a majority of the prime daytime hours of children's lives from age five to sixteen are under the control of the public school. There certainly is time for the family and for churches and other religious associations to have a crucial influence on the lives of children, but many feel that they are in a competitive disadvantage with the schools, with their monopolization of children's daytime hours; elaborate instructional materials; professional, highly trained personnel; and high status. The degree of controversy in this area is also increased by the fact that well into the twentieth century, elements of the informal, de facto nineteenth-century Protestant establishment of religion remained in the public schools. Until after World War II, Bible reading, prayers, Christmas and Easter celebrations, and other Christian religious exercises were commonplace in many public schools. A series of Supreme Court decisions have had the effect of rooting out long-established practices. It is not surprising that opposition and controversy have accompanied these efforts.

In dealing with cases in this area, the Supreme Court has generally taken a strong position against allowing religious observations and exercises into the public schools. . . . Offering state-composed, nonsectarian prayers, Bible reading, reading of the Lord's Prayer, posting the Ten Commandments in classrooms, a minute of silence for meditation and prayer, teaching scientific evidences in support of creation along with those for evolution, and praying at graduation ceremonies are all in violation of the establishment provision of the First Amendment. On the other hand, it has ruled that released-time programs for religious instruction held off school property, objective teaching about religion, a minute of silence for meditation, and the official recognition of voluntary, student-initiated, and student-led religious clubs are all permissible under the First Amendment. As these listings reveal, what the Court has disallowed is greater than what it has allowed. The basis for these decisions has generally been the Court's insistence that the state may not engage in or support any activity that could reasonably be interpreted as advancing or endorsing religion over nonreligion. . . .

Positive neutrality begins what it considers a much more theoretically sound approach to religion in the public schools with a basic point: the inaccuracy of the underlying assumption that a true neutrality between religion and secularism is gained by the removal from the public schools of all practices or references that are favorable to specific religions or to religion generally. The absence of religion in the life of the school in any sort of a favorable context—even one as minor as a moment of silence designated for prayer or meditation—is to send the implicit message that religion as a living, controlling force is unnecessary and irrelevant to most of life. Alone among the opinions of Supreme Court justices to raise this issue in clear terms is the dissent of Justice Potter Stewart in *Abington School District v. Schempp*. . . .

> If religious exercises are held to be an impermissible activity in schools, religion is placed at an artificial and state-created disadvantage. Viewed in this light, permission of such exercises for those who want them is necessary if the schools are truly to be neutral in the matter of religion.

And a refusal to permit religious exercises thus is seen, not as the realization of state neutrality, but rather as the establishment of a religion of secularism. . . .

The response that positive neutrality makes to most church-state issues—guided by the concepts of pluralism, which inform it—is to allow the full and free play of all religious groups and of both religion and secularism. Thus, positive neutrality's approach to the posting of the Ten Commandments in the public schools would be to allow their posting, as long as comparable, key writings of other religious or secular traditions represented in the classroom and community are also periodically displayed. The basic principle is not to try to achieve a neutrality by driving all religion out of the classroom—which results in a false neutrality that, in fact, favors a secular cultural ethos, but by welcoming and recognizing all religions and secular philosophies and mind-sets alike. . . .

. . . I would suggest three additional approaches in keeping with positive neutrality that would help to assure greater pluralism in the public schools than is now the case. All three are aimed at developing appropriate means to recognize and accommodate a diversity of religious beliefs to which students and their families hold, while also recognizing and accommodating the beliefs of those of no religious faith. One approach consists of moments of meditation and prayer at the beginning of the school day, and perhaps at lunch time and the end of the day as well. Here, school children are totally free to speak (or not to speak) to the Deity in any way they please as long as they are not disruptive of others' prayer or meditation. Those who are nonreligious can meditate or reflect on the upcoming day, or, for that matter, plan their after-school television viewing.

The Supreme Court's rejection of such an option in *Wallace v. Jaffree* (1985) went squarely against the religious neutrality that the Court itself has often professed. It did so on the basis that the Alabama law implicitly (and perhaps explicitly) endorsed religion by specifically mentioning prayer along with meditation as a purpose of the minute of silence. In one sense, the Court was right. Of course, the Alabama statute endorsed prayer, but that is beside the point. . . . The norm of neutrality is not violated as long as all religions, as well as religion and secular points of view, are equally endorsed or supported. Under positive neutrality, the relevant question is whether the statute favored any one form of prayer and whether it favored prayer over nonprayer. Neutrality means evenhandedness among religions and between religion and nonreligion. By mandating a one-minute period of silence "for meditation or voluntary prayer," Alabama law was neutral. The religious individuals could pray in whatever form they wished; the irreligious could meditate on anything to which their beliefs or values would lead. Religion and secularism were equally endorsed, yet to single out the endorsement of religion—or, more specifically, religious traditions that accept the possibility and need for human communication with the Deity—as unconstitutional, and not to hold the endorsement of meditation unconstitutional, is to favor secularism and religions not believing in prayer over religions believing in prayer. In contrast, structural pluralism and positive neutrality hold that one appropriate—that is, neutral—way in which to introduce religion into the public schools is to allow times of silence for personal, individual, voluntary prayer; otherwise, due deference to the religious traditions represented in the classroom is bound to be lost. . . .

A second way in which religion can be accommodated within the existing public schools is through the equal access approach approved by the Supreme Court in *Westside Community Schools v. Mergens* (1990) and released-time programs such as the one that was rejected in *McCollum v. Board of Education* (1948). Positive neutrality says that students surely should be free to meet for religious purposes if they meet voluntarily during noninstructional times, as long as all religious traditions and similar or parallel secularly based student groups are equally free to organize and meet. They should be free to meet on school property, to invite outside speakers in, and to advertise their meetings—just as all other student groups are free to do. The key here is a neutrality or evenhandedness by the school officials. Positive neutrality says that both the majority and the dissenting justices were wrong when they decided the *Mergens* case on whether in their judgment religion was being endorsed by the school. Endorsement or nonendorsement of religion is not the issue; equal treatment of all religious points of view and religion and nonreligion is.

Similarly, a plurality of religious points of view can be recognized and given their due without any one being favored or coerced by way of released-time programs. Here, various religious groups are invited to come into the public schools and teach the students who are adherents of their faith each week during an hour or so that has been set aside for such purposes. All religious faiths are invited to teach students of their faiths. Adherents of ethical or value-oriented associations that are not technically religious organizations could also have their representatives come in to teach their students, while those of no faith would have an extra study period.

The Supreme Court, from the point of view of structural pluralism, got it wrong back in 1948 when it judged a released-time program in Champaign, Illinois, on the basis of whether religion was being helped. Of course religion was being helped, but no more so than secularism, and no one religion any more than any other religion. It was religiously neutral. However, the Court simply asserted that the "wall between Church and State . . . must be kept high and impregnable" and then went on to note that the state's tax-supported public school buildings [were being] used for the dissemination of religious doctrines." As far as the Court was concerned, that sealed the fate of Champaign's released-time program. The support or endorsement of religion was enough to find the practice unconstitutional. The question that pluralism considers to be the key one—namely, whether all religions, as well as secular perspectives, were being treated equally—was never brought up. . . .

A third and final way in which positive neutrality suggests dealing with the issue of religion in the public schools is to make certain that religion is given its full due in an objective sense and that secular philosophies and points of view are also given their due, but no more than their proper due. Public schools today often do not even give religion the recognition and consideration it can be given without running afoul of the Supreme Court's church-state doctrines. This fact came out in a 1987 District Court case in the United States District for the Southern District of Alabama (*Smith v. Board of School Commissioners of Mobile County*, No. 82-0544-BH, 1987). Although the District Court's decision—which found that certain public school textbooks used in the Alabama schools promoted the religion of secular humanism in violation of the establishment clause of the First Amendment—was attacked by many commentators and was overturned by the Federal Court of Appeals, yet it brought to light some startling facts. For example, it noted the findings of Timothy Smith of Johns Hopkins University's History Department, which documented a systematic tendency to slight the role that religion has played in U.S. history:

> The pattern in these books is the omission of religious aspects to significant American events. The religious significance of much of the history of the Puritans is ignored. The Great Awakenings are generally not mentioned. Colonial missionaries are either not mentioned or represented as oppressors of native Americans. The religious influence on the abolitionist, women's suffrage, temperance, modern civil rights and peace movements is ignored or diminished to insignificance. The role of religion in the lives of immigrants and minorities, especially southern blacks, is rarely mentioned. After the Civil War, religion is given almost no play.

Positive neutrality—with its emphasis on genuine governmental neutrality among religions and between religion and secular perspectives— says that to drive the role religion has played in U.S. and world history out of textbooks and public school classrooms and to fail to acknowledge what various religious traditions have said in regard to issues such as sexual ethics, personal values, and economic relationships is to do violence to neutrality. The goal should be the fair, unbiased, equal representation of religion's views and perspectives—as fair, unbiased, and equal as those given views and perspectives of secular origin. Positions and evidence on various sides of controversial issues should be presented honestly and accurately.

When Louisiana enacted legislation requiring that so-called creation science be taught along with evolutionary explanations of human origins, it was acting within the spirit of this third approach. Whether this particular Louisiana law was the proper way in which to go about assuring that religion and secularism were treated evenhandedly is not the crucial issue (I personally have serious doubts); however, the underlying goal of "equal time" is. Assuring that a variety of religious and secular points of view are aired and treated fairly and respectfully is a key way in which to assure that the public schools practice a genuine neutrality toward religion and do not end up supporting a secular cultural ethos due to religion being left out of the curriculum.

Piety Versus "Secular Humanism": A Phony War

MARVIN E. FRANKEL

The decision of the Supreme Court in 1962 outlawing the bland triviality composed as a prayer by the New York Board of Regents, and then the succeeding year's ruling against Bible reading in the public schools, led to a thunder of opposition that keeps rolling and resounding over the years. There was outrage that God had been "expelled" from the public schools. A senator declared that the Supreme Court had "made God unconstitutional." Proposed constitutional amendments to overturn those decisions became staple contributions to the congressional hopper. A measure supporting public-school prayers became a central plank of the Republican platform, endorsed by President Reagan with the kind of folksy passion that lifted his high popularity ratings. While that position has never commanded the two-thirds vote in Congress required to launch an amendment, it appears steadily to enlist a large majority in American public opinion polls. It is reflected, too, in a wide and persistent defiance of the Supreme Court's ruling as local communities, especially in the South, cheer schoolteachers for their classroom prayers, promote prayers on athletic fields, and continue to act as if officially directed sanctimony might be a path to salvation.

A strong band of pious politicians have campaigned during the last third of the twentieth century for the right of students, as it is said, to engage in voluntary, silent prayer in the public schools. A number of states in the 1980s enacted statutes to implement this goal. To avoid the constitutional rule against open and explicit group prayers in the schools, legislators combined religious zeal with legal genius. A more or less standard law simply ordered a "moment of silence" during the school day, when every student individually could think about nothing, solve mathematical puzzles, fantasize about sex, or even—perhaps—pray. In a number of instances the state law said nothing at all about prayer, providing only for the brief period of silence. These paths for God's re-entry into the public schools have for the most part run into judicial roadblocks, though the cases have not been unanimous and the struggle is not yet over.

Alabama's silent-prayer law reached, and expired in, the Supreme Court in 1985. The statute struck down in that case provided for a period of silence in the public schools "for meditation or voluntary prayer." Ishmael

Jaffree, father of two second-graders and one kindergartner, sued to have that enactment invalidated. Sustaining his position (over the dissents of Chief Justice Warren Burger and Justices Byron White and William Rehnquist), the Supreme Court found that the purpose of passing the law was, as an Alabama senator put it, "to return voluntary prayer to our public schools." That violated the state's duty of neutrality with respect to religion under the Establishment Clause.

However, two of the Justices in the majority said, and four broadly intimated, that a law merely providing for a period of silence would pass constitutional muster. And that echoed a long-running debate that remains at most only partially resolved. The idea of legislatively decreed moments of silence in the public schools has appealed to the lawmakers of more than half the states. It has led to a spate of judicial opinions one way or another and a small shelf of scholarly writing. For all the devout attention they have received, these state laws exhibit only two or three salient—and to me regrettable—characteristics.

First, they all emerge in the wake of the Supreme Court's banning of officially sponsored prayer and Bible reading in the schools. Their background leaves no question about their essential purpose, to evade or fight in the rearguard against that ban.

Second, in a number of cases the sponsors of these acts make no bones about their view that the majority has taken more than an acceptable amount of guff from minorities, and that the preponderant sentiment favoring school prayer should have its way. A New Jersey state assemblyman sponsoring one of the bills was asked in debate about its effect on atheists. The question may have wrongly implied that only atheists would oppose this sort of law. The answer in its way dismissed all sorts of opponents when the assemblyman said that "they were so few in number their views could be discounted." That position is by no means rare. In an opinion upholding the Nebraska legislature's regular payment and use of a Presbyterian minister to open its sessions with a prayer, Chief Justice Burger wrote that this was "simply a tolerable acknowledgement of beliefs widely held among the people of this country." Expressions like these, made in upholding religious exercises under government sponsorship, give less than enthusiastic support to the proposition that the Religion Clauses vouchsafe minority rights, not indulgences for the majority.

A third characteristic of the moment-of-silence laws is a common claim of their sponsors: that they are merely neutral provisions for a time of repose in the school day, when students can do as they please, even pray if the spirit moves them. This has august support, in the Supreme Court and among notable legal scholars. I'll explain below my dissent from this position.

At this point, to conclude on the state of the law as of now, I report that the majority of the lower federal courts that have considered the question have held these moment-of-silence statutes unconstitutional. They have perceived usually a more or less veiled purpose to sponsor or to promote prayer. . . .

To be sure, the decreed time of silence may be used to daydream or ogle, etc. But how did it happen that in all the decades before the school-prayer cases no powerhouse of daydreamers and oglers (who represent all of us, after all) demanded laws compelling stated periods of silence? Rhetorical questions don't need answers. As a relevant tangent, however, one recalls the long stretches of silence, in study halls and classrooms, that characterized life in public school. There was always plenty of time to pray or ogle. No law proclaimed a specific moment of silence. No occasion arose when anybody was questioned about the failure to use the silent time for praying. The moment-of-silence laws are, in one word, charades.

Ruses of this kind remind us of the essentially sleazy uses to which politicians put their professed devotion to God. The Christians among them notably forget the lesson Christ taught about this:

> Beware of practicing your piety before men in order to be seen by them; for then you will have no reward from your Father who is in heaven.

Instead, in a kind of guerrilla war against the First Amendment, periodic bursts of public religious displays by government officials are offered up as substitutes for statesmanship. A further example or two may be enough illustration.

During the Civil War, when the fate of the nation seemed precarious, the Union cause was buttressed in 1864 by the placement of the national motto, "In God We Trust," on a two-cent piece. Blessed by the Congress, that sentiment on the money continued unquestioned until it came to be noticed by President Theodore Roosevelt. It struck him as being "close to sacrilege." He noted that this form of affirmation had tended to produce jokes rather than accesses of elevated faith. In a letter to a clergyman he wrote:

> Every one must remember the innumerable cartoons and articles based on phrases like "In God we trust for the other eight cents"; "In God we trust for the short weight"; "In God we trust for the thirty-seven cents we do not pay"; and so forth, and so forth.

More repelled than amused, Roosevelt ordered that the motto be deleted from the currency.

One man's sacrilege is a lot of other people's holiness. The Congress was appalled by the President's vandalism and ordered the slogan put back onto the money. Both our metal and paper forms of legal tender have been graced ever since by the religious motto.

Do you feel better protected by those words on the money? Does it perhaps help to keep the dollar sound? Do you in fact have any awareness that the words are there? Probably the answer for most of us is that by this time it is a matter of little or no consequence. If it was thought about, however, one might hope, though possibly in vain, that more of us would be ready to join in Theodore Roosevelt's sentiments. For the genuinely devout, the vote of confidence in God, on money, of all places, might fairly seem an affront. For the nonreligious or for those, like Buddhists, among others, to whom the trust in God is an alien concept, the routine affirmation by their government might grate. It is difficult to know in the end how in a country never accused of insufficiently worshipping money anyone finds strength or solace in this practice. At least in my judgment, all of us, and the still generally shared concept of God, are diminished a little by such cheap public expressions of religiosity.

The thought was put more felicitously by a sensitive Harvard law teacher in a lovely book attending devotedly to the springs of religious sentiment as well as to the sound place of democratic government. Speaking of the easy manifestations of official spirituality, he counted these as instances of "chauvinism and religiosity" combining "to produce a triumphant vulgarity" that congratulates God for the wisdom of favoring America and Americans over lesser, less godly nations. . . .

In the same class, though perhaps more debatably, I'd put the improvement on the Pledge of Allegiance fashioned by Congress in 1954. That was a year, it will be recalled, when Senator Joseph McCarthy was still exploring how low we might be sunk in his ersatz but grimly destructive crusade against "subversives." It was also a year McCarthy's colleagues found it meet to insert the words "under God" after the reference to this "one nation" in the pledge. The House Report on the bill that became this law said that "it would serve to deny the atheistic and materialistic concepts of communism with its attendant subservience of the individual." Some very brief remarks on the floor reaffirmed that inserting the words "under God" would "strengthen the national resistance to communism." The only cerebration manifested on the subject of the bill had to do with the number and placement of commas in the revised pledge—i.e., whether it should be simply "one nation under God" or "one Nation, under God," as the legislative judgment finally determined. The short debate on this subject was suitably placid. There was no debate at all on the merits of the revision and no vote against it. Who, after all, would be caught in the open excluding God?

The uses of God as a "ceremonial and patriotic" implement go forward steadily in more obtrusive and questionable forms. The insistent demand to have crèches and menorahs in public sites continues to present tough questions. . . . The legal issues are tricky enough to promise a continued supply of test cases. To oversimplify a lot, the hardest cases—where private groups want to put their crèches or menorahs in the public park or on City Hall plaza—pit the First Amendment free-speech rights of those groups against the claim of the objectors that this placement of the symbols indicates government endorsement of the religion symbolized. Without questioning the difficulty of these cases, it is fair to conjure with the question why they keep happening. The answer lies, I think, in the very nature of hostile and competitive patriotism out of which one might wish that God could have been kept. The crèche on the public square—to "put Christ back into Christmas," as its sponsors regularly say—plants the religious flag of the angry nativists winning theirs back from the alien, infidel intruders. (Who do they think they are?) The menorah sponsors are a kindred but more pathetic story. (If the *goyim* can do it, so can we.) Both are joined together as enemies of the mutual forbearance that is at the heart of religious freedom in a pluralist society.

The gist of the demand is that the muscle of your religion be displayed in the public space. The subject, as is usual with facile shows of patriotism, is power. It is put, to be sure, as a matter of free expression by the crèche and menorah advocates, but that is largely fraud or self-delusion. There are ample private spaces in every community, amply visible, for displaying religious icons. The insistence on the *public* space, the space that belongs to all of us, is to show those others, the nonadherents. The distinction is readily, if not always malevolently, blurred. Leonid Feldman, an earnest cleric, raised as an atheist and abused as a Jew in the former Soviet Union, serves now as a conservative rabbi in Florida. He says he is now "frightened by secularism" and perplexed by those, Jews and others, who oppose the installation of menorahs. He states his case in a few moving words: "I fought the KGB for the right to light a menorah. Forgive me if I don't want to eliminate menorahs from America's lawns."[1] Moving his words may be. They also reflect, in brief compass, an entire confusion about what church-state separation means in the United States.

The fear of "secularism" is a chimera. "Secular" is what our government is supposed to be. That has nothing to do with the *imposed* religion of atheism that Rabbi Feldman suffered in the U.S.S.R. As for the right to light menorahs on "America's lawns," the rabbi should surely have realized by now that it is a right fully respected under our law (leaving aside blights like private anti-Semitism and other "antis" that continue to sully religious, racial, and ethnic relationships in our country and most others).

Whatever misunderstandings may beset a recent refugee from Soviet atheism, there is no ground for similar confusion, and probably no similar confusion, among most people who want their religious symbols standing on public property. The symbols make a statement—not of religious faith. They are not needed for that. They assert simply and starkly, as I've said, power over the nonbelievers. This was underscored for me in a fleeting moment of a case that ended 4–4 in the Supreme Court, the equal division (Justice Powell was ill and absent) resulting in a defeat for the village of Scarsdale (with me as unsuccessful counsel) when it sought to deny a place for a crèche in a public circle. In the course of that proceeding, one of the sponsors of the crèche was asked about his interest in viewing it while it stood on Scarsdale's Boniface Circle during the Christmas season. To my surprise as the questioner, it turned out that he never bothered to go look at the crèche at all, let alone to admire or draw inspiration from it. But on reflection that should not have been so surprising. The crèche was not there

---

1. KGB is an acronym for the Soviet secret police.

for him to see or appreciate for its intrinsic spiritual value in his religious universe. It was there for others, who professed other religions or none, so that the clout of his religious group should be made manifest—above all to any in the sharply divided village who would have preferred that it not be there. This is the low road followed by at least a good number of those who seek for their religion and its symbols the imprimatur of government. If it is religious at all, this stance betokens a weak and self-doubting species of faith.

Much more blatant and unsettling than the crèches and menorahs, and even the tasteless evasions of moment-of-silence laws, is the ongoing course of flat-out defiance of the Supreme Court's ban against organized prayer in the public schools. It is ironic at best that in God's name, while tracing the blessings of democracy to their religion, so many people hack at the most vital of democratic organs: the rule of law, including the acceptance of authoritative decisions by those commissioned to expound the Constitution. Ironic or not, the practice continues, at a steep price in human anguish and political subversion. One more example helps to sharpen the picture.

In 1993, the Federal Court of Appeals embracing Texas heard the case of a junior-high-school basketball coach who regularly led his girls' team in a recitation of the Lord's Prayer at the beginning and end of each practice session. At games against other schools, the members of the team were brought to the center of the court, where they got on their hands and knees while the coach stood over them, and with their heads bowed, recited the Lord's Prayer. The prayer was also said before they left school for games away from home and at critical times in games like last-second buzzer-beater shots. A twelve-year-old team member objected to the prayer. When her father spoke to the assistant superintendent of schools about her objection, that official said that "unless [the father] had grandparents buried in the Duncanville Cemetery, he had no right to tell [the assistant superintendent] how to run his schools." When Jane Doe decided not to participate in the team prayers, the coach had her stand aside at games while the others prayed. Her fellow students asked, "Aren't you a Christian?" One spectator stood up after a game and yelled, "Well, why isn't she praying? Isn't she a Christian?" Her history teacher called her "a little atheist" during one class lecture.

The court upheld an injunction forbidding this practice. No one can doubt the correctness of the decision. What causes doubt and worry is that the coach and the superintendent should have found it justifiable to require that such a lawsuit be brought. If they have done useful service at all, it is to remind us of the misery inflicted by self-righteous tyrants like these on young people and others who do not share their religious convictions (assuming in their favor that people of this sort have genuine inner "convictions" rather than merely devices for oppressing their neighbors). It is doubtful that the coach, serving as backup minister, thought this performance made his team play more effectively.

But who knows? The uses to which athletes and others put their God are multifarious and often surprising. I recall, having made a note of it, the night of October 25, 1986, when the New York Mets won the critical sixth game of the World Series on a dubious fielding effort by the Boston Red Sox first baseman. As a proper Mets fan, I stayed with the telecast to hear some post-game wisdom. Two of the star Mets players gave similar explanations for their victory. Third baseman Ray Knight explained that the Good Lord had been on their side. Catcher Gary Carter attributed the victory to the favor shown the Mets by Jesus Christ. Even a Mets fan was led to wonder how the Deity had come to nurse hostility toward the Red Sox.

Seemingly more spacious and high-minded are the clerics and philosophers who do not invoke a necessarily partisan God but argue earnestly that the secularization of government in our time leaves a moral vacuum that will be filled with false, evil, probably fascistic substitutes for true religion. A lively proponent of this position is Roman Catholic Father Richard John Neuhaus, whose famous book, *The Naked Public Square: Religion and Democracy in America,* was published in 1984, when he was a Lutheran minister. When the public square becomes naked, he taught, of religious affirmations and frankly religious morality, we lose the most basic need of a good society, some "final inhibition of evil." That inhibition, he makes clear, is found in the Christian—he sometimes says "Judeo-Christian"—tradition. He faults the Supreme Court for straying in recent years from its earlier sound perception, for it remains correct in his view to acknowledge that "this is, as the Supreme Court said in 1931, a Christian people." While the majority of the Court and most legal scholars rejoice that the Court would shun a repetition of that arrogant thought (as Justice Brennan called it), Father Neuhaus deems this a tragic retreat. This epitomizes, in my opinion, the profound error of his way.

. . . It is plain wrong to aver that the fundamental morality of our strikingly diverse people is tied to Christian, or even Judeo-Christian, doctrine or observance. Throughout American history, the great politico-moral issues that have troubled and divided us have seen the Christian and Jewish clergy about as divided as everyone else. Abortion in our time, capital punishment, equal rights for women, even capitalism versus socialism have all had religious leaders on both sides. The most tragic of our national sins, slavery, saw a similar division, with the majority of ministers siding, as is usual, with the status quo throughout the centuries before emancipation. At least one thoughtful religious scholar finds the belief in an inerrant Bible, including its literal approval of slavery, a still significant strand of fundamentalist thought in the American South. None of this is to doubt for an instant the value of spiritual leaders for their followers. It is only to stress again that this is a value that should be neither enforced nor endorsed by the state.

The notion that government must somehow be religious because most of our people are religious is a gross error. The astute observer Tocqueville concluded in the 1830s that it was precisely the separation of church and state that led to both the peaceful careers of varying sects and the flourishing of religion in general. Times have undoubtedly changed since then, but he found among both priests and laypeople a unanimity of opinion on this score. That opinion was sound in Tocqueville's day. We should cherish and preserve it.

■ DISCUSSION QUESTIONS

1. How should we interpret the First Amendment's words on religious freedom? Do we emphasize the philosophical convictions of Madison and Jefferson or the practices of government support for religion that prevailed at the time and for many years afterward?

2. Should there be a strict separation between church and state, as the Supreme Court has proclaimed? Or should religion occupy a greater place in public institutions so long as measures are taken to safeguard everyone's freedom of conscience, including nonbelievers'?

3. Should we allow prayers in the schools and religious symbols on public property so long as all faiths (and nonbelievers) are allowed representation, or would such expressions of religion favor the faiths of the majority and prove coercive to the minority?

4. Should religious expression be considered a normal and usually healthy contributor to political life, or should it be kept a personal matter lest it produce divisiveness or intolerance in politics?

■ SUGGESTED READINGS
AND INTERNET RESOURCES

For a sympathetic and wide-ranging discussion of religion's place in American politics, see Garry Wills, *Under God: Religion and American Politics* (New York: Simon and Schuster, 1990). For a prominent criticism of what the author regards as the dominant culture's antipathy to public expressions of faith, see Stephen L. Carter, *The Culture of Disbelief: How American Law and Politics Trivialize Religious Devotion* (New York: Basic Books, 1993). A political theorist and a historian attack the constitutional argument presented by the Christian right and emphasize the secular intentions of America's founders in Isaac Kramnick and R. Laurence Moore, *The Godless Constitution: The Case Against Religious Correctness* (New York: Norton, 1996). A comprehensive treatment of religious liberty issues is John Witte Jr., *Religion and the American Constitutional Experiment: Essential Rights and Liberties* (Boulder, Colo: Westview Press, 1999). Historical perspective on the struggles for civil liberties and civil rights is provided in

James MacGregor Burns and Stewart Burns, *A People's Charter: The Pursuit of Rights in America* (New York: Vintage Books, 1993).

American Civil Liberties Union
www.aclu.org/issues/religion/hmrf.html
The ACLU, the nation's oldest civil liberties organization, highlights recent events pertinent to First Amendment religious issues, lists resources, and provides links to other religious freedom sites.

The American Center for Law and Justice
www.aclj.org
This Christian legal foundation's site on "Defending the Rights of Believers" includes a booklet on student rights in the public schools, news releases, information letters, and references to important court cases.

7

Civil Rights:
How Far Have
We Progressed?

Almost half a century after the U.S. Supreme Court ruled in *Brown* v. *Board of Education of Topeka* (1954) that racial segregation was a violation of the Constitution, where do relations between the races stand? And what kinds of public policies are still needed to address issues of racial inequity? Have we made considerable progress toward becoming "one nation, indivisible," as claimed by Stephan Thernstrom and Abigail Thernstrom, authors of the first selection that follows? Or do pervasive racial divisions continue to make us "a country of strangers," the title of our second selection, by David Shipler? Should we abandon affirmative action programs, as the Thernstroms recommend, because they impede progress toward a "colorblind" society, or do we need them, as Shipler suggests, because African Americans continue to face handicaps and prejudices in schools and workplaces?

Few Americans today question the landmark civil rights laws and court decisions of the 1950s and 1960s, even though they were enormously controversial in their day. After hundreds of years of slavery and racial segregation, the argument of the civil rights movement that racial discrimination is incompatible with democracy has at last attained official status. But since its heroic phase ended in the late 1960s with the assassination of Martin Luther King Jr., the civil rights struggle has become embroiled in one bitter debate after another. Leaders and groups associated with the old civil rights movement have continued to call for strong legal measures to advance racial equality, including school busing and affirmative action in education and employment. Critics of the movement, black as well as white, challenge these measures, contending that they actually obstruct racial progress by undermining black self-help and by sowing fresh resentments among whites.

The dilemmas of race continued to trouble American society throughout the 1990s, as dramatically evidenced in the Los Angeles riots of 1992 and the antithetical reactions of African Americans and whites to the O. J. Simpson murder trial in 1994–1995. President Bill Clinton claimed that a top priority of his second term was a national dialogue focused on these dilemmas. But critics on the left disparaged Clinton's initiative on race as talk without action, while critics to the right saw it as merely a sounding board for bankrupt liberal nostrums such as affirmative action.

President Clinton was a defender of affirmative action, responding to mounting criticisms of it with the call to "mend it, don't end it." But after he became president, affirmative action programs faced a series of legal and political setbacks. In 1995, the U.S. Supreme Court ruled in *Adarand* v. *Peña* that government programs that provide preferential treatment on the basis of race are unconstitutional unless a pattern of prior discrimination against minorities can be demonstrated. In 1996, voters in California approved Proposition 209, which forbade public agencies and schools in the state from employing racial or gender preferences. That same year, a federal appeals court decided in *Hopwood* v. *Texas* that the state university could not continue to admit minorities with lower grades and test scores in the name of promoting diversity. In 1998, voters in the state of Washington approved a measure similar to California's Proposition 209.

With a Republican in the White House and several cases involving higher education heading for the Supreme Court, affirmative action faces an even more clouded future in the first decade of the new century. President Bush received only 8 percent of the African-American vote in 2000, and his razor-thin margin of victory in Florida was aided by the disproportionate disqualification of black voters. Neither ideology nor political interests predispose his administration to defend affirmative action as the Clinton administration had done. The composition of the Supreme Court has not changed since the *Adarand* decision, so the perspective of its majority about affirmative action remedies is not likely to be sympathetic.

How we view civil rights policies such as affirmative action depends in large part on how we understand and evaluate relations between the races in the United States today. Stephan and Abigail Thernstrom argue in our first selection that purveyors of racial gloom have distorted public debate, particularly by obscuring the evidence that racial attitudes in the United States have been growing more tolerant for decades. Relying heavily on public opinion surveys, the Thernstroms see whites and blacks as coming increasingly closer to one another since the days of Jim Crow segregation, even forming bonds of friendship across the boundaries of race. While not denying that African Americans suffer from higher rates of crime and poverty than whites and score lower on various educational measures, the Thernstroms are most impressed by the signs of African-American advancement, such as the rise of a black middle class. The Thernstroms oppose affirmative action. Although it may spring from benevolent intentions, they argue, it has had pernicious consequences and has blocked further progress toward a "colorblind society."

David Shipler studies race relations differently from the Thernstroms and reaches very different conclusions. Shipler's work is based not on public opinion surveys but on interviews and observations about race relations in schools, workplaces, and communities around the nation. He believes that race continues to draw a line between white and black Americans, with uncertainty, discomfort, and anxiety on both sides. To Shipler, talk of "colorblindness" is unrealistic: "there is scarcely a consequential interaction between a black and a white in the United States in which race is not a factor."

Like many supporters of affirmative action, Shipler expresses some ambivalence, conceding that the policy can play into old racial stereotypes. But to him, affirmative action is needed so long as African Americans face educational and economic handicaps and subtle prejudices that undermine genuine equality of opportunity.

Race relations in the United States have profound implications for our understandings of democracy, freedom, and equality. How do you view the current state of American race relations? Are you more persuaded by the surveys cited by the Thernstroms that we are becoming a more tolerant interracial society or by the interviews and observations presented by Shipler that racial tensions and grievances continue to prevail along an American color line? What measures should our society take to deal with remaining racial inequalities? Is affirmative action still needed? If affirmative action were abolished, would we at last create a level playing field where everyone could compete on equal terms, or would white males reassert their traditional advantages?

One Nation, Indivisible

STEPHAN THERNSTROM
AND ABIGAIL THERNSTROM

I n 1991, 13 percent of the whites in the United States said that they had generally "unfavorable" opinions about black Americans. In an ideal world, that number would be zero. But such a world is nowhere to be found. In Czechoslovakia that same year, 49 percent of Czechs had "unfavorable" attitudes toward the Hungarian ethnic minority living within the boundaries of their country. Likewise, 45 percent of West Germans disliked the Turks living in Germany; 54 percent of East Germans regarded Poles negatively; 40 percent of Hungarians frowned on the Romanians who lived among them; and 42 percent of the French disdained Arab immigrants from North Africa. In only two of the dozen European countries surveyed—Britain and Spain—was the proportion of majority group members who expressed dislike for the principal minority group less than twice as high as in the United States. . . .

Against this yardstick the racial views of white Americans look remarkably good. But are seemingly tolerant whites simply more hypocritical than Czechs or French? Perhaps they have learned to keep their animus hidden from public view. We think not. Although different ways of framing questions about racial prejudice yield slightly different answers, the bulk of the evidence squares with the 1991 survey results: when it comes to intergroup tolerance, Americans rate high by international standards. . . .

America Since Myrdal

This is a profound change. When Gunnar Myrdal first trained his microscope on the American racial scene in the closing years of the Great Depression, he was struck by the radical difference between the status of immigrants and that of African Americans.[1] The United States stood out for its success in absorbing millions of immigrants from other lands into the melting pot. Myrdal believed that American social scientists were too preoccupied with "the occasional failures of the assimilation process" and the "tension" that immigration created in the society. They lacked the perspective available to "the outside observer," to whom the "first and greatest riddle to solve" was how "the children and grandchildren of these unassimilated foreigners" so quickly became "well-adjusted Americans." Part of the answer to the puzzle, Myrdal suggested, was "the influence upon the immigrant of a great national *ethos,* in which optimism and carelessness, generosity and callousness, were so blended as to provide him with hope and endurance."

In those days, the "optimism" and "generosity" Myrdal found did not extend to the descendants of enslaved Africans, though the "callousness" certainly did. Blacks had not been coaxed or coerced into the American melting pot; they had been forcibly kept out of it. Everyone was eager to "Americanize" the immigrants, Myrdal noticed, and viewed "the preservation of their separate national attributes and group loyalties as a hazard to American institutions." The recipe for African Americans was the reverse. They were "excluded from assimilation," and advised "even by their best friends in the dominant white group" to "keep to themselves and develop a race pride of their own."

In the South, where the large majority of African Americans lived, an elaborate legal code defined their position as a separate and inferior people.

---

1. Gunnar Myrdal was a Swedish social scientist who published a landmark study of U.S. race relations, *An American Dilemma: The Negro Problem and American Democracy,* in 1944.

Poorly educated in segregated schools, and confined to ill-paid, insecure, menial jobs, they were a subordinate caste in a society dedicated to white supremacy. Moreover, in countless ways blacks were daily reminded of their status as a lesser breed; they entered only the back door of a white home, never shook hands with a white person, and grown men were habitually addressed as "boy" or simply by their first names. In the North, blacks could vote, and the color line was less rigid and lacked the force of law. But many of the semiskilled and skilled industrial positions that gave immigrants the chance to climb out of poverty were off-limits, and blacks lived for the most part in a world separate from whites. A color line in the housing market confined black families to black neighborhoods; swimming in the "white" part of a public beach was dangerous; and many restaurants would not serve black customers. As Myrdal found, nine out of ten of even the most liberal and cosmopolitan northerners whom he encountered in the 1940s blanched at the thought of interracial marriage.

None of the public opinion surveys conducted in the Depression or World War II years included a specific question about whether whites had "favorable" or "unfavorable" opinions about blacks. But there can be no doubt about the answer such an inquiry would have yielded. The polling data we reviewed . . . demonstrated that large majorities of whites held strongly racist sentiments. African Americans were a stigmatized group, assumed to be a permanent caste that would forever remain beyond the melting pot.

That world has now vanished. In the spring of 1995, in the wake of attacks on affirmative action, Georgia congressman and one-time civil rights hero John Lewis complained that he sometimes felt as if he were reliving his life. "Didn't we learn?" he asked. He felt "the need to . . . tell people we've got to do battle again." But yesterday is not today, as many do recognize—including, we suspect, Lewis himself. "We black folk should never forget that our forefathers were slaves," Florida congresswoman Carrie P. Meek said in 1994. But then she added, "though my daughter says, 'Enough, Mom, enough of this sharecropper-slave stuff.'" Meek was born in 1926, and in her own lifetime the rigidly oppressive caste system delineated in *An American Dilemma* gave way to the far more fluid social order of today.

From rigid caste system to a more fluid social order . . . we reviewed decades of amazing change.

. . . We did not neglect the bad news. In 1995 half of all the murder victims in the United States were African Americans, though they comprised just one-eighth of the population; more than half of those arrested for murder were also black. The black poverty rate that same year was still 26 percent; 62 percent of children in female-headed families were poor. Perhaps most ominously, in 1994, on average, blacks aged seventeen could read only as well as the typical white child just thirteen years old. The racial gap in levels of educational performance permanently stacks the deck against too many African American youngsters as they move on to work or further schooling.

To stress the bad news is to distort the picture, however. Equally important is the story of enormous change, of much more progress than many scholars have recognized. For instance, between 1970 and 1995 the proportion of African Americans living in suburban communities nearly doubled, and residential segregation decreased in almost all the nation's metropolitan areas with the largest black populations. One of the best kept secrets of American life today is that over 40 percent of the nation's black citizens consider themselves members of the middle class. The black male unemployment rate has gotten much press, but, in fact, of those who are in the labor force (working or looking for work), 93 percent had jobs in 1995. We have let the underclass define our notion of black America; it is a very misleading picture.[2]

Over the last half century, the positions of African Americans thus improved dramatically by just about every possible measure of social and economic achievement: years of school completed, occupational levels, median incomes, life expectancy at birth, poverty rates, and homeownership rates. Much of the change took place before the civil rights movement. And while key decisions made by political and legal authorities in this early period were undeniably important (President Truman's order abolishing segregation in the armed forces, for example, and *Brown v. Board of Education*), the impersonal economic and demographic forces that transferred so many blacks from the southern countryside to the northern city were more fundamental.

In addition, white racial attitudes were gradually liberalized. Racist beliefs that were once firmly held by highly educated and uneducated whites alike lost all claim to intellectual respectability by the 1950s, and that changed racial climate finally opened doors. For instance, the door to the Brooklyn Dodgers' locker room. Had the visionary Branch Rickey believed Dodger fans were unreconstructed racists, he would not have put Jackie Robinson on the field and risked plunging ticket sales. As it was, his feel for changing racial attitudes brought championships to Brooklyn.

Social contact between the races has also increased enormously. By 1989, five out of six black Americans could name a white person whom they considered a friend, while two out of three whites said their social circle included someone who was black. By 1994 it had become not the least bit unusual for blacks and whites to have brought someone of the other race home to dine (a third of white families and a majority of the black families had done so), and most blacks and whites said someone of the other race lived in their neighborhood. When a sample of people in the Detroit metropolitan area were asked in 1992 whether they had contact on the job with people of the other race, 83 percent of blacks and 61 percent of whites said, yes. That same year, 72 percent of blacks and 64 percent of whites reported having interracial conversations on the job "frequently" or "sometimes." Even in the most intimate of relations, there had been substantial

---

2. *Underclass* refers to residents of the nation's poorest areas.

change. By 1993, 12 percent of all marriages contracted by African Americans were to a spouse of the other race.

Two Nations: Black and White, Separate, Hostile, Unequal, Andrew Hacker called his best-selling book. Our book is in many ways an answer to Hacker. *One* nation (we argue), no longer separate, much less unequal than it once was, and by many measures, less hostile. Moreover, the serious inequality that remains is less a function of white racism than of the racial gap in levels of educational attainment, the structure of the black family, and the rise in black crime.

We quarrel with the left—its going-nowhere picture of black America and white racial attitudes. But we also quarrel with the right—its see-no-evil view. It seems extraordinarily hard for liberals to say we have come a long way; the Jim Crow South is not the South of 1997. But it seems very hard for conservatives to say, yes, there was a terrible history of racism in this country, and too much remains.

Conservatives seem to think that they concede too much if they acknowledge the ugliness of our racial history and the persistence of racism (greatly diminished but not gone)—that if they do so, they will be committed to the currently pervasive system of racial preferences and indeed to reparations. And liberals, from their different perspective, also fear concession. To admit dramatic change, they seem to believe, is to invite white indifference. As if everything blacks now have rests on the fragile foundation of white guilt . . .

The Road to Progress

Much racial progress has been made. And much has *yet* to be made. How to keep moving forward? It is a question that can be answered only by knowing the route by which African Americans have come to where they are today.

There is no mystery as to how they got from there to here, most writing on racial change in recent decades assumes. The story began with the civil rights movement, which, with a boost from *Brown v. Board of Education,* created turmoil in the nation and forced Congress and the White House to act. The civil rights and voting rights legislation of the mid-1960s destroyed Jim Crow institutions and gave equal legal status to African Americans. These colorblind measures, however, failed to remedy deeper economic and social inequalities rooted in race. Color-conscious policies that set specific numerical goals and timetables attacked the underlying problems. In fact, only the adoption of preferential policies could have created a black middle class and brought about other economic and educational gains.

From this account, a simple policy conclusion flows: preferential policies are the key to future progress. And thus Supreme Court decisions and other actions that constrain the use of racial classifications by public authorities are viewed by some as truly dangerous—a threat to black well-being comparable to the end of Reconstruction.

Such alarm ignores the historical record, we have argued, although the great strides forward have since been somewhat obscured by the gains and disappointments of subsequent years. The civil rights revolution reached a climax in a burst of legislation that destroyed the Jim Crow system, but that legislation promised more than it could quickly deliver. As Dr. King and others understood, the legal fix would not tomorrow solve the problem of economic and educational inequalities so long in the making. Blacks were understandably impatient. They had already waited much too long—almost a century since the passage of the great Reconstruction Amendments to the Constitution. It was tempting to seek shortcuts, ways of accelerating social change, and thus the demand for "freedom now" soon became a call for "equality as a fact and as a result," as Lyndon Johnson put it in 1965.

That call for equality as a "fact" and "result" was the first step down the road to racial preferences. Much celebrated in the civil rights community for the benefits they have brought, preferences are in fact difficult to assess. . . . In 1995 the historian Roger Wilkins described himself as the happy recipient of racial preferences. "I'd rather be an assistant attorney general who was a beneficiary of affirmative action than a GS 14."[3] he said. It's hard to believe Wilkins is really convinced he would have been languishing at the bottom of a bureaucratic heap had he not been rescued by preferential policies. His tale certainly does not square with the larger picture, as we understand it.

In a few respects the overall rate of black progress did accelerate after preferential policies were introduced. Rates of entry into law and medical schools are one example. But lawyers and doctors are a tiny fraction of the black middle class. And by many other measures progress slowed—and in some cases stopped altogether. One recent study found that the racial gap in median wages, labor-force participation, and joblessness was wider in 1992 than in 1967. As a consequence of the huge rise in female-headed households among African Americans, the ratio of black to white family income has fallen somewhat since the 1960s. And the poverty rate for blacks in the 1990s is about as high as it was a generation ago.

Thus, on many counts the socioeconomic gains made by African Americans in the affirmative action era have been less impressive than those that occurred before preferential policies. On the basis of that historical record, however, we cannot conclude that affirmative action did nothing significant. In the 1940s and 1950s, big strides forward were relatively easy to take—blacks were so far behind whites. Thereafter, the rate of progress naturally slowed. Moreover, preferential policies may indeed have benefited some African Americans (those with better educational credentials) without dramatically improving the position of the group as a whole.

The slower growth of the American economy since the early 1970s further complicates the task of assessment. Groups on the lower rungs of the

---

3. GS stands for General Schedule, the system that classifies federal civil servants; GS14 denotes a middle-level position in the federal bureaucracy.

socioeconomic ladder usually find it far easier to improve their position when the economy is booming, as it was to an extraordinary degree in the 1950s and 1960s. And perhaps without affirmative action, the slow economy would have been even harder on African Americans than it was. It's a what-might-have-been argument that cannot be settled. But those who assume that ending affirmative action will end black progress must reconcile the history of pre-1970s progress with their fear of a future that returns to the past.

Even assuming that affirmative action rescued Roger Wilkins and others from professional oblivion, an important question remains: have the benefits outweighed the costs? The issue was implicitly raised in a surprising 1993 letter. The mayors of Minneapolis and four other large American cities wrote to Attorney General Janet Reno, calling for an end to the collection and dissemination of any crime statistics broken down by race. "We believe," the mayors said, "that the collection and use of racial crime statistics by the federal government perpetuate racism in American society." Such data, the mayors went on, were "largely irrelevant" and conveyed the erroneous impression that race and criminality were causally linked. "Racial classifications," the letter continued, were "social constructs" and had "no independent scientific validity." An earlier letter from the Minneapolis mayor had expressed concern about the " 'we' vs. 'they' mentality" that racial classifications created.

The crime statistics had wonderfully concentrated the mayors' minds. Momentarily, at least, they recalled what liberals had always believed until the late 1960s but had chosen to forget when they were converted to affirmative action: racial classifications perpetuate racism. The mayors did not object to racial body counts on principle, as liberals once had. They were simply troubled by the publication of statistics that made African Americans look bad. Racial statistics showing that black poverty and unemployment rates were higher than those of whites, that our colleges and universities did not have "enough" African American students, and that our corporations were short on black executives: these racial classifications apparently were not mere "social constructs" with "no scientific validity." They were essential to enlightened public policy. It was only the black crime rate to which the mayors objected.

But racial data used to distribute benefits inevitably creates the we-versus-they outlook that worried them. American society has paid, it seems to us, a very high price for well-intentioned race-conscious policies. Particularly those built into our law, for the law delivers messages that ripple through both the public and private sectors. And thus unlike the mayors, we hold to Justice Harlan's belief that "our Constitution is color-blind, and neither knows nor tolerates classes among citizens."[4]

---

4. Justice John Marshall Harlan was the lone dissenter to the 1896 Supreme Court decision in *Plessy* v. *Ferguson* that legitimated the "separate-but-equal" system of racial segregation.

In 1896, Justice Harlan was under no illusion that American *society* was color-blind; his was a statement about how to read the Constitution. Nor did Thurgood Marshall in 1947 suppose the country had become oblivious to race when he argued that "classifications based on race or color have no moral or legal validity in our society."[5] We're not naïve; we don't think Americans have to think twice about the color of someone they meet. And we do know that for many whites color still carries important connotations: a young black man on an urban street in the evening appears much more menacing than one who is white. Even middle-class black neighbors may still seem less appealing than white ones to too many white families. It is, in fact, precisely the problem of ongoing racism and just plain color-consciousness that makes race-blind public policy so imperative. Policies that work to heighten the sense of racial separatism spell disaster in a nation with an ugly history of racial subordination and a continuing problem, albeit dramatically diminished, of racial intolerance.

Race-conscious policies make for more race-consciousness; they carry American society backward. We have a simple rule of thumb: that which brings the races together is good; that which divides us is bad. Of course, which policies have what effect is a matter of deep contention. To tear down affirmative action "could start a race war that would make Bosnia look like a kindergarten party," Arthur Fletcher, a former assistant secretary for employment standards, said in 1995. The . . . research we have frequently cited suggests quite a different picture: a racial divide widened by preferences. Others argue that "diversity" strategies bring whites and blacks together; it is not our view. Only those policies that recognize differences among *individuals* can create a true community.

A nation in which individuals are judged as individuals: it was the dream of the 1960s, and we still cherish it. "There *is* a proper object for all the loathing in this country," *New Republic* literary editor Leon Wieseltier has said. "That object is: race. Instead of race hatred, the hatred of race. Instead of the love of what is visible about the person, the love of what is invisible about the person." Does the Wieseltier view ask black Americans to turn their back on all things "black"—to deny all cultural differences associated with group membership? Of course not. Jews haven't; Armenians haven't; Ukrainians haven't. Many Americans arrange their private lives so as to spend much of their time with others of the same background. Purging all racial distinctions from our law and our public life would pose no threat to those who wish to live in a predominantly black neighborhood, attend an all-black church, and otherwise associate primarily or even exclusively with their fellow African Americans.

Racist Americans have long said to blacks, the single most important thing about you is that you're black. Indeed, almost the only important

---

5. Justice Thurgood Marshall was the principal lawyer in the battle by the National Association for the Advancement of Colored People (NAACP) against "separate-but-equal"; later he served on the U.S. Supreme Court.

thing about you is your color. And now, black and white Americans of seeming good will have joined together in saying, we agree. It has been—and is—exactly the wrong foundation on which to come together for a better future. "There can be no empathy and persuasion across racial lines," the economist Glenn C. Loury has said, unless we understand "that the conditions and feelings of particular human beings are universally shared. Such an understanding can be had, but only if we look past race to our common humanity." Ultimately, black social and economic progress largely depend on the sense that we are one nation—that we sink or swim together, that black poverty impoverishes us all, that black alienation eats at the nation's soul, and that black isolation simply cannot work. . . .

True Equality

"The contest between white suburban students and minority inner-city youths is inherently unfair," the chancellor of the University of California at Berkeley, Chang-Lin Tien, said in the summer of 1995. It was not a very persuasive argument for the racial double standards he was defending. If inner-city youngsters are educationally deprived, surely the real solution—indeed the only effective and just solution—has to be one that attacks the problem of K–12 education directly. But in any case, most of the beneficiaries were not the inner-city youths upon whom Tien chose to focus; 30 percent of the black students in the 1994–1995 freshmen class came from families with annual incomes over $70,000. In fact, the Berkeley admissions office, studying the question, found that preferences reserved only for students from low-income families would have reduced the black enrollment by two-thirds. Relatively privileged students—by the measure of economic well-being—had acquired privileges on the basis of the color of their skin.

Affirmative action is class-blind. Students who fall into the category of protected minority will benefit whatever the occupation and income of their parents. As the *Boston Globe* has put it, "officials at even the most selective schools recruit minority scholars with the zeal of a Big 10 football coach." The overwhelming majority of four-year institutions buy expensive lists of minority students and their scores from the Educational Testing Service. Admissions counselors and a network of thousands of alumni comb the country, visiting schools and the special preparatory programs that Phillips Academy in Andover and other private high schools run. Some universities, like Tufts, start the recruitment process in the elementary school years; others, like Boston College, have been known to bring minority students, all expenses paid, for a visit, complete with a chauffeured tour of the area. And if that student can already afford the air fare and more? That's not relevant. Until 1996, when the policy was changed, the African-American student whom the Harvard Graduate School wanted automatically qualified for a Minority Prize Fellowship—even if that student was the son or daughter of a black millionaire.

It's not a process likely to encourage its beneficiaries to work hard in high school. The message is clear: color is the equivalent of good grades. If you don't have the latter, the former will often do. When the University of California regents decided in July 1995 to abolish racial and ethnic preferences in admissions, the executive director of a YWCA college-awareness program told students that the UC vote meant that their "application would be sent in with everybody else's—people who are on college tracks and are prepared." One of the minority students at the session, Jesley Zambrano, reacted at first with anger: "The schools are mostly run by white people. If they don't help us get in, how are we going to get in?" she asked. But then she answered the question herself: "I guess I have to work harder," she said.

That was exactly the point Martin Luther King had made in a speech Shelby Steele heard as a young student in Chicago.[6] "When you are behind in a footrace," King had said, "the only way to get ahead is to run faster than the man in front of you. So when your white roommate says he's tired and goes to sleep, you stay up and burn the midnight oil." As Steele went on to say, "academic parity with all other groups should be the overriding mission of black students. . . . Blacks can only *know* they are as good as others when they are, in fact, as good. . . . Nothing under the sun will substitute for this." And nothing under the sun except hard work will bring about that parity, as King had said. Challenge the students academically rather than capitulate to their demands for dorms with an ethnic theme, Steele has urged universities. And dismantle the machinery of separation, break the link between difference and power. For as long as black students see themselves as *black* students—a group apart, defined by race—they are likely to choose power over parity.

A Country of Strangers

DAVID K. SHIPLER

 line runs through the heart of America. It divides Oak Park from Chicago's West Side along the stark frontier of Austin Boulevard, splitting the two sides of the street into two nations, separating

---

6. Shelby Steele is an African-American scholar who has been one of the most prominent critics of affirmative action.

the carefully integrated town from the black ghetto, the middle class from the poor, the swept sidewalks from the gutters glistening with broken glass, the neat boutiques and trim houses from the check-cashing joints and iron-grilled liquor stores.

The line follows stretches of the Santa Monica Freeway in Los Angeles and Rock Creek Park in Washington, D.C. It runs along the white picket fence that divides the manicured grounds from the empty field where the slaves' shacks once stood at Somerset Place plantation in North Carolina. It cuts across the high, curved dais of the Etowah County Commission in Alabama, where one black member sits with five whites. It encircles the "black tables" where African-Americans cluster together during meals at Princeton University, Lexington High School in Massachusetts, and a thousand corporate cafeterias across the country.

At eleven o'clock Sunday morning, which has been called the most segregated hour in America, the line neatly separates black churches from white churches. It intertwines itself through police departments and courtrooms and jury rooms, through textbooks and classrooms and dormitories, through ballot boxes and offices, through theaters and movie houses, through television and radio, through slang and music and humor, and even through families. The line passes gently between Tony and Gina Wyatt of Florida; he is black, she is white, and they both reach gracefully across the border. It tangles the identity of their teenage son, Justin, who looks white but feels black.

"The problem of the Twentieth Century is the problem of the color-line," W. E. B. Du Bois wrote in 1901; the prophetic words became the opening declaration of his lyrical work *The Souls of Black Folk*.[1] In the succeeding decades, that line has been blurred and bent by the demise of legal segregation and the upward movement of many blacks through the strata of American opportunity. But it remains forbidding to black people left behind in poverty and to others, more successful, who may suddenly confront what Du Bois called a "vast veil"—the curtain of rejection drawn around those whose ancestors were brought in chains from Africa. Today, when sensibilities have been tuned and blatant bigotry has grown unfashionable in most quarters, racist thoughts are given subtler expression, making the veil permeable and often difficult to discern. Sometimes its presence is perceived only as a flicker across a face, as when a white patient looks up from her hospital bed to discover that an attending physician is an African-American.

And so, as the close of the century now approaches, I offer this journey along the color line. It is a boundary that delineates not only skin color and race but also class and culture. It traces the landscape where blacks and whites find mutual encounters, and it fragments into a multitude of fissures

---

1. W. E. B. Du Bois was a leading African-American scholar and political activist whose career stretched from the 1890s to the 1960s.

that divide blacks and whites not only from each other, but also among themselves.

Americans of my generation, who were youngsters when the civil rights movement began in the 1950s, grew up on awful, indelible images. I am haunted still by the cute little white girls who twisted their faces into screams of hatred as black children were escorted into schools. I saw for the first time that the face of pristine innocence could be merely a mask.

Here was the enemy. And the solution seemed obvious: Break down the barriers and let people mingle and know one another, and the importance of race would fade in favor of individual qualities. Blacks would be judged, as Martin Luther King Jr. was preaching, not by the color of their skin but by the content of their character. The perfect righteousness of that precept summoned the conscience of America. . . .

. . . As the Jim Crow segregation laws were overturned, less tractable problems were revealed, and they frustrated King toward the end of his life as he tried to bring his campaign to cities in the North. There, villainy was less easily identified. Rooted in the prejudices, the poverty, the poor education, and the culture of hopelessness that divided blacks and whites, the racial predicament proved too deeply embedded in the society to be pried out by mere personal contact and legal equality. Perhaps it was naïve to think that all that would have to happen was for people to look into each other's eyes, to give blacks as many opportunities as whites, to open the doors. I put this to Reverend Bill Lawson, the black pastor of the Wheeler Avenue Baptist Church in Houston, who had been in the movement and had a long perspective. . . .

. . . "I think that there has been a redefinition of relationships over the last, say, forty years," he said. "There has been, on the one hand, a push toward eliminating the old segregation laws and, on the other hand, a resistance to changing community and neighborhood patterns. So there has been a tension between what we felt was right and what we felt was expedient. There has been the allowance of public contacts. Blacks can ride in the fronts of buses or eat at lunch counters. There has not been a significant change in intimate, personal attitudes. There is still some feeling that we don't want to live too close together, that we don't want to have too many close connections in places [where] we worship, or that we don't want to have too much family contact. We still have some problems with dating and marriage. So in the more public relationships, there has been at least a tolerance that says, let's each one have our own freedom. But anything that becomes more intimate or personal, we tend to have a little bit more resistance."

In Birmingham, Alabama, an old civil rights warrior, Reverend Abraham Lincoln Woods of the St. Joseph Baptist Church, saw the movement's accomplishments as more cosmetic than substantive. "Birmingham has gone through tremendous changes," he said, "and the fact that we have gone from a city where blacks were shut out of the process to having a black mayor and a predominantly black city council—we now have black policemen, in fact we have a black chief now—many things have changed of that kind. But I find that in spite of what seems to be a tolerance of the races and a working together, I find still, somewhat beneath the surface, sometimes not too deeply, those same old attitudes."

But it is behavior, not attitudes, that concerns David Swanston, a white advertising executive whose wife, Walterene, is black. He sat in his handsome town house in McLean, Virginia, one evening and took the measure of America in terms of his own interracial marriage. "It was against the law in a number of states twenty-five years ago," he observed. "It just seems to me that this world was institutionally significantly more racist, overtly racist, than today. Now, each individual black and white within the country may be about the same place they were twenty-five years ago, as regarding interracial marriages and other issues. But it seems to me that's very secondary to the fact that institutionally, we are much beyond that—and it's the institutions that hurt you, that can have the impact on your lives. And by and large, if the twenty people we see in the mall don't like it, and those twenty people wouldn't have liked it twenty-five years ago, I don't really care. The fact that our marriage is recognized by the Commonwealth of Virginia, that we're not criminals, those are the areas where it just seems to me incredible change has been made." . . .

There is scarely a consequential interaction between a black and a white in the United States in which race is not a factor. Even as it goes unmentioned, as it normally does, race is rarely a neutral element in the equation. It may provoke aversion, fear, or just awkwardness, on the one hand, or, on the other, eager friendliness and unnatural dialogue. Even in easy contacts that are fleeting and impersonal—between a diner and a waiter, a customer and a salesperson, a passenger and a bus driver—race does not always drop to zero; it possesses weight and plays some role in the chemical reaction. "There's always something there," said a young white Princeton graduate working for the *National Journal*, a Washington magazine. "It can be mitigated or it can be worsened by a lot of other factors: social class, culture, the status hierarchy in the office." But it never quite goes away, as he realized when he observed how the mixture of race, class, and hierarchy led him to feel more comfortable with the white reporters than with the black secretaries and receptionists.

If race distorts individual relations, it also magnifies most major social and policy issues facing the American public. Poverty, crime, drugs, gangs, welfare, teenage pregnancy, chronic joblessness, homelessness, illiteracy, and the failure of inner-city public schools are usually viewed through the racial prism. They are seen as black problems or as problems created by blacks. The most popular solutions—cuts in welfare for teenage mothers and long sentences for repeat offenders—are codes for cracking down on blacks' misdeeds. Where race enters the realms of politics, health care, economic injustice, and occasionally foreign policy (as in Haiti and South Africa), the debates are charged with an additional layer of emotion. Despite the upheavals brought by the Supreme Court's 1954 ruling against segregated schools in *Brown* v. *Board of Education,* by the civil rights movement, and by the resulting 1964 Civil Rights Act and the 1965 Voting Rights Act, race is still central to the American psychological experience, as it has been for more than two hundred years.

Over their entire history on this continent, African-Americans have struggled as a people in every conceivable way, short of widespread armed insurrection, to share in the pursuit of happiness. By social reflex or by calculation, by happenstance or ideology, blacks have been servile and militant, passive and hardworking, dependent and self-sufficient. They have used the church, the mosque, the schoolhouse, the university, the military, and the corporation in an effort to advance. They have tried to go back to Africa, and they have tried to function within the political system of the United States. They have tried peaceful demonstrations and violent street riots. They have tried sweet reason and angry rhetoric, assimilation and separatism. They have appealed to the nation's conscience and to its fears. It would be wrong to say that none of this has worked: Individuals have succeeded. But neither deference nor defiance has been effective for black Americans as a whole. No degree of personal success quite erases the stigma of black skin, as many achieving blacks realize when they step outside their family, neighborhood, or professional environment into a setting where their rank and station and accomplishments are not known. "I didn't come from a deprived family," says Floyd Donald, who owns a small radio station in Gadsden, Alabama. "I grew up with books. I grew up with china. I grew up with silver. My background is impeccable, so far as my education and my parents' education and their positions in life and their abilities and so forth. So I had that advantage. However, out of my community, I was just another black. You see, it doesn't make much difference about the status that a black achieves. He is black in America."

In five years of crisscrossing the country to research this book, I was struck by the ease with which most blacks I interviewed were able to discuss race and the difficulty most whites had with the subject. . . .

. . . [B]lack Americans were enormously generous of spirit and time in reaching into their experiences to lay them out for me. Gradually, I came to understand what should have been obvious at the outset: that a black person cannot go very long without thinking about race; she has already asked herself every question that I could possibly pose.

By contrast, most whites rarely have to give race much thought. They do not begin childhood with advice from parents about how to cope with racial bias or how to discern the racial overtones in a comment or a manner. They do not have to search for themselves in history books or literature courses. In most parts of America, their color does not make them feel alone in a crowd; they are not looked to as representatives of their people. And they almost never have to wonder whether they are rejected—or accepted— because of their genuine level of ability or the color of their skin. As a result, few whites I interviewed had considered the questions I put to them. Many struggled to be introspective, but most found that I was taking them into uncharted territory, full of dangers that they quickly surrounded with layers of defensiveness. . . .

Many whites are confused over how they should be thinking about racial issues now. Some adopt an air of smooth indifference, an emotional distance. They often hesitate to say what's on their minds, lest they be accused of racism. Others work quietly, sometimes in frustration, to improve blacks' opportunities in their companies or universities or military units; indeed, I have discovered that more sincere effort goes on than ever gets reflected in press portrayals of America's racial problems. But nothing adds up to a neat sum anymore. How does a white person—even a liberal—sort out the anti-white prejudices, the black self-segregation, the manipulation of history, the endless message of white guilt, the visible achievements of prominent blacks coupled with the deepening poverty and violence of the inner cities? Across much of the spectrum of white America run common themes of distress and impatience with the subject of race, a national mood of puzzlement and annoyance. . . .

The question most often asked me by whites is whether racial matters are getting better or worse. It is an odd inquiry for people to make about their own country. I am used to being asked by Americans how things are going in Russia or in the Middle East, where I have lived and traveled and they perhaps have not.[2] But to have so little feel for the situation right at home betrays the corrosive nature of our racial legacy: how it eats away at our equilibrium, our sense of direction, our navigational skills. We simply do not know where we are, and we are not even quite sure where we have been.

What's more, there is no neat answer to the question. Sometimes I ask in return, "What is your reference point? Slavery? Jim Crow? The height of the civil rights movement? The last five years? Are we measuring economic success or personal attitudes? Are we counting black college graduates or anti-black hate crimes? And what if we decide that pockets of hopefulness are tucked into the midst of despair? Shall we feel virtuous and relax?"

If any sum can be reckoned, it is one of acute contradiction. In the 1920s, the Ku Klux Klan had about two million members; by the mid-1990s, the estimated membership was down to between 2,500 and 3,000, out of 20,000 or 25,000 altogether in various hate groups, including skinheads and militias. Furthermore, prospects have improved for blacks with high skills or advanced degrees in the sciences, business, law, medicine, and other professions as more and more white-run institutions have grown eager to find talented African-American men and women to serve diverse constituencies, improve profits, and demonstrate a commitment to "equal opportunity." But other black people, dragged down by the whirlpool of

---

2. Shipler was a foreign correspondent for the *New York Times*.

poverty and drugs, have fewer and fewer exits. The United States has more black executives and more black prison inmates than a decade ago.

The answer may be that things are getting better and worse at the same time. Racially, America is torn by the crosscurrents of progress and decay. Practically every step forward is accompanied by a subtle erosion of the ground beneath. . . .

On a late summer day in the early 1990s, the dean, who was white, rose to welcome the black and Hispanic students entering one of the country's leading law schools. They had been invited a week early for special orientation, and he had a delicate message for them. His remarks were born of anguish, for he knew something that they did not: They had been admitted with lower average scores than their white classmates had earned on the Law School Aptitude Test.

He wanted to warn them but not defeat them. He could not tell them of the disparities in test scores, because his school, like virtually all others, tried to keep such information secret. So he took an oblique approach. He himself had come from a small town, not an intellectual background, he told the new students. To overcome that deprivation, he had been forced to apply enormous effort, and so would they. "If you work extremely hard," he remembered himself saying, "you can make up for differences in past credentials."

His talk was as welcome as an earthquake. "I was deeply criticized by a number of faculty who felt I had hurt these people on their first day at the institution," he said. "I felt terrible."

The issue confronted him more directly when a group of Hispanic students approached him for reassurance. They were being tormented by white classmates who insisted that Hispanics had scored lower than whites on the LSAT and did not deserve to be there. They wanted the smear refuted. "I tried to be very candid with them," the dean recalled. It was true, he told them: Their scores had been somewhat lower, but with hard work they could erase the deficiencies of their pasts.

An awful silence descended. "I just looked into their eyes as I was talking," the dean remembered, "and I thought, 'I can't bear this; it's too painful.' Their hopes and expectations about what would be said were defeated. There was just a feeling of betrayal."

So goes the conversation about one of the most critical methods used to pry open doors long locked against Hispanics, blacks, and other minorities. The truth cannot be told on any campus without stigmatizing those being aided, without giving a weapon to conservative opponents of such efforts. This law school cannot be identified, the dean cannot be named. He cannot be quoted, except anonymously, as he reveals that if only scores and not race were taken into account, only five or six blacks would be admitted each year instead of forty or fifty. A full and honest discussion of how colleges and graduate schools increase the numbers of African-Americans in their ranks cannot be had.

But why not? How shameful can it be, after generations of imprisonment in inferior educational systems, to score lower on a standardized test? How unfair can it be, after three hundred years of white advantage, to spend thirty years redressing the imbalance? And how unwise can it be, after failing to tap the vast resources of black America, to search affirmatively past the sterile test scores into a rich human potential not easily measured? . . .

Although SAT scores are reliable predictors of freshman grades, they forecast later achievement less accurately. Harvard studied alumni in its classes of '57, '67, and '77 and found that graduates with low SAT scores and blue-collar backgrounds displayed a high rate of "success"—defined by income, community involvement, and professional satisfaction. Here is where race and socioeconomic background mix; some admissions officers believe that if affirmative action were aimed particularly at lower-class students, it would generate less opposition. But it would also yield fewer blacks, since two-thirds of eighteen-year-olds below the poverty line are white. Furthermore, giving preference to students who need financial aid would cost more in scholarships than most colleges have. Consequently, some universities seek upper-middle-class blacks, who can bring diversity and also afford the tuition. However, other elite schools, such as Dartmouth, Harvard, and the Massachusetts Institute of Technology, do give a nod to lower-class applicants. "We have particular interest in students from a modest background," said Marlyn McGrath Lewis, director of admissions for Harvard and Radcliffe. "Coupled with high achievement and a high ambition level and energy, a background that's modest can really be a help. We know that's the best investment we can make: a kid who's hungry."

The two words "affirmative action" were first put together during the inauguration of President John F. Kennedy in 1961, when Vice President Lyndon Johnson, standing in a receiving line, buttonholed a young black attorney named Hobart Taylor Jr. and asked him to help advisers Arthur Goldberg and Abe Fortas write Executive Order 10925 barring federal contractors from racial discrimination in hiring. "I was searching for something that would give a sense of positiveness to performance under that executive order, and I was torn between the words 'positive action' and the words 'affirmative action,' " Taylor recalled in an interview for the Lyndon Baines Johnson Library. "And I took 'affirmative action' because it was alliterative."

From that poetic genesis has come an array of requirements and programs that stir resentment in most of white America. An elastic concept with many definitions, affirmative action is broadly seen as unnatural and unfair, yet it has begun to work its way into the standard practices of so many universities, corporations, and government agencies that it seems sustained as much now by habit and ethic as by law. Even as the courts whittle away at affirmative action's constitutional rationales, more and more institutions are following the military's lead in justifying racial diversity as pragmatic, not merely altruistic. They strive to avoid not only legal punishment but the punishment of a marketplace that is producing fewer and fewer white males as a percentage of workers and customers. As the Pentagon realized after the draft ended in 1973, if the armed services were to compete for good people and tap the entire reservoir of potential recruits, those who were not white men would have to be convinced that unfettered opportunities existed in the ranks. Some corporations have experienced a similar epiphany of self-interest, and at many universities, an admissions officer observed, "success in minority recruitment has become a kind of coin of the realm to indicate institutional success.". . .

. . . [T]he problem created by the solution of affirmative action is this: It allows whites to imagine themselves as victims. Polls find about two-thirds of Americans believing that a white has a smaller chance of getting a job or a promotion than an equally or less qualified black does. When asked why they think this, however, only 21 percent can say that they have seen it at work, 15 percent that it has happened to a friend or relative, and just 7 percent that they have experienced it personally. "With blacks, who are such a small fraction of the population," says Barbara Bergmann, an economist at American University, "the lost opportunities to white men are really minuscule."

Furthermore, some of the personal experience is suspect. Affirmative action transports long-standing biases against blacks into the realm of reasonable discussion: It gives whites permission to affirm the stereotype of blacks as less competent by saying, or thinking, that this or that African-American was not good enough to have been admitted, hired, or promoted without a racial preference. Unscrupulous white supervisors contribute to the slander either by hiring less qualified blacks, just to get their numbers up and avoid discrimination suits, or by disingenuously telling whites, "Gee, I'd love to promote you, but I have to take a black or a woman." Affirmative action thus becomes, in the first case, an excuse for sloppy recruiting and, in the second, a handy pretext to spare a manager the discomfort of telling a white colleague why he doesn't deserve to be promoted.

These are perversions of affirmative action's purpose, and they undermine its viability. In its many forms, from intensive recruiting to hiring goals to set-aside contracts for minority-owned businesses, the effort is designed to remedy unjustified exclusion by seeking out qualified people from the excluded groups and accepting the best of them. It recognizes that passive color blindness is not enough, that people do not deal with one another purely as individuals, and that even if overt discrimination is eliminated, the handicaps of poor schooling and impoverished family life, of subtle prejudice and institutional intolerance, remain severe obstacles to advancement by African-Americans.

DISCUSSION QUESTIONS

1. What is the best way to obtain information and insight into American race relations? What are the advantages and disadvantages of using public opinion surveys to gauge race relations? What are the advantages and disadvantages of using interviews and observations to gauge race relations?

2. One point of contention between the Thernstroms and Shipler concerns inter-racial friendships. Looking at the campuses or workplaces with which you are familiar, do you think that whites and blacks have grown more comfortable with one another on a personal level, or do you think that racial separatism is growing?

3. If laws and other measures bar racial discrimination, has American society treated both races with justice? Or do further steps need to be taken to compensate for past racial injustices and to counteract subtly persisting prejudices?

4. Do affirmative action programs only encourage greater white prejudice against blacks? Or do they bring whites into contact with blacks and allow them to see real individuals rather than racial stereotypes?

5. What would American society look like today if affirmative action programs had never been instituted? What would it look like tomorrow if affirmative action programs were abolished?

SUGGESTED READINGS AND INTERNET RESOURCES

Shelby Steele's *The Content of our Character* (New York: St. Martin's Press, 1990) is a passionate call for personal responsibility and an attack on affirmative action by a black scholar. Black journalist Ellis Cose provides a sober critique of the anti-affirmative-action position in *Color-Blind: Seeing Beyond Race in a Race-Obsessed World* (New York: HarperCollins, 1997). For an extensive assault on affirmative action by a former member of the Reagan administration, see Terry Eastland, *Ending Affirmative Action: The Case for Colorblind Justice* (New York: Basic Books, 1996). A detailed case for affirmative action, for women as well as racial minorities, can be found in Barbara Bergmann, *In Defense of Affirmative Action* (New York: Basic Books, 1996). As the title suggests, *Two Nations: Black and White, Separate, Hostile, Unequal* (New York: Ballantine Books, 1993), by political scientist Andrew Hacker, offers a grim account, laden with numerous statistics, of American racial divisions.

Center for Equal Opportunity
www.ceousa.org
A conservative organization for the promotion of "colorblind" public policies, the Center for Equal Opportunity concentrates on the issues of racial

preferences, immigration, and multicultural education; its site provides commentary and extensive access to articles and links on these issues.

National Association for the Advancement of Colored People
www.naacp.org
The nation's oldest civil rights organization's official site provides commentary on current civil rights controversies and offers research tools.

American Civil Liberties Union
www.aclu.org/issues/racial/hmre.html
This site of a section of the ACLU that focuses on race relations and civil rights provides current news and extensive research tools and links.

8

Public Opinion: The American People After September 11

O n September 11, 2001, the world watched in horror as thousands of innocent people died in the ruins of buildings that had symbolized American
power and invulnerability. In the aftermath of September 11, much has
changed. The United States is engaged in a new "war on terrorism" of uncertain duration and consequences. Federal budget priorities have shifted
from dividing up a surplus accumulated in the late 1990s to instituting a new
era of deficit spending, with new large increases in military expenditures and
billions for "homeland security." New federal laws and security measures have
shifted the nation's focus from individual freedom to order. President George
W. Bush, who once lagged in the polls, has gained widespread popularity as a
"war president" and strong leader. In the time since 9/11, the national political
agenda has shifted to concerns about both domestic and international
terrorism. Issues such as social security, taxes, medical care, and education
have been pushed to the back burner.

In the immediate aftermath of the terrorist attacks, many commentators
predicted a widespread transformation of American tastes, opinions, and social
views. From the 1980s through the beginning of the new millennium, many
observers had discerned a shift toward the individualistic strains in American
culture—government and collective life just weren't as important as they had
been, and people were turning their attention to private life. The new economy of the 1980s and 1990s exalted entrepreneurs, individual consumption,
and innovative and trendy lifestyles, not collective concerns. After Septem-

ber 11, the attacks, as well as an uncertain economy and stock market, seemed to bring this era to an end.

For elite and popular democrats alike, these events present dilemmas and opportunities. On the one hand, the aftermath of September 11 presented stirring moments of national unity and community. In New York City, the heroism of residents, firefighters, and police officers inspired the nation. Charitable organizations were flooded with individual donations, and some studies pointed to much increased levels of volunteerism and civic commitment. Government, scorned by some in the 1980s and 1990s as inefficient, ineffective, and wasteful, gained new respect. After September 11, Americans seemed to embrace an old idea: our society is not a loose collection of individuals, but a nation in which we must depend on each other to survive.

On the other hand, there was a dark side to the new sense of solidarity and unity. For those who care about civil liberties, new measures passed by Congress seemed to pose dangerous precedents, as hundreds of immigrants were held without charges and the Bush administration proposed special military tribunals for accused terrorists. Responding to the public mood, much of the news media seemed to censor themselves and simply ceased covering many stories that might raise questions about the new war and the crackdown on real or "potential" terrorists. Congress seemed cowed before many debatable presidential initiatives and delegated to the executive branch many powers. While abroad many friendly governments scorned President Bush's talk about an "axis of evil," at home there seemed to be few willing to question the president about his foreign policy or the particulars of his massive increases in military spending. At least in the first months after September 11, the interest groups and social movements that usually animate American democracy had every reason to remain silent, as every element of complaint or conflict could be labeled petty or unpatriotic.

How, and to what extent, did September 11 and its aftermath change the basic political opinions of the American people? Would long-standing views about the role of government in society and the economy, about the political parties, about racial equality, and about civil liberties be altered? Students of public opinion have observed that basic public attitudes about government, policies, and parties change pretty slowly. While military intervention abroad initially almost always receives widespread popular support, in time controversies and debates about foreign as well as domestic policies have usually returned. But the present war on terrorism may be different, because it was provoked by a direct, dramatic, and brutal attack on innocent civilians in U.S. territory. This is a different kind of war against a shadowy and secretive enemy, not against an identifiable nation-state.

The two essay reprinted here present dramatically contrasting pictures of the American people and their opinions after September 11. David Brooks, senior editor at the conservative *Weekly Standard* and PBS commentator, argues in the first essay that September 11 will indeed reshape public concerns and sentiments and the terms of political debate. Liberals skeptical of the use of military power as well as antigovernment conservatives intent on slashing budgets will each become increasingly marginalized, Brooks contends. A new tough-mindedness will predominate, and Americans will become surer and more resolute in our exercise of power against enemies, as well as more intolerant of dissenters. In contrast, journalist and documentary producer Bill Moyers argues that September 11 will prompt new public debates about what has happened to our democracy. In a time of supposedly shared sacrifice, the glaring economic and political inequalities that separate ordinary citizens from control of their own government will become more evident. We must, Moyers says, seize the opportunity provided by September 11 to renew our democracy.

While reading the essays, you might ask the following: How does each author define patriotism? Which qualities does each see as important in public opinion and U.S. political culture? Could both writers be incorrect in their mutual assumption that September 11 has and will change Americans all that much?

The Age of Conflict: Politics and Culture After September 11

DAVID BROOKS

"**A** singular fact of modern war," the historian Bruce Catton once wrote, "is that it takes charge. Once begun it has to be carried to its conclusion, and carrying it there sets in motion events that may be beyond men's control. Doing what has to be done to win, men perform acts that alter the very soil in which society's roots are nourished." Catton was writing about the Civil War, but his observation applies to most wars, and it will likely apply to the war to which we are now committed. If this conflict lasts as long as it is likely to last—as long as the president has warned us it will—it will reshape our culture and our politics. It will constitute a hinge moment in American history.

We had probably entered a time of transition even before the September 11 attack. The collapse of the dot-com economy already meant that Silicon Valley and the wonders of high technology were not going to hold the nation's attention during the next ten years the way they did during the last ten. The economic slowdown had already brought one boom to an end; the next economic recovery was bound to have different growth sectors, a different personality. George W. Bush's Washington was bound to be different from Bill Clinton's. But September 11 brought the 1990s to a close all at once. And the ensuing war will mean that the next few years will not only feel different from the last few; they will feel dramatically different. Subjects that used to seem riveting will seem stale. Can anybody imagine why we cared about *Inside.com*? . . . Can anybody get interested in think tank reports on Social Security lockboxes or charitable choice? Are there liberals still intrigued by the disease of "affluenza" or the menace of corporate branding? . . .

Obviously nobody knows what the future years will feel like, but we do know that the next decade will have a central feature that was lacking in the last one: The next few years will be defined by conflict. And it's possible to speculate about what that means. The institutions that fight for us and defend us against disorder—the military, the FBI, the CIA—will seem more important and more admirable. The fundamental arguments won't be over economic or social issues, they will be over how to wield power—whether to use American power aggressively or circumspectly. We will care a lot more about ends—winning the war—than we will about means. We will debate whether it is necessary to torture prisoners who have information about future biological attacks. We will destroy innocent villages by accident, shrug our shoulders, and continue fighting. In an age of conflict, bourgeois virtues like compassion, tolerance, and industriousness are valued less than the classical virtues of courage, steadfastness, and a ruthless desire for victory.

Looking back, the striking thing about the 1990s zeitgeist was the presumption of harmony. The era was shaped by the idea that there were no fundamental conflicts anymore. The Cold War was over, and while the ensuing wars—like those in Bosnia and Rwanda—were nettlesome, they were restricted to global backwaters. Meanwhile, technology was building bridges across cultures. The Internet, Microsoft ads reminded us, fostered communication and global harmony. All around the world there were people casting off old systems so they could embrace a future of peace and prosperity. Chinese Communists were supposedly being domesticated by the balm of capitalist success. Peace seemed in the offing in Northern Ireland and, thanks to the Oslo process, in the Middle East.

Bill Clinton and George W. Bush were elected president of the United States. Neither had performed much in the way of military service. Neither was particularly knowledgeable about foreign affairs. Both promised to be domestic-policy presidents. In that age of peace and prosperity, the top sitcom was *Seinfeld,* a show about nothing. Books appeared with titles like *All Connected Now: Life in the First Global Civilization.* Academics analyzed the twilight of national sovereignty. Commerce and communications seemed much more important than politics.

Defense spending was drastically cut, by Republicans as well as Democrats, because there didn't seem to be any clear and present danger to justify huge budgets. The army tried to recruit volunteers by emphasizing its educational benefits, with narcissistic slogans like "An Army of One." Conservatives, of all people, felt so safe that they became suspicious of the forces of law and order. Conservative activists were heard referring to police as "bureaucrats with badges"; right-wing talk radio dwelt on the atrocities committed by the FBI, the DEA, and other agencies at places like Ruby Ridge and Waco. Meanwhile, all across the political spectrum, interest in public life waned, along with the percentage of adults who bothered to vote. An easy cynicism settled across the land, as more people came to believe that national politics didn't really matter. What mattered instead, it seemed, were local affairs, community, intimate relations, and the construction of private paradises. When on rare occasions people talked about bitter conflict, they usually meant the fights they were having with their kitchen renovators.

Historians who want to grasp the style of morality that prevailed in the 1990s should go back to the work of sociologist Alan Wolfe. In books like *One Nation, After All* and *Moral Freedom,* Wolfe called the prevailing ethos "small scale morality." Be moderate in your beliefs, and tolerant toward people who have other beliefs. This is a moral code for people who are not threatened by any hostile belief system, who don't think it is worth it to stir up unpleasantness. "What I heard as I talked to Americans," Wolfe wrote of his research, "was a distaste for conflict, a sense that ideas should never be taken so seriously that they lead people into uncivil, let alone violent, courses of action."

But now violence has come calling. Now it is no longer possible to live so comfortably in one's own private paradise. Shocked out of the illusion of self-reliance, most of us realize that we, as individuals, simply cannot protect ourselves. Private life requires public protection. Now it is not possible to ignore foreign affairs, because foreign affairs have not ignored us. It has become clear that we are living in a world in which hundreds of millions of people hate us, and some small percentage of them want to destroy us. That realization is bound to have cultural effects.

In the first place, we will probably become more conscious of our American-ness. During the blitz in 1940, George Orwell sat in his bomb shelter and wrote an essay called "England Your England." It opened with this sentence: "As I write, highly civilised human beings are flying overhead, trying to kill me." What struck him at that moment of danger was that it really does matter whether you are English or German. The nation is a nursemaid that breads certain values and a certain ethos. Orwell went on to describe what it meant to be English.

Now Americans are being killed simply because they are Americans. Like Orwell, Americans are once again becoming aware of themselves as a nationality, not just as members of some ethnic community or globalized Internet chat group. Americans have been reminded that, despite what the multiculturalists have been preaching, not all cultures are wonderfully equal hues in the great rainbow of humanity. Some national cultures, the ones that have inherited certain ideas—about freedom and democracy, the limits of the political claims of religion, the importance of tolerance and dissent—are more humane than other civilizations, which reject those ideas.

As criticism of our war effort grows in Europe, in hostile Arab countries, and in two-faced countries like Egypt and Saudi Arabia, which dislike our principles but love our dollars, Americans will have to articulate a defense of our national principles and practices. That debate in itself will shape American culture. We will begin to see ourselves against the backdrop of the Taliban. During the Cold War, we saw ourselves in contrast to the Soviet Union. Back then, we faced a godless foe; now we are facing a god-crazed foe. As we recoil from the Islamic extremists, we may be less willing to integrate religion into political life. That would mean trouble for faith-based initiatives and religion in the public square.

On the other hand, democracies tend to become patriotic during wartime, if history is any guide, and this will drive an even deeper wedge between regular Americans and the intellectual class. Literary critic Paul Fussell, a great student of American culture in times of war, wrote a book, *Wartime,* on the cultural effects of World War II. Surveying the culture of that period, he endorsed the view of historian Eileen Sullivan, who wrote, "There was no room in this war culture for individual opinions or personalities, no freedom of dissent or approval; the culture was homogeneous, shallow and boring."

The earnest conformity that does prevail in wartime drives intellectuals—who like to think of themselves as witty, skeptical, iconoclastic dissidents—batty. They grow sour, and alienated from mainstream life. For every regular Joe who follows the Humphrey Bogart path in *Casablanca*, from cynicism to idealism, there is an intellectual like Fussell, whose war experiences moved him from idealism to lifetime cynicism.

There are other cultural effects. For example, commercial life seems less important than public life, and economic reasoning seems less germane than cultural analysis. When life or death fighting is going on, it's hard to think of Bill Gates or Jack Welch as particularly heroic. Moreover, the cost-benefit analysis dear to economists doesn't really explain much in times of war. Osama bin Laden is not motivated by economic self-interest, and neither are our men and women who are risking their lives to defeat him. To understand such actions, you need to study history, religion, and ethics. The people who try to explain events via economic reasoning begin to look silly. Here is the otherwise intelligent economist Steve Hanke, in *Forbes*, analyzing bin Laden:

> Don't make the mistake of interpreting the events of Sept. 11 purely in terms of terrorism and murder. . . . The terrorists are a virulent subset of a much larger group of anticapitalists, one that includes many politicians, bureaucrats, writers, media types, academics, entertainers, trade unionists and, at times, church leaders. The barbarians at the gates are more numerous than you thought.

But the most important cultural effect of conflict is that it breeds a certain bloody-mindedness or, to put it more grandly, a tragic view of life. Life in times of war and recession reminds us of certain hard truths that were easy to ignore during the decade of peace and prosperity. Evil exists. Difficulties, even tragedies, are inevitable. Human beings are flawed creatures capable of monstrosity. Not all cultures are compatible. To preserve order, good people must exercise power over destructive people.

That means that it's no longer sufficient to deconstruct ideas and texts and signifiers. You have to be able to construct hard principles so you can move from one idea to the next, because when you are faced with the problem of repelling evil, you absolutely must be able to reach a conclusion on serious moral issues.

This means you need to think in moral terms about force—and to be tough-minded. During the Cold War, Reinhold Niebuhr was a major intellectual figure. In 1952, he wrote *The Irony of American History*. The tragedy of the conflict with communism, he argued, was that, "though confident of its virtue, [America] must yet hold atomic bombs ready for use so as to prevent a possible world conflagration." The irony of our history, he continued, is that we are an idealistic nation that dreams of creating a world of pure virtue, yet in defeating our enemies we sometimes have to act in ways that are not pure. "We take, and must continue to take, morally hazardous action to preserve our civilization," Niebuhr wrote. "We must exercise our power." We have to do so while realizing that we will not be capable of perfect disinterestedness when deciding which actions are just. We will be influenced by dark passions. But we still have to act forcefully because our enemies are trying to destroy the basis of civilization: "We are drawn into an historic situation in which the paradise of our domestic security is suspended in a hell of global insecurity."

Niebuhr's prescription was humble hawkishness. He believed the United States should forcefully defend freedom and destroy its enemies. But while doing so, it should seek forgiveness for the horrible things it might have to do in a worthy cause.

To reach this graduate-school level of sophistication, you have to have passed through elementary courses in moral reasoning. It will be interesting to see whether we Americans, who sometimes seem unsure of even the fundamental moral categories, can educate ourselves sufficiently to engage in the kind of moral reasoning that Niebuhr did.

The greatest political effect of this period of conflict will probably be to relegitimize central institutions. Since we can't defend ourselves as individuals against terrorism, we have to rely on the institutions of government: the armed forces, the FBI, the CIA, the CDC, and so on. We are now only beginning to surrender some freedoms, but we will trade in more, and willingly. As Alexander Hamilton wrote in the Federalist Papers, "Safety from external danger is the most powerful director of national conduct. Even the ardent love of liberty will, after a time, give way to its dictates. . . . To be more safe, [people] at length become willing to run the risk of being less free." Moreover, we will see power migrate from the states and Capitol Hill to the White House. "It is of the nature of war to increase the executive at the expense of the legislative authority," Hamilton continued.

This creates rifts on both left and right, because both movements contain anti-establishment elements hostile to any effort to relegitimize central authorities. . . . Many literary and academic liberals . . . have built a whole moral system around powerlessness. They champion the outgroups. They stand with the victims of hegemony, patriarchy, colonialism, and all the other manifestations of central authority. Sitting on their campuses, they are powerless themselves, and have embraced a delicious, self-glorifying identity as the out-manned sages who alone can see through the veils of propaganda in which the powerful hide their oppressive schemes. For these thinkers, virtue inheres in the powerless. The weak are sanctified, not least because they are voiceless and allegedly need academics to give them voices. These outgroup leftists dislike the Taliban, but to ally themselves with American power would be to annihilate everything they have stood for and the role they have assigned themselves in society.

The splits on the right have been quieter, but no less important. Anti-establishmentarianism on the right comes in libertarian and populist forms.

Its adherents have noticed that during wartime, the power of the state tends to expand. "Wars are nasty things: They make governments grow," Grover Norquist of Americans for Tax Reform told the *Washington Post*. This skepticism applies not only to any new social programs that might emerge in this centralizing moment, but to proposals to strengthen the forces of law and order. "We don't like the bad guys either. But let's not sacrifice our freedoms because the FBI and CIA want more power," Norquist told the *Boston Globe.*

Since September 11, conservatives have broken down into two camps: those who fear that Bush will go squishy on Iraq, and those who fear that he will go squishy on capital gains. The conservatives who fear that the United States won't take out Saddam are national security conservatives. They don't think it's worth getting into a big fight over reducing taxes at a moment of national crisis. They value free market reforms, but believe that right now other conservative agenda items should take a back seat to national security.

The libertarian, anti-government, "leave us alone" conservatives, such as Dick Armey and Tom DeLay, believe Bush should use his popularity to push through capital gains tax reductions and the like. They detest the domestic bipartisanship that Bush has cultivated on Capitol Hill. They believe that national security arguments should not be used to strengthen the hand of Washington.

On balance, George W. Bush is behaving more like a national security conservative. . . . He embraces every Democrat he can wrap his arms around. He has tried to reduce partisan conflict on the stimulus package. He would not even think of raising divisive social issues. He seeks to clear the domestic front so he can focus on the fight against terror. No longer the compassionate conservative, he has, with impressive decisiveness, turned himself into a fighting conservative.

What the Bush administration is now presenting, and what the public seems to want, is Rudy Giuliani-ism on a global scale. Giuliani took over a city plagued by crime and apparently ungovernable. He didn't stop to ponder the root causes of crime, or whether the '60s had sent American into irreversible decline. Giuliani is not even particularly interested in the general moral fabric of the city. He's not conservative on the social issues. Instead, he's interested in preventing acts of disorder. He is a guy who sits around with his friends watching the *Godfather* movies and reciting the lines. He simply went after the bad guys and the actual things they did to create disorder. He and his police commissioners worked aggressively to arrest people who broke the law.

By doing this, Giuliani restored order, so that New Yorkers could go out and live whatever sorts of lives they wanted to lead. His approach was: Every morning you strap on your armor and you go out to battle the evil ones. It's more important to be feared than loved. You maneuver situations so as to get your rivals in the place where you want them to be. Then they have to make concessions. His instinct was always: Give me authority. Hold me accountable.

For Bush, the leader of the free world, the issue is terrorism, not street crime. But now he too is engaged in the effort to restore order so that people can go about their lives. He is the one rounding up the posse, forsaking social issues and other moral debates for a straightforward act of international prosecution. He is reasserting authority to show that under Pax Americana, the world *is* governable.

What we may end up with, therefore, is an America in which the old split between hawks and doves is no longer relevant. Instead our political landscape will have a few intellectuals on the fringes, while the main argument unfolds—to borrow Machiavelli's terms—between the lions and the foxes. Lions believe in the aggressive use of power. For them the main danger is appeasement. They worry that we will be half-hearted and never really tackle our problems. Foxes, by contrast, believe you have to move cleverly and subtly. They worry that America will act unilaterally and tear its coalition and trample upon our own freedoms.

It's interesting that the people who are lions on foreign policy also tend to be lions on domestic policy, while the foxes are fox-like both abroad and at home. So we have new arguments. Do we give higher priority to cracking down on domestic terror or preserving civil liberties? Do we give higher priority to destroying all terrorist states, or to preserving our alliances? In these debates, so far, the *Weekly Standard,* the *New Republic,* and the *Washington Post* have made the case for the lions. The *New York Times,* Robert Novak, Hillary Clinton, Colin Powell, Barney Frank, and Jack Kemp have supported the foxes. It may truly be a strange new world.

At the start of the Civil War, nobody could have foreseen how the war would alter the domestic political culture, producing a raft of legislation ranging from the Homestead Act to the transcontinental railway to currency reform. The war ended with a grand march by the Union armies through Washington, an event that symbolized America's emergence as a unified nation and a superpower in the making. "Neither party expected for the war the magnitude or the duration which it has already attained," Lincoln declared in his Second Inaugural. "Each looked for an easier triumph, and a result less fundamental and astounding."

It's impossible to know if the renewed confidence in government that we already see will translate into a new sort of big government activism, as some liberals are predicting. . . . The war, Randolph Bourne observed in 1917, "is the health of the state."

But history never repeats itself neatly. No one can predict the political and cultural consequences of a war, any more than the course of the war itself. But it does seem clear that we have moved out of one political and cultural moment and into another. We have traded the anxieties of affluence for the real fears of war. We have moved from an age of peace to an age of conflict, and in times of conflict people are different. They go to extremes. Some people, and some nations, turn cowardly or barbaric. Other people, and other nations, become heroic, brave, and steadfast. It all depends on what they have in them. War isn't only, as Bourne said, the health of the state. It's the gut-check of the nation.

Which America Will We Be Now?

BILL MOYERS

For the past several years I've been taking every possible opportunity to talk about the soul of democracy. "Something is deeply wrong with politics today," I told anyone who would listen. And I wasn't referring to the partisan mudslinging, the negative TV ads, the excessive polling or the empty campaigns. I was talking about something fundamental, something troubling at the core of politics. The soul of democracy—the essence of the word itself—is government of, by and for the people. And the soul of democracy has been dying, drowning in a rising tide of big money contributed by a narrow, unrepresentative elite that has betrayed the faith of citizens in self-government.

But what's happened since the September 11 attacks would seem to put the lie to my fears. Americans have rallied together in a way that I cannot remember since World War II. This catastrophe has reminded us of a basic truth at the heart of our democracy: No matter our wealth or status or faith, we are all equal before the law, in the voting booth and when death rains down from the sky.

We have also been reminded that despite years of scandals and political corruption, despite the stream of stories of personal greed and pirates in Gucci scamming the Treasury, despite the retreat from the public sphere and the turn toward private privilege, despite squalor for the poor and gated communities for the rich, the great mass of Americans have not yet given up on the idea of "We, the People." And they have refused to accept the notion, promoted so diligently by our friends at the Heritage Foundation, that government should be shrunk to a size where, as Grover Norquist has put it, they can drown it in a bathtub.

These ideologues at Heritage and elsewhere, by the way, earlier this year teamed up with deep-pocket bankers—many from Texas, with ties to the Bush White House—to stop America from cracking down on terrorist money havens. How about that for patriotism? Better that terrorists get their dirty money than tax cheaters be prevented from hiding theirs. And these people wrap themselves in the flag and sing "The Star-Spangled Banner" with gusto.

Contrary to right-wing denigration of government, however, today's heroes are public servants. The 20-year-old dot-com instant millionaires and the preening, pugnacious pundits of tabloid television and the crafty celebrity stock-pickers on the cable channels have all been exposed for what they are—barnacles on the hull of the great ship of state. In their stead we have those brave firefighters and policemen and Port Authority workers and emergency rescue personnel—public employees all, most of them drawing a modest middle-class income for extremely dangerous work. They have caught our imaginations not only for their heroic deeds but because we know so many people like them, people we took for granted. For once, our TV screens have been filled with the modest declarations of average Americans coming to each other's aid. I find this good and thrilling and sobering. It could offer a new beginning, a renewal of civic values that could leave our society stronger and more together than ever, working on common goals for the public good.

Already, in the wake of September 11, there's been a heartening change in how Americans view their government. For the first time in more than thirty years a majority of people say they trust the federal government to do the right thing at least "most of the time." It's as if the clock has been rolled back to the early 1960s, before Vietnam and Watergate took such a toll on the gross national psychology. This newfound respect for public service— this faith in public collaboration—is based in part on how people view what the government has done in response to the attacks. To most Americans, government right now doesn't mean a faceless bureaucrat or a politician auctioning access to the highest bidder. It means a courageous rescuer or brave soldier. Instead of our representatives spending their evenings clinking glasses with fat cats, they are out walking among the wounded.

There are, alas, less heartening signs to report. It didn't take long for the wartime opportunists—the mercenaries of Washington, the lobbyists, lawyers and political fundraisers—to crawl out of their offices on K Street determined to grab what they can for their clients. While in New York we are still attending memorial services for firemen and police, while everywhere Americans' cheeks are still stained with tears, while the President calls for patriotism, prayers and piety, the predators of Washington are up to their old tricks in the pursuit of private plunder at public expense. In the wake of this awful tragedy wrought by terrorism, they are cashing in. Would you like to know the memorial they would offer the thousands of people who died in the attacks? Or the legacy they would leave the children who lost a parent in the horror? How do they propose to fight the long and costly war on terrorism America must now undertake? Why, restore the three-martini lunch—that will surely strike fear in the heart of Osama bin Laden. You think I'm kidding, but bringing back the deductible lunch is one of the proposals on the table in Washington right now. And cut capital gains for the wealthy, naturally that's America's patriotic duty, too. And while we're at it, don't forget to eliminate the corporate alternative minimum tax, enacted fifteen years ago to prevent corporations from taking so many credits and deductions that they owed little if any taxes. But don't just repeal their minimum tax; refund to those corporations all the minimum tax they have ever been assessed.[1]

---

1. These measures were supported by House Republicans and President Bush in the Fall of 2001.

What else can America do to strike at the terrorists? Why, slip in a special tax break for poor General Electric, and slip inside the EPA while everyone's distracted and torpedo the recent order to clean the Hudson River of PCBs. Don't worry about NBC, CNBC or MSNBC reporting it; they're all in the GE family. It's time for Churchillian courage, we're told. So how would this crowd assure that future generations will look back and say "This was their finest hour"? That's easy. Give those coal producers freedom to pollute. And shovel generous tax breaks to those giant energy companies. And open the Alaska wilderness to drilling—that's something to remember the 11th of September for. And while the red, white and blue waves at half-mast over the land of the free and the home of the brave—why, give the President the power to discard democratic debate and the rule of law concerning controversial trade agreements, and set up secret tribunals to run roughshod over local communities trying to protect their environment and their health. If I sound a little bitter about this, I am; the President rightly appeals every day for sacrifice. But to these mercenaries sacrifice is for suckers. So I am bitter, yes, and sad. Our business and political class owes us better than this. After all, it was they who declared class war twenty years ago, and it was they who won. They're on top. If ever they were going to put patriotism over profits, if ever they were going to practice the magnanimity of winners, this was the moment. To hide now behind the flag while ripping off a country in crisis fatally separates them from the common course of American life.

Some things just don't change. When I read that Dick Armey, the Republican leader in the Senate, said "it wouldn't be commensurate with the American spirit" to provide unemployment and other benefits to laid-off airline workers, I thought that once again the Republican Party has lived down to Harry Truman's description of the GOP as Guardians of Privilege. And as for Truman's Democratic Party—the party of the New Deal and the Fair Deal—well, it breaks my heart to report that the Democratic National Committee has used the terrorist attacks to call for widening the soft-money loophole in our election laws. How about that for a patriotic response to terrorism? Mencken got it right when he said, "Whenever you hear a man speak of his love for his country, it is a sign that he expects to be paid for it."

Let's face it: These realities present citizens with no options but to climb back in the ring. We are in what educators call "a teachable moment." And we'll lose it if we roll over and shut up. What's at stake is democracy. Democracy wasn't canceled on September 11, but democracy won't survive if citizens turn into lemmings. Yes, the President is our Commander in Chief, but we are not the President's minions. While firemen and police were racing into the fires of hell in downtown New York, and now, while our soldiers and airmen and Marines are putting their lives on the line in Afghanistan, the Administration and its Congressional allies are allowing multinational companies to make their most concerted effort in twenty years to roll back clean-air measures, exploit public lands and stuff the pockets of their executives and shareholders with undeserved cash. Against such crass exploitation, unequaled since the Teapot Dome scandal, it is every patriot's duty to join the loyal opposition. Even in war, politics is about who gets what and who doesn't. If the mercenaries and the politicians-for-rent in Washington try to exploit the emergency and America's good faith to grab what they wouldn't get through open debate in peacetime, the disloyalty will not be in our dissent but in our subservience. The greatest sedition would be our silence. Yes, there's a fight going on—against terrorists around the globe, but just as certainly there's a fight going on here at home, to decide the kind of country this will be during and after the war on terrorism.

What should our strategy be? Here are a couple of suggestions, beginning with how we elect our officials. As Congress debates new security measures, military spending, energy policies, economic stimulus packages and various bailout requests, wouldn't it be better if we knew that elected officials had to answer to the people who vote instead of the wealthy individual and corporate donors whose profit or failure may depend on how those new initiatives are carried out?

That's not a utopian notion. Thanks to the efforts of many hardworking pro-democracy activists who have been organizing at the grassroots for the past ten years, we already have four states—Maine, Arizona, Vermont and Massachusetts—where state representatives from governor on down have the option of rejecting all private campaign contributions and qualifying for full public financing of their campaigns. About a third of Maine's legislature and a quarter of Arizona's got elected last year running clean— that is, under their states' pioneering Clean Elections systems, they collected a set number of $5 contributions and then pledged to raise no other money and to abide by strict spending limits.

These unsung heroes of democracy, the first class of elected officials to owe their elections solely to their voters and not to any deep-pocketed backers, report a greater sense of independence from special interests and more freedom to speak their minds. "The business lobbyists left me alone," says State Representative Glenn Cummings, a freshman from Maine who was the first candidate in the country to qualify for Clean Elections funding. "I think they assumed I was unapproachable. It sure made it easier to get through the hallways on the way to a vote!" His colleague in the Statehouse, Senator Ed Youngblood, recalls that running clean changed the whole process of campaigning. "When people would say that it didn't matter how they voted, because legislators would just vote the way the money wants," he tells us, "it was great to be able to say, 'I don't have to vote the way some lobbyist wants just to insure that I'll get funded by him in two years for re-election."

It's too soon to say that money no longer talks in either state capital, but it clearly doesn't swagger as much. In Maine, the legislature passed a bill creating a Health Security Board tasked with devising a detailed plan to implement a single-payer healthcare system for the state. The bill wasn't everything its sponsor, Representative Paul Volenik, wanted, but he saw real progress toward a universal healthcare system in its passage. Two years ago, he noted, only fifty-five members of the House of Representatives (out of 151) voted for the bill. This time eighty-seven did, including almost all the Democrats and a few Republicans. The bill moved dramatically further, and a portion of that is because of the Clean Elections system they have there, Volenik said.

But the problem is larger than that of money in politics. Democracy needs a broader housecleaning. Consider, for example, what a different country we would be if we had a Citizens Channel with a mandate to cover real social problems, not shark attacks or Gary Condit's love life, while covering up Rupert Murdoch's manipulations of the FCC and CBS's ploy to filch tax breaks for its post-terrorist losses.[2] Such a channel could have spurred serious attention to the weakness of airport security, for starters, pointing out long ago how the industry, through its contributions, had wrung from government the right to contract that security to the lowest bidder. It might have pushed the issue of offshore-banking havens to page one, or turned up the astonishing deceit of the NAFTA provision that enables secret tribunals to protect the interests of investors while subverting the well-being of workers and the health of communities. Such a channel— committed to news for the sake of democracy—might also have told how corporations and their alumni in the Bush administration have thwarted the development of clean, home-grown energy that would slow global warming and the degradation of our soil, air and water, while reducing our dependence on oligarchs, dictators and theocrats abroad.

Even now the media elite, with occasional exceptions, remain indifferent to the hypocrisy of Washington's mercenary class as it goes about the dirty work of its paymasters. What a contrast to those citizens who during those weeks of loss and mourning have reminded us that the kingdom of the human heart is large, containing not only hatred but courage. Much has been made of the comparison to December 7, 1941. I find it apt. In response to the sneak attack on Pearl Harbor, Americans waged and won a great war, then came home to make this country more prosperous and just. It is not beyond this generation to live up to that example. To do so, we must define ourselves not by the lives we led until September 11 but by the lives we will lead from now on. If we seize the opportunity to build a stronger country, we too will ultimately prevail in the challenges ahead, at home and abroad. But we cannot win this new struggle by military might alone. We will prevail only if we lead by example, as a democracy committed to the rule of law and the spirit of fairness, whose corporate and political elites recognize that it isn't only firefighters, police and families grieving their missing kin who are called upon to sacrifice.

---

2. Rupert Murdoch is the CEO of the News Corporation, and the owner of many newspapers, satellite TV networks, and the Fox network.

DISCUSSION QUESTIONS

1. Both writers see the war on terrorism as a catalyst for widespread changes in U.S. society. What kind of "sacrifices" does each author call for, and how do these sacrifices reveal their visions of a democratic America?

2. Since these essays were written, some say the memories of September 11 have faded. How relevant do you think September 11 is to present debates and to the current political agenda?

3. How might Moyers respond to the revelations of the Enron scandal? How might Brooks? To what degree do you believe that the war on terrorism should affect discussions of issues like corporate power and wealth and income inequality?

4. How do Moyers and Brooks define freedom?

SUGGESTED READINGS AND INTERNET RESOURCES

The two selections in this chapter are based on their authors' reading of public opinion before, as well as after, September 11. Many prominent scholars paint a diverse portrait of U.S. public opinion in Carol Glynn, ed., *Public Opinion* (New York: HarperCollins, 1999). A comprehensive look at U.S. public opinion is provided by Robert Erikson and Kent Tedin, *American Public Opinion* (6th ed.; Boston: Allyn and Bacon, 2001). Two works with radically different views of America after September 11 are Strobe Talbott, *America and the World After September 11th* (New York: Basic Books, 2002); and Michael Parenti, *The Terrorism Trap: September 11 and Beyond* (San Francisco: City Lights Press, 2002).

Public Agenda
www.publicagenda.org
This is an outstanding source for all kinds of polling data, along with helpful assessments about how to read surveys and their findings critically.

Pew Research Center for the People and the Press
www.people-press.org
Pew, an independent opinion research group that conducts surveys about popular perceptions of the media, the visibility of public policy issues, and public figures, is known for its in-depth analyses of basic and long-term trends in public opinion.

Policy.com
www.policy.com
This is perhaps the best and most comprehensive site for all political news. Click on "polling" in the subject column for links to all major international and national polling organizations.

9

The New Media and the Internet: Corporate Wasteland or Democratic Frontier?

In this information-rich age, the mass media play a crucial and powerful set of roles in the lives of citizens. In periods of trauma and crisis, we depend on the media to inform, alert, and even comfort us. After the September 11 attacks, almost all Americans turned in horror to cable and network news stations, and ratings for a whole range of new and old media from newspapers to the Internet soared to record levels. More than ever, we also depend on the media to mirror ourselves, interpret the actions of others, and guide political debate.

The crucial role of press freedom is enshrined in the Constitution's First Amendment. The founders hoped that the press would use its special protections to educate the public and ferret out facts, opinions, and interpretations that promote public debate. At the same time, the media are supposed to reflect and express the wide range of interests and views among the citizenry, however controversial they may be. For advocates of popular democracy, the media's most important role may be to speak "truth to power." Media diversity is crucial to seeking truth. While any single media source may be incorrect, variety provides some assurance that different and even competing versions of political truth will emerge.

Just how have the mass media performed these democratic tasks? While people rely on the mass media more than ever, criticism and distrust of the news media abound. The most vocal critics lampoon the media for liberal or

conservative biases. Others accuse the media of crass commercialism and sensationalism in their relentless pursuit of profits. To others, the definition of news
has been trivialized, as in-depth stories are pushed to the side in favor of "features" and "infotainment." Even as the needs of a democratic society require a
broad debate, some argue that media are cowed and complacent, a part of the
system rather than an independent voice.

Contemporary U.S. and global media are dominated by two major trends.
The first seems ironic in light of the second: from two hundred TV stations to
thousands of magazines and millions of Internet sites, the mass media seem
more diverse and decentralized than ever, providing new choices for everyone,
while at the same time ownership of the major mass media outlets has consolidated into fewer and fewer hands. Corporate megagiants from AOL–Time
Warner to Viacom, Disney, and General Electric produce the bulk of the nation's
books, films, and TV programs, and own most of the radio and TV stations.
While thousands of new channels and films are produced in the media
marketplace, fewer and fewer sellers draw the most consumers.

Nevertheless, the case for a wide and increasingly participatory marketplace seems to be bolstered by the growth of digital communication, especially
the Internet and World Wide Web. On the Internet, everyone can become a
media source—at least in theory—by building a web page. On the web and
through email, information and opinions travel with the speed of light. Low
start-up costs allow millions of people to interchange ideas and information.
Seemingly unmediated and unfiltered by corporations and government, the
Internet seems to provide choice and democratic diversity.

In the two essays that follow, the authors agree about the Internet's
potential: it could expand democratic possibilities. Yet agreement leads to
debate when it comes to the obstacles that threaten this potential. In the first
article, University of Chicago law professor Cass Sunstein heralds the World
Wide Web, but he worries that individuals will use it to insulate themselves from
others who don't share their identities, tastes, and politics. Sunstein argues that
individual consumer choices will mesh with emerging technologies to produce
a "Daily Me"—Internet "favorites" that will insulate people from the public
realm and separate them from a wider vision of nation and community.

Robert McChesney shares some of Sunstein's concerns but traces a very different source for the problem: corporate control of the Internet. McChesney
asks whether corporate power and its search for profits create a nation of
passive consumers, not active citizens, and exacerbate the isolating and insulat-
ing effects of the Internet. McChesney and Sunstein both point to public
policies and new ideas that may help the Internet to become a more
democratic medium.

While reading these two essays, you might ask the following questions of
them: How do the authors see the role of government and public policy in
creating a "democratic" Internet? How would each author define democratic
values? Does the Internet reflect a free market or corporate domination of
access to it?

The Daily We

CASS R. SUNSTEIN

I s the Internet a wonderful development for democracy? In many ways it certainly is. As a result of the Internet, people can learn far more than they could before, and they can learn it much faster. If you are interested in issues that bear on public policy—environmental quality, wages over time, motor vehicle safety—you can find what you need to know in a matter of seconds. If you are suspicious of the mass media, and want to discuss issues with like-minded people, you can do that, transcending the limitations of geography in ways that could barely be imagined even a decade ago. And if you want to get information to a wide range of people, you can do that via email and websites; this is another sense in which the Internet is a great boon for democracy.

But in the midst of the celebration, I want to raise a note of caution. I do so by emphasizing one of the most striking powers provided by emerging technologies: the growing power of consumers to "filter" what they see. As a result of the Internet and other technological developments, many people are increasingly engaged in a process of "personalization" that limits their exposure to topics and points of view of their own choosing. They filter in, and they also filter out, with unprecedented powers of precision. Consider just a few examples:

1. Broadcast.com has "compiled hundreds of thousands of programs so you can find the one that suits your fancy. . . . For example, if you want to see all the latest fashions from France 24 hours of the day you can get them. If you're from Baltimore living in Dallas and you want to listen to WBAL, your hometown station, you can hear it."
2. Sonicnet.com allows you to create your own musical universe, consisting of what it calls "Me Music." Me Music is "A place where you can listen to the music you love on the radio station YOU create. . . . A place where you can watch videos of your favorite artists and new artists."
3. Zatso.net allows users to produce "a personal newscast." Its intention is to create a place "where you decide what's news." Your task is to tell "what TV news stories you're interested in," and Zatso.net turns that information into a specifically designed newscast. . . .
4. George Bell, the chief executive officer of the search engine Excite, exclaims, "We are looking for ways to be able to lift chunks of content off other areas of our service and paste them onto your personal page so you can constantly refresh and update that 'newspaper of me.'" . . .

Of course, these developments make life much more convenient and in some ways much better: we all seek to reduce our exposure to uninvited noise. But from the standpoint of democracy, filtering is a mixed blessing. An understanding of the mix will permit us to obtain a better sense of what makes for a well-functioning system of free expression. In a heterogeneous society, such a system requires something other than free, or publicly unrestricted, individual choices. On the contrary, it imposes two distinctive requirements. First, people should be exposed to materials that they would not have chosen in advance. *Unanticipated encounters,* involving topics and points of view that people have not sought out and perhaps find irritating, are central to democracy and even to freedom itself. Second, many or most citizens should have a range of *common experiences.* Without shared experiences, a heterogeneous society will have a more difficult time addressing social problems and understanding one another.

Individual Design

Consider a thought experiment—an apparently utopian dream, that of complete individuation, in which consumers can entirely personalize (or "customize") their communications universe.

Imagine, that is, a system of communications in which each person has unlimited power of individual design. If some people want to watch news all the time, they would be entirely free to do exactly that. If they dislike news, and want to watch football in the morning and situation comedies at night, that would be fine too. If people care only about America, and want to avoid international issues entirely, that would be very simple; so too if they care only about New York or Chicago or California. If people want to restrict themselves to certain points of view, by limiting themselves to conservatives, moderates, liberals, vegetarians, or Nazis, that would be entirely feasible with a simple point-and-click. If people want to isolate themselves, and speak only with like-minded others, that is feasible too.

At least as a matter of technological feasibility, our communications market is moving rapidly toward this apparently utopian picture. A number of newspapers' websites allow readers to create filtered versions, containing exactly what they want, and no more. . . . To be sure, the Internet greatly increases people's ability to expand their horizons, as millions of people are now doing; but many people are using it to produce narrowness, not breadth. Thus MIT professor Nicholas Negroponte refers to the emergence of the "Daily Me"—a communications package that is personally designed, with components fully chosen in advance.

Of course, this is not entirely different from what has come before. People who read newspapers do not read the same newspaper; some people do not read any newspaper at all. People make choices among magazines based on their tastes and their points of view. But in the emerging situation, there is a difference of degree if not of kind. What *is* different is a dramatic increase in individual control over content, and a corresponding decrease in the power of general interest intermediaries, including newspapers, magazines, and broadcasters. For all their problems, and their unmistakable limitations and biases, these intermediaries have performed some important democratic functions.

People who rely on such intermediaries have a range of chance encounters, involving shared experience with diverse others and exposure to material that they did not specifically choose. You might, for example, read the city newspaper and in the process come across a range of stories that you would not have selected if you had the power to control what you see. Your eyes may come across a story about Germany, or crime in Los Angeles, or innovative business practices in Tokyo, and you may read those stories although you would hardly have placed them in your "Daily Me." . . . Reading *Time* magazine, you might come across a discussion of endangered species in Madagascar, and this discussion might interest you, even affect your behavior, although you would not have sought it out in the first instance. A system in which you lack control over the particular content that you see has a great deal in common with a public street, where you might encounter not only friends, but a heterogeneous variety of people engaged in a wide array of activities (including, perhaps, political protests and begging).

In fact, a risk with a system of perfect individual control is that it can reduce the importance of the "public sphere" and of common spaces in general. One of the important features of such spaces is that they tend to ensure that people will encounter materials on important issues, whether or not they have specifically chosen the encounter. When people see materials that they have not chosen, their interests and their views might change as a result. At the very least, they will know a bit more about what their fellow citizens are thinking. As it happens, this point is closely connected with an important, and somewhat exotic, constitutional principle.

Public (and Private) Forums

In the popular understanding, the free speech principal forbids government from "censoring" speech of which it disapproves. In the standard cases, the government attempts to impose penalties, whether civil or criminal, on political dissent, and on speech that it considers dangerous, libelous, or sexually explicit. The question is whether the government has a legitimate and sufficiently weighty basis for restricting the speech that it seeks to control.

But a central part of free speech law, with large implications for thinking about the Internet, takes a quite different form. The Supreme Court has also held that streets and parks must be kept open to the public for expressive activity. Governments are obliged to allow speech to occur freely on public streets and in public parks—even if many citizens would prefer to have peace and quiet, and even if it seems irritating to come across protesters and dissidents whom one would like to avoid. . . .

The public forum doctrine serves three important functions. First, it ensures that speakers can have access to a wide array of people. If you want to claim that taxes are too high, or that police brutality against African Americans is common, you can press this argument on many people who might otherwise fail to hear the message. Those who use the streets and parks are likely to learn something about your argument; they might also learn the nature and intensity of views held by one of their fellow citizens. Perhaps their views will be changed; perhaps they will become curious, enough to investigate the question on their own.

Second, the public forum doctrine allows speakers not only to have general access to heterogeneous people, but also to specific people, and specific institutions, with whom they have a complaint. Suppose, for example, that you believe that the state legislature has behaved irresponsibly with respect to crime or health care for children. The public forum ensures that you can make your views heard by legislators simply by protesting in front of the state legislature building.

Third, the public forum doctrine increases the likelihood that people generally will be exposed to a wide variety of people and views. When you go to work, or visit a park, it is possible that you will have a range of unexpected encounters, however fleeting or seemingly inconsequential. You cannot easily wall yourself off from contentions or conditions that you would not have sought out in advance, or that you would have chosen to avoid if you could. Here, too, the public forum doctrine tends to ensure a range of experiences that are widely shared—streets and parks are public property—and also a set of exposures to diverse circumstances. . . .

. . . Society's general interest intermediaries—newspapers, magazines, television broadcasters—can be understood as public forums of an especially important sort, perhaps above all because they expose people to new, unanticipated topics and points of view.

When you read a city newspaper or a national magazine, your eyes will come across a number of articles that you might not have selected in advance, and if you are like most people, you will read some of those articles. Perhaps you did not know that you might have an interest in minimum wage legislation, or Somalia, or the latest developments in the Middle East. But a story might catch your attention. And what is true for topics of interest is also true for points of view. You might think that you have nothing to learn from someone whose view you abhor; but once you come across the editorial pages, you might read what they have to say, and you might benefit from the experience. . . .

Television broadcasters have similar functions. Most important in this regard is what has become an institution: the evening news. If you tune into the evening news, you will learn about a number of topics that you would not have chosen in advance. Because of their speech and immediacy, television broadcasts perform these public forum–type functions more than general interest intermediaries in the print media. The "lead story" on the networks is likely to have a great deal of public salience; it helps to define central issues and creates a kind of shared focus of attention for millions of people. . . .

None of these claims depends on a judgment that general interest intermediaries are unbiased, or always do an excellent job, or deserve a monopoly over the world of communications. The Internet is a boon partly because it breaks that monopoly. So too for the proliferation of television and radio shows, and even channels, that have some specialized identity. (Consider the rise of Fox News, which appeals to a more conservative audience.) All that I am claiming is that general interest intermediaries expose people to a wide range of topics and views and at the same time provide shared experiences for a heterogeneous public. Indeed, intermediaries of this sort have large advantages over streets and parks precisely because they tend to be national, even international. Typically they expose people to questions and problems in other areas, even other countries.

Specialization and Fragmentation

In a system with public forums and general interest intermediaries, people will frequently come across materials that they would not have chosen in advance—and in a diverse society, this provides something like a common framework for social experience. A fragmented communications market will change things significantly.

Consider some simple facts. If you take the ten most highly rated television programs for whites, and then take the ten most highly rated programs for African Americans, you will find little overlap between them. Indeed, more than half of the ten most highly rated programs for African Americans rank among the ten *least* popular programs for whites. With respect to race, similar divisions can be found on the Internet. Not surprisingly, many people tend to choose like-minded sites and like-minded discussion groups. Many of those with committed views on a topic—gun control, abortion, affirmative action—speak mostly with each other. It is exceedingly rare for a site with an identifiable point of view to provide links to sites with opposing views; but it is very common for such a site to provide links to like-minded sites.

With a dramatic increase in options, and a greater power to customize, comes an increase in the range of actual choices. Those choices are likely, in many cases, to mean that people will try to find material that makes them feel comfortable, or that is created by and for people like themselves. This is what the Daily Me is all about. Of course, many people seek out new topics and ideas. And to the extent that people do, the increase in options is hardly bad on balance; it will, among other things, increase variety, the aggregate amount of information, and the entertainment value of actual choices. But there are serious risks as well. If diverse groups are seeing and hearing different points of view, or focusing on different topics, mutual understanding might be difficult, and it might be hard for people to solve problems that society faces together. . . .

We can sharpen our understanding of this problem if we attend to the phenomenon of *group polarization*. The idea is that after deliberating with one another, people are likely to move toward a more extreme point in the direction to which they were previously inclined, as indicated by the median of their predeliberation judgments. With respect to the Internet, the implication is that groups of people, especially if they are like-minded, will end up thinking the same thing that they thought before—but in more extreme form.

Consider some examples of this basic phenomenon, which has been found in over a dozen nations. (a) After discussion, citizens of France become more critical of the United States and its intentions with respect to economic aid. (b) After discussion, whites predisposed to show racial prejudice offer more negative responses to questions about whether white racism is responsible for conditions faced by African Americans in American cities. (c) After discussion, whites predisposed not to show racial prejudice offer more positive responses to the same question. (d) A group of moderately profeminist women will become more strongly profeminist after discussion. . . .

The phenomenon of group polarization has conspicuous importance to the current communications market, where groups with distinctive identities increasingly engage in within-group discussion. If the public is balkanized, and if different groups design their own preferred communications packages, the consequence will be further balkanization, as group members move one another toward more extreme points in line with their initial tendencies. At the same time, different deliberating groups, each consisting of like-minded people, will be driven increasingly far apart, simply because most of their discussions are with one another. . . .

Group polarization is a human regularity, but social context can decrease, increase, or even eliminate it. For present purposes, the most important point is that group polarization will significantly increase if people think of themselves . . . as part of a group having a shared identity and a degree of solidarity. If . . . a group of people in an Internet discussion group think of themselves as opponents of high taxes, or advocates of animal rights, their discussions are likely to move toward extreme positions. As this happens to many different groups, polarization is both more likely and more extreme. Hence significant movements should be expected for those who listen to a radio show known to be conservative, or a television program dedicated to traditional religious values or to exposing white racism. . . .

Group polarization is occurring every day on the Internet. Indeed, it is clear that the Internet is serving, for many, as a breeding ground for extremism, precisely because like-minded people are deliberating with one another, without hearing contrary views. Hate groups are the most obvious example. Consider one extremist group, the so-called Unorganized Militia, the armed wing of the Patriot movement, "which believes that the federal government is becoming increasingly dictatorial with its regulatory power over taxes, guns and land use." A crucial factor behind the growth of the Unorganized

Militia "has been the use of computer networks," allowing members "to make contact quickly and easily with like-minded individuals to trade information, discuss current conspiracy theories, and organize events." . . .

Of course we cannot say, from the mere fact of polarization, that there has been a movement in the *wrong* direction. Perhaps the more extreme tendency is better; indeed, group polarization is likely to have fueled many movements of great value, including the movement for civil rights, the antislavery movement, the movement for sex equality. All of these movements were extreme in their time, and within-group discussion bred greater extremism; but extremism need not be a word of opprobrium. If greater communications choices produce greater extremism, society may, in many cases, be better off as a result. . . .

The basic issue here is whether something like a "public sphere," with a wide range of voices, might not have significant advantages over a system in which isolated consumer choices produce a highly fragmented speech market. The most reasonable conclusion is that it is extremely important to ensure that people are exposed to views other than those with which they currently agree, that doing so protects against the harmful effects of group polarization on individual thinking and on social cohesion. This does not mean that the government should jail or fine people who refuse to listen to others. Nor is what I have said inconsistent with approval of deliberating "enclaves," on the Internet or elsewhere, designed to ensure that positions that would otherwise be silenced or squelched have a chance to develop. Readers will be able to think of their own preferred illustrations. . . .

Consider in this light the ideal of "consumer sovereignty," which underlies much of contemporary enthusiasm for the Internet. Consumer sovereignty means that people can choose to purchase, or to obtain, whatever they want. For many purposes this is a worthy ideal. But the adverse effects of group polarization show that, with respect to communications, consumer sovereignty is likely to produce serious problems for individuals and society at large—and these problems will occur by a kind of iron logic of social interactions.

The phenomenon of group polarization is [also] closely related to the widespread phenomenon of "social cascades." Cascade effects are common on the Internet, and we cannot understand the relationship between democracy and the Internet without having a sense of how cascades work.

It is obvious that many social groups, both large and small, seem to move both rapidly and dramatically in the direction of one or another set of beliefs or actions. These sorts of "cascades" often involve the spread of information; in fact they are driven by information. If you lack a great deal of private information, you may well rely on information provided by the statements or actions of others. A stylized example: If Joan is unaware whether abandoned toxic waste dumps are in fact hazardous, she may be moved in the direction of fear if Mary seems to think that fear is justified. If Joan and Mary both believe that fear is justified, Carl may end up thinking so too, at least if he lacks reliable independent information to the contrary.

If Joan, Mary, and Carl believe that abandoned toxic waste dumps are hazardous, Don will have to have a good deal of confidence to reject their shared conclusion.

The example shows how information travels, and often becomes quite entrenched, even if it is entirely wrong. The view, widespread in some African-American communities, that white doctors are responsible for the spread of AIDS among African Americans is a recent illustration. Often cascades of this kind are local, and take different form in different communities. Hence one group may end up believing something and another group the exact opposite, and the reason is the rapid transmission of one piece of information within one group and a different piece of information in the other. In a balkanized speech market, this danger takes a particular form: different groups may be lead to quite different perspectives, as local cascades lead people in dramatically different directions. The Internet dramatically increases the likelihood of rapid cascades, based on false information. Of course, low-cost Internet communication also makes it possible for truth, and corrections, to spread quickly as well. But sometimes this happens much too late. In the event, balkanization is extremely likely. As a result of the Internet, cascade effects are more common than they have ever been before. . . .

I hope that I have shown enough to demonstrate that for citizens of a heterogeneous democracy, a fragmented communications market creates considerable dangers. There are dangers for each of us as individuals; constant exposure to one set of views is likely to lead to errors and confusions, or to unthinking conformity (emphasized by John Stuart Mill). And to the extent that the process makes people less able to work cooperatively on shared problems, by turning collections of people into non-communicating confessional groups, there are dangers for society as a whole.

Common Experiences

In a heterogeneous society, it is extremely important for diverse people to have a set of common experiences. Many of our practices reflect a judgment to this effect. National holidays, for example, help constitute a nation, by encouraging citizens to think, all at once, about events of shared importance. And they do much more than this. They enable people, in all their diversity, to have certain memories and attitudes in common. At least this is true in nations where national holidays have a vivid and concrete meaning. In the United States, many national holidays have become mere days-off-from-work, and the precipitating occasion—President's Day, Memorial Day, Labor Day—has come to be nearly invisible. This is a serious loss. With the possible exception of the Fourth of July, Martin Luther King Day is probably the closest thing to a genuinely substantive national holiday, largely because that celebration involves something that can be treated as concrete and meaningful—in other words, it is *about* something.

Communications and the media are, of course, exceptionally important here. Sometimes millions of people follow the presidential election, or the Super Bowl, or the coronation of a new monarch; many of them do so because of the simultaneous actions of others. The point very much bears on the historic role of both public forums and general interest intermediaries. Public parks are places where diverse people can congregate and see one another. General interest intermediaries, if they are operating properly, give a simultaneous sense of problems and tasks.

Why are these shared experiences so desirable? There are three principal reasons:

1. Simple enjoyment is probably the least of it, but it is far from irrelevant. People like many experiences more simply because they are being shared. Consider a popular movie, the Super Bowl, or a presidential debate. . . .

2. Sometimes shared experiences ease social interactions, permitting people to speak with one another, and to congregate around a common issue, task, or concern, whether or not they have much in common with one another. In this sense they provide a form of social glue. They help make it possible for diverse people to believe that they live in the same culture. Indeed they help constitute that shared culture, simply by creating common memories and experiences, and a sense of common tasks.

3. A fortunate consequence of shared experiences—many of them produced by the media—is that people who would otherwise see one another as unfamiliar can come to regard one another as fellow citizens, with shared hopes, goals, and concerns. This is a subjective good for those directly involved. But it can be objectively good as well, especially if it leads to cooperative projects of various kinds. . . .

How does this bear on the Internet? An increasingly fragmented communications universe will reduce the level of shared experiences having salience to a diverse group of Americans. This is a simple matter of numbers. When there were three television networks, much of what appeared would have the quality of a genuinely common experience. The lead story on the evening news, for example, would provide a common reference point for many millions of people. To the extent that choices proliferate, it is inevitable that diverse individuals, and diverse groups, will have fewer shared experiences and fewer common reference points. It is possible, for example, that some events that are highly salient to some people will barely register on others' viewscreens. And it is possible that some views and perspectives that seem obvious for many people will, for others, seem barely intelligible.

This is hardly a suggestion that everyone should be required to watch the same thing. A degree of plurality, with respect to both topics and points of view, is highly desirable. Moreover, talk about "requirements" misses the point. My only claim is that a common set of frameworks and experiences is valuable for a heterogeneous society, and that a system with limitless options, making for diverse choices, could compromise the underlying values.

Changing Filters

My goal here has been to understand what makes for a well-functioning system of free expression, and to show how consumer sovereignty, in a world of limitless options, could undermine that system. The point is that a well-functioning system includes a kind of public sphere, one that fosters common experiences, in which people hear messages that challenge their prior convictions, and in which citizens can present their views to a broad audience. I do not intend to offer a comprehensive set of policy reforms or any kind of blueprint for the future. . . . But it will be useful to offer a few ideas, if only by way of introduction to questions that are likely to engage public attention in coming years.

In thinking about reforms, it is important to have a sense of the problems we aim to address, and some possible ways of addressing them. If the discussion thus far is correct, there are three fundamental concerns from the democratic point of view. These include:

(a) the need to promote exposure to materials, topics, and positions that people would not have chosen in advance, or at least enough exposure to produce a degree of understanding and curiosity;
(b) the value of a range of common experiences;
(c) the need for exposure to substantive questions of policy and principle, combined with a range of positions on such questions. . . .

Drawing on recent developments in regulation generally, we can see the potential appeal of five simple alternatives. Of course, different proposals would work better for some communications outlets than others. I will speak here of both private and public responses, but the former should be favored: they are less intrusive, and in general they are likely to be more effective as well.

Disclosure: Producers of communications might disclose important information on their own, about the extent to which they are promoting democratic goals. To the extent that they do not, they might be subject to disclosure requirements (though not to regulation). In the environmental area, this strategy has produced excellent results. The mere fact that polluters have been asked to disclose toxic releases has produced voluntary, low-cost reductions. Apparently fearful of public opprobrium, companies have been spurred to reduce toxic emissions on their own. . . .

The same idea could be used far more broadly. Television broadcasters might, for example, be asked to disclose their public interest activities. On a quarterly basis, they might say whether and to what extent they have provided educational programming for children, free air time for candidates, and closed captioning for the hearing impaired. They might also be asked whether they have covered issues of concern to the local community and allowed opposing views a chance to speak. The Federal Communications Commission has already taken steps in this direction; it could do a lot more. . . .

Self-Regulation: Producers of communications might engage in *voluntary self-regulation.* Some of the difficulties in the current speech market stem from relentless competition for viewers and listeners, competition that leads to a situation that many broadcast journalists abhor about their profession, and from which society does not benefit. The competition might be reduced via a "code" of appropriate conduct, agreed upon by various companies, and encouraged but not imposed by government. In fact, the National Association of Broadcasters maintained such a code for several decades, and there is growing interest in voluntary self-regulation for both television and the Internet. The case for this approach is that it avoids government regulation while at the same time reducing some of the harmful effects of market pressures. Any such code could, for example, call for an opportunity for opposing views to speak, or for avoiding unnecessary sensationalism, or for offering arguments rather than quick soundbites whenever feasible. . . .

Subsidy: The government might *subsidize speech,* as, for example, through publicly subsidized programming or publicly subsidized websites. This is, of course, the idea that motivates the Public Broadcasting System. But it is reasonable to ask whether the PBS model is not outmoded. Other approaches, similarly designed to promote educational, cultural, and democratic goals, might well be ventured. Perhaps government could subsidize a "Public.net" designed to promote debate on public issues among diverse citizens—and to create a right of access to speakers of various sorts.

Links: Websites might use links and hyperlinks to ensure that viewers learn about sites containing opposing views. A liberal magazine's website might, for example, provide a link to a conservative magazine's website, and the conservative magazine might do the same. The idea would be to decrease the likelihood that people will simply hear echoes of their own voices. Of course many people would not click on the icons of sites whose views seem objectionable; but some people would, and in that sense the system would not operate so differently from general interest intermediaries and public forums. . . .

Public Sidewalk: If the problem consists in the failure to attend to public issues, the most popular websites in any given period might offer links and hyperlinks, designed to ensure more exposure to substantive questions. Under such a system, viewers of especially popular sites would see an icon for sites that deal with substantive issues in a serious way. It is well established that whenever there is a link to a particular webpage from a major site, such as MSNBC, the traffic is huge. Nothing here imposes any requirements on viewers. People would not be required to click on links and hyperlinks. But it is reasonable to expect that many viewers would do so, if only to satisfy their curiosity. The result would be to create a kind of Internet "sidewalk" that promotes some of the purposes of the public forum doctrine. . . .

These are brief thoughts on some complex subjects. My goal has not been to evaluate any proposal in detail, but to give a flavor of some possibilities for those concerned to promote democratic goals in a dramatically changed media environment. . . .

Beyond Anticensorship

My principal claim here has been that a well-functioning democracy depends on far more than restraints on official censorship of controversial ideas and opinions. It also depends on some kind of public sphere, in which a wide range of speakers have access to a diverse public—and also to particular institutions, and practices, against which they seek to launch objections.

Emerging technologies, including the Internet, are hardly an enemy here. They hold out far more promise than risk, especially because they allow people to widen their horizons. But to the extent that they weaken the power of general interest intermediaries and increase people's ability to wall themselves off from topics and opinions that they would prefer to avoid, they create serious dangers. And if we believe that a system of free expression calls for unrestricted choices by individual consumers, we will not even understand the dangers as such. Whether such dangers will materialize will ultimately depend on the aspirations, for freedom and democracy alike, by whose light we evaluate our practices. What I have sought to establish here is that in a free republic, citizens aspire to a system that provides a wide range of experiences—with people, topics, and ideas—that would not have been selected in advance.

The Power
of the Producers

ROBERT MCCHESNEY

More than forty years ago, C. Wright Mills published *The Power Elite*. In his book, Mills discusses the paradox of the postwar United States. On the one hand, it is a nation abuzz with technology, celebrity and commercialism, a radical society in which tradition has been torn asunder and all that is solid melts into air. On the other hand, it is a highly depoliticized society—only formally democratic in many key respects—where most important political decisions are made by the few for the few, with public relations to massage the rabble should they question their status.

Robert McChesney, "Power of the Producers." Copyright © 1999 *Rich Media, Poor Democracy: Communication Politics in Dubious Times* by Robert W. McChesney. Reprinted by permission of The New Press. (800) 233-4830.

We are today dazzled by a mind-boggling explosion of new technologies, seemingly lifted from the pages of a science fiction novel, that promise unprecedented consumer choice. On the other hand, the clear tendencies of our media and communication world tend toward ever greater corporate concentration, media conglomeration, and hypercommercialism. There is really no paradox in this, as Mills knew: the illusions of consumer choice and individual freedom merely provide the ideological oxygen necessary to sustain a media system that serves the few while making itself appear accountable and democratic. The digital revolution and the Internet seem less a process of empowering the less powerful than a process that will further the corporate and commercial penetration and domination of life in the United States.

Cass Sunstein has done a great service by raising the anti-democratic implications of the emerging wired world. Much of his critique is on target, and I found myself nodding my head vigorously time after time. In two fundamental areas, however, my train of thought diverges from his. One is a matter of contextualization: In what kind of political and social contexts do people feel the need to construct what Sunstein calls a "Daily Me"? The second is a disagreement over a core assumption: Sunstein seems to assume that consumer sovereignty actually exists, yet I would argue that there are many reasons for doubt on this score.

It may be true, as Sunstein says, that people will tend to look for opinions that reinforce what they already believe. Yet the desire to construct a Daily Me that threatens democracy may not be inherent in the species. Nothing in our genetic code makes the bulk of us, especially those among us who are poorer and younger, narrowly self-obsessed and depoliticized in the ways Sunstein describes. In my view it is fairly clear that since the advent of universal adult suffrage powerful interests have worked tirelessly to promote depoliticization and social demoralization. Sometimes these interests seem to have liberal concerns, or at other times they are frankly elitist, but the point is always the same: it is best for the unwashed not to have too much interest in politics or too much control over important decisions. To the liberals, an active and democratic public will lead to outcomes offensive to the educated; to the elitists, it will lead to outcomes offensive to the wealthy. In either case—and the two groups tend to overlap on core issues—nothing good comes from too much democracy.

A viable democracy depends upon minimal social inequality and a sense that an individual's welfare is determined in large part by the welfare of the general community. It is difficult to imagine an inegalitarian social order like the United States surviving as a democracy if the bottom half of the population put as much interest into political affairs as the top 5 or 10 percent. What better example of this than the 2000 presidential election, where exit polls showed that the richest 20 percent of Americans accounted for about one-half of all voters.

How this process of depoliticizing people plays out is of course tremendously complex; my own work has emphasized the role that the commercial media system has played in making the world safe for vibrant capitalism and weak democracy. It does this partly through a vapid journalism. Because investigative journalism or coverage of foreign affairs makes no economic sense for profit-driven media, it is discouraged as being too expensive. There is appalling schlock journalism for the masses, based upon lurid tabloid-style-type stories. For the occasional serious story, there is the mindless regurgitation of press releases from one source or another, with the range of debate mostly limited to what is being debated among the elites. As with entertainment, at times the corporate media giants generate first-rate journalism, but it is a minuscule fraction of their output and often causes just the sort of uproar that corporate media firms prefer to avoid.

At another level, however, the hypercommercial entertainment culture has been the result of, and necessary condition for, the rise of a global market for goods and services dominated by a few hundred trans-national corporations. The global commercial media system and the growth and emergence of a global economy are predicated upon pro-business deregulation policies worldwide. Just following rational market calculations, the media system exists to provide light escapist entertainment. Dominated by a handful of massive firms, advertisers, and the firms' billionaire owners, the whole media system is spinning in a hypercommercial frenzy with little trace of public service or public accountability.

Is the Internet any different? I believe that Sunstein exaggerates the extent of "consumer sovereignty" on the Internet. Recall the countless pronouncements of the 1990s that the rise of the Internet would spell the doom of the media giants, as entrepreneurs would use the Internet to launch commercially viable competitors to the conglomerates. Supposedly, Internet users could pick from billions of choices, and were there any modicum of demand for something that did not exist, a plucky entrepreneur would surely respond. Hundreds of millions, even billions, of dollars were invested to seize the opportunity to introduce online competition to the media industries. And guess how many commercially viable Internet content providers this flurry of investment generated?

Zero.

It is true that anyone can start a website at a nominal expense and that there may well be billions of websites in the coming decades. It is also true that one can access the global media instantaneously on the Web, which breaks down barriers of time and space. While these are truly astonishing and world-historical developments, they do not however lead to consumer sovereignty, which requires intense competition among producers. Ironically, the evidence suggests that the effect of the Internet on our media culture may well be, strangely enough, to generate even greater *producer* sovereignty.

How can this be?

The principal reason is that the two dozen or so media firms that rule the U.S. media system have spectacular advantages over nascent online competitors. Firms like AOL-Time Warner have digital programming already and need not create something entirely new; they have known brand names; they can advertise their Web activities in their traditional media, a striking advantage over someone who has to pay for that level of promotion. They can bring their advertisers over to their websites; they get "pole position" from browsers, portals, and search engines. Plus, the media giants have a much longer time horizon with regard to the Web. They will take huge losses every year because they know that by doing so they can make sure no one can use the Internet to destroy their existing empires. An investor without an existing media empire to protect recognizes early on that there are better locations for profitable investment. Indeed, the Internet may well be likely to increase concentration rather than competition in the media and other industries as they move online. This is the lesson of Amazon.com: whoever gets the jump on an online industry, because the margins are low, requires massive scale to make a profit. Once the scale reaches a certain point, it is virtually impossible for newcomers to invade the market. Just recently, Borders has thrown in the towel as an Internet bookseller. If Borders, with its massive warehouses of books, cannot compete with Amazon, who can?

So, when individuals are selecting from billions of websites to construct their Daily Me, as Sunstein suggests they are doing, they will not be exercising consumer sovereignty. More than likely, they will be selecting from a much smaller group of options directed by the largest media firms in the world. While the Internet will permit the occasional interloper to break a story, and it will change many aspects of political organizing, the journalism that receives the funding and attention will do so under the same commercial auspices and terms that offline journalism operates under. In my view, that is bad news for the sort of informed, participatory democracy that both Sunstein and I advocate.

The simple truth is that for those atop our economy success is based in large part on *eliminating* competition, not encouraging it. I am being somewhat facetious, because in the end capitalism is indeed a war one against all, since every capitalist is in competition with all the others. But competition is also something successful capitalists learn to avoid like the plague. The less competition a firm has, the less risk it faces and more profitable it tends to be. In general, most markets in the United States in the twentieth century have gravitated not to monopoly but to oligopolistic status. This means that a small handful of firms—this ranges from two to three to as many as a dozen or so—thoroughly dominate the market's output and maintain barriers to entry that effectively keeps new market entrants at bay.

So how should we expect the Internet to develop? Exactly as it has so far. Despite now having the technological capacity to compete, the largest firms are extremely reticent about entering new markets and forcing their way into highly lucrative communications markets. It is safe to say that *some* new communications giants will be established during the coming years, much as Microsoft attained gigantic status during the 1980s. But most of the great new fortunes will be made by start-up firms who develop a profitable idea and then sell out to one of the existing giants. Witness Microsoft, which spent over $2 billion between 1994 and 1997 to purchase or take a stake in some fifty communications companies.

The market system may "work" in the sense that goods and services are produced and consumed, but it is no means fair in any social or political or ethical sense of the term. Wealthy individuals have significant advantages over poor or middle class individuals in terms of participating as capitalists. A tremendous amount of talent simply never gets an opportunity to develop and contribute to the economy. It is unremarkable that "self-made" billionaires like Bill Gates, Ted Turner, Michael Eisner, Rupert Murdoch, and Sumner Redstone all come from privileged backgrounds. And on the demand side of the market, power is determined by how much money an individual has; it is a case of one dollar, one vote, rather than one person, one vote. In this sense, the political system to which the media and Internet market is most similar is the limited suffrage days of pre-twentieth century democracies, where propertyless adults could not vote and their interests were studiously ignored.

What this all means is clear. To have the Internet contribute to a democratization of our society requires that we work to democratize our political economy and reform our media system. The most important area of political activity ultimately is to organize to change media policies. The core problem with the U.S. media systems relates to how it is owned, its profit motivation, and its reliance upon advertising. Corporate media power must be confronted directly, and reduced. Here are some suggestions:

1. *Building nonprofit and commercial media.* The starting point for media reform is to build up a viable, nonprofit, noncommercial media sector. Such a sector currently exists in the U.S., and produces much of value, but is woefully small and underfunded. It can be developed independently of changes in laws and regulations—foundations and organized labor could and should contribute far more to nonprofit media. Government subsidies and policies have played a key role in establishing lucrative commercial media; now new policies could also foster a nonprofit media sector.

2. *Public broadcasting.* Establishing a strong nonprofit sector to complement the commercial media giants is not enough. Therefore, it is important to establish and maintain a noncommercial, nonprofit, public radio and television system, which could include national networks, local stations, public access television, and independent community radio stations. Every community should also have a stratum of low power television and micropower radio stations.

3. *Regulation.* A third main plank is to increase regulation of commercial broadcasting in the public interest. Experience in the U.S. and abroad indicates that if commercial broadcasters are not held to high public service standards, they will generate the easiest profits by resorting to the crassest commercialism and overwhelm the balance of the media culture. The solution to this problem is clear: Commercial broadcasters

should receive their government licenses for only eighteen hours per day. The remaining six hours should be taken out of their control and dedicated to public service.

4. *Antitrust.* Break up the largest firms and establish more competitive markets, thus shifting some control from corporate suppliers to citizen consumers. The contemporary political power implied in the consolidation of media into a handful of corporate behemoths rivals that of the great trusts of the Gilded Age. We need a new media antitrust statute, which emphasizes the importance of ideological diversity and non-commercial editorial content.

There are, of course, some specific policy reforms we should seek for the Internet: for example, guaranteeing universal public access at low rates, perhaps for free. But in general terms, we might do better to regard the Internet as the corporate media giants regard it. It is part of the emerging media landscape, not its entirety. So when we create more and smaller media firms, when we create public and community radio and television networks and stations, when we create a strong public service component to commercial news and children's programming, when we use government policies to spawn a nonprofit media sector, all these will have a tremendous effect on the Internet's development. Why? Because websites will not be worth much if they do not have the resources to provide a quality product. And all the new media that result from media reform will have websites as a mandatory aspect of their operations, much like the commercial media. By creating a vibrant and more democratic traditional media culture, we will go a long way toward creating a more democratic cyberspace.

◼ DISCUSSION QUESTIONS

1. In 2000, the largest media company on earth (Time-Warner) joined with the largest Internet access provider (America Online). How might each author respond to the implications of this merger? Does it promote public access to the Net, represent a new version of the "Daily Me," or signal a blatant corporate takeover?

2. Both Sunstein and McChesney see a certain democratic potential in the Internet. For each author, what would have to happen for this democratic potential to be realized?

3. Because almost anyone with minimal expertise can set up a web site, the Internet has been heralded as the ultimate participatory medium. In what ways is the Internet an extension of the established traditional media of print, TV, and newspapers? In what ways is it a departure?

4. Both authors suggest alternatives to the present Internet system. Which reforms do you find the most convincing, and why? Do you have

suggestions of your own for changing the Internet? Do they reflect a larger assessment of the state of democracy in the United States?

■ SUGGESTED READINGS AND INTERNET RESOURCES

At least partly, debates about the Internet's impact are related to larger ideas about what has happened to the more traditional media. Are the media lapdogs or are they watchdogs when it comes to governmental and corporate power in U.S. society? How diverse are the traditional media, and what new influences might shape the news coverage of networks, cable stations, and newspapers? One book that envisages an important, if problematic, role for modern journalists is James Fallows, *Breaking the News: How the Media Undermine American Democracy* (New York: Pantheon Books, 1995). See also Doris Graber, *Mass Media and American Politics* (Washington, D.C.: Congressional Quarterly Press, 2000). For a wild ride through the history of public relations and advertising, written by a former booster of the Internet, see Douglas Rushkoff, *Coercion: Why We Listen to What "They" Say* (New York: Riverhead Books, 1999). For an alternative view, see Bernard Goldberg, *Bias* (Arlington, Va.: Regnery Publishing, 2002). A good conventional account of the effect of the Internet on mass politics is Richard Davis, *The Web of Politics* (New York: Oxford University Press, 1999).

Fairness and Accuracy in Reporting (FAIR)
www.fair.org
This New York City–based watchdog group reports inaccuracies and biases in mainstream news programs, with an emphasis on the undemocratic effects of corporate control.

Media Access Project
www.mediaacess.org
This is the web site of the only U.S. law firm dedicated to preserving public space on the increasingly commercial airwaves.

Pew Research Center for the People and the Press
www.people-press.org
This web site contains excellent polling information on changing patterns of media use by Americans. Use the archives selection.

10

Political Parties and Elections: The 2000 Presidential Election and U.S. Democracy

lections in America are trumpeted as the defining moments of U.S. democratic political identity. And there is good reason for such a declaration: since the founding of the Republic, regular elections between or among competing candidates and parties have provided a stable and dignified way in which the people's voice is heard.

Yet elections and parties can also fall well short of a reasonable democratic standard. Women, African Americans, and the propertyless were excluded by law or custom from the polls throughout much of the nineteenth century. Indeed, Jim Crow laws were not struck down until the 1960s. The struggle to create a wide and inclusive electorate required blood, sweat, and tears over many years and many contexts. And in 2000 the nation learned that electoral institutions and practices are far from pristine—the battle for a fully democratic suffrage is hardly over and is bound to remain contentious.

Are American elections broadly representative of the conflicts and divisions among the U.S. population? Some analysts have doubts. U.S. presidential elections draw only about half of the eligible electorate to the polls, and off-year congressional elections draw only one-third. There's a substantial middle- and upper-class tilt to the voting electorate: while people with college and graduate degrees vote in high percentages, working-class and poor voters are much less likely to vote. The young vote much less than the middle-aged and elderly, and, with some exceptions, recent immigrants who've become citizens are less likely to show up at the polls than people born in the United States. Compared to other wealthy countries, the United States ranks at the bottom in voting participation rates. The kinds of people who don't vote the most are disproportionately those who lack other means to influence politics—money, contacts, and leisure time to study the issues.

From another perspective, however, there is little wrong with this system. Since the 1960s voter registration rules have eased, and people have ample opportunities to become involved in politics, even if many choose not to do so, either out of apathy or disgust. According to most surveys, nonvoters generally hold the same public policy and partisan views as do those who vote. These factors suggest that modern elections do reflect the citizenry's real choices and diversity, in all their complexity.

Nevertheless, issues about the legitimacy of U.S. electoral procedures came to a head in the razor-edged 2000 presidential election. In that year Democratic candidate Al Gore lost to Republican George W. Bush because Bush won the electoral votes of Florida, even though Gore won the overall popular vote by 1 percent. Bush secured Florida's electoral votes through a Supreme Court decision, *Bush v. Gore,* that struck down a Florida Supreme Court decision to recount votes in contested counties.

For many, the Bush victory raised a host of larger issues about U.S. elections as well as about the legitimacy of the Florida vote. Media organizations found that a disproportionate number of probable Gore voters had been disfranchised because their votes had been spoiled. The Federal Civil Rights Commission found numerous violations of federal election laws, from outright disfranchisement of minority, poor, and immigrant voters to antiquated ballot machines and confusing ballots in poorer counties. Others contested an electoral college system that denied the popular majority a victory. Still others questioned the fundamentals of an electoral system that awarded a "majority" all the representation while denying to "minorities" any representation at all. Still others wondered how a system in which only half the electorate voted could be called democratic at all.

For many commentators, such criticisms were sour grapes. No tanks had run through the streets of Palm Beach County; the U.S. legal system had worked the way it was supposed to work, and the victor was George W. Bush. If people objected to the electoral college system, then there was a process for getting rid of it. The point was that the 2000 presidential election had been undeniably close but nevertheless had faithfully reflected the democratic debate in all its complexity.

The two essays excerpted here reflect very different perspectives on the 2000 election and its meanings. In the first, *Weekly Standard* editor and PBS commentator David Brooks writes about the genuine differences in the "Blue" America where Al Gore received a majority and the "Red" America where George Bush did (on election night electoral maps colored Gore states blue and Bush states red). In his journeys, Brooks finds two Americas, which are divided from each other by consumption patterns and attitudes toward life, work, and religion. Despite these differences, Brooks finds, especially since the September 11 attacks, an underlying unity and harmony to Blue and to Red America. Lani Guinier, a Harvard Law School professor and long-time social activist, sees the 2000 election in different terms. Where Brooks sees an underlying harmony, Guinier sees a system of basic injustice and the absence of real democracy. Guinier argues that the rule and procedures of U.S. elections discourage participation, distort potential popular majorities, and subdue America's diverse and conflicted voices. Guinier contends that U.S. elections perpetuate racial privilege, class inequality, and undemocratic practices.

While reading these two contrasting essays, you might consider the following: Which points about U.S. society do these two essays hold in common, and which are points of contention? For each author, what are the fundamental conflicts and debates in U.S. society? What would Guinier say about Brooks's Red America, and what would Brooks say about Guinier's disfranchised voters?

One Nation, Slightly Divisible

DAVID BROOKS

Sixty-five miles from where I am writing this sentence is a place with no Starbucks, no Pottery Barn, no Borders or Barnes & Noble. . . . The place I'm talking about goes by different names. Some call it America. Others call it Middle America. It has also come to be known as Red America, in reference to the maps that were produced on the night of the 2000 presidential election. People in Blue America, which is my part of America, tend to live around big cities on the coasts. People in Red America tend to live on farms or in small towns or small cities far away from the coasts. Things are different there. . . .

Different sorts of institutions dominate life in these two places. In Red America churches are everywhere. In Blue America Thai restaurants are everywhere. In Red America they have QVC, the Pro Bowlers Tour, and hunting. In Blue America we have NPR, Doris Kearns Goodwin, and socially conscious investing. In Red America the Wal-Marts are massive, with parking lots the size of state parks. In Blue America the stores are small but the markups are big. . . .

We in the coastal metro Blue areas read more books and attend more plays than the people in the Red heartland. We're more sophisticated and cosmopolitan—just ask us about our alumni trips to China and Provence, or our interest in Buddhism. But don't ask us, please, what life in Red America is like. We don't know. . . .

All we know, or all we think we know, about Red America is that millions and millions of its people live quietly underneath flight patterns, many of them are racist and homophobic, and when you see them at highway rest stops, they're often really fat and their clothes are too tight. . . .

Crossing the Meatloaf Line

Over the past several months . . . I have every now and then left my home in Montgomery County, Maryland, and driven sixty-five miles northwest to Franklin County, in south-central Pennsylvania. Montgomery County is one of the steaming-hot centers of the great espresso machine that is Blue America. It is just over the border from northwestern Washington, D.C., and it is full of upper-middle-class towns inhabited by lawyers, doctors, stockbrokers, and establishment journalists like me—towns like Chevy Chase, Potomac, and Bethesda (where I live). Its central artery is a burgeoning high-tech corridor with a multitude of sparkling new office parks housing technology companies such as United Information Systems and Sybase, and pioneering biotech firms such as Celera Genomics and Human Genome Sciences. When I drive to Franklin County, I take Route 270. After about forty-five minutes I pass a Cracker Barrel—Red America condensed into chain-restaurant form. I've crossed the Meatloaf Line; from here on there will be a lot fewer sun-dried-tomato concoctions on restaurant menus and a lot more meatloaf platters.

Franklin County is [Bush's] Red America. It's a rural county, about twenty-five miles west of Gettysburg, and it includes the towns of Waynesboro, Chambersburg, and Mercersburg. . . .

I shuttled back and forth between Franklin and Montgomery Counties because the cultural differences between the two places are great, though the geographic distance is small. The two places are not perfect microcosms of Red and Blue America. The part of Montgomery County I am here describing is largely the Caucasian part. Moreover, Franklin County is in a Red part of a Blue state: overall, Pennsylvania went for Gore. And I went to Franklin County aware that there are tremendous differences within Red America, just as there are within Blue. Franklin County is quite different from, say, Scottsdale, Arizona, just as Bethesda is quite different from Oakland, California.

Nonetheless, the contrasts between the two counties leap out, and they are broadly suggestive of the sorts of contrasts that can be seen nationwide. When Blue America talks about social changes that convulsed society, it tends to mean the 1960s rise of the counterculture and feminism. When Red America talks about changes that convulsed society, it tends to mean World War II, which shook up old town establishments and led to a great surge of industry. . . .

[In Red America] there . . . seems to be an important distinction between men who work outdoors and men who work indoors. The outdoor guys wear faded black T-shirts they once picked up at a Lynyrd Skynyd concert and wrecked jeans that appear to be washed faithfully at least once a year. They've got wraparound NASCAR sunglasses, maybe a NAPA auto parts cap, and hair cut in a short wedge up front but flowing down over their shoulders in the back—a cut that is known as a mullet, which is sort of a cross between Van Halen's style and Kenny Rogers's, and is the ugliest hairdo since every hairdo in the seventies. . . .

The guys who work indoors can't project this rugged proletarian image. It's simply not that romantic to be a bank-loan officer or a shift manager at the local distribution center. So the indoor guys adopt a look that a smart-ass, sneering Blue American might call Bible-academy casual—maybe Haggar slacks, which they bought at a dry-goods store best known for its appliance department, and a short-sleeved white Van Heusen shirt from the Bon-Ton. . . .

The kinds of distinctions we make in Blue America are different. In my world the easiest way to categorize people is by headroom needs. People who went to business school or law school like a lot of headroom. They buy humongous sport-utility vehicles that practically have cathedral ceilings over the front seats. They live in homes the size of country clubs, with soaring entry atriums so high that they could practically fly a kite when they come through the front door. These big-headroom people tend to be predators: their jobs have them negotiating and competing all day. . . .

Small-headroom people tend to have been liberal-arts majors, and they have liberal-arts jobs. They get passive-aggressive pleasure from demonstrating how modest and environmentally sensitive their living containers are. They hate people with SUVs, and feel virtuous driving around in their low-ceilinged little Hondas, which often display a RANDOM ACTS OF KINDNESS bumper sticker or one bearing an image of a fish with legs, along with the word "Darwin," just to show how intellectually superior to fundamentalist Christians they are.

Some of the biggest differences between Red and Blue America show up on statistical tables. Ethnic diversity is one. In Montgomery County 60 percent of the population is white, 15 percent is black, 12 percent is Hispanic, and 11 percent is Asian. In Franklin County 95 percent of the population is white. White people work the gas-station pumps and the 7-Eleven counters. (This is something one doesn't often see in my part of the country). Although the nation is growing more diverse, it's doing so only in certain spots. . . .

Another big thing is that, according to 1990 census data, in Franklin County only 12 percent of the adults have college degrees and only 69 percent have high school diplomas. In Montgomery County 50 percent of the adults have college degrees and 91 percent have high school diplomas. The education gap extends to the children. . . .

Because the information age rewards education with money, it's not surprising that Montgomery County is much richer than Franklin County. According to some estimates, in Montgomery County 51 percent of households have annual incomes above $75,000, and the average household income is $100,365. In Franklin County only 16 percent of households have incomes above $75,000, and the average is $51,872.

A major employer in Montgomery County is the National Institutes of Health, which grows like a scientific boomtown in Bethesda. A major economic engine in Franklin County is the interstate highway Route 81. Trucking companies have gotten sick of fighting the congestion on Route 95, which runs up the Blue corridor along the northeast coast, so they move their stuff along 81, farther inland. Several new distribution centers have been built along 81 in Franklin County, and some of the workers who were laid off when their factories closed, several years ago, are now settling for $8.00 or $9.00 an hour loading boxes.

The two counties vote differently, of course—the differences, on a nationwide scale, were what led to those red-and-blue maps. Like upscale areas everywhere, from Silicon Valley to Chicago's North Shore to suburban Connecticut, Montgomery County supported the Democratic ticket in last year's presidential election, by a margin of 63 percent to 34 percent. Meanwhile, like almost all of rural America, Franklin County went Republican, by 67 percent to 30 percent. . . .

From Cracks to a Chasm?

These differences are so many and so stark that they lead to some pretty troubling questions: Are Americans any longer a common people? Do we have one national conversation and one national culture? Are we loyal to the same institutions and the same values? How do people on one side of the divide regard those on the other? . . .

Toward the end of my project the World Trade Center and the Pentagon were attacked. This put a new slant on my little investigation. In the days immediately following September 11 the evidence seemed clear that despite our differences, we are still a united people. American flags flew everywhere in Franklin County and in Montgomery County. Patriotism surged. Pollsters started to measure Americans' reactions to the events. Whatever questions they asked, the replies were near[ly] unanimous. Do you support a military response against terror? More than four fifths of Americans said yes. Do you support a military response even if it means thousands of U.S. casualties? More than three fifths said yes. There were no significant variations across geographic or demographic lines.

A sweeping feeling of solidarity was noticeable in every neighborhood, school, and workplace. Headlines blared, "A NATION UNITED" and "UNITED STATE." An attack had been made on the very epicenter of Blue America—downtown Manhattan. And in a flash all the jokes about and seeming hostility toward New Yorkers vanished, to be replaced by an outpouring of respect, support, and love. The old hostility came to seem merely a sort of sibling rivalry, which means nothing when the family itself is under threat.

But very soon there were hints that the solidarity was fraying. . . .

It started to seem likely that these cracks would widen once the American response got under way, when the focus would be not on firemen and rescue workers but on the Marines, the CIA, and the special-operations forces. If the war was protracted, the cracks could widen into a chasm, as they did during Vietnam. Red America, the home of patriotism and military service (there's a big military-recruitment center in downtown Chambersburg), would undoubtedly support the war effort, but would Blue America (there's a big gourmet dog [food] bakery in downtown Bethesda) decide that a crude military response would only deepen animosities and make things worse?

So toward the end of my project I investigated Franklin County with a heightened sense of gravity and with much more urgency. If America was not firmly united in the early days of the conflict, we would certainly not be united later, when the going got tough.

"The People Versus the Powerful"

There are a couple of long-standing theories about why America is divided. One of the main ones holds that the division is along class lines, between the haves and the have-nots. This theory is popular chiefly on the left. . . .

According to this theory, during most of the twentieth century gaps in income between the rich and the poor in America gradually shrank. Then came the information age. The rich started getting spectacularly richer; the poor started getting poorer, and wages for the middle class stagnated, at best. Over the previous decade, these writers emphasized, remuneration for top-level executives had skyrocketed: now the average CEO made 116 times as much as the average rank-and-file worker. Assembly-line workers found themselves competing for jobs against Third World workers who earned less than a dollar an hour. Those who had once labored at well-paying blue-collar jobs were forced to settle for poorly paying service-economy jobs without benefits.

People with graduate degrees have done well over the past couple of decades: their real hourly wages climbed by 13 percent from 1979 to 1997. . . . But those with only some college education saw their wages fall by nine percent, while those with only high school diplomas saw their wages fall by 12 percent, and high school dropouts saw a stunning 26 percent decline in their pay.

Such trends have created a new working class . . . not a traditional factory-and-mill working class but a suburban and small-town working class, made up largely of service workers and low-level white-collar employees. . . .

[Pollster] Stanley Greenberg tailored Al Gore's presidential campaign to appeal to such voters. Gore's most significant slogan was "The People Versus the Powerful," which was meant to rally members of the middle class who felt threatened by "powerful forces" beyond their control, such as

HMOs, tobacco companies, big corporations, and globalization, and to channel their resentment against the upper class. Gore dressed down throughout his campaign in the hope that these middle-class workers would identify with him.

Driving from Bethesda to Franklin County, one can see that the theory of a divide between the classes has a certain plausibility. . . .

When the locals are asked about their economy, they tell a story very similar to the one that . . . the wage-stagnation liberals recount. There used to be plenty of good factory jobs in Franklin County, and people could work at those factories for life. But some of the businesses, including the textile company J. Schoeneman, once Franklin County's largest manufacturer, have closed. Others have moved offshore. The remaining manufacturers, such as Grove Worldwide and JLG Industries, which both make cranes and aerial platforms, have laid off workers. The local Army depot, Letterkenny, has radically shrunk its work force. The new jobs are in distribution centers or nursing homes. People tend to repeat the same phrase: "We've taken some hits."

And yet when they are asked about the broader theory, whether there is class conflict between the educated affluents and the stagnant middles, they stare blankly as if suddenly the interview were being conducted in Aramaic. I kept asking, Do you feel that the highly educated people around, say, New York and Washington are getting all the goodies? Do you think there is resentment toward all the latte sippers who shop at Nieman Marcus? Do you see a gulf between high-income people in the big cities and middle-income people here? I got only polite, fumbling answers as people tried to figure out what the hell I was talking about.

When I rephrased the question in more-general terms, as Do you believe the country is divided between the haves and the have-nots?, everyone responded decisively: yes. But as the conversation continued, it became clear that the people saying yes did not consider themselves to be among the have-nots. Even people with incomes well below the median thought of themselves as haves.

What I found was entirely consistent with the election returns from November of last year. Gore's pitch failed miserably among the voters it was intended to target: nationally he lost among non-college-educated white voters by 17 points and among non-college-educated white men by 29 points. But it worked beautifully on the affluent, educated class: for example, Gore won among women with graduate degrees by 22 points. The lesson seems to be that if you run a campaign under the slogan "The People Versus the Powerful," you will not do well in the places where "the people" live, but you will do fantastically well in the places where "the powerful" live. This phenomenon mirrors, on a larger scale, one I noted a couple of years ago, when I traveled the country for a year talking about *Bobos in Paradise,* a book I had written on upscale America. The richer the community, the more likely I was to be asked about wage inequality. In middle-class communities the subject almost never came up.

Hanging around Franklin County, one begins to understand some of the reasons that people there don't spend much time worrying about economic class lines. The first and most obvious one is that although the incomes in Franklin County are lower than those in Montgomery County, living expenses are also lower—very much so. . . .

The biggest difference is in real-estate prices. In Franklin County one can buy a nice four-bedroom split-level house with about 2,200 square feet of living space for $150,000 to $180,000. In Bethesda that same house would cost about $450,000. . . .

Some of the people I met in Franklin County were just getting by. Some were in debt and couldn't afford to buy their kids the Christmas presents they wanted to. But I didn't find many who assessed their own place in society according to their income. Rather, the people I met commonly told me that although those in affluent places like Manhattan and Bethesda might make more money and have more-exciting jobs, they are the unlucky ones, because they don't get to live in Franklin County. They don't get to enjoy the beautiful green hillsides, the friendly people, the wonderful church groups and volunteer organizations. They may be nice people and all, but they are certainly not as happy as we are.

Another thing I found is that most people don't think sociologically. They don't compare themselves with faraway millionaires who appear on their TV screens. They compare themselves with their neighbors. . . . One man in Mercersburg, Pennsylvania, told me about a friend who had recently bought a car. "He paid twenty-five thousand dollars for that car!" he exclaimed, his eyes wide with amazement. "He got it fully loaded." I didn't tell him that in Bethesda almost no one but a college kid pays as little as $25,000 for a car.

Franklin County is a world in which there is little obvious inequality, and the standard of living is reasonably comfortable. Youth-soccer teams are able to raise money for a summer trip to England; the Lowe's hardware superstore carries Laura Ashley carpets; many people have pools, although they are almost always above ground; the planning commission has to cope with an increasing number of cars in the county every year, even though the population is growing only gradually. But the sort of high-end experiences that are everywhere in Montgomery County are entirely missing here. . . .

No wonder people in Franklin County have no class resentment or class consciousness; where they live, they can afford just about anything that is for sale. (In Montgomery County, however—and this is one of the most striking contrasts between the two counties—almost nobody can say that. In Blue America, unless you are very, very rich, there is always, all around you, stuff for sale that you cannot afford.) And if they sought to improve their situation, they would look only to themselves. If a person wants to make more money, the feeling goes, he or she had better work hard and think like an entrepreneur. . . .

People do work extremely hard in Franklin County—even people in supposedly dead-end jobs. You can see it in little things, such as drugstore shelves. The drugstores in Bethesda look the way Rome must have looked after a visit from the Visigoths. But in Franklin County the boxes are in perfect little rows. Shelves are fully stocked, and cans are evenly spaced. The floors are less dusty than those in a microchip-processing plant. The nail clippers on a rack by the cash register are arranged with a precision that would put the Swiss to shame.

There are few unions in Franklin County. People abhor the thought of depending on welfare; they consider themselves masters of their own economic fate. . . .

In sum, I found absolutely no evidence that a Stanley Greenberg–prompted Democratic Party (or a Pat Buchanan–led Republican Party) could mobilize white middle-class Americans on the bias of class consciousness. I found no evidence that economic differences explain much of anything about the divide between Red and Blue America. . . .

Pew has conducted a broad survey of the differences between Red and Blue states. The survey found that views on economic issues do not explain the different voting habits in the two regions. There simply isn't much of the sort of economic dissatisfaction that could drive a class-based political movement. Eighty-five percent of Americans with an annual household income between $30,000 and $50,000 are satisfied with their housing. Nearly 70 percent are satisfied with the kind of car they can afford. Roughly two thirds are satisfied with their furniture and their ability to afford a night out. These levels of satisfaction are not very different from those found in upper-middle-class America.

The Pew researchers found this sort of trend in question after question. Part of the draft of their report is tilted "Economic Divide Dissolves."

A Lot of Religion but Few Crusaders

This leaves us with the second major hypothesis about the nature of the divide between Red and Blue America, which comes mainly from conservatives: America is divided between two moral systems. Red America is traditional, religious, self-disciplined, and patriotic. Blue America is modern, secular, self-expressive, and discomfited by blatant displays of patriotism. Proponents of this hypothesis in its most radical form contend that America is in the midst of a culture war, with two opposing armies fighting on behalf of their views. . . .

The values-divide school has a fair bit of statistical evidence on its side. Whereas income is a poor predictor of voting patterns, church attendance . . . is a pretty good one. Of those who attend religious services weekly (42 percent of the electorate), 59 percent voted for Bush, 39 percent for Gore. Of those who seldom or never attend religious services (another 42 percent), 56 percent voted for Gore, 39 percent for Bush.

The Pew data reveal significant divides on at least a few values issues. Take, for example, the statement "We will all be called before God on

Judgment Day to answer for our sins." In Red states 70 percent of the people believe that statement. In Blue states only 50 percent do. . . .

Chambersburg and its vicinity have eighty-five churches and one synagogue. The Bethesda–Chevy Chase area, which has a vastly greater population, has forty-five churches and five synagogues. Professors at the local college in Chambersburg have learned not to schedule public lectures on Wednesday nights, because everybody is at prayer meetings. . . .

Life is complicated, however. Yes, there are a lot of churches in Franklin County; there are also a lot of tattoo parlors. And despite all the churches and bumper stickers, Franklin County doesn't seem much different from anywhere else. People go to a few local bars to hang out after softball games. Teenagers drive recklessly along fast-food strips. Young women in halter tops sometimes prowl in the pool halls. The local college has a gay-and-lesbian group. One conservative clergyman I spoke with estimated that 10 percent of his congregants are gay. He believes that church is the place where one should be able to leave the controversy surrounding this sort of issue behind. Another described how his congregation united behind a young man who was dying of AIDS. . . .

Franklin County is probably a bit more wholesome than most suburbs in Blue America. (The notion that deviance and corruption lie underneath the seeming conformism of suburban middle-class life, popular in Hollywood and in creative-writing workshops, is largely nonsense.) But it has most of the problems that afflict other parts of the country: heroin addiction, teen pregnancy, and so on. Nobody I spoke to felt part of a pristine culture that is exempt from the problems of the big cities. . . .

If the problems are the same as in the rest of America, so are many of the solutions. Franklin County residents who find themselves in trouble go to their clergy first, but they are often referred to psychologists and therapists as part of their recovery process. Prozac is a part of life.

Almost nobody I spoke with understood, let alone embraced, the concept of a culture war. Few could see themselves as fighting such a war, in part because few have any idea where the boundary between the two sides lies. People in Franklin County may have a clear sense of what constitutes good or evil (many people in Blue America have trouble with the very concept of evil), but they will say that good and evil are in all neighborhoods, as they are in all of us. People take the Scriptures seriously but have no interest in imposing them on others. One finds little crusader zeal in Franklin County. For one thing, people in small towns don't want to offend people whom they'll be encountering on the street for the next fifty years. Potentially controversial subjects are often played down. . . .

Certainly Red and Blue America disagree strongly on some issues, such as homosexuality and abortion. But for the most part the disagreements are not large. For example, the Pew researchers asked Americans to respond to the statement "There are clear guidelines about what's good or evil that apply to everyone regardless of their situation." Forty-three percent of people in Blue states and 49 percent of people in Red states agreed. Forty-seven percent of Blue America and 55 percent of Red America agreed with the statement "I have old-fashioned values about family and marriage." Seventy percent of the people in Blue states and 77 percent of the people in Red states agreed that "too many children are being raised in day-care centers these days." These are small gaps. And, the Pew researchers found, there is no culture gap at all among suburban voters. In a Red state like Arizona suburban voters' opinions are not much different from those in a Blue state like Connecticut. The starkest differences that exist are between people in cities and people in rural areas, especially rural areas in the South.

The conservatism I found in Franklin County is not an ideological or a reactionary conservatism. It is a temperamental conservatism. People place tremendous value on being agreeable, civil, and kind. They are happy to sit quietly with one another. They are hesitant to stir one another's passions. They appreciate what they have. They value continuity and revere the past. They work hard to reinforce community bonds. Their newspapers are filled with items about fundraising drives, car washes, bake sales, penny-collection efforts, and auxiliary thrift shops. Their streets are lined with lodges: VFW, Rotarians, Elks, Moose. Luncheons go on everywhere. Retired federal employees will be holding their weekly luncheon at one restaurant, Harley riders at another. . . .

These are the sorts of things that really mobilize people in Franklin County. Building community and preserving local ways are far more important to them than any culture war.

The Ego Curtain

The best explanation of the differences between people in Montgomery and Franklin Counties has to do with sensibility, not class or culture. If I had to describe the differences between the two sensibilities in a single phrase, it would be conception of the self. In Red America the self is small. People declare in a million ways, "I am normal. Nobody is better, nobody is worse. I am humble before God." In Blue America the self is more commonly large. People say in a million ways, "I am special. I have carved out my own unique way of life. I am independent. I make up my own mind."

In Red America there is very little one-upmanship. Nobody tries to be avant-garde in choosing a wardrobe. The chocolate-brown suits and baggy denim dresses hanging in local department stores aren't there by accident; people conspicuously want to be seen as not trying to dress to impress.

For a person in Blue America the blandness in Red America can be a little oppressive. But it's hard not to be struck by the enormous social pressure not to put on airs. If a Franklin County resident drove up to church one day in a shiny new Lexus, he would face huge waves of disapproval. If one hired a nanny, people would wonder who died and made her queen. . . .

I sometimes think that Franklin County takes its unpretentiousness a little too far. I wouldn't care to live there, because I'd find it too unchanging.

I prefer the subtle and not-so-subtle status climbing on my side of the Ego Curtain—it's more entertaining. Still, I can't help respecting the genuine modesty of Franklin County people. It shows up strikingly in data collected by Mediamark Research. In survey after survey, residents of conservative Red America come across as humbler than residents of liberal Blue America. About half of those who describe themselves as "very conservative" agree with the statement "I have more ability than most people," but nearly two thirds of those who describe themselves as "very liberal" agree. Only 53 percent of conservatives agree with the statement "I consider myself an intellectual," but 75 percent of liberals do. Only 23 percent of conservatives agree with the statement "I must admit that I like to show off," whereas 43 percent of liberals do.

A Cafeteria Nation

These differences in sensibility don't in themselves mean that America has become a fundamentally divided nation. As the sociologist Seymour Martin Lipset pointed out in *The First New Nation* (1963), achievement and equality are the two rival themes running throughout American history. Most people, most places, and most epochs have tried to intertwine them in some way.

Moreover, after bouncing between Montgomery and Franklin Counties, I became convinced that a lot of our fear that America is split into rival camps arises from mistaken notions of how society is shaped. Some of us still carry the old Marxist categories in our heads. We think that society is like a layer cake, with the upper class on top. And, like Marx, we tend to assume that wherever there is class division there is conflict. Or else we have a sort of *Crossfire* model in our heads: where would people we meet sit if they were guests on that show?

But traveling back and forth between the two counties was not like crossing from one rival camp to another. It was like crossing a high school cafeteria. Remember high school? There were nerds, jocks, punks, bikers, techies, druggies, God Squadders, drama geeks, poets, and Dungeons & Dragons weirdoes. All these cliques were part of the same school: they had different sensibilities; sometimes they knew very little about the people in the other cliques; but the jocks knew there would always be nerds, and the nerds knew there would always be jocks. That's just the way life is.

And that's the way America is. We are not a divided nation. We are a cafeteria nation. We form cliques (call them communities, or market segments, or whatever), and when they get too big, we form subcliques. Some people even get together in churches that are "nondenominational" or in political groups that are "independent." These are cliques built around the supposed rejection of cliques.

We live our lives by migrating through the many different cliques associated with the activities we enjoy and the goals we have set for ourselves.

Our freedom comes in the interstices; we can choose which set of standards to live by, and when.

We should remember that there is generally some distance between cliques—a buffer zone that separates one set of aspirations from another. People who are happy within their cliques feel no great compulsion to go out and reform other cliques. The jocks don't try to change the nerds. . . .

What unites the two Americas, then, is our mutual commitment to this way of life—to the idea that a person is not bound by his class, or by the religion of his fathers, but is free to build a plurality of connections for himself. . . .

Never has this been more apparent than in the weeks following the September 11 attacks. . . .

. . . If I had to boil down all the conversations I have had in Franklin and Montgomery Counties since September 11, the essence would be this: A horrible thing happened. We're going to deal with it. We're going to restore order. We got through Pearl Harbor. We're going to get through this. . . .

If the September 11 attacks rallied people in both Red and Blue America, they also neutralized the political and cultural leaders who tend to exploit the differences between the two. Americans are in no mood for a class struggle or a culture war. The aftermath of the attacks has been a bit like a national Sabbath, taking us out of our usual pleasures and distractions and reminding us what is really important. Over time the shock will dissipate. But in important ways the psychological effects will linger, just as the effects of John F. Kennedy's assassination have lingered. The early evidence still holds: although there are some real differences between Red and Blue America, there is no fundamental conflict. There may be cracks, but there is no chasm. Rather, there is a common love for this nation—one nation in the end.

What We Must Overcome

LANI GUINIER

For years many of us have been calling for a national conversation about what it means to be a multiracial democracy. We have enumerated the glaring flaws inherent in our winner-take-all form of voting, which has produced a steady decline in voter participation, underrepresentation of women and racial minorities in office, lack of meaningful competition and choice in most elections, and the general failure of politics to mobilize, inform, and inspire half the eligible electorate. Still, nothing changed. Democracy was an asterisk in political debate and the diagnosis for what ailed it was encompassed in vague references to "campaign finance reform." But the harm was not just in the money and its sources; the problem has been the rules of American democracy itself. Enter Florida and the surprising intervention by the United States Supreme Court in *Bush v. Gore.* On December 12, 2000, the Supreme Court selected the next president when, in the name of George W. Bush's rights to equal protection of the laws, it stopped the recounting of votes. Excoriated at the time for deciding an election, the Court majority's stout reading of equal protection is an invitation not just to future litigation but to a citizens' movement for genuine participatory democracy. The Court's decision—and the colossal legal fight that preceded it—might stimulate a real national debate about democracy. At minimum the ruling calls on us to consider what it means to be a multiracial democracy that has equal protection as its first principle. . . .

The *Bush v. Gore* majority, which went out on a limb to protect the rights of a single litigant, George W. Bush, has been noticeably less exercised about arbitrary or disparate treatment when such considerations are raised by voters who are racial minorities. Indeed, in a 1994 concurring opinion, when the claim to a meaningful and equally valued vote was raised by black litigants, Justice Clarence Thomas declared that the Court should avoid examining "electoral mechanisms that may affect the 'weight' given to a ballot duly cast." Even where congressional statutes, such as the Voting Rights Act, explicitly define the term "voting" to "include all action necessary to make a vote effective," Justice Thomas urged the Court to ignore the actual text of the statute.

The *Bush v. Gore* invitation to value votes equally, in order to "sustain the confidence that all citizens must have in the outcome of elections," should be heeded, but not in the form of legal wrangling before a judge. That it is time for political agitation rather then judicial activism may be the most important contribution of the *Bush v. Gore* opinion. . . .

Indeed, the Court's choice of language explicitly valuing "no person's vote over another's" ought to launch a citizen's movement similar to the 1960s civil rights marches that led to the Voting Rights Act, demonstrations in which citizens carried banners with the "one person, one vote" slogan. One vote, one value—meaning that everyone's vote should count toward the election of someone he or she voted for—should be the rallying cry of all who wish to restore the confidence that even the conservative Court majority agrees "all citizens must have in the outcome of elections." This movement, let's recall, began in the streets, was cautiously then boldly embraced by liberal politicians, and eventually led to raised grass-roots consciousness as well as national legislation. That is how democratic movements change the course of events—and in the process enrich and renew democracy.

Where's the Outrage?

Certainly many people outside the legal academy continue to feel alienated by the outcome of this presidential election. A survey released in early December from the Harvard Vanishing Voter project suggests that large majorities of the American people believe election procedures have been "unfair to the voters." Not surprisingly, nationwide those most likely to feel disenfranchised are blacks. In December 2000, almost 90 percent of black voters felt that way. One out of 10 blacks reported that they or someone in their family had trouble voting, according to a national report produced by Michael Dawson and Lawrence Bobo, of the Center for the Study of Race, Politics and Culture, and the W. E. B. Du Bois Institute. A CBS News poll, made public on the eve of the inauguration, found that 51 percent of the respondents said they considered Bush's victory a legitimate one, but only 19 percent of Democrats and 12 percent of blacks said so.

The anger over what happened in Florida has only been reinforced by the failure of the Democratic Party leadership to move quickly and seriously to engage the legitimacy issue. Right after November 7, when the perception first emerged that the election was being hijacked, the Gore campaign actively discouraged mass protest. On January 12, when Al Gore presided over the counting of the electoral college votes, it was only members of the Congressional Black Caucus (CBC) who rose, one by one, to protest the filing of Florida's votes. They could not get a single Democratic senator (from a body that includes not a single black representative) to join their objection. The silence of the white Democrats in Congress turned the CBC demonstration into an emphatic recapitulation of the election drama. As the presiding officer, Al Gore overruled the protests. The moment was especially poignant, because the Black Caucus members, in speaking out for Floridians whose votes were not counted, were speaking out for all Americans, while even their progressive white colleagues sat in awkward silence. E. J. Dionne, a columnist for *The Washington Post,* watched the drama unfold on television. Turning to his eight-year-old son, seated next to him, Dionne explained, "They are speaking out for us too." . . . As [James] Carroll wrote, "Those who sit atop the social and economic pyramid always speak of love, while those at the bottom always speak of justice."

The CBC protest shows that outrage over the election continues. But the CBC protest also speaks to the fact that the conversation about the true meaning of democracy is not happening yet, at least not at the highest levels of government. There is talk, of course, about fixing the mechanics of election balloting; but it is the rules themselves, and not just the vote-counting process, that are broken. This is all the more reason that the conversation, which needs to address issues of justice, not just compassion, also needs to rise up from communities as a citizen's movement.

Those who were disenfranchised—disproportionately black, poorer, and less well educated—were not asking for pity; they wanted democracy. Stories of long lines at polling places, confusing ballots, and strict limitations on how long voters could spend in the voting booth help explain why turnout numbers are skewed toward those who are wealthy, white, and better educated. We are a democracy that supposedly believes in universal suffrage, and yet the different turnout rates between high-income and low-income voters are far greater than in Europe, where they range from 5 percent to 10 percent. More than two-thirds of people in America with incomes greater than $50,000 voted, compared with one-third of those with incomes under $10,000. Many poor people are also less literate; for them time limits and complex ballots proved disabling when the menu of candidates was organized around lists of individuals rather than easily identified icons for political parties. Indeed, more ballots were "spoiled" in the presidential race than were cast for so-called spoiler Ralph Nader. The shocking number of invalid ballots is a direct result of antiquated voting mechanics, an elitist view of the relationship between education and citizenship, and an individualistic view of political participation that would shame any nation that truly believes in broad citizen participation.

Class, Race, and Balloting

In addition to class, the window into the workings of Florida's balloting allowed us to see how race affects—and in turn is affected by—voting rules and procedures. The election debacle revealed gaps not just in our democracy but in the way our democracy racializes public policy and then disenfranchises the victims of those policies. Old voting machines, more likely to reject ballots not perfectly completed, were disproportionately located in low-income and minority neighborhoods. These problems contributed to stunning vote-rejection numbers. According to *The New York Times,* black precincts in Miami-Dade County had votes thrown out at twice the rate of Hispanic (primarily Cuban and Republican) precincts and at close to four times the rate of white precincts. In that county alone, in predominantly black precincts, the *Times* said, "one in 11 ballots were rejected . . . a total of 9,904"—thousands more than Bush's margin of victory.

The balloting rules in Florida did not just incidentally disenfranchise minority voters; they apparently resulted from what many think were aggressive efforts to suppress black turnout. *The New York Times* also reported that county officials in Miami-Dade gave certain precincts—mostly the Hispanic (that is, Cuban and Republican) ones—laptop computers so that they could check names against the central county voter file. In black precincts, where there were a lot of recently registered voters whose names didn't appear on the local list, the precinct workers were not given computers and were supposed to call the county office to check the list—but no one answered the phones or the lines were busy, so countless voters, who were in fact registered, were just sent away.

Florida's minority residents and many others faced another structural hurdle to having their voices heard. Anyone convicted of a felony is permanently banned from voting in Florida and 12 other states (disproportionately from the Old Confederacy) even after they have paid their debt to society. As a result, 13 percent of black men nationwide and in some southern states as many as 30 percent of black men are disenfranchised. In Florida alone, more than 400,000 ex-felons, almost half of them black, could not vote last November. Also worth noting is that before the election Florida's secretary of state hired a firm to conduct a vigorous cleansing of the voting rolls—not just of Florida's felons, but also of ex-offenders from other states whose rights had been restored in those states and who were thus still legally eligible to vote in Florida. The Hillsborough County elections supervisor, for example, found that 54 percent of the voters targeted by the "scrub" were black, in a county where blacks make up 11 percent of the voting population. While Canada takes special steps to register former prisoners and encourage citizenship, Florida and other states ostracize them. . . .

The Soul of a Democracy Movement

Unfortunately, in pursuit of bipartisan civility, the Democratic Party leadership appears to be marching to a false harmony: Charmed by compassionate conservatism and conscious of middle-of-the-road swing voters' aversion to conflict, top Democrats have ignored issues of justice and the troubling disenfranchisement of many of the party's most loyal supporters. If we learn anything from the Supreme Court's role in the 2000 election travesty, it must be that when the issue is justice, the people—not the justices of the Court or the Democratic leaders in Washington—will lead. And if anything is true about the fiasco in Florida, it is the need for new leaders who are willing to challenge rather than acquiesce to unfair rules. New leadership will not come from a single, charismatic figure orchestrating deals out of Washington, D.C.; nor will it be provided by a group devoted only to remedying the disenfranchisement of black voters. What is needed instead is a courageous assembly of stalwart individuals who are willing to ask the basic questions the Black Caucus members raised—questions that go to the very legitimacy of our democratic procedures, not just in Florida but nationwide. These are likely to be individuals organized at the local level, possibly even into a new political party that is broadly conceived and dedicated to real, participatory democracy. Such a movement could build on the energy of black voter participation, which between 1996 and last year went from 10 percent to 15 percent in Florida and from 5 percent to 12 percent in Missouri.

But while black anger could fuel a citizens' movement or a new, European-style political party that seeks reforms beyond the mechanics of election day voting, the danger is that whites will be suspicious of the struggle if they perceive that its aim is simply to redress wrongs done to identifiable victims or to serve only the interests of people of color. And people of color can alienate potential supporters if they focus exclusively on vindicating the rights of minority voters and fail to emphasize three dramatic distortions in our present rules that undermine the ability of low-income and working people, women, and progressives, as well as racial minorities, to participate in a genuinely democratic transformation. These rules (1) limit voting to 12 hours on a workday and require registration weeks or even months in advance; (2) disenfranchise prisoners for the purpose of voting but count them for the purpose of allocating legislative seats . . . ; and (3) waste votes through winner-take-all elections. A pro-democracy movement has a good chance to succeed if it focuses on unfair rules whose dislocations may be felt first by blacks but whose effects actually disempower vast numbers of people across the country.

A pro-democracy movement would need to build on the experience of Florida to show how problems with disenfranchisement based on race and status signify systemic issues of citizen participation. Such mobilization would seek to recapture the passion in evidence immediately after the election as union leaders, civil rights activists, black elected officials, ministers, rabbis, and the president of the Haitian women's organization came together at a black church in Miami, reminded the assembly of the price their communities had paid for the right to vote, and vowed never to be disfranchised again. . . .

Although not encouraged by Democratic Party leaders, by joining their voices these Florida voters were beginning to realize their collective potential—as ordinary citizens—to become genuine democrats (with a small *d*). By highlighting our nation's wretched record on voting rules and practices, these impassioned citizens were raising the obvious questions: Do those in charge really want large citizen participation, especially if that means more participation by poor people and people of color? Even more, do Americans of all incomes and races realize that everyone loses when we tolerate disenfranchisement of some? And how can we tolerate the logjam of winner-take-all two-party monopoly, especially at the local level?

Enriching Democratic Choice

As the Florida meltdown suggests, the problem includes mechanical defects, but it is the rules themselves, not just old technology, that limit the political clout of entire communities. Weak democracy feeds on itself. There are some technical fixes worth pursuing. . . . But reform of voting mechanisms—while important—is not enough. The circumstances of this last election call for a larger focus on issues of representation and participation. A longer-term and more-far-ranging solution to the problems in Florida as well as those around the country would be to enrich democracy by broadening ways of reflecting and encouraging voter preferences.

For example, in South Africa, where the black majority now shares political power with the white minority, there is a successful system of proportional representation. Voters cast their ballots for the political party they feel most represents their interests, and the party gets seats in the legislature in proportion to the number of votes it receives. Instead of a winner-take-all situation in which there are losers who feel completely unrepresented when their candidate doesn't capture the top number of votes, each vote counts to enhance the political power of the party of the voters' choice. Under South Africa's party-list system, the party that gets 30 percent of the vote gets 30 percent of the seats. Or if the party gets only 10 percent of the vote, it still gets 10 percent of the seats in the legislature. Only because of this system does South Africa's white minority have any representation in the national legislature. Ironically, South Africa, only seven years out of apartheid, is more advanced in terms of practicing democratic principles than the United States is 150 years after slavery and 40 years after Jim Crow.

As June Zeitlin, executive director of the Women's Environment and Development Organization points out, proportional representation systems also benefit women. In a letter that *The New York Times* declined to publish, Zeitlin wrote: "Women are grossly underrepresented at all levels of government worldwide. However, women fare significantly better in proportional representation electoral systems. . . . The 10 countries with the highest percentage of women in parliament have systems that include proportional representation." . . .

Proportional representation reforms for legislative bodies, even Congress, would not even require an amendment to the U.S. Constitution. Nothing in the Constitution says that we have to use winner-take-all single-member districts. Since seizing the initiative in 1995, two Democratic members of the Congressional Black Caucus, Representatives Cynthia McKinney of Georgia and Mel Watt of North Carolina, have repeatedly introduced legislation called the Voter Choice Act, which provides for states to choose proportional representation voting. It's a system that should have great appeal not just for African Americans but for every group that has ever felt disenfranchised.

A pro-democracy movement would look seriously at forms of proportional representation that could assure Democrats in Florida, Republicans in Democratic-controlled states, and racial minorities and women in all states fair representation in the state legislatures. It would focus renewed attention on the importance of minority voters—racial, political, and urban minorities—gaining a more meaningful voice as well as a real opportunity to participate throughout the democratic process and not just on election day. The five-member Supreme Court majority allowed the interests of the Florida legislature (in obtaining the safe-harbor benefits of a congressional statute for certifying electors) to trump any remedy to protect the rights of the voters, about whom it was ostensibly so solicitous.

If legislatures are to enjoy such power to speak for all citizens, it is imperative that voters' voices be reflected in fully representative legislative bodies. Florida voters are closely divided along party lines, but in the legislature they are represented by an overwhelmingly Republican leadership. And the partisan acts of the Florida legislature in the 2000 election should focus renewed attention on how the winner-take-all system in a state legislature can fail to recognize the will of racial and political minorities: It wastes the votes of those whose ballots are cast and tabulated but don't lead to the election of any candidate they selected.

If we are not to abolish the electoral college, we might at least mitigate its winner-take-all effect and apportion electoral votes based on the popular split. In Florida, where all of the state's 25 electoral votes went to the Republican candidate, Bush could have gotten 13 votes and Gore 12 (or vice versa!). Such a system is perfectly constitutional and can be readily enacted by the state legislature. Two states do this already, although they use unfairly gerrymandered congressional districts rather than statewide proportions to allocate electoral college votes.

Proportional representation voting, which is used in most of the world's democracies, ensures that each voter's ballot counts when it is cast. Voters essentially "district" themselves by how they mark their ballots. The method thus eliminates the problem of gerrymandering by incumbents protecting their seats. Proportional voting could also encourage the development of local political organizations to educate and mobilize voters. Only when voters are vigilant, even after the voters are counted, shall we return to a government of, by, and for the people. Developing local grass-roots organizations that can monitor not only elections but also legislative actions is especially important in 2001, a year when every state legislature will be engaged in the decennial task of redistricting. The spread of such organizations—which a proportional representation system makes possible because the participants actually have a chance to win elections—could also fuel a new era of issue-centered politics in which people exercise their political views through advocacy groups focused on issues of concern to them. As Richard Berke has written in *The New York Times*:

> The first half of the last century was dominated by party-centered politics. Then came candidate-centered politics. Now, some foresee an era where the power moves to activists, who create local coalitions around specific issues. That could happen because, with the rise of the Internet, activists have far greater access to communication and organizing tools—and no longer have to rely on help from campaigns or party committees.

Local grass-roots and issue-centered coalitions are more likely if we adopt proportional representation because it rewards those who mobilize directly with seats in the local collective-decision-making body. And local multiparty organizing could effectively generate citizen engagement and meaningful participation not merely on election day but in between elections, too.

Of course, there are downsides to a politics that depends primarily on activists building multiple coalitions of overlapping constituencies through issue-oriented organizing. Creating such coalitions requires enormous energy; they often have to be built from scratch, and for every one that gets it together, dozens will fall short. . . .

But the upside is that coalitions that start with narrowly focused issues and then engage multiple constituencies can create sustainable alliances even after an election. They can grow into institutions that use their aggregated power again and again—getting organized labor to join fights that affect Latinos and gays, civil rights groups to join labor, and so forth. These coalitions can also aspire to an electoral strategy and nurture leaders who can eventually become candidates.

Over time, the best of these permanent coalitions might begin to look a little bit like parties: presumably they would have broad platforms, sizable but loose constituencies, and candidates and elected officials allied to them. Proportional representation would lower the bar to successful cross-constituency and multiracial-coalition organizing. But even with a proportional voting system, realizing a fully democratic movement would still require us to fight fragmentation and to aggregate, rotate, and share power among progressive interests in a lasting and sustainable way.

"One vote, one value," a notion underscored by the conservative Supreme Court majority, ironically could become the rallying cry of a multiracial and multi-issue grass-roots movement of voters throughout the nation. It could herald a new era of issue-centered rather than candidate-centered politics. Black leaders may be key in some communities; union activists or environmentalists in others. But in the end, an aroused and engaged citizenry—one committed to a broad, multiracial democracy—will be our best, indeed our only protection to ensure that every vote counts and that every citizen can truly vote. Mobilizing citizens requires local, grass-roots political organizations accountable to the people themselves instead of ad hoc candidate machines that are too often driven by money. Voting should not be an obstacle course of arbitrary deadlines, lousy lists, untrained poll workers, and outdated ballot technology. Rather, voting should be just the first step in a democratic system by which we, the people—through democratic institutions that are accountable to all of us—actually rule.

DISCUSSION QUESTIONS

1. For both Guinier and Brooks, what are the fundamental conflicts in U.S. society? Do elections reflect these debates or deflect them?

2. How would Guinier comment on Brooks's assertion that sensibility differences are the fundamental divide between Red and Blue America? How would Brooks comment on Guinier's idea that U.S. society is divided between races and classes?

3. Brooks dismisses observers who see big class differences among Americans. How would Guinier argue with his assertion?

4. Guinier sees a potential social movement for greater democracy as a potential reform force in U.S. politics. What would Brooks say about the state of democracy and the potential for a reform movement?

▪ SUGGESTED READINGS AND INTERNET RESOURCES

For the most exhaustive account on the state of political participation in America, see Sidney Verba, Kay Lehman Schlozman, and Henry Brady, *Voice and Equality* (Cambridge, Mass.: Harvard University Press, 1995). The most thought-provoking book is Robert Putnam, *Bowling Alone: The Collapse and Revival of American Community* (New York: Simon and Schuster, 2000). For general accounts of the 2000 election, see Gerald Pomper, ed. *The Election of 2000* (Chatham, N.J.: Chatham House Publishers, 2001); and Michael Nelson, ed. *The Elections of 2000* (Washington, D.C.: Congressional Quarterly Press, 2001). For specifics about the legal controversies of the 2000 election, see Richard Posner, *Breaking the Deadlock,* (Princeton; N.J.: Princeton University Press, 2001); and E. J. Dionne and William Kristol, *Bush v. Gore: The Court Cases and the Commentary* (Washington, D.C.: Brookings Institution Press, 2001).

VoterMarch
www.votermarch.org
This is the web site of a major group that is still contesting the outcome of the 2000 election.

Electronic Policy Network
www.epn.org
This web site is that of many nonpartisan but liberal groups who support Lani Guinier's approaches to the 2000 elections.

Committee for the Study of the American Electorate
www.csae.org
This site provides interesting data on voter turnout in recent elections.

Center for Democracy and Citizenship
www.publicwork.org
This site offers information about various projects to increase citizen participation.

11

Campaigns and Elections: Organized Money Versus (Dis)Organized People?

rom the nineteenth century's camp meetings and torchlight parades to today's sound bites and attack ads, political campaigns are part of American democratic folklore. Despite their hoopla and hype, electoral campaigns are serious business. Without them, voters wouldn't have a choice, couldn't get organized, and would judge their would-be rulers in ignorance and isolation.

Today, however, a chorus of critics complains about campaigns. Campaigns often seem to be personality contests that trivialize issues rather than engage the electorate. Supercharged accusations fly between candidates, without much sense of their truth value. The media often compound the problem through sensationalized coverage. Campaign professionals and spin doctors seem to orchestrate images and manipulate voters rather than respond to their deeper aspirations. Sensing that they're being used, many citizens become cynical spectators or withdraw from the electoral process entirely.

While there are few unqualified fans of modern campaigns, there are some defenders of the process. Most of the voters, most of the time, seem to learn something from campaigns, and when voters care enough to participate, the democratic debate seems to improve. The 1992 and 1994 electoral contests, some say, were more substantive because many voters demanded precision and substance from the candidates and the parties. Perhaps campaigns are no better or worse than the society from which they emerge.

High-tech campaigns may also be inevitable. Old-style, door-to-door campaigning just isn't possible in a country of 280 million people, whose attention is constantly distracted from politics by the burdens of work and family and the diversions of entertainment. Politicians and parties have to rely on costly and sophisticated advertising, focus groups, and public opinion polls because it is impossible to know every voter and because there is considerable competition for attention. In any case, perhaps campaigns are no worse than they used to be; competitive elections have always been messy affairs, and perhaps today's critics romanticize the past.

Nonetheless, there are some notable developments in modern election campaigns that deserve extended scrutiny. Successful campaigns have always had ample amounts of cash, but today the new technology of politics—polls, advertising, and image-makers—requires money in amounts that seem to utterly exclude the unconnected or the unrich. Today, political campaigns may be monopolized by interests and candidates concerned less with addressing the needs of voters than those of the privileged, that slender slice of American society that contributes the cash that makes campaigns effective.

Raising money has almost always mattered in modern U.S. electoral campaigns, but the elections of the 1990s and 2000 witnessed a quantum leap in expenditures. In 2000, the total cost of federal elections soared to $3 billion. The presidential contest's price was $250 million, while winning House candidates spent an average of $900,000 apiece—double the 1992 amount. To get around federal caps on contributions to individual candidates, the major political parties have pioneered new ways to collect and disperse funds. The parties spent over $480 million in so-called soft money in 2000, and interest groups spent an estimated (and undisclosed) $300 million in so-called issue advocacy efforts.

The vast bulk of the growing cash pile is donated by very affluent individuals, corporations, and trade associations organized into political action committees. This phenomenon has sparked an intense movement for reform, spurred in part by Arizona senator John McCain, a Republican, and leading House and Senate Democrats.

After six years of procedural maneuvering and delay, both houses of Congress passed, and President Bush reluctantly signed, a major revision of campaign finance laws in early 2002. The new law banned soft money contributions, raised the allowable limits for individual contributions to candidates, and called for a ban on political ads sponsored by interest groups. The new law's constitutionality was immediately questioned, and the Supreme Court will be hearing arguments as early as 2003. Campaign finance reformers relished this long-sought victory. Yet may labelled the "McCain-Feingold" bill a modest first step toward a more extensive reform. This would be a voluntary system that promoted public financing of political campaigns—a practice already in effect in Maine, Vermont, Massachusetts, and Arizona.

Is the cost of money-driven campaigns too high? Or is the right to contribute money to candidates an expression of a lively democracy? Answers to these questions provide judgment about the state of American democracy itself. For people who believe in popular democracy, today's campaigns have to be judged by how well or poorly they promote talk and participation by ordinary voters. While money, advertising, polling, and professional marketing may never disappear from contemporary campaigns, do these drown out democratic activity by volunteers and organizations that have little money to give? Popular democrats look to a historical standard by which to judge modern campaigns. Which is more important: organized money or organized people? Do modern campaigns mean that only candidates who are wealthy or backed by wealthy people can succeed? And does money undermine the egalitarian spirit of one citizen, one vote, which is supposed to be the basis of democracy itself?

For elite democrats, money's corrupting role is far from clear. Money is said to promote effective free speech, for to be heard requires resources and organization. Reformers, in their zeal to create a wall between money and politics, don't understand why generations of reformers have been ineffective; no matter what the laws intend, organized money in a free society will always find a way to be heard. The best that we can hope for in a free society is that the sources of money be made known to the electorate. Existing laws passed in the 1970s could be beefed up to further disclosure, and there are already ample laws on the books to limit the size of contributions to individual candidates. Anything more than that, elite democrats say, would be a violation of the democratic norm of free speech and would backfire on democracy itself.

The two essays reprinted here both articulate and expand on these arguments. Bradley Smith, an Ohio law professor and a GOP appointee to the Federal Election Commission, provides a persuasive case against further efforts to regulate campaign contributions. He finds little evidence to support the charges of people who believe that campaign donations corrupt the political process and much evidence that limits on campaign spending would prevent full debate and discussion of contentious political issues. Sociologists Dan Clawson, Alan Neustadtl, and Mark Weller respond with a careful study of what corporate contributors expect from politicians as they hand out the cash. These authors argue that business campaign contributions "subvert democracy" for numerous reasons, and they propose a system of public financing of campaigns to level the playing field.

While reading these essays, you might think about the following questions: How would the "Dollars and Votes" authors respond to Smith's charge that regulating campaign money never works? How would Smith deal with the problem of the amount of time politicians must devote to fund-raising? All the authors rely on a historical standard of democracy to defend their claims. What do the authors of each essay mean by the term?

Free Speech Requires Campaign Money

BRADLEY A. SMITH

In 1974, Congress passed amendments to the Federal Elections Campaign Act that, for the first time in our nation's history, seriously undertook to regulate political campaigns. Most states followed suit, and virtually overnight, politics became a heavily regulated industry.

Yet we now see, on videotape and in White House photos, shots of the President of the United States meeting with arms merchants and drug dealers; we learn of money being laundered through Buddhist nuns and Indonesian gardeners; we read that acquaintances of the President are fleeing the country, or threatening to assert Fifth Amendment privileges to avoid testifying before Congress.[1] Regulation, we were told two decades ago, would free our elected officials from the clutches of money, but they now seem to devote more time than ever before to pursuing campaign cash. The 1974 reforms, we were promised, would open up political competition, yet the purely financial advantage enjoyed by incumbents in congressional races has increased almost threefold. Regulation was supposed to restore confidence in government, yet the percentage of Americans who trust their government to "do what is right most of the time" is half what it was before the 1974 act, and campaigns themselves seem nastier and less informative.

Well, say apologists for the law, if we have failed, it is only because our labors have just begun. If our goals seem further away, we must redouble our efforts. We must ban political action committees (PAC's). We must prevent "bundling," a procedure whereby a group collects contributions from its members and delivers them all at once to a candidate's election committee. We must ban large contributions to political parties ("soft money"). . . .

If existing regulation has failed so spectacularly, and existing laws are being broken seemingly at will, is more regulation the solution? Before we rush off on another round, it may be worthwhile to examine the premises on which the impulse to regulate campaign finance is based. Each of them is severely flawed. . . .

II

The first assumption underlying proposals for campaign-finance regulation is that too much money is being spent on political campaigning. The amounts are

---

1. Smith is writing about allegations regarding the Clinton White House's fundraising practices during the 1996 election.

often described in near-apocalyptic terms. Candidates, we are informed, amass "huge war chests" from "fat cats" who "pour their millions" into campaigns and "stuff the pockets" of representatives in an "orgy" of contributions. Expenditures "skyrocket," leaving legislators "awash" in "obscene" amounts of cash.

Hyperbole aside, however, the amount spent each year on all political activity in the United States, from every ballot referendum to races for every office from dog catcher to President, is less than the amount spent on potato chips. Total spending on congressional races in 1995–96 was less than what is spent annually on Barbie dolls. Total PAC contributions in federal elections in 1995–96 were just about equal to the amount needed to produce the most recent *Batman* movie.

On a per-voter basis, our expenditures are equally low: less than $2.50 per eligible voter per year, or about the cost of a single video rental, for all congressional races, including all primaries. . . .

Perhaps more relevant than any of these comparisons are the amounts spent on political campaigning versus other types of advertising. In 1996, the Home Depot corporation alone spent more on advertising than federal law allowed Bill Clinton, Bob Dole, and Ross Perot put together to spend on the general election. Although Michael Huffington was roundly criticized for "exorbitant" spending in his 1994 race for a Senate seat from California, it cost him less than what Sony International spent in the same year to promote a single compact disc by Michael Jackson. . . .

The plain truth is that it costs money to communicate, and there is no reason to expect that political communication should come free. This is the crucial insight of the Supreme Court's 1976 decision in *Buckley* v. *Valeo,* a case issuing from a challenge to the 1974 Federal Elections Campaign Act by a broad coalition of groups ranging from the ACLU to the Conservative and Libertarian parties. There the Court struck down mandatory limits on campaign spending as well as limits on what a candidate could spend from his own personal funds. The Court did not say, as its critics have alleged, that money equals speech; rather, it recognized that limits on spending can restrict speech just as surely as can a direct prohibition. Imagine, for example, if newspapers were limited to $100,000 a year for publishing costs: most would go out of business, and those that remained would become very thin indeed. . . .

Spending on political advertisements is important to educate voters, increasing their interest in elections and their knowledge of candidates and issues. Repetition plays an important part in this process: the electorate's hatred of 30-second campaign ads is surpassed only by its desire to get its political information by means of those same ads. And the ads cost money.

Although campaign-finance reformers often appeal to the public's unhappiness with negative ads, negativity has long been a feature of political campaigns, and money is not the source of it. (As long ago as 1796, the presidential candidate Thomas Jefferson was attacked as "an atheist, anarchist, demagogue, coward, mountebank, trickster, and Francomaniac." . . .) In fact, if the goal is to have positive campaigns, even *more* money would be needed, for the simple reason that positive ads are less memorable than negative ones and hence need to be repeated more frequently. Besides, a limit on spending would mean that candidates would have to depend more on the media to get their message across, and the press is often more negative in its campaign coverage than the contestants themselves.

There is, finally, no objective criterion by which to measure whether "too much" is being spent on political campaigns. But as we have seen, spending in this country is not high. Considering the vital importance of an informed electorate to democratic government, it is hard to discern why it should be lower.

The hidden premise behind the idea that too much is being spent on campaigns is that money "buys" election results—a second assumption of reformers. It is true that the candidate who spends the most money wins most of the time. But the cause-and-effect relationship between spending and victory is nowhere near so straightforward as this might suggest.

For one thing, the formulation neglects the desire of donors to give to candidates likely to win. In other words, it may be the prospect of victory that attracts money, not the other way around. . . . Or a candidate's fundraising edge may simply reflect the relative status of his popularity, later to be confirmed or disconfirmed at the polls.

Even when the ability to raise and spend money actually succeeds in changing the outcome of a race, it is ballots, not dollars, that ultimately decide who wins, and ballots reflect the minds of voters. All that spending can do is attempt to change those minds. It would be a strange First Amendment that cut off protection for speech at the point where speech began to influence people's views, and it reflects a remarkable contempt for the electorate to suggest that it is incapable of weighing the arguments being tendered for its consideration.

Indeed, there is ample evidence that the electorate does so discriminate, and that higher spending in behalf of a losing argument will not necessarily translate into electoral triumph. In the Republican takeover of Congress in 1994, for example, the 34 victorious challengers spent, on average, just two-thirds of the amount spent by their Democratic opponents, who also enjoyed the inherent advantage of incumbency. By contrast, in the 1996 race for the Republican presidential nomination, Phil Gramm, who raised the most money, was the first to have to drop out. As Michael Malbin of the Rockefeller Institute of Government has observed, "Having money means having the ability to be heard; it does not mean that voters will like what they hear."

The key variable in elections is not which candidate spends the most, but whether or not challengers are able to spend enough to overcome the advantage of incumbency and make their names and issues known to voters. Once they reach this threshold, races are up for grabs. For example, in the 1996 House races, 40 percent of challengers who spent over $600,000 won, as opposed to just 3 percent who spent less than $600,000. Once the threshold was crossed, it mattered little whether or not the challenger was outspent, or by how much. The problem, if it can be called that, is not that some candidates "buy" elections by spending too much, but that others spend too little to get their message to the voters.

Still another assumption of reformers is that, if we truly cared about self-government and participatory democracy, we would be better off if campaigns were funded by many small contributors rather than by fewer large ones.

In fact, the burden of financing political campaigns has *always* fallen to a small minority, both in the United States and in other democracies. Nearly eighteen million Americans now make contributions to a political party, candidate, or PAC during an election cycle. Although this figure is higher than at any other time in American history, and represents a broader base of voluntary public support than has been enjoyed by any other system of campaign funding anywhere, it still comes to less than 10 percent of the voting-age population.

Which sorts of candidates are typically able to raise large sums of money in small amounts, as the reformers prefer? In the years prior to federal funding of presidential campaigns, the two most successful in this respect were Barry Goldwater and George McGovern. The former raised $5.8 million from over 400,000 contributors in 1964, only to suffer a landslide defeat, while the latter, who raised almost $15 million from donors making average contributions of about $20, lost in an even bigger landslide eight years later. More recently, Oliver North raised approximately $20 million, almost all from small contributors, for his 1994 U.S. Senate race, outspent his rival by almost four to one, and still lost to a candidate plagued by personal scandal—primarily because the electorate, rightly or wrongly, viewed him as too "extreme."

What these examples suggest is that the ability to raise large sums in small contributions can be a sign less of broad public support, as reformers assert, than of fervent backing by an ideological minority. Other groups positioned to exert influence by this means tend to be those (like unions) in possession of an ongoing structure for mobilizing their constituents or those we usually call "special interests." It is the inchoate, grass-roots public that more often fails to make its interests known, and is therefore frequently reliant on individuals with large fortunes to finance movements that will represent it. . . .

Ironically, the banning of large contributions, which means that no single gift is likely to make much difference in a political race, gives potential donors little incentive to become involved. A radical campaign can overcome this difficulty: its supporters tend to be motivated more by ideology than by rational calculations of a candidate's chances of winning. But this just further underscores the way in which banning large contributions can help render the political system more rather than less vulnerable to forces on the fringes of the mainstream—hardly, one presumes, the result the reformers have in mind.

A corollary fallacy entertained by reformers is that the financial resources placed at a candidate's disposal should ideally reflect his level of popular support. But this is to confuse the purpose of elections with the purpose of campaigns. The former do measure popular support. The latter, however, are about something else: persuading voters, and *improving* one's level of support. This, as we have seen, requires monetary expenditures, and it is a sign of health in a democracy when such expenditures are forthcoming. . . .

Perhaps no belief is more deeply rooted in the psyche of reformers—and of the public at large—than that the money drawn into the system through political campaigns corrupts not only the campaigns themselves but, once a candidate is elected, the entire legislative process. Many office-holders have themselves complained about the influence of money in the legislature. But political scientists and economists who have studied this matter have consistently concluded otherwise. As John Lott and Stephen Bronars, the authors of one such study, conclude: "Our tests strongly reject the notion that campaign contributions buy politicians' votes. . . . Just like voters, contributors appear able to sort [out] politicians who intrinsically value the same things that they do."

The primary factors affecting a legislator's voting record are personal ideology, party affiliation, and constituent wishes—not contributions. Does anybody really think [Texas GOP Senator] Phil Gramm would suddenly drop his opposition to gun control if the National Rifle Association (NRA) ceased contributing to his campaigns? Of course not: the NRA supports Gramm *because* he opposes gun control, and so, almost certainly, do many if not most of his Texas constituents.

This makes perfect sense. Individuals who enter politics usually do so because they have strong views on political issues; party support is almost always more important to election than any one contribution; and, to repeat, a legislator wins with votes, not dollars. For a politician to adopt an unpopular or unwise position that will cost him voter support in exchange for a $5,000 campaign contribution—the maximum amount allowed under federal law—would be counterproductive, to say the least.

This is not to say that other factors never come into play. A legislator may be concerned about how his vote will be reported in the press, or whether an opponent can easily caricature him in a negative ad. Personal friendships may affect a voting decision, as may the advice of aides and staff, itself often influenced by ideology. Money is another such secondary factor, but it is only one, and not necessarily the political commodity of greatest value. Many of the most influential Washington lobbying groups, including the American Association of Retired Persons, the National Education Association, and the American Bar Association, do not make political contributions. The NRA does have a large PAC, but it also has nearly two million members who care intensely about its issues. Although gun-control advocates complain that the NRA outspends them, the more important fact is that it also outvotes them.

Finally, most issues find well-financed lobbies on both sides. A seemingly dull proposal to introduce a one-dollar coin, for example, may line up metal companies, vending-machine manufacturers, and coin laundries on one side, paper and ink companies on the other. Similarly with higher-profile issues like tort reform, where well-financed insurance interests take one position and equally well-financed trial lawyers the other. At least one set of these contributors, and often both, will suffer enormous *losses* in the legislative process, a fact often ignored by reformers.

When push comes to shove, even the most ardent reformers are rarely able to point to a specific instance of corruption. Ask a reformer to name which of our 535 Congressmen and Senators are acting contrary to what they believe to be the public good, or to what their constituents desire, because of campaign contributions, and the answer every time is some variation of "It's the system that's corrupt." But if we cannot name individuals corrupted by the system, on what basis are we to conclude that corruption is a problem intrinsic to the "system"?

III

When it came time to fight the American Revolution, the founders of this nation did not go to the king seeking matching funds with which to finance their revolt. Instead, in the Declaration of Independence, they pledged their fortunes as well as their lives and sacred honor.

Today, in order to cure the alleged problem of fortunes in politics, reformers offer a variety of complex schemes aimed at *preventing* private citizens from demonstrating their commitment to democratic political change. Former Senator Bill Bradley and House Minority Leader Richard Gephardt claim that we need a constitutional amendment to overturn the *Buckley* decision. In Gephardt's sweeping formulation, there is a "direct conflict" between "freedom of speech and our desire for healthy campaigns in a healthy democracy," and "you can't have both." Their proposed amendment, if enacted, would grant a greater degree of protection to commercial speech, flag burning, and Internet porn than to the discussion of political candidates and issues.

Meanwhile, "moderate" reformers continue to push the McCain-Feingold bill, lately shorn of a ban on PAC's that even its sponsors admit was "probably" unconstitutional. Even so, this bill would place vast new limits on the freedom of political discussion, ban most contributions to political parties to pay for voter registration, slate cards, rallies, and get-out-the-vote drives, and restrict speech in ways directly prohibited by standing Supreme Court decisions.[2]

If it is not the case that too much money is spent on campaigns, or that money, rather than the character of a handful of elected officials, is the source of political corruption, or that large contributors buy elections or in some way frustrate "true democracy," why should we tolerate such gross infringements of traditional First Amendment freedoms? What would be accomplished by measures like those being proposed by the reformers that would not be better accomplished by minimal disclosure laws that simply require the reporting of all sources of financial support?

Of course, disclosure laws may also be broken, as they appear to have been in the 1996 campaign. Character matters, and the rule has yet to be invented that someone will not succeed in violating. But what all the reformers overlook, from the most extreme to the most moderate, is that we already have, in the First Amendment, a deeply considered response to the problems

2. Opposition from Senate Republicans and Senate Majority Leader Trent Lott (R-Mississippi) prevented the McCain-Feingold bill from reaching the Senate floor in 1998. In early 2002, a modified version of McCain-Feingold was passed by Congress and signed by President Bush.

inherent in democratic elections—and one that is far superior to the supposedly enlightened system of regulation with which we are now saddled.

By assuring freedom of speech and the press, the First Amendment allows for exposure of government corruption and improper favors, whether these consist of White House meetings with drug dealers or huge tax breaks for tobacco companies. By keeping the government out of the electoral arena, it allows for robust criticism of government itself, and prevents incumbents from manipulating the election-law machinery in their own favor. It frees grass-roots activists and everyday speech alike from suffocating state regulation, thereby furthering the democratic aim of political discussion. And it allows candidates to control their own message rather than having to rely on the filters of the press or the vagaries of bureaucrats and judges called upon to decide which forms of speech are to be limited as "endorsements or attacks," and which allowed as "genuine debate."

In the vast muddle that has been made by our decades-old regulatory folly, the only real question concerns whose logic we will now follow: the logic of those who gave us our existing campaign-finance laws and who, despite a disastrous record, now want license to "reform" them still further, or the logic of the founders who gave us the First Amendment. For most Americans, I suspect, the choice would be an easy one.

Dollars and Votes

DAN CLAWSON,
ALAN NEUSTADTL, AND
MARK WELLER

I magine the November election is just a few weeks away, and your friend Sally Robeson is seriously considering running for Congress two years from now. This year the incumbent in your district, E. Chauncey DeWitt III, will (again!) be reelected by a substantial margin, but you and Sally hate Chauncey's positions on the issues and are convinced that with the right campaign he can be beaten. Sally is capable, articulate, well informed, respected in the community, politically and socially connected, charming, good at talking to many kinds of people, and highly telegenic. She has invited you and several other politically active friends to meet with her immediately after the election to determine what she would need to do to become a viable candidate.

From "Follow the Money" and "Scandal or System," which appear in *Dollars and Votes: How Business Campaign Contributions Subvert Democracy*, by Dan Clawson, Alan Neustadtl, and Mark Weller. Reprinted by permission of Temple University Press. © 1988 by Temple University. All Rights Reserved.

The meeting that takes place covers a host of topics: What are the key issues? On which of these are Sally's stands popular, and on which unpopular? What attacks, and from what quarters, will be launched against her? What individuals or groups can she count on for support? How, why, and where is the incumbent vulnerable? But lurking in the background is the question that cannot be ignored: *Can Sally (with the help of her friends and backers) raise enough money to be a contender?*

This is the *money primary, the first, and, in many instances, the most important round of the contest.* It eliminates more candidates than any other hurdle. Because it eliminates them so early and so quietly, its impact is often unobserved. To make it through, candidates don't have to come in first, but they do need to raise enough money to be credible contenders. Although having the most money is no guarantee of victory, candidates who don't do well in the money primary are no longer serious contenders. . . .

How much is needed? If Sally hopes to win, rather than just put up a good fight, she, you, and the rest of her supporters will need to raise staggering amounts. (At least they are staggering from the perspective of most Americans. . . .) In order to accumulate the *average* amount for major-party congressional candidates in the general election, you will collectively need to raise $4,800 next week. And the week after. And *every* week for the next two years.

But even that is not enough. The average amount includes many candidates who were never "serious"; that is, they didn't raise enough to have a realistic hope of winning. If you and your friends want to raise the average amount spent by a *winning* candidate for the House, you'll have to come up with $6,730 next week and every single week until the election, two years away.[1]

Well, you say, your candidate is hardly average. She is stronger, smarter, more politically appealing, and more viable than the "average" challenger. You think she can win even if she doesn't raise $6,730 a week. Let's use past experience—the results of the 1996 elections—to consider the likelihood of winning for challengers, based on how much money they raised. In 1996 more than 360 House incumbents were running for reelection; only 23 of them were beaten by their challengers. The average successful challenger spent $1,045,361—that is, he or she raised an average of over $10,000 every week for two years. What were the chances of winning without big money? Only one winning challenger spent less than $500,000, 12 spent between a half-a-million and a million dollars, and 10 spent more than a million dollars. Furthermore, 13 of the 23 winning challengers outspent the incumbent. A House challenger who can't raise at least a half-million dollars doesn't have a one percent chance of winning. . . .

In the Senate, even more money is needed. Suppose your candidate were going to run for the Senate, and started fundraising immediately after an election, giving her six years to prepare for the next election. How much money would she need to raise each and every week for those *six* years? The average winning Senate candidate raised approximately $15,000 per week.

---

1. In 2000, the figure was around $9,000.

For presidential candidates, the stakes are, of course, much higher: "The prevailing view is that for a politician to be considered legitimate, he or she must collect at least $20 million by the first of January 2000." Presumably any candidate who does not do so is "illegitimate" and does not belong in the race.[2]

If you collectively decide that the candidate you plan to back will need to raise $7,000 per week (for the House; $15,000 per week for the Senate), how will you do it? Suppose you hold a $10-per-person fundraiser—a barbecue in the park on Memorial Day or Labor Day. Even if 500 people attend, the affair will gross only $5,000, and net considerably less, no matter how cheap the hot dogs and hamburgers. And that takes no account of the problems of persuading 500 people to attend—just notifying them of the event is a major undertaking—or what it would mean to hold such an event every week, not just on Labor Day. In order to get through the money primary, an alternative strategy is needed, so candidates, especially incumbents, increasingly prefer to raise money at "big ticket" events. Selling 10 tickets for a $1,000-per-person fundraiser brings in more than twice as much as the 500-person barbecue in the park.

Who is likely to cough up a thousand bucks to attend a fundraiser? . . . A disproportionate number of such contributors are corporate political action committees (PACs), executives, and lobbyists. One typical version of the $1,000-per-person fundraiser is a breakfast: The candidate and 10 to 30 PAC officers and lobbyists from a particular industry (trucking, banking, oil and gas exploration). Even with a lavish breakfast, the candidate's net take is substantial. If enough lobbyists and corporate executives can be persuaded to come, perhaps the candidate could get by on one fundraiser every couple of weeks.

Coming up with the money is a major hassle; even for incumbents, it requires constant effort. *National Journal,* probably the single most authoritative source on the Washington scene, reports that "there is widespread agreement that the congressional money chase has become an unending marathon, as wearying to participants as it is disturbing to spectators," and quoted an aide to a Democratic senator as observing, "During hearings of Senate committees, you can watch senators go to phone booths in the committee rooms to dial for dollars." . . .

Long before the 1996 election, politicians felt that they had no choice: The Senate majority leader reported that "public officials are consumed with the unending pursuit of money to run election campaigns." Senators not only leave committee hearings for the more crucial task of calling people to beg for money. They also chase all over the country, because their reelection is more dependent on meeting rich people two thousand miles from home than on meeting their own constituents. Thomas Daschle, the current Democratic leader in the Senate, reports that, in the two years prior to his election to the Senate, he "flew to California more than 20 times to meet with prospective contributors," going there almost as often as he went to the largest city in his home state of South Dakota. . . .

---

2. Each of the major candidates had raised more than $30 million by January 2000. George W. Bush alone raised $67 million by January 2000.

Not only is it necessary to raise lots of money; it is important—for both incumbents and challengers—to raise it early. Senator Rudy Boschwitz, Republican of Minnesota, was clear about this as a strategy. He spent $6 million getting reelected in 1984, and had raised $1.5 million of it by the beginning of the year, effectively discouraging the most promising Democratic challengers. After the election he wrote, and typed up himself, a secret evaluation of his campaign strategy:

> "Nobody in politics (except me!) likes to raise money, so I thought the best way of discouraging the toughest opponents from running was to have a few dollars in the sock. *I believe it worked.* . . . *From all forms of fundraising I raised $6 million plus and got 3 or 4 (maybe even 5) stories and cartoons* that irked me," he said. "In retrospect, I'm glad I had the money. . . ."

The Contributors' Perspective

Candidates need money, lots of it, if they are to have any chance of winning. The obvious next question . . . is who gives, why, and what they expect for it.

Contributions are made for many different reasons. The candidate's family and friends chip in out of loyalty and affection. Others contribute because they are asked to do so by someone who has done favors for them. People give because they agree with the candidate's stand on the issues, either on a broad ideological basis or on a specific issue. Sometimes these donations are portrayed as a form of voting—people show that they care by putting their money where their mouth is, anyone can contribute, and the money raised reflects the wishes of the people. Even for these contributions, however, if voting with dollars replaces voting at the ballot box, then the votes will be very unequally distributed: the top 1 percent of the population by wealth will have more "votes" than the bottom 90 percent of the population. In the 1996 elections, less than one-fourth of one percent of the population gave contributions of $200 or more to a federal candidate. PACs and large contributors provide most of the money, however; small contributors accounted for under one-third of candidate receipts.

It is not just that contributions come from the well-to-do. Most contributors have a direct material interest in what the government does or does not do. Their contributions, most of them made directly or indirectly by business, provide certain people a form of leverage and "access" not available to the rest of us. The chair of the political action committee at one of the twenty-five largest manufacturing companies in the United States explained to us why his corporation has a PAC:

> The PAC gives you access. It makes you a player. These congressmen, in particular, are constantly fundraising. Their elections are very expensive, and getting increasingly expensive each year. So they have an ongoing need for funds. . . .
>
> You know, some congressman has got X number of ergs of energy and here's a person or a company who wants to come see him and give

him a thousand dollars, and here's another one who wants to just stop by and say hello. And he only has time to see one. Which one? So the PAC's an attention getter.

So-called soft money, where the amount of the contribution is unlimited, might appear to be an exception: Isn't $100,000 enough to buy a guaranteed outcome? . . . It is *not,* at least not in any simple and straightforward way. PAC contributions are primarily for members of Congress; they are for comparatively small amounts, but enough to gain access to individual members of Congress. The individual member, however, has limited power. Soft money donations are best thought of as a way of gaining access to the president, top party leaders, and the executive branch. These individuals are more powerful than ordinary members of Congress, so access to them comes at a higher price. . . . It does not—and is not expected to—*guarantee* a quid pro quo. . . .

Why Business?

In business-government relations most attention becomes focused on instances of scandal. The real issue, however, is not one or another scandal or conflict of interest, but rather the *system* of business-government relations, and especially of campaign finance, that offers business so many opportunities to craft loopholes, undermine regulations, and subvert enforcement. . . .

Business and the way it uses money and power . . . subverts the democratic process. This runs counter to the conventional wisdom, which treats all campaign contributions as equally problematic. A "balanced" and "objective" approach would, we are told, condemn both business and labor; each reform that primarily restricts business should be matched by one that restricts labor. We've heard these arguments, thought them over, and rejected them. They assume that what we have now is "balance" and that all changes should reinforce the existing relations of power. We see no reason to accept that as an a priori assumption.

Why are business campaign contributions more of a problem than contributions by labor (or women, or environmentalists)? First, because business contributes far more money. According to a study by the Center for Responsive Politics, in [1996] business outspent labor by an 11 to 1 margin.[3] Most reports about campaign finance give the impression that labor contributes roughly as much as business—a distortion of the reality.

Second, . . . beyond the world of campaign finance, business has far more power than labor, women's groups, or environmentalists.

Third, business uses campaign contributions in a way few other groups do, as part of an "access" process that provides corporations a chance to shape the details of legislation, crafting loopholes that undercut the stated

---

3. The disparity was 14 to 1 in 2000.

purpose of the law. Other groups do this on rare occasions; business does so routinely. Businesses are far more likely than other donors to give to *both* sides in a race; nearly all the soft money donors who gave to both sides were corporations. . . .

Fourth, there is a fundamental difference between corporate and labor PAC contributions. That difference is democracy; unions have it, corporations don't. This overwhelmingly important distinction is concealed by almost all public discussion. No one talks about it, no one seems to take it seriously. There is a virtual embargo on any mention of this fact, but it merits serious consideration.

The original legislation ratifying the creation of PACs, passed in 1971 and amended in 1974 after Watergate, intended that corporations and labor unions be treated in parallel fashion. In each case, the organization was permitted a special relationship to the group that democratically controlled it—stockholders in the case of corporations, members in the case of labor unions. The organization was permitted to communicate with those individuals and their families on any issue (including political issues), to conduct registration and get-out-the-vote campaigns, and to ask those people for voluntary contributions to a political action committee.

In the 1975 SUN–PAC decision, the Federal Election Commission, for almost the only time in its existence, took a bold step. In fact, it essentially threw out a key part of the law and then rewrote it, permitting corporations to solicit PAC contributions not just from their stockholders but also from their managerial employees. This had two consequences. First, corporate PACs—but no others—are able to coerce people to contribute. Second, corporate PACs are not, even in theory, democratically controlled. Each of these consequences needs to be examined.

Neither stockholders nor union members can be coerced to contribute—the organization doesn't have power over them, they have power over the organization. Managers, however, can be coerced. As a result, virtually all corporate PAC money comes from employees rather than stockholders. If your boss comes to you and asks for a contribution, saying he or she hopes that all team players will be generous, it's not easy for you, an ambitious young manager, to say no. Some companies apparently do not pressure employees to contribute, but others do. For example, at one company we studied, the head of government relations told us that each year he and the company's lobbyist go to each work unit and hold an employee meeting: "We talk about the PAC and what it means to the company and what it means to them as individuals, and we solicit their membership; if they are members, we solicit an increase in their gift." Then the employees' boss is asked "to get up and say why they are members and why they think it's important for an employee to be a member." The upper-level manager clearly has no confidentiality, which in itself sends a key message to others. A number of coercive elements converge in this solicitation: The meeting is public, employees are to commit themselves then and there in the public meeting, the boss recommends that subordinates contribute, and an impression is probably conveyed that the boss will be evaluated on the basis of his or her employees' participation rate. . . . No one is told they will be fired for failing to contribute, but it seems probable that they will assume their boss will be disappointed and that their contribution or noncontribution will be remembered at promotion time.

The second consequence of the 1975 SUN–PAC decision is even more important. Corporate PACs are *not* democratic. Many corporations have steering committees that vote to decide to whom the PAC will contribute, but the committees are appointed, the corporate hierarchy selects individuals who are expected to take the corporate purpose as their own, and managers know that they will be evaluated on their performance on the committee. As one senior vice president explained: "Policy is made by the top of the company, and it filters down. They tell you what they want, and you do it."

The internal functioning of corporate PACs suggests how they relate to and value democracy. Most aspects of the political system are beyond the *direct* control of corporations, but they *can* determine how their PACs operate and make decisions. As a result, in all but a handful of corporate PACs democratic control is not even a theoretical possibility. . . .

The only corporation that reported having *some* contested elections agreed that, in general: "It is an elected-appointive; it's kind of a pseudo-election I guess is what it amounts to."

We might expect those ideological corporations that stress general principles of support for democracy and the "free" enterprise system to be exceptions to the undemocratic organization of corporate PACs. Not at all. At one corporation that boasted about its wholehearted support of the "free enterprise system," the chair of the PAC Committee matter-of-factly noted: "If our [company] chairman said we are going to have a certain kind of PAC, then we'd have an option of resigning or doing it the way he wanted." . . .

The nondemocratic character of corporate PACs is consistent with the principles guiding the corporation as a whole. Corporations are not run on democratic principles; employees don't vote on corporate leadership or policies. Many corporate executives are dubious about democracy in general. Leonard Silk and David Vogel attended a set of meetings organized by the Conference Board for top executives. They concluded:

> While critics of business worry about the atrophy of American democracy, the concern in the nation's boardrooms is precisely the opposite. For an executive, democracy in America is working all too well—*that is the problem.*

Campaign contributions are (part of) the solution to the "problem" of democracy. . . .

Business Is Different

Power, we would argue, is not just the ability to force someone to do something against their will; it is most effective (and least recognized) when it shapes the field of action. Moreover, business's vast resources, influence on the economy, and general legitimacy place it on a different footing from other campaign contributors. Every day a member of Congress accepts a $1,000 donation from a corporate PAC, goes to a committee hearing, proposes "minor" changes in a bill's wording, and has those changes accepted without discussion or examination. The changes "clarify" the language of the bill, legalizing higher levels of pollution for a specific pollutant, or exempting the company from some tax. The media do not report this change and no one speaks against it. On the other hand, if a PAC were formed by Drug Lords for Cocaine Legalization, no member would take their money. If a member introduced a "minor" wording change to make it easier to sell crack without bothersome police interference, the proposed change would attract massive attention, the campaign contribution would be labeled a scandal, the member's political career would be ruined, and the changed wording would not be incorporated into the bill. Drug Lords may make an extreme example, but approximately the same holds true for many groups: At present, equal rights for gays and lesbians could never be a minor and unnoticed addition to a bill with a different purpose.

Even groups with great social legitimacy encounter more opposition and controversy than business faces for proposals that are virtually without public support. One example is the contrast between the largely unopposed commitment of tens or hundreds of billions of dollars for the savings and loan bailout, compared to the sharp debate, close votes, and defeats for the rights of men and women to take *unpaid* parental leaves. The classic term for something non-controversial that everyone must support is "a motherhood issue," and while it costs little to guarantee every woman the right to an *un*paid parental leave, this measure nonetheless generated intense scrutiny and controversy—going down to defeat under President Bush, passing under President Clinton, and then again becoming a focus of attack after the 1994 Republican takeover of Congress. Few indeed are the people publicly prepared to defend pollution or tax evasion. Nonetheless, business is routinely able to win pollution exemptions and tax loopholes. . . .

Corporations are unlike other "special interest" groups not only because business has far more resources, but also because of its acceptance and legitimacy. When people feel that "the system" is screwing them, they tend to blame politicians, the government, the media—but rarely business. In terms of campaign finance, while much of the public is outraged at the way money influences elections and public policy, the issue is almost always posed in terms of politicians, what they do or don't do. This is part of a pervasive double standard that largely exempts business from criticism. We, however, believe it is vital to scrutinize business as well. . . .

. . . Corporations are so different, and so dominant, that they exercise a special kind of power, what Antonio Gramsci called hegemony. Hegemony can be regarded as the ultimate example of a field of power that structures what people and groups do. It is sometimes referred to as a worldview, a way of thinking about the world that influences every action, and makes it difficult to even consider alternatives. But in Gramsci's analysis it is much more than this, it is a culture and set of institutions that structure life patterns and coerce a particular way of life. . . .

. . . Today business has enormous power and exercises effective hegemony, even though (perhaps because) this is largely undiscussed and unrecognized. *Politically,* business power today is similar to white treatment of blacks in 1959—business may sincerely deny its power, but many of the groups it exercises power over recognize it, feel dominated, resent this, and fight the power as best they can. At least until very recently, *economically,* business power was more like gender relations in 1959: Virtually no one saw this power as problematic. The revived labor movement is beginning to change this, and there are signs that a movement is beginning to contest corporate power. Nonetheless, if the issue is brought to people's attention, many still don't see a problem: "Well, so what? how else could it be? maybe we don't like it, but that's just the way things are." . . .

Everyone is talking about campaign finance reform. But what kind of reform? The answer varies. If the problem is occasional abuses by renegade fundraisers, then the only change needed is a system of improved enforcement. . . . If the problem is that the public has (momentarily? irrationally?) lost faith in the system, and now sees democracy for sale, then the solution is to address the most visible symbol of this—soft money—and make cosmetic changes elsewhere, loudly proclaiming that this is a thorough reform. For campaign finance insiders—a tiny fraction of the population, but crucial for policy decisions—the problem is that politicians are having to work too hard to raise money. The solution is to find some way to reduce the cost of campaigns (typically, through limited free television time), while seeing to it that the margin of success continues to depend on campaign contributions from big-money donors, which is, after all, the system that put these politicians into office. Most campaign finance experts analyze the issue in ways generally similar to the political insiders. Academic "expertise," and certainly media punditry, generally depends on possessing views certified as "reasonable" by those with power—that is, by politicians, the media, business, and big-money campaign contributors. For most members of the American public—and for us—the problem is an entire system that is institutionally corrupt, that coerces politicians to put dollars over voters, that buys off democracy. The solution, therefore, must be a complete overhaul and the introduction of a fundamentally new system. . . .

Public Financing

. . . As long as our society continues to have vast inequalities of wealth, income, and power, the people with the most money will be able to find ways around restrictive rules. Virtually all current [reform] proposals are intended to limit the ways in which money can be funneled into campaigns. It is extremely difficult to impose limitations, because however many rules and barriers are erected, the ingenuity of the rich, or their hirelings, will always find ways to evade the regulations. Clinton's Deputy Chief of Staff Harold Ickes explains, "Money is like water. . . . If there is a crack, water will find it.

Same way with political money." Moreover, virtually no meaningful penalties are imposed on those caught violating the rules. As a result, the regulators are always one step behind the evaders and shysters.

The alternative approach is to cut the Gordian knot of restrictions by instituting public financing of election campaigns. In the early 1990s, such proposals seemed utopian. In 1992, we argued that Congress and the president would not institute public financing unless a popular movement put a gun to their heads. As we predicted, Washington didn't budge, but state-level referendum campaigns may do what Congress would never do. In 1996, Maine voters adopted a public financing system, and Public Campaign, a new organization dedicated to taking special interest money out of elections, is spearheading a movement around the country to bring about public campaign financing, one state at a time, if necessary. Real reform, with full public financing, is no longer a utopian dream—it's on today's political agenda. Other proposals are of course possible, but Public Campaign's model law is an excellent framework, *and* it has helped mobilize and coordinate a major grassroots campaign. Our discussion therefore focuses on this proposal.

Public Campaign, and its Clean Money Campaign Reform (CMCR), are—at least for now—bypassing Congress, which has shown an amazing ability to sidetrack and frustrate reform efforts, and focusing instead on state-by-state efforts, most notably by putting referendum questions on the ballot. By taking the issue directly to the voters in a ballot referendum, it's possible to pass a full reform proposal. The normal legislative process is highly likely to bury reform in committee and then change "just a few" details in order to make the proposal "more realistic"—that is, to be sure that special interest money continues to provide a decisive margin in most contests.

State-level campaigns necessarily mean that there will be minor variations from one place to another. And any effort to present a campaign finance proposal confronts a dilemma: Readers want enough detail to be sure the proposal is viable—that it won't encounter an insoluble contradiction—but don't want to be bogged down in minor provisions of interest only to technocrats and political junkies. In its broad outlines, Clean Money Campaign Reform limits campaign spending, prohibits special interest contributions to those candidates who participate in the system, provides public financing for participating candidates, and guarantees a level playing field. The system is completely voluntary. . . .

The arguments in favor of [public financing of campaigns] are . . . powerful. . . . Elections would be far more competitive. Although challengers would still have less name recognition than incumbents, they would have enough money to mount credible campaigns, and for the first time challengers as a group would have as much to spend as incumbents.

Special interests could no longer use campaign money to increase their access and win benefits for themselves. It is not only that a member would not be indebted for a past donation. Members would also know they would never need to depend on a future donation and could never gain a campaign advantage by soliciting or accepting such a donation. Corporations would continue to have substantial clout based on their wealth, power, and respectability, their ability to maintain a staff of lobbyists, their advocacy advertising, their networks, connections, and friendships. But *one* of their major special interest weapons would have been eliminated.

The guarantee of public funding for campaigns would give members of Congress more time to spend on legislation and on keeping in touch with constituents who are *not* campaign contributors. . . .

People sometimes argue that such reforms only make the system more stable and resistant to change. Perhaps that is true in some instances. In other instances, what Andre Gorz called a "non-reformist reform" provides immediate benefits to people *and* makes it easier to win future reforms. Did the auto safety campaign Nader launched produce a significant change in the way people think about business? Yes. Did it make people more or less willing to consider additional reforms? Obviously, much more willing.

We would argue that Clean Money Campaign Reform is also a "nonre-formist reform." It proposes a reform that can be won, and one that if won will substantially weaken business power. By itself, will it transform American society? No. Will it have an impact? Yes. Will the end of corporate campaign contributions and the emergence of public financing make it easier or more difficult to make future political changes? Clearly, easier. Will continued struggle be necessary to elect good people and to fight business power? Certainly. Will electoral politics be enough? No. Business exercises power on many different fronts and that power must be opposed on every front.

DISCUSSION QUESTIONS

1. Smith claims that campaign contributors don't buy favors or votes from candidates but that contributions simply register support for candidates' political positions. How would Smith deal with the contention that contributions buy privileged access to candidates and that to get access requires contributions?

2. In *Buckley* v. *Valeo* (1976), the U.S. Supreme Court seemed to agree with Smith's idea that campaign contributions are protected by the First Amendment as free speech. Are proposals for public financing of campaigns such as those submitted by the authors of "Dollars and Votes" a violation of free speech?

3. In 1999 and 2000, the House leadership blocked campaign reform initiatives from coming to a vote. If money is such a corrupting influence in campaigns, why aren't voters more supportive of the kinds of initiatives proposed to limit its effects? What are the obstacles to forming a grassroots movement that supports campaign finance reform?

4. Assuming that money has become crucial in modern campaigns, devise a plausible campaign strategy for a cash-poor but volunteer-rich candidate for a House seat. Could volunteers be used to balance the high-tech campaign? Under what circumstances?

■ SUGGESTED READINGS
AND INTERNET RESOURCES

A comprehensive look at campaign finance reform is provided by Trevor Potter, Anthony Corrado, and Daniel Ortiz, *The New Campaign Finance Sourcebook* (Washington, D.C.: Brookings Institution Press, 2001). For a skeptical account of the effects of campaign finance reform, see Michael Malbin and Thomas Gais, *The Day After Reform* (Albany, N.Y.: Rockefeller Institute Press, 1998). A devastating look at money in politics is Charles Lewis, *The Buying of the President 2000* (New York: Avon Books, 2000). A short and effective set of proposals for public financing of campaigns can be found in David Donnelly, Janice Fine, and Ellen Miller, *Money and Politics* (Boston: Beacon Press, 1999).

Federal Election Commission (FEC)
www.fec.gov
The FEC's site provides access to the financial reports of all candidates for federal offices and press releases summarizing monthly trends in campaign fundraising.

Center for Responsive Politics
www.opensecrets.org
This is the most comprehensive site for data and analysis of FEC data, with a concentration on the role of monied interests and their effects on the political process.

Public Campaign
www.publiccampaign.org
Here are news and views from the major advocacy organization favoring public financing of political campaigns.

Democracy Network
www.dnet.org
This League of Women Voters–sponsored site provides state-by-state access to candidate information and ways to contact and interact with campaign organizations.

Campaign Finance Institute
www.cfinst.org
This nonpartisan institute's mission is to assess the effectiveness of campaign finance reform. The institute's web site features reports on pending legislation, easy access to donor lists, and news of key congressional races where money is the chief factor.

12

Local Democracy: Is Suburban Sprawl the Realization or Violation of Democratic Values?

I n his classic history of suburbanization, *Crabgrass Frontier,* Kenneth Jackson describes how the United States differs from other nations: "The United States has thus far been unique in four important respects that can be summed up in the following sentence: affluent and middle-class Americans live in urban areas that are far from their work places, in homes that they own, and in the center of yards that by urban standards elsewhere are enormous." Increasingly, the American pattern of low-density suburban development has become the center of a heated political controversy.

Critics call spread-out urban development "sprawl"—a term that suggests a process that is unattractive and undisciplined. Defenders of low-density suburban development have long decried the use of the term. Residents of St. Charles, Missouri, a suburban county north of St. Louis, have rejected even using the term, saying that such development should be called "urban choice" instead. Notwithstanding the derogatory connotations, the term sprawl has stuck—giving opponents a verbal victory, if nothing else.

Opposition to sprawling suburban development goes back to the Regional Planning Association's 1927 plan for the New York metropolitan area calling for a small number of suburban job centers that would cluster development instead of sprawling across the countryside. But the early visionary regional plans had little impact on urban development, flying, as they did, in the face of America's longstanding tradition of local control over land use. By the 1970s, American cities were sprawling out over the countryside at an incredible pace. Motivated largely by environmental concerns, a "Quiet Revolution" in state land planning in the 1970s gave many state governments the power to override local land-use laws in certain cases. In 1972, President Richard Nixon proposed a national land-use, planning law that would have greatly strengthened the power of state planning agencies. Attacked as a usurpation of local privileges, the bill was ultimately defeated in the wake of the Arab oil boycott (which undermined environmental arguments) and the Watergate scandal (which crippled the Nixon administration).

The sprawl debate pretty much died out in the 1980s. Democrats realized that in opposing sprawl, they risked alienating suburban voters who feared that the federal government would foist low-income public housing and other unwanted developments on them. Much of the credit for the quieting of the sprawl issue, however, must go to President Ronald Reagan, who won two presidential elections partly on his promise to move decision making down the ladder from the federal government to states and, ultimately, to localities. With public opinion behind devolution (see Chapter 3), critics of sprawl had a tougher time defending enhanced state and federal land-use powers to overcome fragmented local planning.

In the 1990s, the sprawl debate returned with a vengeance. The sustained economic boom of the 1990s caused American metropolitan areas to sprawl out as never before. Americans could afford bigger houses on bigger lots, and they did not hesitate to spend the money. Partly to afford this new level of consumption, women entered the workforce in droves. As a result, most suburban households owned two cars, with many owning three or more. Probably the biggest impetus for the revival of sprawl as a political issue was the tremendous increase in traffic congestion in American metropolitan areas in the 1990s. As people sat in traffic jams on the way to and from work, they had plenty of time to question the benefits of low-density suburban development. Road rage became part of the American vocabulary. In 1999 *USA Today* published a special report on "National Gridlock," with story after story about horrible traffic jams.

An interesting wrinkle in the contemporary sprawl debate, compared to the earlier debate in the 1970s, is that opponents of sprawl have also raised the issue of whether sprawl harms economic growth. According to this view, competition in the new economy is not between nation-states or cities but between regions. Regions that are highly sprawled out and that have weak central cities will be at a disadvantage in the competition for jobs and investment. Syndicated columnist Neal Peirce coined the term "citistates" to refer to regions that successfully collaborate to succeed in the global economy. Business, however, has been divided on the question of whether regional collaboration is a good way to stimulate economic growth. Some business leaders embrace the idea of regional collaboration, while others shun it for requiring too much government planning.

Critics of sprawl have also been motivated by aesthetic and community concerns. In 1994 a group of planners and architects joined together to form the Congress for the New Urbanism. New urbanists charge that suburban developments lacking sidewalks and front porches undermine human connections. They also charge sprawl with the sin of ugliness: suburbs lack graceful public spaces, and the ugly strip malls all look alike. The writer James Howard Kunstler calls this the "geography of nowhere." Defenders of sprawl attack these views as cultural elitism: if low-density suburbs are so ugly and inhuman, why do people keep flocking to them?

In truth, the anti-sprawl movement has been more effective with words than it has been with action. Portland, Oregon is the only major metropolitan area to aggressively control sprawl. It has the nation's only European-style greenbelt around the metropolitan area, where intensive development is forbidden. An elected regional government, known as "Metro," enforces the growth boundary. Interestingly, a moderate Republican governor, Tom McCall, provided the leadership behind Oregon's innovative state land-use planning in the 1970s.

In recent years, both Republican and Democratic politicians have endorsed so-called smart growth policies. The idea behind smart growth is to discourage development on the urban fringe that will require new infrastructure, such as sewer lines and roads, if there is room for development in the older parts of the region where infrastructure is already in place. Under the leadership of Democratic governor Parris Glendenning, Maryland has led the way in smart growth policies, but little is known at this point about whether they have had much effect on sprawl. Many states have borrowed money to purchase land on the urban fringe to preserve it from development. In 1998, Republican governor Christine Todd Whitman of New Jersey helped to persuade voters in her state to borrow $1 billion, with the goal of acquiring 1 million acres of open space.

In the 2000 presidential race, Vice President Al Gore, as part of what he called his "livability agenda," promised to make urban sprawl a central issue in his campaign. In fact, sprawl played almost no role in that campaign. (The Clinton administration pushed a number of small programs to preserve open space and limit sprawl.) Gore's opponent, George W. Bush, refused to address the issue, saying that it should be left to state and local governments.

The essay by Gregg Easterbrook, an award-winning author and journalist, casts doubt on Gore's "livability agenda." The impetus behind the anti-sprawl campaign, Easterbrook maintains, comes from those who already have nice homes in the suburbs and do not want more strip malls or traffic to reduce the quality of their lives. The problem is that the only way to stop sprawl is to prevent others from building new houses or businesses on the urban fringe. The anti-sprawl movement, therefore, is basically exclusionary and elitist. Educated intellectuals may prefer crowded and diverse cities, but they shouldn't foist their tastes on average Americans, who prefer large houses on large lots.

The costs of sprawl, according to Easterbrook, are exaggerated. The amount of land consumed is infinitesimal considering the total American landmass, and the car is really more efficient than mass transit at getting people where they want to go quickly. Anti-sprawl laws, Easterbrook implies, are misguided efforts at social engineering that contradict American values.

Todd Swanstrom, a professor of public policy, argues that sprawl is not an expression of American values but a violation of them. Far from being a product of free choice in the market, sprawl is heavily subsidized by public policies. If households that moved out to the urban fringe were required to pay the full costs of the new roads and sewer and water lines that service them, Swanstrom argues, sprawl would be greatly reduced. Moreover, sprawl has costs, such as air pollution, traffic congestion, and even obesity, that are not taken into account. Limiting sprawl would benefit the entire society. Sprawl also damages democracy, Swanstrom argues. As people sprawl out, they segregate themselves along class and racial lines into independent suburban governments. Local public services become highly unequal, and citizens treat local government as a consumption good, not an arena for civic activism. Swanstrom concludes that sprawl, by segregating different groups of people from one another, can lead to greater intolerance and misunderstanding.

The debate over sprawl is more than a conflict over how to measure the cost and benefits of our present pattern of suburban development. Both the opponents and the defenders of sprawl invoke fundamental democratic values, such as freedom and equality (see Introduction). Defenders of sprawl often root their argument in the value of freedom: people should be able to move wherever they want without any outside interference from government. Opponents of sprawl often base their argument on equality: sprawl leads to inequities in local government services, with those left behind in poor central cities being denied access to equal opportunity. If you carefully read the essays that follow, however, you will find that the value positions are, in fact, more complex. Defenders of sprawl also invoke equality (equal access to the good life in the suburbs), and critics of sprawl argue that people do not presently have true freedom of movement (because public policies tilt the playing field in favor of sprawl). Sorting out the factual and value-based claims in the sprawl debate, you will find, is a challenging task.

Suburban Myth

GREGG EASTERBROOK

The ideal restaurant would have terrific food, moderate prices, and would be unpopular, so lines would never inconvenience diners. Legislatures could make restaurants less crowded by, say, mandating that some tables be kept vacant even when customers are queued. Those already seated would surely benefit. But others would stew over being denied service, while business and jobs would be lost.

It's worth remembering this as politicians begin to tackle the issue of suburban "sprawl," currently emerging as a primary topic in the run-up to Campaign 2000. Polling data and focus groups show that sprawl has hot political Q-scores; last fall, state and local voters approved nearly 200 ballot measures to limit development or preserve green space. Vice President Gore has unveiled a "livability agenda" to ease traffic and other frustrations of suburban commuters. As Gore notes, "Parents want to spend more time with their kids and less time stuck behind a steering wheel." And Gore is hardly alone. New Jersey Governor Christine Todd Whitman, a Republican, is leading the charge for a $1 billion program to set aside half the state's remaining wildland. Even Ralph Reed is touting sprawl politics.

Of course, everybody wishes there were fewer cars on the road, fewer strip malls, and less demand for living space or commercial square footage. But how do you discourage such things without denying a place at the table to those who have not yet been seated—especially in a country whose population is growing? If suburbs are where Americans choose to live—and that verdict is in, the suburban class now constituting the majority of Americans—then brainpower should be applied to making burbs as livable as possible. It's a good sign that policy organizations such as the Brookings Institution are turning their attention to such tasks as planning for "smart growth."

But, as an issue, sprawl can also sound awfully similar to exclusionary zoning and other pull-up-the-ladder ideas that comfortable communities have used in the past to keep out unwanted arrivistes—often minorities and immigrants. One person's greenspace preservation is another's denied housing permit. So here are a few qualms about the emerging national buzz on sprawl:

Sprawl is infuriating but not statistically significant. The footprint of the United States reflects an ever-bigger shoe size; the Chicago metropolitan area, for example, grew 46 percent from 1970 to 1990. The Sierra Club estimates that

400,000 acres per year are being converted to developed use. Yet are these figures really as worrisome as they seem? Four hundred thousand acres, for example, sounds like the circumference of the Crab Nebula but represents 0.02 percent of the U.S. land mass: 50 years of sprawl at the current rate would be required to consume a single percent of America's expanse.

Just 3.4 percent of the United States is urban, suburban, or otherwise "built up," according to federal figures. If roads are added to the calculation, the total concrete-ized area of the country rises to 4.8 percent. The forested portion of the United States is, by contrast, 20.4 percent, meaning there are four acres of woodland for every acre of development. Even if the definition of "developed" is expanded in the most liberal way, to include all land used for crops or grazing, the United States is still two-thirds wild, one-third under the hand of man. Sprawl is a local problem, not an all-encompassing effect.

Recent concerns about agricultural land-use patterns, often spun in the media and by lobbyists as a crisis of "vanishing farms," also diminish on close examination. "Land in farms" fell 16 percent between 1964 and 1997, according to the Agriculture Department. But this much-cited category incorporates considerable acreage that owners were calling farms only for tax purposes. Since the 1960s, "total cropland" is down only about one percent, while "harvested cropland," or land under cultivation, is up eight percent. And production per acre—what matters most—is way, way up, thanks to high-yield crop strains.

Moreover, the trend line is toward the *decline* of sprawl, relative to people at least. David Rusk, a theorist of the smart-growth movement, estimates that U.S. metro development covered 208,000 square miles in 1950 and by 1990 had sprawled out to 345,000 square miles. But, through that period, the population of those areas rose from 84 million to 159 million. This translates to a 66 percent increase in physical area for a population increase of 89 percent. America isn't gobbling up more space per capita; it's gobbling less—mainly because developers are responding to market incentives to use land more efficiently. Sprawl theory assumes that builders despoil the land without restraint. Yet price is already an important restraint; land is an expensive resource.

People fled city centers because they wanted to. One motivator for suburban expansion was white desire to escape contact with blacks. As *Brookings Review* recently noted, "Race has been a major factor in the spatial configuration of our metropolitan areas." That aspect of sprawl does not reflect well on American society, but the rest of the phenomenon is mainly a voluntary choice. Blacks are now sprawling, too: mainly African American, middle-class burbs are expanding in Georgia, Maryland, and elsewhere. Detached homes, verdant lawns, lower crime rates—for many millions of Americans, including many millions of minority Americans, such things represent a lifelong dream. People of all races seek the sprawled areas because that's what they *like*.

People also sought the suburbs to escape the corruption and mismanage-ment of urban government—especially the disastrous inner-city school sys-tems. Suburban government is usually clean and responsive, if ho-hum; if people like honest government supervising their driveways and lawns, why should public policy argue with that judgment? Intellectuals have long dis-dained the expansion of the burbs, despite works such as *The Levittowners* that demonstrate little urban-suburban distinction in sophistication. Of course, many suburbanites have trite values and nothing to say, but then the same goes for many who reside in Upper West Side walk-ups and hold subscription seats for the opera. And, for reasons never entirely clear, twentieth-century liberalism swooned for Le Corbusier's contention that human beings deserve to be packed into high-density tower housing that rises from the landscape like so many vertical penitentiaries. Maybe there was once a reason to believe that such structures were the only way to bring decent living standards to the masses, but now it's clearly possible to bring detached homes to the masses. That's an important social achievement, not a cause for angst.

We know from the choices of housing buyers, and from the unhappi-ness of housing-project residents, that most Americans despise living in cramped quarters. Despite this, some sprawl theorists assert that, since the average density of an American metro area is one-fourth the density of metro areas in nations such as Germany, public policy should strive to force a dramatic compression of American living space. But if Germany, or any of many other European or Asian countries, had more land area, its citizens would clamor for detached homes and lawns, too. The fact that other na-tions lack the expanse in which to offer the majority of their citizens, homeownership hardly means that America, blessed with such space, should prevent citizens from occupying it.

Sprawl has economic utility. Some cities have spread out in a jumbled, ill-thought-through manner that causes awful traffic bottlenecks, wasted fuel, and an excessively asphaltized ambiance. But it is not the case that tract housing, overpasses, multilane roads, malls, and other aspects of suburbia happen solely because of rapacious developers or civic pandemonium. Most happen because they are economically efficient.

Subdivision development is nowhere near as tasteful as an elm-shaded, turn-of-the-century Cape Cod in the university district, but it has the virtue of being affordable to many more families. Malls may be stupefying, but they are a furiously efficient means of retailing. Two-car, two-earner fami-lies with husband and wife commuting in opposite directions may lead to daily stress but might also be one reason for the American economy's flexi-bility. The United States has experienced unprecedented economic growth, low unemployment, and improvement in living standards during the very period of burb explosion and traffic jams. Maybe these factors are positively correlated, not negatively.

Consider the assumption that road construction is odious. Roads are not only much cheaper to build than mass transit systems; they are also more flexible. The excellent subway system in Washington, D.C., which I ride to work, is fixed in its downtown-outward configuration: tens of billions of dollars would be required to rebuild the system to reflect the between-burb commuting that has been the main urban transportation trend of the past 20 years. Roads, on the other hand, can reflect changes in commuter patterns instantly—people just point their cars at different destinations.

Cars, in turn, are consumers of money and fossil fuel, and we belittle ourselves when we regard them as status symbols. But automobiles also promote economic efficiency and personal freedom; there are good reasons why even anti-sprawlers want to own one. As new cars approach negligible levels of pollution emissions, environmental objections to them decline. And an annoying little secret of suburban life is that, even with traffic congestion, it's almost always faster to get somewhere in a car than by riding public transit. Cars are ubiquitous partly because people make rational time-money tradeoffs regarding their use, and those sorts of judgments, though sometimes wrong on the micro scale, are usually logical on the macro scale.

Thus, the fact that the federal government spends about $28 billion a year on road construction, compared with about $6 billion on mass transit, isn't necessarily the outrage that current sprawl politicking suggests. It surely can be argued that shifting some spending toward mass transit makes sense, though such purposes can be far more quickly and flexibly achieved by better bus service than by the rail lines that urban planners adore. But roads and car culture aren't a crazed anti-people conspiracy. The challenge is to make roads and cars serve us better while bugging us less.

The Michigan Land Use Institute, an impressive new smart-growth organization, recently proposed a sensible middle course along these lines for Traverse City, Michigan. Local officials currently plan to bracket the metro area with a high-speed highway bypass. The Michigan Land Use Institute offered a detailed alternative plan for improving existing major arteries and left-turn lanes, speeding up traffic within the city but preventing cars from being sucked away from established commercial zones. Compromises like this admit that the automobile is here to stay as America's primary means of transportation but seek to adjust car culture to avoid construction that isn't really needed.

Sprawl is caused by affluence and population growth, and which of these, exactly, do we propose to prohibit? The Census Bureau projects that the American population will expand to 394 million by the year 2050, half again the level of today, with almost all that growth attributable to (legal) immigration, which currently runs at about 900,000 arrivals per year. Do we want to halt or deeply restrict immigration? Unless we do, the country's stock of houses, roads, commercial space, and other construction must substantially enlarge in decades to come.

Meanwhile, the reason Americans keep buying more housing, more SUVs, more swimming pools, and other space-consuming items is that they can afford these things. And so ... affluence is bad? The literature on sprawl is rife with sarcastic references to the square footage of the typical new home and to the spread of McMansions—"spacious" is a sneer word in this context—as if cramped quarters or adjoining walls are what human beings ought to prefer, damn it! There are many philosophical reasons why people might be more content with a modest lifestyle. But these are arguments about materialistic culture and the modern soul, not about appropriate housing-lot size. If prosperity puts the four-bedroom house within reach for the typical person, it's hard to see why public policy should look askance at that.

Sprawl complaints might justify exclusionary zoning. If political opposition to sprawl leads to smarter growth, or more parks and wildlife habitats, or better bus service, or better traffic regulation, then the public good is served. The trouble is, some sprawl concerns would not serve the public good.

Aspects of environmentalism have long been criticized as using ostensible concerns about nature to serve private purposes such as property values. Sprawl theory is now being hailed as an alternative to this. Since every person, rich or poor, is equally inconvenienced by being stuck in traffic, *The New York Times* recently opined, Gore's livability initiative will "take the lingering elitist tinge off environmentalism." Actually, it's the other way around. Sprawl control has much greater potential to wander into have-and-have-not inequity than does, say, regulation of CFCs or dioxin.

In a passage of his 1992 book *Earth in the Balance*, Gore worries about a glade of trees removed to build a new housing subdivision near what was then his Virginia home. "As the woods fell to make way for more concrete," he writes, "more buildings, more parking lots, the wild things that lived there were forced to flee." When he wrote these words, Gore was himself living in a large suburban house built on cleared woodland and parking his car on concrete. Why are comfortable homes and long driveways all right for those who already possess them, but threatening when others ask for the same?

Adopting smart-growth policies and better transportation plans is something every community should do. But, if communities take the kind of steps that would really stop sprawl, they would confer a windfall on those already entrenched, while damaging the prospects of those who long to attain the detached-home lifestyle. It's not for nothing that the Supreme Court has long taken a dim view of regulations whose official purpose is to keep communities leafy and quiet but whose effective result is to lock in the favored at the expense of new arrivals.

Everybody wants symbolic action against sprawl, but real action would drive people crazy. Gore's "livability agenda" matches great p.r. ring with hardly any content. Its chief plank is federal support for about $9.5 billion in local land-preservation bonds. This is a fine idea, though a one-shot infusion that won't change the larger panorama of land-use politics. (For my own admittedly politically improbable proposal to require developers to preserve at least one acre of land for every new one they build on, thus making ever-greater increments of land preservation a permanent part of American public policy, see "Greener Pastures," *TNR*, March 2, 1998.) The rest of Gore's initiative are inoffensive, small-change items, such as $10 million to help schools become "community centered" or $17.2 million for safeguarding ex-urban agricultural lands—an amount that will buy roughly two farms per state.

Announcing the livability initiative, Gore mused about "the Lakota storytellers who described the vast clearness of the Western sky as a metaphor for inner courage." It's easy to see why he would rather discuss the Lakota than the emphatic actions that would really cut down on sprawl. One would be exclusionary zoning. Another would be the denial of environmental or sewer permits, which brings business expansion to a halt. Another would be revoking the hugely popular mortgage-interest deduction. Another real-world restriction would be raising gasoline taxes.

If mortgage interest were not tax-deductible, and gasoline prices were quadrupled (putting them on a par with Europe's), demand for those sinister spacious homes would wane, enthusiasm for public transportation would rise, and the market could be relied on to take care of the rest. But do *you* want to be the politician who advocates a $3-per-gallon gasoline tax? Think of Bill Clinton's panicky 1996 retreat from a 4.3-cents-per-gallon gas-tax increase—not exactly a metaphor for inner courage. There is little chance any major candidate will advocate higher gasoline taxes during Campaign 2000. And, if the political world is afraid of this moderate reform—which would not imperil car culture, just trim some of the tonnage off our SUVs—where is the will for real change?

Other anti-sprawl proposals have similar implausibility quotients. Rusk and other theorists, for example, call for consolidating urban and suburban governments to prevent local entities from playing one off the other in development contests. It's an admirable idea, and a few cities and their suburbs have voluntarily combined, notably Indianapolis and Jacksonville. But, if you live in the ring burbs around Newark, Detroit, or Washington, D.C., you'd have to be dragged kicking and screaming into combination with their corrupt, incompetent governments. Some have proposed that combining tax bases of suburban and urban jurisdictions would reduce sprawl contests and promote equity by improving schools in poorer neighborhoods. The latter goal is totally justified, but where is the political support for this idea? Tax-base sharing is currently foundering in Vermont, one of the most liberal states.

And, if you want decisive action against sprawl, don't you want land-use planning? Imagine how poll numbers will shoot up for the candidate who proposes that! Regional land-use planning has done well by the city of Portland, which has both controlled its boundaries and seen its economy prosper. But Portland is a special case; its geography imposes physical limits on growth.

Portland's high land values and high quality of life tell us land-use planning and prosperity are not incompatible, which is an important lesson for local officials who traditionally have felt compelled to approve any and all construction. But the kind of land-use planning that's worked in Portland may not work nationally, especially since Portland has pretty much closed its doors to population growth, which is not an option for the country as a whole.

Hey, these movie-theater lines are too long! You bet the lines at the movie theater are too long. My proposed solution is to forbid you from going to the movies. Your proposed solution is to forbid me. We both claim a noble public purpose—the shorter movie line. But sometimes what seems like concern for the public square is really a declaration of "me first."

Thoughtful study of smart-growth alternatives is in everyone's interest and will lead to improvements in suburban livability. But many of the people who now grouse about sprawl themselves live in spacious houses, own an SUV, owe their good fortunes to the growth economy, and would be entirely outraged if there were not ample roads, stores, restaurants, and parking wherever they went. They wish everybody else would get off the highway so that they can have the road to themselves. In this way, the sprawl issue touches on the selfish downside of democracy. Smart growth is a smart idea, but those who pursue it must be wary of favoring the enfranchised and the organized, which our politics does too much of already.

The Case Against Sprawl

TODD SWANSTROM

The defenders of sprawl base their argument on one critical point: sprawl is a product of free markets and therefore is simply an expression of what the American people want. Americans love their big yards, big homes, and big cars. By implication, anyone who criticizes sprawl is an elitist who wants to use the coercive powers of government to tell people where and how to live.

In fact, sprawl is not a free market phenomenon but is a product of politics. Public policies pushed by land developers, homebuilders, the highway lobby, and automobile interests have tilted the field of metropolitan development in favor of sprawl. Real estate developers do not pay for the full costs of sprawl, which include loss of green space, air pollution, and traffic congestion. Finally, even if developers wanted to build compact, mixed-use developments, they wouldn't be able to because of local zoning laws.

Sprawl not only has political causes but political consequences, as well—consequences that are disturbing for democracy. By drawing away the white middle and upper classes from the central cities and older suburbs, sprawl worsens racial and class polarization. The poor, especially minorities, become trapped in areas of concentrated poverty, far from most jobs and with access to inferior public services, especially schools. Sprawl undermines the principle of equal opportunity, and by putting greater distance between groups in the population, nurtures stereotypes that poison the political atmosphere.

The Myth of Free Choice

Sprawl is an elusive term. It is useful to start out by defining it. Most obviously, sprawl means low-density suburban development—single-family homes on large lots, less than two or three to the acre. But it also means more than that. Under sprawl, land uses are separated; office and retail functions are located far from residential neighborhoods. As a result, almost all trips require an automobile. (Public transit needs a certain level of population density to succeed.) Fundamentally, sprawl is the opposite of what we associate with traditional cities—high levels of density with different functions (housing, shops, offices) mixed together in the same area.

To defenders of sprawl, low-density sprawl is good, not because it is inherently better than other forms, but because it is what Americans want. At first glance, they are right: according to one survey, if given the choice, 80 percent of American citizens would prefer to live in low-density, single-family homes.

Although it is true that people choose where to live in the United States, *they do not choose the rules that govern their choices.* Land markets are not free and never have been. More than any other market, land markets are socially and politically constructed—and for good reason. We don't care who buys the next ballpoint pen after us. But we do care who buys the lot next to our house. By manipulating land use decisions, land developers have made low-density suburban sprawl much more attractive than it otherwise would have been. In effect, sprawl has been subsidized at the same time that compact, mixed-use developments have been burdened.

People's preferences in housing are shaped by the options that are presented to them. In free markets, demand is supposed to determine supply; in the case of suburban sprawl, supply determines demand. Dense and diverse central cities are generally characterized by higher taxes, inferior public services, higher crime rates, and poorly performing schools. At the same time, homebuyers in outer-ring suburbs usually get more house (square footage) for their money, lower crime rates, and better and cheaper public services, including schools. No wonder people prefer sprawl!

Defenders of sprawl maintain that the advantages of sprawl are inherent: low-density suburbs are more attractive than crowded central cities, especially to hardworking middle-class families. Density and diversity, on the other hand, generate negative behaviors, like crime and social disorder; they become the areas of last resort for families who cannot afford to move to thriving suburbs.

In fact, the choice between sprawled-out suburbs and dense central cities has been rigged by government policies. Sprawl wins not because it is inherently better but because it has unfair advantages. It's as if in the race between sprawl and more compact forms of development, sprawl was given a head start while dense and diverse cities were forced to carry 50-pound sacks of rocks on their backs.

The defenders of sprawl tout it as a product of free choice. Ironically, sprawl undermines choice. Because of sprawl, the automobile is a necessity, not a choice. In most metropolitan areas, few if any neighborhoods exist where households can dispense with the automobile for a significant proportion of their trips. In other nations, compact, mixed-use areas serviced by mass transit provide an alternative to the auto culture. Italians, for instance, make 54 percent of all trips by foot or bicycle. Compare this to the United States where a pitiful 10 percent are made this way (though the figure is higher in pedestrian-friendly, mixed-use neighborhoods).

You can't blame people for making the choices that provide the most benefits for their families. (In truth, some critics of sprawl are guilty of cultural elitism—looking down their noses at those who choose the suburban lifestyle.) The problem is not with the choices that families make, but with the alternatives that are offered to them.

Government Subsidizes Sprawl

A few years ago, 149 leading urban scholars were asked to identify the most significant influences on American metropolitan development since 1950. At the top of the list they put the policies of the federal government, such as interstate highways and homeowner tax breaks, which "intentionally or unintentionally promoted suburbanization and sprawl."

Far from being biased toward sprawl, the public perception is that the government heavily subsidizes central cities with generous welfare payments paid for mostly from the taxes of hardworking suburbanites. Like the free market in land, this is another myth. True, social welfare programs, such as public assistance, are targeted to the mostly urban poor, but these expenditures are vastly outweighed by other programs that mostly benefit middle- and upper-class suburbanites.

Take housing, for example. In 2000 the federal government spent a total of $30 billion on all subsidized housing programs for the poor. This is a significant sum of money and most of it was spent in central cities and inner-ring suburbs. But housing programs that favor wealthy suburbs and new single-family homes dwarf programs for the urban poor. The federal government allows homeowners to deduct mortgage interest and property taxes from their incomes, thus saving them money on their federal taxes. In 2000, homeowner tax breaks cost the federal government over $103 billion, almost 3.5 times the amount of money spent on the poor. The homeowner tax breaks effectively subsidize sprawl by increasing the demand for large expensive homes. Meanwhile, there is no corresponding tax break for renters, who tend to live in more compact cities.

The same bias toward sprawl is evident in federal transportation policies. Between 1975 and 1995, the United States spent $1.15 trillion on roads and highways and only about one-sixth of that on all forms of mass transit. Defenders of auto-driven sprawl will tell you that most of this came out of earmarked gasoline taxes and therefore drivers are simply paying for what they get. The problem with this argument is that earmarked gasoline taxes don't come close to covering the true costs of the automobile. The World Resources Institute estimated that if drivers were forced to pay for all the hidden costs of air pollution, congestion, and parking, the cost of gasoline would soar to $7 a gallon. In addition, the defenders of sprawl rarely mention the approximately 40,000 traffic deaths and over 3 million injuries every year from our auto-dependent transportation system. Clearly, not all these deaths can be attributed to sprawl, but if more people lived in pedestrian-friendly neighborhoods and could use mass transit, fewer people would be killed or maimed in traffic accidents.

In general, sprawl is not good for our health, and we all pay for the resulting medical problems in our taxes and health insurance premiums. The increase in vehicle miles traveled, partly caused by sprawl, has harmed air quality. Vehicle-related air pollutants are responsible for 20,000 to 40,000 cases of chronic respiratory illness each year. Obesity is now at epidemic levels in the United States. The cost of caring for patients with entirely preventable obesity-related illnesses tops $70 billion per year, with about half of the tab picked up by the taxpayers. Sprawled out suburbs, often lacking sidewalks and public parks, are a major reason why Americans do not exercise enough. A 1999 editorial in the *Journal of the American Medical Association* blamed the obesity epidemic partly on our over-reliance on the car, suggesting that the solution would require "substantial changes in community or regional design."

Although policies still favor sprawl, successful efforts to provide alternatives to sprawl challenge the assumption that Americans simply prefer the low-density suburban lifestyle. New urbanist planners and architects have succeeded in developing hundreds of compact, mixed-use, pedestrian-friendly communities. When Americans are given a choice of compact communities with good schools, low crime, and decent public services (the main factors that attracted many people to the suburbs in the first place), a significant proportion choose compactness over sprawl. This is true whether the choice is an older city, like Portland, Oregon, or a new community built from scratch, like Seaside, Florida.

Is Sprawl Economically Efficient?

Defenders of sprawl also argue that it is economically efficient. Once again, the argument is simple: if housing and jobs are moving out to the urban fringe, it must because it is more efficient and, therefore, profitable. What this ignores is that jobs and housing are attracted to the urban fringe not just by the inherent advantages of low-density development but by massive public investments in roads, sewers, and water lines.

Study after study has demonstrated that the public expense to service sprawl is much greater than with more compact development. The increased distances between developments means that sewer lines, water lines, roads, and other services are more expensive than under more compact development. A study conducted by the Center for Urban Policy Research at Rutgers University estimated that, compared to low-density sprawl, compact development saves 20 to 25 percent on road costs and 15 to 20 percent on utility costs. The public infrastructure costs of each new home in a low-density development can be $20,000 to $30,000. The problem is that the developers and new homeowners do not pay the full costs. The taxpayers as a whole pay for the new roads and highways, and the ratepayers in the sewer and water district pay for the new lines. In effect, the residents of older parts of metropolitan areas are forced to subsidize suburban flight, leading to urban blight and fiscal stress in their own cities.

At the same time that we are subsidizing new development on the fringe, we are abandoning infrastructure in central cities and inner-ring suburbs. Cleveland had a population of 914,808 in 1950; by 2000 it was down to 478,403. The local government still has to service the same number of miles of roads, sewers, and other public services with income from far fewer taxpayers. So-called smart growth policies are designed to reverse this process. Enacted in many states, including Oregon and Maryland, smart growth policies encourage locating new housing and jobs where the roads and sewers already exist before spending money on new infrastructure on the urban fringe. The Rutgers study mentioned earlier concluded that a nationwide smart growth strategy could save the country $250 billion over the next 25 years. (This assumes that about one-third of the marketplace will change their behavior and live closer to town centers.)

As alternatives to sprawl are being developed, the choice should not be between low-density and high-density job development. Metropolitan areas are interdependent wholes that need both. Some economic activities, like routine manufacturing and back-office functions, thrive in low-density settings, while others, such as specialty manufacturing and skilled service-sector employment, require high levels of density to perform best. Advocates of sprawl express little concern that sprawl causes older compact areas to decline. For them, that is just the verdict of the marketplace and this decline will have little effect on other parts of the metropolitan area. But to speak of one area as being independent from the rest makes as much sense as talking about the human brain being independent from the heart. Excessive sprawl weakens the heart of metropolitan areas, their central cities. And when the central city goes down, it can pull the whole region with it.

The Marketplace of Governments

Proponents of sprawl base their arguments not just on a free market in land, but a free market in local public policies. The average metropolitan area in the United States has over a hundred local governments that offer a wide range of taxing and spending policies. According to public choice theory—

the application of market economics to politics—the proliferation of local governments is good because households can "vote with their feet" for the package of services and taxes that best satisfy their preferences. Households will sort themselves into different local governments according to their preferences for local public goods. The proliferation of governments maximizes choice and increases the likelihood that each household will find a government that meets its taxing and spending priorities.

According to defenders of sprawl, people moved to the suburbs, as Gregg Easterbrook puts it, "to escape the corruption and mismanagement of urban government." Sprawl is thus an expression of consumer sovereignty in the marketplace of governments. Public choice sounds good in theory, but it is deeply flawed in practice. First, households do not primarily sort themselves according to their preferences for local public goods; they segregate themselves by race and class. Local governments do not aim to attract just any households; they seek to attract households that contribute more in taxable resources than they consume in services. The middle class and rich are well-served by the marketplace of governments. The poor are served badly, if at all.

The best evidence that suburban sprawl is not a free market phenomenon is the widespread use of exclusionary zoning regulations by local governments. The most common method is to exclude apartments, but many communities go further and require each house to be built on 2, 3, or 4-acre lots. In 1952, Westchester County, north of New York City, was zoned for 3.2 million residents. By the early 1960s, downzoning had reduced the county's population capacity to 1.8 million. By the 1980s apartments were permitted on less than one-half of one percent of the developable land in Westchester County. Exclusionary zoning promotes leapfrog development: developers are forced to leap over suburbs that exclude and build housing further and further out. With construction of new housing, especially apartments, coming almost to a halt in Westchester County due to zoning regulations, developers have leapfrogged to Putnam, Dutchess, and even Ulster counties—with commutes of fifty miles or more into New York City becoming commonplace.

Sprawl does not just spread people out, it segregates them by income and race. Because of exclusionary zoning, working-class families are unable to follow the jobs out to the suburbs. Because minorities tend to be poorer than whites, they are harmed the most. Central cities and poor inner-ring suburbs become areas of concentrated poverty, with all the resultant problems: poor schools, high crime, inferior public services, and high tax rates. The spatial segregation inherent in sprawl violates equal opportunity by denying those who are left behind equal access to education and to jobs, especially if they don't own a car. Not only do people trapped in areas of concentrated poverty earn less, independent of their own skills or effort, but they also spend more for goods and services on the private market. An extensive literature has documented that the ghetto poor, lacking access to high-volume supermarkets, pay more for groceries—anywhere from 5 to 35 percent more. They also pay more for car and homeowner's insurance and have inferior access to medical services.

Scholars have long debated whether suburbanization has been primarily caused by the "pull" of new housing and cheaper land or by the "push" of families trying to escape the problems of central cities. Although the exact mix is unclear, push factors are obviously an important cause of suburban sprawl. One of the reasons households move out to the urban fringe is to get as far away as possible from the problems of concentrated poverty. To the extent that push factors are important, sprawl is not a product of the free market but is caused by social processes of decay and abandonment. And the process can become self-reinforcing: suburban flight creams off the most prosperous families from older, compact neighborhoods, accelerating social decay and motivating even more families to flee.

Is Sprawl Good for Democracy?

According to its defenders, sprawl reflects consumer preferences, not just for consumer goods and suburban lifestyles but for local government services. Households are able to "vote with their feet," leaving behind large, bureaucratic, and expensive central city governments to embrace small, responsive suburban governments. For centuries political theorists have maintained that democracy flourishes best in small homogeneous republics. Homogeneity nurtures consensus on the ends of government and forestalls divisive conflicts. Smallness enhances civic participation because citizens can more readily see the connection between their own well-being and the well-being of the community. Suburban governments are the modern realization of Jeffersonian democracy. In short, sprawl is good for democracy.

In *Democracy in Suburbia* J. Eric Oliver uses national survey data to examine the effect of suburban governments on civic participation. His research shows that people who live in racially and economically homogenous suburbs display lower levels of civic participation. Politics in homogeneous suburban settings is like an old sweater—comfortable but boring. It lacks the burning economic and social issues that motivate people to become politically involved. A local government can hardly serve as an effective democratic training ground, if the most pressing issue is whether to paint the benches in front of city hall red, white, or blue. In addition, the spread-out nature of suburban life eats away at the time available for community affairs. Robert Putnam (see Chapter 4) reports that adding ten minutes in daily commuting time reduces involvement in community affairs by 10 percent.

Homogeneity makes politics superfluous. Indeed, if everybody is like everybody else, there is hardly any need for politics at all. Any randomly selected person can represent everyone else. In the marketplace of governments, citizenship has been reduced to a consumption good. Citizens vote with their feet on the type of government they want. Settled amidst others just like themselves, they do not need to bother with politics anymore.

Independent suburban governments are good at serving the immediate needs of their residents. The problem is that they have no incentive to address the issues that the different suburbs share in common. Like individual shepherds who continue grazing their sheep on common land until all the grass is killed off, suburban governments, if left unchecked, will kill off the resources and common understandings that make successful regions possible. (This is known as the "tragedy of the commons.") Whether the issue is traffic congestion, air pollution, or regional identity, it will tend to be ignored by independent suburban governments. Each tree will be well cared for but the forest ecology will be despoiled.

If sprawl created only apathy and inaction, it would be troubling enough. But it also nurtures intolerance and division. The issues forced off the agenda by sorting the population into small suburban governments don't go away. The costs of unaddressed racial and class divisions end up sneaking through the back door and biting people, whether they are aware of them or not. When poverty-stricken central city and inner suburban school districts fail to educate students to the demands of the modern job market, economic growth in the region is choked off and social problems proliferate. What does it mean for the quality of life when suburbanites are afraid to drive into the city to enjoy live theater or a concert because of crime? When people of different classes and races rarely encounter each other socially and seldom rub elbows in public spaces, stereotypes and prejudice can thrive.

It is one thing for different racial and economic groups to live in separate neighborhoods, divided by railroad tracks or a park. It is something quite different when they live in entirely different municipalities, separated by many miles of low-density development. Sprawl not only severs social relations between groups, it severs political relations. Surely, that is not healthy for our democracy.

◾ DISCUSSION QUESTIONS

1. What type of community did you grow up in (rural, small town, suburban, or urban)? From your own experience, what were the strengths and weaknesses of the physical environment you grew up in?

2. How racially or economically diverse was the community you grew up in? Do you think exposure to people who are different makes people more tolerant or less tolerant?

3. Do you think Americans have a "love affair with the automobile"? Or do you think it is more accurately characterized as an "arranged marriage"? Would you be willing to pay more and give up owning a car in order to live

in an area with pedestrian access to many services and excellent mass transit?

4. Everyone agrees that local governments should not be allowed to exclude people on the basis of race or religion. Presently, they are allowed to exclude people on the basis of income. Do you agree or disagree with this practice?

5. What do you think American metropolitan areas will look like fifty years from now?

■ SUGGESTED READINGS AND INTERNET RESOURCES

In *Cities Without Suburbs* (Washington, D.C.: Woodrow Wilson Center Press, 1993), David Rusk, the former mayor of Albuquerque, argues that metropolitan areas divided into many governments are more economically and racially polarized. Peter Dreier, John Mollenkopf, and Todd Swanstrom emphasize the relationship between sprawl and central city decline in their *Place Matters: Metropolitics for the Twenty-first Century* (Lawrence: University Press of Kansas, 2001). A good introduction to new urbanism is Andres Duany, Elizabeth Plater-Zyberk, and Jeff Speck, *Suburban Nation: The Rise of Sprawl and the Decline of the American Dream* (New York: North Point Press, 2000). In *Edge City: Life on the New Frontier* (New York: Doubleday, 1991), Joel Garreau maintains that Americans are "pretty smart cookies" and that they have gotten the kind of suburban development they want and need. For a compendium of articles defending sprawl, see Jane S. Shaw and Ronald D. Utt, eds., *A Guide to Smart Growth: Shattering Myths, Providing Solutions* (Washington, D.C.: Heritage Foundation, 2000).

Sprawl Watch Clearinghouse
www.sprawlwatch.org
This research center, generally critical of sprawl, provides information on sprawl, smart growth, and livable communities.

Sprawl-Busters Consultants
www.sprawl-busters.org
This web site is dedicated to helping small towns and suburbs oppose new Wal-Marts, which are viewed as draining the life from older city centers.

Reason Public Policy Institute
www.rppi.org
This web site is generally supportive of sprawl from a conservative, free market perspective.

13

Congress: Can It Serve the Public Good?

O f the three branches of the federal government, Congress provides the most direct representation, and it is sometimes called "the people's branch." But public disenchantment with Congress was on the rise in the late 1980s and early 1990s. When members of Congress voted themselves a pay raise in 1989, talk radio shows erupted with vehement denunciations of the nation's legislators as a privileged elite out of touch with the citizens who had sent them to Washington. The House banking scandal of 1992 added to the image of privilege the taint of corruption. Meanwhile, congressional inability to get mounting deficits under control or to pass major legislation created a picture of a profligate and inefficient legislature. Then came the electoral "earthquake" of 1994, when the voters took out their unhappiness on the Democrats who had long controlled Congress and established a new Republican majority pledged to transform the institution.

Under the leadership of the new Speaker of the House, Newt Gingrich, the Republicans moved swiftly to enact a "revolution" in Congress. Playing to popular democratic grievances, House Republicans took the lead in cutting down some of the symbols of congressional privilege. More importantly, congressional Republicans pushed a far-reaching conservative agenda that would shift power away from Washington to the states and private industry, cut taxes, and balance the budget through major spending cuts.

Perhaps the most remarkable aspect of the Republican "revolution" of 1995 was the attempt to transform fundamentally how Congress works. During the years of Democratic control, the most influential force in shaping congressional behavior had been the individual members, whose concern for reelection fostered close attention to district or state interests. Congress as an institution was relatively decentralized, with committees and subcommittees shaping legislation more than did the parties or their leadership. It was the goal of Speaker Gingrich and his followers to change the congressional culture by placing the unifying forces of leadership and party above the fragmenting forces of committee power and individualism. Through new rules and bold assertions of authority, Gingrich and his team consolidated power and kept the focus on their party's agenda.

Gingrich's congressional revolution was stymied by the end of 1995, once a majority of Americans blamed the Republicans for a government shutdown caused by a stalemate with President Clinton over the budget. A subsequent series of blows to Gingrich's power and reputation, culminating in Republican electoral disappointment in 1998, led to the Speaker's resignation. Republicans held on to their control of the House, but by increasingly narrow margins. The Senate returned to Democratic control in June 2001 when a Republican moderate, Senator James Jeffords of Vermont, announced that he was leaving the Republican party to become an independent and vote with the Democrats on leadership and organizational matters.

As the Republican revolution in Congress faded, the forces of individualism and committee power reasserted themselves. Yet the postrevolutionary Congress is a changed institution in an important respect: Partisanship is more intense and party leaders are more influential than they were before 1994. On major bills before the House and Senate, it is now common to find almost all Republicans on one side and almost all Democrats on the other. This partisan polarization was evident in the impeachment and trial of President Clinton in 1998–1999. Even the shock of the terrorist attacks on September 11, 2001 brought only a temporary halt to partisan conflict in Congress. Within a few weeks of September 11, the sharp division between Republicans and Democrats on economic policy had reemerged.

Although political scientists who study Congress did not anticipate the electoral explosion of 1994, the revolution of 1995, or the partisan polarization that we find today, they have long been concerned with the problems of the institution. Many have agreed with the electorate that the contemporary Congress has not been working well. Others, however, believe that Congress has strengths that disenchanted citizens (and disenchanted political scientists) fail to recognize.

Morris Fiorina, the author of our first selection, believes that both legislators and the people who elect them are motivated by calculations of self-interest. For members of Congress, the goal of self-interested behavior is reelection. For their constituents, the goal of self-interested behavior is pork-barrel projects, which bring federal dollars into their district, and assistance from the legislator in handling problems with federal bureaucrats ("casework"). Fiorina stresses how the bureaucratic state is a godsend to congressional incumbents, who get credit for establishing new programs that expand the bureaucracy and then win still further credit by denouncing the inevitable bureaucratic blunders that ensue. Note that in Fiorina's picture of congressional politics, neither representatives nor voters are paying much attention to legislation that seeks to address the nation's problems.

In the second selection, Joseph Bessette takes issue with Fiorina's sardonic account of Congress. Bessette argues that Congress still contains members who uphold James Madison's hopes for a deliberative and public-spirited legislature—elite democracy at its best. While not denying that the reelection motive affects members of Congress, he disputes the claim that it is the best explanation for congressional behavior. Bessette finds evidence that Congress is influenced by "serious lawmakers" who want to improve national well-being, seek the respect of their colleagues as much as the votes of their constituents, do the hard work of developing expertise in particular policy areas, sway fellow legislators through reasoned persuasion, and even are willing to take personal risks for the sake of the public good.

The debate between Fiorina and Bessette raises important questions about the character of representation in the contemporary Congress. It also may prove enlightening to set their accounts of Congress against the conception put forward during the Republican revolution of 1995. Are representatives and voters locked into a system of self-interested and short-term exchanges while no one devotes sufficient care to the long-term welfare of the nation? Can lawmakers engage in a deliberative search for the public good, and are there congressional reforms that will enhance such deliberation? Do stronger leadership and greater party unity make Congress more effective, or do they undercut deliberation about the public good?

The Rise of the Washington Establishment

MORRIS P. FIORINA

Dramatis Personae

I assume that most people most of the time act in their own self-interest. This is not to say that human beings seek only to amass tangible wealth but rather to say that human beings seek to achieve their own ends—tangible and intangible—rather than the ends of their fellow men. I do not condemn such behavior nor do I condone it (although I rather sympathize with Thoreau's comment that "if I knew for a certainty that a man was coming to my house with the conscious design of doing me good, I should run for my life"). I only claim that political and economic theories which presume self-interested behavior will prove to be more widely applicable than those which build on more altruistic assumptions.

What does the axiom imply when used in the specific context of this book, a context peopled by congressmen, bureaucrats, and voters? I assume that the primary goal of the typical congressman is reelection. Over and above the $57,000 salary plus "perks" and outside money, the office of congressman carries with it prestige, excitement, and power.[1] It is a seat in the cockpit of government. But in order to retain the status, excitement, and power (not to mention more tangible things) of office, the congressman must win reelection every two years. Even those congressmen genuinely concerned with good public policy must achieve reelection in order to continue their work. Whether narrowly self-serving or more publicly oriented, the individual congressman finds reelection to be at least a necessary condition for the achievement of his goals.

Moreover, there is a kind of natural selection process at work in the electoral arena. On average, those congressmen who are not primarily interested in reelection will not achieve reelection as often as those who are interested. We, the people, help to weed out congressmen whose primary motivation is not reelection. We admire politicians who courageously adopt the aloof role of the disinterested statesman, but we vote for those politicians who follow our wishes and do us favors.

---

1. The $57,000 salary was the salary for a member of Congress in 1977, when the first edition of Fiorina's book was published.

What about the bureaucrats? A specification of their goals is somewhat more controversial—those who speak of appointed officials as public servants obviously take a more benign view than those who speak of them as bureaucrats. The literature provides ample justification for asserting that most bureaucrats wish to protect and nurture their agencies. The typical bureaucrat can be expected to seek to expand his agency in terms of personnel, budget, and mission. One's status in Washington (again, not to mention more tangible things) is roughly proportional to the importance of the operation one oversees. And the sheer size of the operation is taken to be a measure of importance. As with congressmen, the specified goals apply even to those bureaucrats who genuinely believe in their agency's mission. If they believe in the efficacy of their programs, they naturally wish to expand them and add new ones. All of this requires more money and more people. The genuinely committed bureaucrat is just as likely to seek to expand his agency as the proverbial empire-builder.

And what of the third element in this equation, us? What do we, the voters who support the Washington system, strive for? Each of us wishes to receive a maximum of benefits from government for the minimum cost. This goal suggests maximum government efficiency, on the one hand, but it also suggests mutual exploitation on the other. Each of us favors an arrangement in which our fellow citizens pay for our benefits.

With these brief descriptions of the cast of characters in hand, let us proceed.

Tammany Hall Goes to Washington

What should we expect from a legislative body composed of individuals whose first priority is their continued tenure in office? We should expect, first, that the normal activities of its members are those calculated to enhance their chances of reelection. And we should expect, second, that the members would devise and maintain institutional arrangements which facilitate their electoral activities. . . .

For most of the twentieth century, congressmen have engaged in a mix of three kinds of activities: lawmaking, pork barreling, and casework. Congress is first and foremost a lawmaking body, at least according to constitutional theory. In every postwar session Congress "considers" thousands of bills and resolutions, many hundreds of which are brought to a record vote (over 500 in each chamber of the 93rd Congress). Naturally the critical consideration in taking a position for the record is the maximization of approval in the home district. If the district is unaffected by and unconcerned with the matter at hand, the congressman may then take into account the general welfare of the country. (This sounds cynical, but remember that "profiles in courage" are sufficiently rare that their occurrence inspires books and articles.) Abetted by political scientists of the pluralist school, politicians have propounded an ideology which maintains that the good of the country on any given issue is simply what is best for a majority of congressional districts.[2] This ideology provides a philosophical justification for what congressmen do while acting in their own self-interest.

A second activity favored by congressmen consists of efforts to bring home the bacon to their districts. Many popular articles have been written about the pork barrel, a term originally applied to rivers and harbors legislation but now generalized to cover all manner of federal largesse. Congressmen consider new dams, federal buildings, sewage treatment plants, urban renewal projects, etc. as sweet plums to be plucked. Federal projects are highly visible, their economic impact is easily detected by constituents, and sometimes they even produce something of value to the district. The average constituent may have some trouble translating his congressman's vote on some civil rights issue into a change in his personal welfare. But the workers hired and supplies purchased in connection with a big federal project provide benefits that are widely appreciated. The historical importance congressmen attach to the pork barrel is reflected in the rules of the House. That body accords certain classes of legislation "privileged" status: they may come directly to the floor without passing through the Rules Committee, a traditional graveyard for legislation. What kinds of legislation are privileged? Taxing and spending bills, for one: the government's power to raise and spend money must be kept relatively unfettered. But in addition, the omnibus rivers and harbors bills of the Public Works Committee and public lands bills from the Interior Committee share privileged status. The House will allow a civil rights or defense procurement or environmental bill to languish in the Rules Committee, but it takes special precautions to insure that nothing slows down the approval of dams and irrigation projects.

A third major activity takes up perhaps as much time as the other two combined. Traditionally, constituents appeal to their congressman for myriad favors and services. Sometimes only information is needed, but often constituents request that their congressman intervene in the internal workings of federal agencies to affect a decision in a favorable way, to reverse an adverse decision, or simply to speed up the glacial bureaucratic process. On the basis of extensive personal interviews with congressmen, Charles Clapp writes:

> Denied a favorable ruling by the bureaucracy on a matter of direct concern to him, puzzled or irked by delays in obtaining a decision, confused by the administrative maze through which he is directed to proceed, or ignorant of whom to write, a constituent may turn to his congressman for help. These letters offer great potential for political

---

2. Pluralist theory in political science argues that power in the United States is dispersed among many different groups, which compete for influence in a process marked by bargaining and compromise.

benefit to the congressman since they affect the constituent personally. If the legislator can be of assistance, he may gain a firm ally; if he is indifferent, he may even lose votes.

Actually congressmen are in an almost unique position in our system, a position shared only with high-level members of the executive branch. Congressmen possess the power to expedite and influence bureaucratic decisions. This capability flows directly from congressional control over what bureaucrats value most: higher budgets and new program authorizations. In a very real sense each congressman is a monopoly supplier of bureaucratic unsticking services for his district.

Every year the federal budget passes through the appropriations committees of Congress. Generally these committees make perfunctory cuts. But on occasion they vent displeasure on an agency and leave it bleeding all over the Capitol. The most extreme case of which I am aware came when the House committee took away the entire budget of the Division of Labor Standards in 1947 (some of the budget was restored elsewhere in the appropriations process). Deep and serious cuts are made occasionally, and the threat of such cuts keeps most agencies attentive to congressional wishes. Professors Richard Fenno and Aaron Wildavsky have provided extensive documentary and interview evidence of the great respect (and even terror) federal bureaucrats show for the House Appropriations Committee. Moreover, the bureaucracy must keep coming back to Congress to have its old programs reauthorized and new ones added. Again, most such decisions are perfunctory, but exceptions are sufficiently frequent that bureaucrats do not forget the basis of their agencies' existence. For example, the Law Enforcement Assistance Administration (LEAA) and the Food Stamps Program had no easy time of it this last Congress (94th). The bureaucracy needs congressional approval in order to survive, let alone expand. Thus, when a congressman calls about some minor bureaucratic decision or regulation, the bureaucracy considers his accommodation a small price to pay for the goodwill its cooperation will produce, particularly if he has any connection to the substantive committee or the appropriations subcommittee to which it reports.

From the standpoint of capturing voters, the congressman's lawmaking activities differ in two important respects from his pork-barrel and casework activities. First, programmatic actions are inherently controversial. Unless his district is homogeneous, a congressman will find his district divided on many major issues. Thus when he casts a vote, introduces a piece of nontrivial legislation, or makes a speech with policy content he will displease some elements of his district. Some constituents may applaud the congressman's civil rights record, but others believe integration is going too fast. Some support foreign aid, while others believe it's money poured down a rathole. Some advocate economic equality, others stew over welfare cheaters. On such policy matters the congressman can expect to make friends as well as enemies. Presumably he will behave so as to maximize the excess of the former over the latter, but nevertheless a policy stand will generally make some enemies.

In contrast, the pork barrel and casework are relatively less controversial. New federal projects bring jobs, shiny new facilities, and general economic prosperity, or so people believe. Snipping ribbons at the dedication of a new post office or dam is a much more pleasant pursuit than disposing of a constitutional amendment on abortion. Republicans and Democrats, conservatives and liberals, all generally prefer a richer district to a poorer one. Of course, in recent years the river damming and stream-bed straightening activities of the Army Corps of Engineers have aroused some opposition among environmentalists. Congressmen happily react by absorbing the opposition and adding environmentalism to the pork barrel: water treatment plants are currently a hot congressional item.

Casework is even less controversial. Some poor, aggrieved constituent becomes enmeshed in the tentacles of an evil bureaucracy and calls upon Congressman St. George to do battle with the dragon. Again Clapp writes:

> A person who has a reasonable complaint or query is regarded as providing an opportunity rather than as adding an extra burden to an already busy office. The party affiliation of the individual even when known to be different from that of the congressman does not normally act as a deterrent to action. Some legislators have built their reputations and their majorities on a program of service to all constituents irrespective of party. Regularly, voters affiliated with the opposition in other contests lend strong support to the lawmaker whose intervention has helped them in their struggle with the bureaucracy.

Even following the revelation of sexual improprieties, Wayne Hays won his Ohio Democratic primary by a two-to-one margin. According to a *Los Angeles Times* feature story, Hays's constituency base was built on a foundation of personal service to constituents:

> They receive help in speeding up bureaucratic action on various kinds of federal assistance—black lung benefits to disabled miners and their families, Social Security payments, veterans' benefits and passports.
>
> Some constituents still tell with pleasure of how Hays stormed clear to the seventh floor of the State Department and into Secretary of State Dean Rusk's office to demand, successfully, the quick issuance of a passport to an Ohioan.

Practicing politicians will tell you that word of mouth is still the most effective mode of communication. News of favors to constituents gets around and no doubt is embellished in the process.

In sum, when considering the benefits of his programmatic activities, the congressman must tote up gains and losses to arrive at a net profit. Pork barreling and casework, however, are basically pure profit.

A second way in which programmatic activities differ from casework and the pork barrel is the difficulty of assigning responsibility to the former as compared with the latter. No congressman can seriously claim that he is responsible for the 1964 Civil Rights Act, the ABM, or the 1972 Revenue Sharing Act.[3] Most constituents do have some vague notion that their congressman is only one of hundreds and their senator one of an even hundred. Even committee chairmen have a difficult time claiming credit for a piece of major legislation, let alone a rank-and-file congressman. Ah, but casework, and the pork barrel. In dealing with the bureaucracy, the congressman is not merely one vote of 435. Rather, he is a nonpartisan power, someone whose phone calls snap an office to attention. He is not kept on hold. The constituent who receives aid believes that his congressman and his congressman alone got results. Similarly, congressmen find it easy to claim credit for federal projects awarded their districts. The congressman may have instigated the proposal for the project in the first place, issued regular progress reports, and ultimately announced the award through his office. Maybe he can't claim credit for the 1965 Voting Rights Act, but he can take credit for Littletown's spanking new sewage treatment plant.

Overall then, programmatic activities are dangerous (controversial), on the one hand, and programmatic accomplishments are difficult to claim credit for, on the other. While less exciting, casework and pork barreling are both safe and profitable. For a reelection-oriented congressman the choice is obvious.

The key to the rise of the Washington establishment (and the vanishing marginals) is the following observation: *the growth of an activist federal government has stimulated a change in the mix of congressional activities.*[4] Specifically, a lesser proportion of congressional effort is now going into programmatic activities and a greater proportion into pork-barrel and casework activities. As a result, today's congressmen make relatively fewer enemies and relatively more friends among the people of their districts.

To elaborate, a basic fact of life in twentieth-century America is the growth of the federal role and its attendant bureaucracy. Bureaucracy is the characteristic mode of delivering public goods and services. Ceteris paribus, the more the government attempts to do for people, the more extensive a bureaucracy it creates. As the scope of government expands, more and more citizens find themselves in direct contact with the federal government. Consider the rise in such contacts upon passage of the Social Security Act, work relief projects, and other New Deal programs. Consider the millions of additional citizens touched by the veterans' programs of the postwar period. Consider the untold numbers whom the Great Society and its aftermath brought face to face with the federal government. In 1930 the federal bureaucracy was small and rather distant from the everyday concerns of Americans. By 1975 it was neither small nor distant.

---

3. The acronym ABM stands for antiballistic missile.
4. *Marginals* refers to congressional incumbents who barely hold on to their seats in close races; instead, most incumbents at the time Fiorina was writing were winning their races by large margins.

As the years have passed, more and more citizens and groups have found themselves dealing with the federal bureaucracy. They may be seeking positive actions—eligibility for various benefits and awards of government grants. Or they may be seeking relief from the costs imposed by bureaucratic regulations—on working conditions, racial and sexual quotas, market restrictions, and numerous other subjects. While not malevolent, bureaucracies make mistakes, both of commission and omission, and normal attempts at redress often meet with unresponsiveness and inflexibility and sometimes seeming incorrigibility. Whatever the problem, the citizen's congressman is a source of succor. The greater the scope of government activity, the greater the demand for his services.

Private monopolists can regulate the demand for their product by raising or lowering the price. Congressmen have no such (legal) option. When the demand for their services rises, they have no real choice except to meet that demand—to supply more bureaucratic unsticking services—so long as they would rather be elected than unelected. This vulnerability to escalating constituency demands is largely academic, though. I seriously doubt that congressmen resist their gradual transformation from national legislators to errand boy–ombudsmen. As we have noted, casework is all profit. Congressmen have buried proposals to relieve the casework burden by establishing a national ombudsman or Congressman Reuss's proposed Administrative Counsel of the Congress. One of the congressmen interviewed by Clapp stated:

> Before I came to Washington I used to think that it might be nice if the individual states had administrative arms here that would take care of necessary liaison between citizens and the national government. But a congressman running for reelection is interested in building fences by providing personal services. The system is set to reelect incumbents regardless of party, and incumbents wouldn't dream of giving any of this service function away to any subagency. As an elected member I feel the same way.

In fact, it is probable that at least some congressmen deliberately stimulate the demand for their bureaucratic fixit services. Recall that the new Republican in district A travels about his district saying:

> I'm your man in Washington. What are your problems? How can I help you?

And in district B, did the demand for the congressman's services rise so much between 1962 and 1964 that a "regiment" of constituency staff became necessary?[5] Or, having access to the regiment, did the new Democrat stimulate the demand to which he would apply his regiment?

---

5. Earlier in his book, Fiorina presented case studies of districts A and B.

In addition to greatly increased casework, let us not forget that the growth of the federal role has also greatly expanded the federal pork barrel. The creative pork barreler need not limit himself to dams and post offices—rather old-fashioned interests. Today, creative congressmen can cadge LEAA money for the local police, urban renewal and housing money for local politicians, educational program grants for the local education bureaucracy. And there are sewage treatment plants, worker training and retraining programs, health services, and programs for the elderly. The pork barrel is full to overflowing. The conscientious congressman can stimulate applications for federal assistance (the sheer number of programs makes it difficult for local officials to stay current with the possibilities), put in a good word during consideration, and announce favorable decisions amid great fanfare.

In sum, everyday decisions by a large and growing federal bureaucracy bestow significant tangible benefits and impose significant tangible costs. Congressmen can affect these decisions. Ergo, the more decisions the bureaucracy has the opportunity to make, the more opportunities there are for the congressman to build up credits.

The nature of the Washington system is now quite clear. Congressmen (typically the majority Democrats) earn electoral credits by establishing various federal programs (the minority Republicans typically earn credits by fighting the good fight). The legislation is drafted in very general terms, so some agency, existing or newly established, must translate a vague policy mandate into a functioning program, a process that necessitates the promulgation of numerous rules and regulations and, incidentally, the trampling of numerous toes. At the next stage, aggrieved and/or hopeful constituents petition their congressman to intervene in the complex (or at least obscure) decision processes of the bureaucracy. The cycle closes when the congressman lends a sympathetic ear, piously denounces the evils of bureaucracy, intervenes in the latter's decisions, and rides a grateful electorate to ever more impressive electoral showings. Congressmen take credit coming and going. They are the alpha and the omega.

The popular frustration with the permanent government in Washington is partly justified, but to a considerable degree it is misplaced resentment. *Congress is the linchpin of the Washington establishment.* The bureaucracy serves as a convenient lightning rod for public frustration and a convenient whipping boy for congressmen. But so long as the bureaucracy accommodates congressmen, the latter will oblige with ever larger budgets and grants of authority. Congress does not just react to big government—it creates it. All of Washington prospers. More and more bureaucrats promulgate more and more regulations and dispense more and more money. Fewer and fewer congressmen suffer electoral defeat. Elements of the electorate benefit from government programs, and all of the electorate is eligible for ombudsman services. But the general, long-term welfare of the United States is no more than an incidental by-product of the system.

Congress and Deliberative Democracy

JOSEPH M. BESSETTE

Deliberation Defined

The deliberation that lies at the core of the kind of democracy established by the American constitutional system can be defined most simply as *reasoning on the merits of public policy*. As commonly and traditionally understood, deliberation is a reasoning process in which the participants seriously consider substantive information and arguments and seek to decide individually and to persuade each other as to what constitutes good public policy. Thus, deliberation includes a variety of activities often called "problem solving" or "analytic": the investigation and identification of social, economic, or governmental problems; the evaluation of current policies or programs; the consideration of various and competing proposals; and the formulation of legislative or administrative remedies. In any genuine deliberative process the participants must be open to the facts, arguments, and proposals that come to their attention and must share a general willingness to learn from their colleagues and others.

So defined, the proximate aim of a deliberative process is the conferral of some public good or benefit. Such a benefit need not necessarily be national in scope (such as a healthy economy or a sound national defense); it may instead be a locally oriented good (such as a flood control project or a new highway), a good directed toward a broad class of citizens (as with civil rights laws or labor legislation), or even transnational in its reach (such as foreign aid). Thus, the existence of deliberation does not turn on the distinction between local and national interests. An overriding desire to serve one's local constituents does not in itself close a legislator to the persuasive effects of information and arguments, although such a legislator will respond to different kinds of appeals than one who seeks to promote national interests. This is true even if the desire to confer local benefits results directly from self-interested calculations, such as the representative's desire to be reelected; for the legislator who seeks singlemindedly to be reelected may well find that in some situations this goal requires him to give real consideration to the merits of legislative proposals designed to benefit his constituents.

From *The Mild Voice of Reason: Deliberative Democracy and American National Government*, by Joseph M. Bessette. Copyright © 1994 by the University of Chicago Press. Reprinted with permission.

Although legislators may deliberate about local, or partial, interests as well as those of a national dimension, there remains a relationship between the likelihood and nature of deliberation in Congress and the scope of the public benefits that legislators seek to confer. Consider, for example, legislators who deliberate about how to promote the well-being of specific interests. If such legislators see their job essentially in terms of doing good for external groups, they will be inclined to accept the groups' determination as to how this should be done; for who knows the groups' interests better than they do? The narrower and more specific the group (wheat farmers, auto workers, coal miners, etc.) the less difference of opinion or conflict there will be and therefore the less need for such a legislator to consider different arguments or to reason about alternative proposals. However, as the scope of the legislator's concerns widens, to encompass more or broader interests, the more difficult it will become to defer to the interests themselves for guidance. A variety of differing and often conflicting opinions will highlight the complexity of the issues at stake and place a greater obligation on the lawmaker to exercise some independent judgment. For the legislator who seeks to promote the national interest, personal deliberation will be essential; insofar as other legislators share the same goal, collective deliberation will be pervasive.

Personal deliberation by individual legislators does not require that others in the lawmaking body share the same goals. A member of the House, for example, could deliberate in a serious way about how the federal government could solve a transportation problem within his or her district even if no House members shared the same concern. Collective deliberation, however, necessarily requires some sharing of goals, purposes, or values. If legislators are to reason together about the merits of public policy, there must be some common ground for the arguments and appeals essential to deliberation. Whether the shared goal is quite specific and well defined (e.g., a national health insurance plan along the British model) or much broader and even somewhat vague (e.g., a healthy economy or a sound national defense), it will provide the basis for legislators, who may have little else in common, to share information and to reason and argue together about public policy.

Although the geographically based representation of the American system of government has a tendency to elevate localized interests and needs over broad programmatic concerns, district and state representation also provides a solid basis for the sharing of goals within Congress. Similar kinds of constituencies are likely to have common interests and needs and therefore similar desires or expectations for national policy. Inner-city residents throughout the nation are likely to have similar desires regarding social welfare policy. Farmers from the Midwest, South, and West are likely to agree on the need for price supports. Blue-collar workers in threatened industries across the country are likely to desire high tariffs or other protectionist measures. Those elected to Congress to represent these kinds of constituents will soon discover that many of their colleagues represent similar electorates and thus share many of the same policy goals. In some cases such like-minded legislators institutionalize and promote their shared policy interests through an informal caucus which helps them to share information and ideas and to coordinate policy efforts.

In describing what deliberation is, it is important to clarify what it is not; for policy deliberation is not just any kind of reasoning involved in the policy process. As understood throughout this book, policy deliberation necessarily involves reasoning about the substantive benefits of public policy, reasoning about some *public* good—some good external to the decision-makers themselves. "Reasoning on the merits" of public policy means reasoning about how public policy can benefit the broader society or some significant portion thereof. Thus, there is a sharp analytical distinction between deliberation and merely self-interested calculations (however complex the relationship between these two in practice). Similarly, deliberation does not include reasoning about legislative tactics, such as drafting a bill to facilitate its referral to a sympathetic committee or determining how to use the rules of the House or Senate to greatest advantage during the legislative process.

Although a deliberative process is per se rational or analytical, the values or dispositions that the participants bring to bear on the determination of good public policy may reflect a host of diverse influences: general upbringing, parental values, personal experiences, the views of friends and acquaintances, influential teachers, partisan attachments, social class, economic status, etc. Thus, it is not surprising that different individuals often reach quite opposed conclusions about the merits of policy proposals even when exposed to the same information and arguments. Such disagreement is not in itself evidence of the absence of deliberation.

Deliberation, as defined here, may take a variety of forms. It may be a largely consensual process in which like-minded individuals work together to fashion the details of a policy they all desire; or it may involve deep-seated conflicts over fundamental issues or principles. It may result in unanimity of view, where no votes are necessary; or it may reveal sharp disagreements that require formal voting to determine the majority view. It may range from private reflection in the quiet of an office or study to an emotionally charged exchange on the floor of the House or Senate. It may take the form of open and public discussions preserved in official records or of private exchanges hidden from public view. It may involve direct discussions among elected officials themselves or, perhaps more frequently, conversations among their staff. It may be limited to those who hold formal positions in the government, either elective or appointive; or it may include the ideas and opinions of interest groups, trade associations, national organizations, or the scholarly community.

Nonetheless, however diverse the various manifestations of deliberation, every deliberative process involves three essential elements: information, arguments, and persuasion. . . .

Bargaining and reelection theories are the two great pillars that support the widespread contemporary view that Congress is not a deliberative institution (at least in any fundamental sense) and, by implication, that American democracy is not a deliberative democracy. We have seen in the previous chapter how little support the case studies of policymaking within Congress provide for the belief that bargaining is the predominant device for reaching collective decisions in the House and Senate. What, then, of the reelection incentive as the principal explanation for individual desires and actions? No one can dispute the analytical attractiveness of *assuming* its dominance, but what does the empirical evidence tell us, fairly reviewed?

We must be careful how we frame the issue. The question here is not whether the reelection incentive matters in Congress. The vast majority of those who serve in the House and Senate give every indication that they desire to remain in office (although some voluntarily resign at each election). Thus, it is reasonable to call the reelection incentive an established fact. This incentive, then, inclines the members of Congress to engage in behaviors helpful to future electoral success. As we have seen, such behaviors are not limited to formal campaigning. They may occur throughout a legislative term (it is not unusual to hear House members complain about campaigning for reelection all the time) and may include activities that are clearly nonlegislative in character, such as tracking down missing Social Security checks, posing for photographs with delegations from home, and the like. That those who serve in the House and Senate devote a certain amount of their time and resources, especially staff time, to nonlegislative activities that will promote reelection is beyond dispute.

Thus the issue here is not whether the members of Congress pursue reelection but rather whether the reelection incentive squeezes out deliberative activities in a way that undermines, or even destroys, Congress's character as a deliberative institution. This could occur in two ways. First, reelection-oriented activities could so consume the time and resources of the member that nothing is left for serious reasoning about public policy. Second, the reelection incentive could intrude upon formal legislative activities in such a way as to distort otherwise deliberative behavior. For example, the committee member who single-mindedly plays to the cameras during some hearing on a controversial matter because it is good politics has allowed his private interests to overcome his deliberative responsibilities.

While it is certainly possible for the reelection incentive to undermine deliberation in these two ways, it is not necessary. The fact that the members of Congress do certain things to promote their reelection is hardly proof that they do not do other things to reach reasoned judgments about the merits of public policy. Indeed, as noted earlier, those who designed the American Congress saw no necessary incompatibility between the reelection incentive and deliberation. The framers believed not only that the legislator's desire to return to Congress would not disable him from engaging in genuine deliberation about national laws, but also that the reelection incentive was the vital link between deliberations in Congress and popular interests and attitudes. Indeed, to argue that the system of public accountability in the modern Congress makes genuine deliberation impossible is virtually the equivalent of saying that deliberation and democracy, as presently constituted in the United States, are incompatible.

It follows, then, that in assessing Congress as a deliberative institution the issue is not so much whether the reelection incentive is a powerful motive in influencing congressional behavior, but rather whether and to what degree legislators in the U.S. Congress embrace and act upon the independent desire to promote good public policy, the end for which deliberation is the means. How much evidence do we have that the ambitious and reelection-seeking members of Congress actually care about and work to promote good public policy? . . .

The High Art of Responsible Lawmaking

. . . A theory of legislative behavior that posits only the low motive of reelection cannot even provide the vocabulary to describe and explain the serious lawmaking evident in the accounts summarized here. To repeat a question asked above, how can the reelection incentive explain why any legislator would choose substance over symbols, hard work over posturing, or responsibility over popularity? And, most incongruous of all, why would any legislator moved primarily by the reelection incentive ever take any political risks for the sake of substantive policy goals?

Conversely, a full understanding and appreciation of the high art of lawmaking allows the low arts of mere self-seeking to reveal themselves fully for what they are. Could it even be said that it is only some sense of what constitutes serious lawmaking that makes it possible to understand fully the nature of the lower self-seeking arts (what Hamilton called "the little arts of popularity")? Consider "posturing," for example, a term that came up in several of the portraits. Lawmakers and those who observe and study lawmakers have little difficulty identifying posturing when they see it; but surely this is because in the back of their minds they possess a rather clear picture or model of what posturing is not: reasoned argument and effort at genuine persuasion. Posturing can be understood fully only in contrast to this thing which it is not, in contrast to something higher than itself.

What, then, are the principal characteristics of those who engage in serious lawmaking in the United States Congress? Insofar as the accounts reviewed here are an accurate guide, the following stand out:

- Serious lawmakers are not satisfied simply to serve in Congress and enjoy its many perks. They want to make a difference, to accomplish something of importance, to make the nation (and perhaps the world) a better place through their governing activities. They believe that there is a public interest, that it is knowable, and that their efforts in Congress can help to achieve it.

- By virtue of their office (membership in the House or Senate, committee and subcommittee chairmanships, leadership positions, etc.) they feel a sense of responsibility to something beyond their personal advantage, a duty to larger ends. It is the accomplishment of these larger ends that is the source of their deepest political satisfaction.

- They seek to earn the respect of their colleagues and of those outside Congress through their deliberative efforts and their substantive achievements. They want to be known as effective legislators. The respect they so earn from their colleagues is a principal source of their power in Congress.

- They develop substantive expertise in the areas under their jurisdiction through careful and thorough analysis, engaging in the hard work necessary to master a subject. Open to facts and arguments, they are willing to learn from others.

- They seek to influence others on legislative matters principally through reasoned persuasion. Although they recognize that raw political bargaining may be necessary to build majorities, their decided preference is to influence through facts and arguments, not through bargains.

- They try to protect the opportunities for responsible lawmaking from the consequences of unrestrained publicity seeking. They have little respect for "legislators" who seek only popularity and reelection.

- Although they wish and seek reelection to Congress, they are, nonetheless, willing to take some political risks for the sake of good public policy.

It would be an understatement to say that these kinds of characteristics are not well accounted for by the reigning self-interest theories of Congress or of American government more generally. Moreover, the point here is not that the 535 members of the House and Senate fall neatly into two categories: the merely ambitious who pursue only narrow self-interest and the high-minded who strive for the public good. Rather these represent something like the extremes of the continuum, from the low to the high, between which the various members of Congress can be found. As this exercise has tried to demonstrate, some members of the U.S. Congress, perhaps especially the leaders within the institution, look more like the serious lawmaker described by these characteristics than like the mere self-seeker we have come to view as the norm. If, as those who created the U.S. Congress believed, the serious lawmaker is nothing less than essential to the success of American democracy, then we ought to have a very great interest indeed in assessing the status and activities of such legislators in the contemporary

Congress: How many members of the institution behave like serious lawmakers and has this changed over time? What electoral conditions promote the election of the serious-minded, public-spirited legislator as opposed to the mere self-seeking politician? How much influence do serious lawmakers have in the two branches? What are the forces that affect their lawmaking behavior? And what procedural or structural reforms, if any, would enhance the prospects of serious lawmaking in Congress? Although it is beyond the scope of this work to address systematically these various questions, a few additional points can be made.

A central issue is how many of our representatives and senators display the characteristics of the serious lawmaker described here—if not all of the time, then at least much of the time. That the serious lawmaker is not so rare as to be analytically uninteresting or irrelevant to the workings of Congress on major policy issues is amply demonstrated by the kinds of detailed portraits of legislators reviewed here, by the large body of evidence demonstrating the importance of the goal of promoting good public policy in attracting members of the House and Senate to many of the leading committees, and by such occasional episodes as the nearly united, and quite unpopular, stand by Senate Republicans in 1985 in favor of a COLA freeze on Social Security payments. . . .

In addition to the evidence that serious lawmakers are more prevalent within Congress than modern theories acknowledge, there is also reason for believing that they have a greater impact on policymaking than their mere numbers (and relative proportion of the membership) might suggest. One reason is that because the serious lawmaker undertakes the kind of substantive legislative work that does not interest the mere self-seeker, he will *ipso facto* influence the details of policy in a way that the self-seeker rarely will. After all, the legislator dominated by the reelection incentive has "only a modest interest in what goes into bills or what their passage accomplishes." He knows that "in a large class of undertakings the electoral payment is for positions rather than for effects." The second reason is that the serious lawmaker may be more prevalent among institutional leaders than among the membership generally. In part this is because the members of Congress may select as their leaders those with a reputation for legislative skill and seriousness of purpose. In addition, for formal leadership positions within committees and subcommittees, where selection is virtually automatic, the office itself may foster a sense of responsibility to ends larger than mere private advantage.

This latter point is one of the conclusions of Martha Derthick and Paul Quirk in their study of the deregulation movement of the Carter and Reagan years:

> There is an unmistakable pattern in our leading cases: presidents, commission chairmen, and congressional committee and subcommittee leaders generally advocated reform. We infer that such leaders are especially induced or constrained to serve broad,

encompassing, diffuse interests. Any officeholder faces conflicting pressures of personal conviction, desire for reputation, and political interest; some of these pressures will encourage service to broader, diffuse interests while others certainly will not. For leaders, the pressures that encourage such service are markedly enhanced by the very fact of leadership, which makes their actions visible to a wider public, exposes them to observation and comment among the political and governmental elite, and tends to elicit a more compelling sense of responsibility.

And as they say about congressional leaders in particular:

> To the extent that a congressman finds or places himself in [a position of leadership on an issue] . . . , two related conditions follow, both of them likely to affect his response: his actions will be more consequential to the outcome; and because they will be more consequential, they will also be more widely observed. Leaders on an issue will be more prone to act on their conception of the public interest, because it is more irresponsible for those in a position of power to do otherwise.

It follows that even a handful of serious, responsible lawmakers in key positions within Congress may have a more consequential effect on the substance of public policy than a much larger number of mere self-seeking politicians who can pursue and achieve private advantage through nonlegislative means.

■ DISCUSSION QUESTIONS

1. What motivates members of Congress in their legislative behavior? What motivates constituents when they decide whom to vote for in a congressional contest? How do Fiorina and Bessette approach questions of motivation, and how do their respective approaches reflect different conceptions of human nature?

2. Can Congress initiate changes that will remove the causes of public disenchantment? Why is Fiorina skeptical about this possibility? How might Bessette explain public disenchantment with Congress? What reforms might he support that would enhance deliberation in Congress *and* the public's respect for the institution?

3. How do we explain lawmaking that serves narrow interests? Have members of Congress become too tied up with the self-seeking objectives of federal bureaucrats and their programs, as Fiorina argues? Or are there other reasons that better explain the inability of Congress to serve the national

interest—for example, the power of monied private interests to influence legislation?

4. Do Fiorina and Bessette neglect the importance of partisanship in congressional politics? Is partisan behavior in Congress closer to Fiorina's focus on self-interest or Bessete's emphasis on deliberation?

SUGGESTED READINGS AND INTERNET RESOURCES

The central place of the electoral motive in congressional behavior is highlighted in David Mayhew, *Congress: The Electoral Connection* (New Haven, Conn.: Yale University Press, 1974). For a rich descriptive account of the interactions of representatives and their constituents, the classic work is Richard Fenno, *Home Style: House Members in Their Districts* (Boston: Little, Brown, 1978). A sophisticated analysis of why members of Congress sometimes support narrow interests and sometimes vote for a broader public interest is R. Douglas Arnold, *The Logic of Congressional Action* (New Haven, Conn.: Yale University Press, 1990). Heightened partisan conflict in Congress is the subject of Jon R. Bond and Richard Fleisher, eds., *Polarized Politics: Congress and the President in a Partisan Era* (Washington, D.C.: Congressional Quarterly Press, 2000). See Lawrence C. Dodd and Bruce I. Oppenheimer, eds., *Congress Reconsidered,* 7th ed. (Washington, D.C.: Congressional Quarterly Press, 2001) for an anthology of insightful articles by leading scholars in the field of congressional politics.

Free Congress Foundation
www.freecongress.org
This web site, reflecting a conservative perspective on Congress, offers numerous publications and Internet links.

National Committee for an Effective Congress
www.ncec.org
This web site, reflecting a liberal perspective on Congress, contains extensive coverage of liberal challengers to conservative incumbents.

Library of Congress
thomas.loc.gov
The Library of Congress web site offers the Congressional Record and information on legislation and committee activity for current and recent Congresses.

14

The Presidency: How Much Difference Does the Individual Make?

The president of the United States is coming to your city. You may not like this president's personality, programs, or ideas, but you are likely to make an effort to see him (someday, her) in the flesh. Why? Because most Americans regard the president—any president—as the embodiment of our nation's history and greatness. The presidency is commonly seen as the personification of American democracy.

This equation of the presidency with democracy would have come as a surprise to the generation that established the American Republic. The men who drafted the U.S. Constitution believed that democracy had been carried too far in the revolutionary era. They conceived of the new president not as a democratic champion of the people but rather as a constitutional officer who would, by the length of his term and the loftiness of his stature, be insulated from the passions and pressures of ordinary citizens. Anti-federalist critics of the Constitution, however, feared that the president would be too remote from the people and too reminiscent of the arbitrary executive that the Revolution had banished.

Neither Federalists nor Anti-federalists viewed the executive as a democratic figure. In sharp contrast, modern presidents present themselves as the only elected representative of the whole people and the very embodiment of democracy itself. Other political actors—members of Congress, bureaucrats, political parties, interest groups—are taken to represent only partial and selfish interests. The president alone can claim to stand for the national interest and the public good.

The modern equation of the presidency with democracy began with Theodore Roosevelt and Woodrow Wilson and reached its zenith with Franklin Roosevelt. After Roosevelt, most journalists, political scientists, and historians came to believe that presidents were the principal agents of democratic purpose in the American political system. Modern media, especially television, offered presidents a vehicle to bring their dramas of democratic leadership directly into people's homes.

Yet even as the bond between the presidency and democracy was celebrated, presidents were extending their powers in ways that threatened democratic values. With the Vietnam War, the Watergate scandal, and later the Iran-contra affair, the undemocratic potential of executive power was revealed. A new and more skeptical perspective toward the presidency began to emerge. At the same time, the perceived failures of most recent presidents left many Americans eager to see a reassertion of an effective presidency as a champion of democracy.

The role of presidents in American democracy depends upon the relationship between an individual leader and an institutional system. For political scientist Fred Greenstein, the critical importance of each chief executive's individual qualities flows from "the highly personalized nature of the modern American presidency." Greenstein suggests that presidential performance will vary depending on how each president measures up on six personal dimensions: "effectiveness as a public communicator"; "organizational capacity"; "political skill"; "vision"; "cognitive style"; and "emotional intelligence." In this excerpt from his book *The Presidential Difference,* Greenstein illustrates the impact of each of these six dimensions with material on modern presidents from Franklin D. Roosevelt to Bill Clinton. No president, he suggests, is likely to be strong on all six dimensions, but the most effective presidents will possess several key skills and avoid the most crippling deficiencies, especially a flawed emotional nature.

Stephen Skowronek, another political scientist, criticizes the idea that individual attributes and skills are the important variables in presidential performance. For Skowronek, all of presidential history (and not just the "modern presidency") can be viewed in light of the rise and fall of political regimes. A regime marks an era in which one party is dominant in its electoral strength, coalition of interest groups, and ideas about the proper relationship between government and society (e.g., the liberal regime that began with Franklin D. Roosevelt and ended with Jimmy Carter). Skowronek suggests that presidents come into office confronting four types of political structures: (1) "a politics of reconstruction," in which the collapsing force of the previously dominant regime provides the opportunity for a president of the opposing coalition to launch a new regime and achieve greatness; (2) "a politics of disjunction," in which a president associated with a regime that is falling apart faces an "impossible leadership situation" and thereby appears incompetent; (3) "a politics of preemption," in which a president opposed to a still-vigorous regime tries to find success by blending the ideas of his own party with those of the dominant party; and (4) "a politics of articulation," in which a president associated with a still-vigorous regime tries to complete its unfinished agenda, at the risk of fostering divisions in the dominant coalition and evoking charges that he has betrayed the true faith set down by the reconstructive president who first formed the regime. In each of these cases, says Skowronek, what most matters about a president is not his character but his place in the changing structures of American politics.

The conflicting perspectives of Greenstein and Skowronek are evident in the respective ways they interpret the presidency of Bill Clinton. Greenstein rates Clinton on each of his six dimensions, finding a mixture of strengths and weaknesses, but his bottom line is Clinton's flawed character. Skowronek describes Clinton as one of a series of preemptive presidents, similar in the opportunities he seized and the constraints he encountered to such predecessors as Woodrow Wilson and Richard Nixon. Thus, whereas Greenstein ascribes Clinton's lack of "a clearly defined point of view" to a personal deficiency in vision, Skowronek finds the source of Clinton's "indeterminate" positions in his political need, as a "third way" president, to adopt the most popular parts of both conservatism and liberalism.

From the perspective of Fred Greenstein, American democracy has a great deal riding on the personal qualities of the individual elected every four years. From the perspective of Stephen Skowronek, the potential of each president is bound up with longer-term political structures that reflect dominant interests, institutions, and ideas. Are presidents, as Greenstein argues, likely to serve democracy well or poorly depending upon the personal qualities they bring with them to their office? Or are presidents, as Skowronek argues, strengthened or weakened by the opportunity structures characteristic of the four types of leadership found throughout presidential history? How much of a difference does the individual in the White House make to the workings of democratic politics in the United States?

Lessons from the Modern Presidency

FRED I. GREENSTEIN

> The executive branch of our government is like a chameleon. To a startling degree it reflects the character and personality of the President.
>
> —Clark M. Clifford, 1972

The highly personalized nature of the modern American presidency makes the strengths and weaknesses of the White House incumbent of the utmost importance. It places a premium on the ability of chief executives to get the most out of their strong points and compensate for their limitations. It also places a great value on the ability of Americans to select presidents with attributes that serve well in the Oval Office. . . .

The Qualities That Bear on Presidential Performance

Effectiveness as a Public Communicator For an office that places so great a premium on the presidential pulpit, the modern presidency has been surprisingly lacking in effective public communicators. Most presidents have not addressed the public with anything approximating the professionalism of countless educators, members of the clergy, and radio and television broadcasters. Roosevelt, Kennedy, and Reagan—and Clinton at his best—are the shining exceptions.

Chief executives who find the most able of the presidential communicators daunting should be relieved to learn that their eloquence was in part the product of effort and experience. Roosevelt, Kennedy, and Reagan took part in drafting their speeches and rehearsed their presentations. In 1910, when Eleanor Roosevelt first heard her husband give a speech, she was taken aback by his long pauses and slow delivery. "I was worried for fear that he would never go on," she recalled. When Kennedy was a freshman congressman, he had a diffident, self-effacing public manner. And for all of Reagan's professionalism, he did not perfect the podium manner of his political years until the 1950s, when his film career drew to a close and he found employment on the speaking circuit.

One president who allowed himself to be fazed by an accomplished predecessor was George Bush, who seems to have concluded that since he

Reprinted with the permission of The Free Press, an imprint of Simon & Schuster Adult Publishing Group from *The Presidential Difference: Leadership Style from FDR to Clinton* by Fred I. Greenstein. Copyright © 2000 by Fred I. Greenstein.

could not compare with Reagan as a communicator, he should be his near antithesis. Bush used the White House briefing room for his public communications, only rarely addressing the nation from the Oval Office, and he instructed his speechwriters to temper his prose. Bush's initial three years of high public approval provide a reminder that formal addresses are not the only way for a president to remain in the good graces of the public. His defeat highlights the costs of a leadership style that gives short shrift to the teaching and preaching side of presidential leadership.

Organizational Capacity   A president's capacity as an organizer includes his ability to forge a team and get the most out of it, minimizing the tendency of subordinates to tell their boss what they sense he wants to hear. It also includes a quite different matter: his proficiency at creating effective institutional arrangements. There is an illuminating postpresidential indicator of a president's success as a team builder—the way that he is remembered by alumni of his administration. Veterans of the Truman, Eisenhower, Kennedy, Ford, and Bush presidencies have nothing but praise for their erstwhile chiefs. In contrast, few Johnson, Carter, and Clinton lieutenants emerged from their White House service with unmixed views of the president they served. Most ambivalent are the former aides of Richard Nixon, a number of whom went to prison for their actions in his service.

Presidents also differ in their ability to avail themselves of a rich and varied fare of advice and information. FDR encouraged diversity in the recommendations that reached him by pitting his assistants against one another. Kennedy's method was to charge his brother Robert and his alter ego Theodore Sorensen with scrutinizing the proposals of his other advisors for flaws and pitfalls. The modern president with by far the greatest and most demanding organizational experience was Eisenhower, who had a highly developed view of the matter. "I know of only one way in which you can be sure you have done your best to make a wise decision," he declared in a 1967 interview:

> That is to get all of the [responsible policymakers] with their different viewpoints in front of you, and listen to them debate. I do not believe in bringing them in one at a time, and therefore being more impressed by the most recent one you hear than the earlier ones. You must get courageous men of strong views, and let them debate with each other.

Not all of the modern presidents have been open to vigorous give and take. Nixon and Reagan were uncomfortable in the presence of face-to-face disagreement. Johnson's Texas-sized personality had a chilling effect on some of his subordinates. His NSC staff member Chester Cooper recalled recurrent fantasies of facing down LBJ at NSC meetings when Johnson sought his concurrence on a matter relating to Vietnam by replying, "I most definitely do not agree." [1] But when LBJ turned to him and asked, "Mr. Cooper, do you agree?" Cooper found himself replying, "Yes, Mr. President, I agree."

---

1. The acronym NSC stands for National Security Council.

The capacity to design effective institutional arrangements has been in even scarcer supply than effective public communication in the modern presidency. In this department, Eisenhower was in a class of his own. The most emulation-worthy of his departures was the set of arrangements that framed his administration's national security deliberations. Each week the top planners in the bodies represented in the NSC hammered out option papers stating the policy recommendations of their agencies. The disagreements were clearly delineated and set before the NSC, where they were the object of sharp, focused debate. The result was as important for preparing Eisenhower's foreign policy team to work together as it was for grounding it in the issues bearing on unfolding global contingencies.

Political Skill   The classic statement of the centrality of political skill to presidential performance is Richard E. Neustadt's *Presidential Power,* which has been described as the closest approximation to Machiavelli's writings in the literature of American politics. The question Neustadt addresses is how the chief executive can put his stamp on public policy in the readily stalemated American political system. Neustadt's prescription is for the president to use the powers of his office assertively, build and maintain public support, and establish a reputation among fellow policymakers as a skilled, determined political operator. If there ever was reason to doubt Neustadt's diagnosis, it was eliminated by the presidential experience of Jimmy Carter.

Lyndon Johnson seemed almost to have taken his methods from the pages of *Presidential Power.* Within hours after Kennedy's assassination, Johnson had begun to muster support for major domestic policy departures. He exhibited will as well as skill, cultivating his political reputation by keeping Congress in session until Christmas 1963 in order to prevail in one of his administration's first legislative contests. His actions won him strong public support, making it apparent to his opposite numbers on Capitol Hill that it would be politically costly to ignore his demands.

Vision   "Vision" is a term with a variety of connotations. One is the capacity to inspire. In this the rhetorically gifted presidents—Kennedy, Reagan, and above all FDR—excelled. In the narrower meaning employed here, "vision" refers to preoccupation with the content of policies, an ability to assess their feasibility, and the possession of a set of overarching goals. Here the standouts are Eisenhower, Nixon, and to a lesser extent Ronald Reagan, whose views were poorly grounded in specifics. Vision also encompasses consistency of viewpoint. Presidents who stand firm are able to set the terms of policy discourse. In effect they serve as anchors for the rest of the political community. George Bush was not alone in his lack of "the vision thing." He falls in a class of presidential pragmatists that includes the great bulk of the modern chief executives. The costs of vision-free leadership include internally contradictory programs, policies that have unintended consequences, and sheer drift.

Cognitive Style   Presidents vary widely in their cognitive styles. Jimmy Carter had an engineer's proclivity to reduce issues to what he perceived to be their component parts. That style served him well in the 1978 Camp David negotiations, but it was ill suited for providing his administration with a sense of direction. Carter's cognitive qualities contrast with the kind of strategic intelligence that cuts to the heart of a problem, as Eisenhower did when he introduced his administration's deliberations on Dien Bien Phu with the incisive observation that the jungles of Indochina would "absorb our divisions by the dozens."

Another example of strategic intelligence is to be had from a chief executive who will never grace Mount Rushmore: Richard Nixon. Two years before entering the White House, Nixon laid down the goals of moving the United States beyond its military involvement in Vietnam, establishing a balance of power with the Soviet Union and an opening with China. By the final year of his first term, he had accomplished his purposes.

Nixon's first-term successes contrast with the paucity of major accomplishments in the two White House terms of the first presidential Rhodes scholar, Bill Clinton. Clinton possesses a formidable ability to absorb and process ideas and information, but his mind is more synthetic than analytic, and his political impulses sometimes lead him to substitute mere rationalization for reasoned analysis.

Two presidents who were marked by cognitive limitations were Harry Truman and Ronald Reagan. Truman's uncritical reading of works of popular history made him susceptible to false historical analogies. Reagan was notorious for his imperfect understanding of a number of his policy initiatives. That both presidents had major policy accomplishments shows that intelligence and information as measured by standardized tests is not the sole cause of presidential effectiveness.

Emotional Intelligence   Three of the eleven modern presidents stand out as fundamentally free of distracting emotional perturbations: Eisenhower, Ford, and Bush. Four others were marked by emotional undercurrents that did not significantly impair their leadership: Roosevelt, Truman, Kennedy, and Reagan. That leaves Johnson, Nixon, Carter, and Clinton, all of whom were emotionally handicapped. The vesuvian LBJ was subject to mood swings of clinical proportions. Jimmy Carter's rigidity was a significant impediment to his White House performance. The defective impulse control of Bill Clinton led him into actions that led to his impeachment.

Richard Nixon was the most emotionally flawed of the presidents considered here. His anger and suspiciousness were of Shakespearean proportions. He more than any other president summons up the classic notion of a tragic hero who is defeated by the very qualities that brought him success. It has been argued that the tortured psyche of a Nixon is a precondition of political creativity. This was the view of Elliot Richardson, who held that if Nixon's "rather petty flaws" had been taken away, "you would probably have removed that very inner core of insecurity that led to his rise."

Richardson's claim is a variant of the proposition that the inner torment of a Van Gogh is the price of his creativity, but other great painters were free of Van Gogh's self-destructiveness, and the healthy-minded Eisenhower was as gifted as Nixon in the positive aspects of leadership. Great political ability does sometimes derive from troubled emotions, but the former does not justify the latter in the custodian of the most destructive military arsenal in human experience. . . .

In the world of imagination it is possible to envisage a cognitively and emotionally intelligent chief executive, who happens also to be an inspiring public communicator, a capable White House organizer, and the possessor of exceptional political skill and vision. In the real world, human imperfection is inevitable, but some imperfections are more disabling than others. Many of the modern presidents have performed adequately without being brilliant orators. Only a few chief executives have been organizationally competent. A minimal level of political skill is a precondition of presidential effectiveness, but political skill is widely present in the handful of individuals who rise to the political summit. Vision is rarer than skill, but only Lyndon Johnson was disastrously deficient in the realm of policy.

Finally there are thought and emotion. The importance of cognitive strength in the presidency should be self-evident. Still, Presidents Johnson, Nixon, Carter, and Clinton had impressive intellects and defective temperaments. They reversed Justice Holmes's characterization of FDR.[2] Clinton's foibles made him an underachiever and national embarrassment. Carter's defective temperament contributed to making his time in office a period of lost opportunity. Johnson and Nixon presided over major policy breakthroughs, but also over two of the most unhappy episodes of the twentieth century. All four presidential experiences point to the following moral: Beware the presidential contender who lacks emotional intelligence. In its absence all else may turn to ashes. . . .

[Bill Clinton]

Public Communication At his best, Clinton is an outstanding public communicator. He is at the top of his form when he is on the defensive and in contexts that evoke his Southern Baptist heritage, such as his 1995 address in Oklahoma City. At his worst, he is long-winded, unfocused, and "off message," which is to say that his rhetoric mirrored the rest of his leadership.

Clinton's rhetorical shortcomings were most evident early in his presidency, when he sometimes stepped on his own lines by making multiple statements in the same news cycle. He also was capable of discarding a pre-

---

2. Supreme Court Justice Oliver Wendell Holmes, Jr., observed that Franklin D. Roosevelt had a "second-class intellect but a first-class temperament."

pared text and ad libbing his way into political trouble. For example, in his September 1993 endorsement of New York's first African American mayor, David Dinkins, for reelection, Clinton offhandedly remarked that New Yorkers who voted against Dinkins might well be guilty of unconscious racism. The assertion was harmful to Dinkins, drawing fire even from some of his supporters.

Organizational Capacity   The oxymoronic organization of the Clinton White House has been compared to a little boys' soccer team with no as- signed positions and each player chasing the ball. The conclusion of vet- eran Washington reporter Elizabeth Drew was that the Clinton White House did not fit the existing models of presidential organization. It fol- lowed neither the "spokes in the wheel" principle, in which the president coordinates his own advisory system, nor the hierarchical model in which the president employs a strong chief of staff. Instead, Clinton's key aides moved freely from issue to issue, and Clinton spent much of his time in meetings in which participation was a function of who showed up.

Despite the freedom Clinton afforded his staff, he has not been the kind of president who is beloved by his aides. His associates found him dif- ficult to advise, because of the inconstancy of his policy positions. He also was subject to fits of anger, and became a source of embarrassment to those of his aides who stood behind his denial of sexual involvement with Mon- ica Lewinsky. It is no wonder that the memoirs of Clinton's former aides are uniformly ambivalent about him.

After the chaotic opening months of his presidency, Clinton managed to find staff members who were able to channel his centrifugal tendencies, for example his second chief of staff, Leon Panetta, and Panetta's successor, Erskine Bowles. Still, there was never a point at which Clinton established a principle of organization that conserved his energy and mitigated the ten- dency of his administration's policies to exist mainly in his own mind.

Political Skill   As one might expect of someone whose adult life was de- voted to politics, Clinton is capable of impressive displays of political skill. He is also susceptible to astonishing missteps and miscalculations. The un- evenness of Clinton's performance was a partial function of his readiness to change his policies in response to political exigencies and his tendency to overreach himself under favorable political circumstances.

The Clinton presidency has been marked by numerous political suc- cesses. The most impressive of them occurred when he was on the defen- sive, as he was in 1995 when he bested the forces of Newt Gingrich.[3] His most notable failure was the defeat of his 1993 health initiative, which is additionally instructive because it might have been avoided if Clinton had

---

3. President Clinton's victory over House Speaker Gingrich came in a showdown over the fed- eral budget at the end of 1995.

taken a lesson from Carter's effort to win support for his similarly complex and politically vulnerable energy initiative.

Vision No American president has exceeded Clinton in his grasp of policy specifics, especially in the domestic sphere, but his was a mastery that did not translate into a clearly defined point of view. Why that was the case is not fully evident, but several factors are at work. Clinton's intelligence enables him to envisage complexity; his verbal facility permits him to express that complexity; and his intensely political nature leads him to modify his positions from context to context.

This is not to suggest that Clinton's policies have lacked a broad pattern. He has tended to take the middle ground on contested issues, and he has faith in government, particularly as a catalyst to private endeavor. There could be no greater contrast than that between a Bill Clinton, whose positions are ever open to modification, and a Ronald Reagan, who was vague about the details of policies but stood for a handful of broad verities.

Cognitive Style There can be no doubt about Clinton's impressive intelligence. He reads omnivorously, alternating between demanding works on public policy and fiction, sometimes while listening to briefings or watching television. He is a sponge for facts and has an ability to synthesize complex material. On one occasion at Oxford, he was given two weeks to prepare an essay on political pluralism in the Soviet Union. Consulting some thirty books and articles, he wrote a paper that his instructor considered a model of clarity and kept as a teaching tool. At Yale Law School Clinton was famed for skipping class, reading a friend's notes just before an examination, and writing a better exam than the note-taker.

There is a less positive side to Clinton's cognitive style, however. While he is a far cry from a Jimmy Carter, whose tendency was to amass specifics, he also seems to lack the ability of an Eisenhower to cut to the core of a problem or make a balanced net assessment of a complex issue. Instead, Clinton fits the description of the lawyer who masters issues with the speed of oil covering water, but sometimes does so at the same depth.

Emotional Intelligence The politically gifted, emotionally challenged William Jefferson Clinton provides yet another indication of the fundamental importance of emotional intelligence in the modern presidency. Clinton's political gifts enabled him to thwart the Republican effort to remove him from office, but his psychic shortcomings were debilitating. Assertions about the impact of an incumbent or recent president are necessarily provisional, but Clinton seems certain to be recognized for moving the Democratic party to the center of the political spectrum and for many incremental policy departures. Yet he is also likely to be remembered as a politically talented underachiever, whose White House experience provides a reminder that in the absence of emotional soundness, the American presidency is a problematic instrument of democratic governance.

The Changing Political Structures of Presidential Leadership

STEPHEN SKOWRONEK

W hen a president does well, our natural inclination is to attribute his success to the special talents and skills he brought to the office; when things go wrong, we look for personal missteps and character flaws. There is something comforting in these judgments, for they sustain confidence in the office of the presidency itself no matter what the experience of the particular incumbent holding power at the moment. So long as performance is tied to the personal attributes of the man, success is always a possibility; it awaits only the right combination of character and skill. So long as the presidency is a true test of the man, its incumbents are free to become as great as they can be.

Much of what is written about the presidency reinforces these conceits. Typically, analysis begins by describing the office that all presidents have shared, a position defined by constitutional arrangements that have undergone remarkable little change since 1789. To this is added a description of the trappings of modernity—of new governing responsibilities imposed on the office in the wake of the Great Depression and World War II and new resources made available to it. These distinguish the leadership situation shared by all presidents after FDR from that of all their predecessors. The effect of this setup is to hold the demands and capacities of the office constant over the latter half of the twentieth century and to present leadership as a problem of how best to apply the resources of the modern presidency to the responsibilities of the modern presidency. In this way, each modern incumbent becomes a new source of insight into what attributes of character and skill work best in the shared context, what strategies are most effective, what it takes to measure up.

But in fact the leadership demands and capacities of the office of the presidency are not the same over successive administrations and closer attention to the changing relationship between the presidency and the political system accounts for much of what we take to be evidence of personal skills and leadership flaws. To access these changing relationships, however, we need to think about presidential history a bit differently. Rather than divide moderns from pre-moderns, we need to connect them to one another, to review the history of presidential leadership as a whole and reconsider the contextual conditions under which great leaders typically arise.

The alternative history I have in mind charts change in American politics through the recurring establishment and disintegration of relatively durable political regimes. This regime-based structure of American political history has been widely observed by political scientists and historians alike. It demarcates the rise and decline of Federalist Nationalism between 1789 and 1800, of Jeffersonian Democracy between 1800 and 1828, of Jacksonian Democracy between 1828 and 1860, of Republican Nationalism between 1860 and 1932, and of New Deal Liberalism between 1932 and 1980. Each of these regimes can be identified with the empowerment of an insurgent political coalition whose reconstruction of basic governing arrangements endured through various subsequent configurations of party power. Just as America's fragmented constitutional system has made sweeping political change rare and difficult to achieve, it has worked similarly to perpetuate the ideological and programmatic commitments of the few insurgencies that have succeeded. To this extent at least, the regime structure of American political history may be considered a byproduct of the constitutional structure of American government.

Looking over the course of each of these regimes suggests a number of typically structured relationships between the presidency and the political system, and thinking about the modern presidents in these terms places each of them in a unique analytic relationship with the presidents of the past. Regime formation and decay are not processes external to presidential leadership; indeed, the active intervention of presidents at various stages in these processes has driven them forward. What I am suggesting is that we understand the political demands and challenges of presidential leadership as variables mediated by the generation and degeneration of political orders, that we reverse the standard analytic procedure by holding personality and skill constant and examining the typical political effects of presidential action in the differently structured political contexts characteristic of our constitutional system.

The Political Structures of Presidential Leadership

Each regime begins with the rise to power of a new political coalition out to construct and legitimize alternative governing arrangements, to recast relations between state and society in ways advantageous to its members. These coalitions will then attempt to extend their claims on power by elaborating and modifying their basic agenda in ways that are responsive to changes in the nation at large. Once they are established, however, coalition interests can have an enervating effect on the governing capacities of these regimes. An immediate and constant problem is posed by conflicts of interest within the dominant coalition. The danger here is that attempts to elaborate the coalition's political agenda will focus a sectarian struggle, weaken regime support through factional disaffection, and open new avenues to power for the political opposition. A longer-range, and ultimately more devastating, problem is posed by changes in the nation at large that throw into question the dominant coalition's most basic commitments of ideology and interest. The danger here, of course, is that the entire political regime will be called into question as an inadequate governing instrument and then repudiated wholesale in a nationwide crisis of political legitimacy.

Considering the history of the presidency in this light, two systemic relationships stand out as especially significant for an analysis of the politics of leadership. First is the president's affiliation with the political complex of interests, institutions, and ideas that dominated state/society relations prior to his coming to office. Second is the current standing of these governmental arrangements in the nation at large. These relationships are, of course, always highly nuanced, but certain variations are easily discerned. For the sake of simplicity we can conceptualize the leadership problem with reference to those institutions with which political regimes are invariably identified in America, namely the political parties. Using this shorthand, the leadership problem confronting each president can be framed by the answers to two simple questions: is the president affiliated with the political party that has defined the government's basic commitments of ideology and interest; are the governmental commitments of that party vulnerable to direct repudiation as failed and irrelevant responses to the problems of the day?

Answers to these questions specify four typical opportunity structures for the exercise of political leadership by a president. In the first, the basic governmental commitments of the previously dominant political party are vulnerable to direct repudiation, and the president is associated with the opposition to them. In the second, basic governmental commitments of the previously dominant political party are again on the line, but this time the president is politically affiliated with them. In the third, the governmental commitments of the previously dominant political party still appear timely and politically resilient, but the president is linked with the political opposition to them. In the fourth, the governmental commitments of the previously dominant political party again appear to hold out robust solutions to the problems of the day and the president is affiliated with them. These four opportunity structures are represented in Table 1,

The Political Structures of Presidential Leadership

		Presidents' Political Identity	
		Opposed	*Affiliated*
Regime party commitments	*Vulnerable*	politics of reconstruction	politics of disjunction
	Resilient	politics of preemption	politics of articulation

with the "previously dominant political party" designated as the "regime party" for easy reference.

Each of these structures defines a different institutional relationship between the presidency and the political system, each engages the president in a different type of politics, and each defines a different kind of leadership challenge. These differences are summarized in the four cells of the table. Before proceeding to a discussion of the table, two points of clarification are in order. First, the table is a schematic presentation of pure types that are only more or less closely approximated in history. In the discussion that follows, the presidents that best fit each type are grouped together. The object is to highlight the distinctive problems and dynamics of political action that adhere to leadership in these situations and by implication to reconsider the problems and prospects faced by leaders in our own day. The procedure radically delimits the play of personality and skill in determining leadership outcomes, but it leaves to others a more precise determination of the significance left to them. The second point is that this typology does not provide an independent explanation of the historical patterns on which it draws. There is no accounting here for whether a regime affiliate or a regime opponent will actually be elected (or otherwise come into office), nor for when in the course of the nation's development a regime's basic governmental commitments will be called into question. The object is to reorganize the analysis of the politics of leadership by cutting into political history at certain typical junctures. My purpose is to suggest the rather blunt ways in which political structure has delimited the political capacities of the presidency and informed the impact of presidential action on the political system as a whole.

The *politics of reconstruction* has been most closely approximated in the administrations of Thomas Jefferson, Andrew Jackson, Abraham Lincoln, Franklin Roosevelt, and Ronald Reagan. Each came to power on the heels of an electoral upheaval in political control of the institutions of the federal government. More specifically, their victories were driven by widespread discontent with the established order of things and were potent enough to displace a long-established majority party from its dominant position in both Congress and the presidency. With political obligations to the past severed in this way, these presidents were thrust beyond the old regime into a political interregnum where they were directly engaged in a systemic recasting of the government's basic commitments of ideology and interest.

These presidents are widely regarded as the most effective of all political leaders in presidential history; what is less well appreciated is that they shared the same basic relationship to the political system at large. All are also known as great communicators; what is less well appreciated is that they all had the same basic message to communicate. Each was free to repudiate received commitments of ideology and interest forthrightly as failed and illegitimate responses to the problems of the day and to identify his leadership with a new beginning, with the salvation of the nation from political bankruptcy. Safe to say, the political preeminence of the presidency is naturally pronounced when the old regime has been widely discredited, when old alliances have been thrown into disarray, and when new interests have been thrust afresh upon governmental institutions.

More important, however, is what the performance of leaders in this situation can tell us about the structured capacities of the presidency as a political institution. Order-shattering elections do not themselves shape the future, but they vastly expand the president's capacities to break prior governmental commitments, to reset the terms and conditions of legitimate national government, and to orchestrate a political reordering of the rules and conditions of state/society relations. It is significant in this regard that none of the presidents who reconstructed the terms and conditions of legitimate national government had much success in actually resolving the tangible problems that gave rise to the nationwide crisis of political legitimacy in the first place. Jefferson's attempt to deal with the problems at issue in the international crisis of 1798 proved a total failure;[1] Jackson's attempt to deal with the long-festering problem of national banking precipitated an economic panic and ultimately exacerbated a devastating depression; Lincoln's proposed solution to the sectional conflict of the 1850's plunged the nation into a civil war; and Roosevelt's New Deal failed to pull the nation out of the Depression. But what these presidents could do that their predecessors could not was to redefine thoroughly the significance of the events they oversaw and to secure the legitimacy of the solutions they proposed. Released from the burden of upholding the integrity of the old regime, these presidents were not restricted in their leadership to mere problem solving. Situated just beyond the old regime, they reformulated the nation's political agenda as a direct response to the manifest failures of the immediate past, presented their solutions as the only alternative to national ruin, and galvanized political support for the release of governmental power on entirely new terms.

The leadership opportunities afforded by this kind of political breakthrough are duly matched by its characteristic political challenges. In penetrating to the core of the political system and orchestrating a political reordering of relations between state and society, these presidents ultimately found it imperative to try to secure a governmental infrastructure capable of perpetuating their new order. The shape of the new regime came to depend on the way party lines were recast and on how institutional relationships within the government were reorganized. Accordingly, it will be observed that these are all great party-building presidencies, and that each president was engaged institutionally as a negative instrument, rooting out the residual institutional supports for the politics of the past. Court battles, Bank Wars, a real Civil War—great confrontations that dislodge entire frameworks of governing are the special province of the reconstructive leader,

---

1. The reference here is to President Jefferson's failed embargo policy in his second term.

and they can be counted on to forge new forms of opposition as well as support.[2] The reconstructive leader passes to his successor a political system that is not only reconfigured in its basic commitments of ideology and interest but newly constricted in its potential for independent action.

The *politics of disjunction* has been most closely approximated in the administrations of John Adams, John Quincy Adams, Franklin Pierce, James Buchanan, Herbert Hoover, and Jimmy Carter. With due regard for the reputations of these men for political incompetence, it is evident in identifying them as a group that they share what is quite simply an impossible leadership situation. Rather than moving to orchestrate a political breakthrough in state/society relations, these presidents are compelled to cope with the breakdown of those relations. Their affiliation with the old regime at a time when its basic commitments of ideology and interest were being called into question turns their office into the focal point of a nationwide crisis of political legitimacy. This situation imparts to them a consuming preoccupation with a political challenge that is really a prerequisite of leadership, that of simply establishing their own political credibility.

Each of the major historical episodes in the politics of disjunction has been foreshadowed by a long-festering identity crisis within the old majority party itself. But the distinctiveness of this juncture goes beyond these simmering tensions within the ranks; it lies in changes within the nation itself that obscure the regime's relevance as an instrument of governance and cloud its legitimacy as caretaker of the national interest. The Adamses, Pierce, Hoover, and Carter are notable for their open recognition of the vulnerabilities of the establishments with which they were affiliated; each promised to solve national problems in a way that would repair and rehabilitate the old order. But presidents are hard pressed to deliver on problem solving plain and simple and in this situation, where they have little else to offer, they find themselves in especially difficult straits. Actions that challenge established commitments in the name of rehabilitation and repair are likely to leave the president isolated from his most likely political allies; actions that reach out to allies and affirm established commitments will provide insurgents with proof positive that the president has nothing new to offer, that he really is nothing more than a symptom of the problems of the day.

Invariably these presidents drive forward the crisis of legitimacy they came into office to forestall. They become the leading symbols of systemic political failure and regime bankruptcy, and provide the essential premise for a reconstructive movement. Certainly it is no accident that the presidents who have set the standard of political incompetence in American political history are succeeded by presidents who set the standards of political mastery. This recurrent coupling of dismal failure with towering success

---

2. Jefferson, Jackson, and Roosevelt tangled with the Supreme Court, while Jackson destroyed the Bank of the United States.

suggests that the contingent political relationship between the presidency and the political system is far more telling of leadership prospects than the contingencies of personality and skill.

The *politics of preemption* has engaged a large number of presidents, some of the more aggressive leaders among them being John Tyler, Andrew Johnson, Grover Cleveland, Woodrow Wilson, Richard Nixon, and Bill Clinton. The men in this grouping stand out as wild cards in American political history. As their experiences indicate, the politics of leadership in this situation are especially volatile, and perhaps least susceptible to generalization. Tyler was purged from the ranks of the party that elected him; Wilson took a disastrous plunge from the commanding heights of world leadership into the political abyss; Johnson and Nixon were crippled by impeachment proceedings. Of all the presidents that might be grouped in this situation, only Dwight Eisenhower finished a second term without suffering a precipitous reversal of political fortune, but this exception is itself suggestive, for Eisenhower alone kept whatever intentions he might have had for altering the shape of national politics well hidden.

As the leader of the opposition to a previously dominant party that can still muster formidable political, ideological, and institutional support, the president interrupts the working agenda of national politics and intrudes into the establishment as an alien power. The exercise of creative political leadership in this situation hinges on expanding and altering the base of opposition support, and here the leader is naturally drawn toward latent interest cleavages and factional discontent within the ranks of the regime's traditional supporters. These leadership opportunities are not hard to find, but the political terrain to be negotiated in exploiting them is treacherous. To preempt the political discourse of an established regime, the president will simultaneously have to maintain the support of the stalwart opposition, avoid a frontal attack on regime orthodoxy, and offer disaffected interests normally affiliated with the dominant coalition a modification of the regime's agenda that they will find more attractive. Testing both the tolerance of the opposition and the resilience of the establishment, the leader openly tempts a massive political reaction from both.

Compared to a president engaged in a politics of disjunction, the leader here has a much greater opportunity to establish and exploit the political independence of the presidential office. All preemptive leaders who were elected to office in the first instance were reelected to second terms. Compared to a president engaged in the politics of reconstruction, however, these leaders face a much greater risk of political isolation. Preemptive leadership is unique in its propensity to provoke impeachment proceedings. Probing alternative lines of political cleavage, the president may well anticipate new party building possibilities, but, short of systemic electoral break with the immediate past and of the concomitant authority to repudiate the received order forthrightly, opposition leadership is hard pressed to secure them. It is more effective in disrupting the established political regime than at replacing it.

The *politics of articulation* has engaged the largest number of presidents; in contemporary politics it would include both George H.W. Bush and George W. Bush. If no more "normal" a situation than any other, this situation does pinpoint the distinctive problems of political leadership that arise when relations between the incumbent and established regime commitments are most consonant. Here the presidency is the font of political orthodoxy and the president, the minister to the faithful. The leadership posture is wholly affirmative; the opportunity at hand is to move forward forthrightly on the outstanding political commitments on the regime's agenda and to update to accord with the times. The corresponding challenge is to mitigate and manage the factional ruptures within the ranks of the regime's traditional supporters that inevitably accompany these alterations in the status quo ante.

In each of America's major political regimes, there has been one particular episode of the politics of articulation that stands out, not only as typical of the problems and prospects this situation holds for presidential leadership but also as pivotal in the course of each regime's development. In the Jeffersonian era, it came in the first term of James Monroe; in the Jacksonian era, in the administration of James Polk; in the Liberal era, in the administration of Lyndon Johnson. These men exercised power in especially propitious circumstances. At the outset of each of these administrations a long-established majority party was reaffirmed in its control of the entire national government, and the national posture was so strong at home and abroad that it left no excuses for not finally delivering on long-heralded regime promises. Each president thus set full sail at a time when it was possible to think about completing the unfinished business of national politics and realizing the regime's highest moral vision for the nation. But if a leadership project of culmination and completion suggests a great leap forward, it also demands the maintenance of certain fundamental political commitments. The curious result was that in each of these presidencies, a regime at the apex of its projection of national power and purpose became mired in the dilemmas of reconciling old commitments with the expansive political possibilities at hand; assiduous efforts by the president to serve all interests in the pursuit of new initiatives set off a political implosion of conflicting expectations. Paradoxically, as these leaders pushed ahead with the received business of national politics, they fomented deep schisms within the ranks and instigated real changes in political commitments that they could not openly defend without aggravating the situation. On the verge of its fullest political articulation as a governing instrument, each president was charged with a betrayal of the faith, and each pulled the regime into an accelerated sectarian struggle over the true meaning of orthodoxy. These presidencies were not undermined by their nominal political opponents but by the disaffection of their ostensible allies.

Whereas in the politics of preemption, political disaffection and factional breakup within the ranks of the dominant party provide opportunities that the leader has every incentive to exploit, here they present risks that the leader is constrained to manage and to try to forestall. Whereas in the politics of reconstruction, the president stands opposed to the old regime and orchestrates the breakthrough to a new one, here the leader is pulled by the competing impulses to maintain the political regime and to fulfill its potential through innovation and change. Finally, just as every episode of the politics of preemption entices the leader to probe for reconstructive possibilities, every episode in the politics of articulation challenges the leader to hold at bay the specter of a political disjunction.

Bill Clinton: A Closer Look

In his rise to power, it was clear that Bill Clinton was not, like Ronald Reagan, the great repudiator of a governing regime in collapse. Nor was he, like George H.W. Bush, the faithful son of an unfinished revolution. A Democrat seeking the presidency in the post-Reagan era, Clinton sought to preempt the Republican revolution by promising a "third way."

To talk about a third way in 1992 was to acknowledge the Democrats' three consecutive losses to liberal-bashing Republicans and to attempt to adjust the Democratic alternative to the new political standards that had been established by the Reagan Revolution. The idea was to dispel the aura of illegitimacy that had surrounded the Democratic Party's posture in national politics since the Carter debacle and to redefine the choices at hand so that the Republicans no longer posed the only alternative to discredited liberalism. To meet this challenge, Clinton cast himself firmly in the mold of an opposition leader. The practical problems he addressed were not those of a regime with which he was politically affiliated, but those of the new regime that had replaced liberalism. Clinton pegged the nation's woes to twelve years of Republican rule, exploited new divisions arising within the Republican coalition, and committed himself to a "new course" that would "put people first." At the same time, however, he acknowledged the Republicans' redefinition of the terms and conditions of legitimate national government. To escape the burdens of older Democratic identities, he rejected the liberal label outright, turned a cold shoulder to familiar icons of the left, and openly proclaimed himself the leader of a "New Democratic Party." By actively disassociating himself from the standard that Reagan had so effectively driven from the field, Clinton promised to take the discussion of political alternatives beyond what he called "the stale, failed rhetoric of the past." His new party was, he said, "neither liberal nor conservative but both and different."

It was, to be sure, a subtle, complicated, and equivocal message. Clinton did not assume the authority to challenge fundamentally the terms in which legitimate national government had come to be understood. From the start, his opposition was more preemptive than reconstructive. Characteristically, the clarity of purpose achieved by great repudiators gives way in such circumstances to leadership that is cooptive, ad hoc, and ultimately indeterminate in its fundamental purposes. What Clinton drew from this opposition stance was a good measure of independence in crafting and altering his political positions. Preemptive leaders have more room to maneuver around received commitments than do orthodox innovators or late-regime affiliates. They are far less beholden to those within their own ranks for their doctrinal purity or for the consistency of their actions with established party priorities. To put it another way, preemptive leaders are not out to establish, uphold, or salvage any political orthodoxy. Theirs is an unabashedly mongrel politics: an aggressive critique of the prevailing political categories and a bold bid to mix them up.

The "third way" finds its distinctive opportunities in the schisms within the ranks of the dominant coalition that affiliated leaders are at such pains to assuage. By taking advantage of these schisms, preemptive leaders bid to appropriate much of the field of action carved out by those who built the regime. They threaten to take over their opponents' most attractive positions and to leave them holding only the most extreme ones. The political contest is thus framed by the president's purposeful blurring of received political identities and by his opponents' stake in keeping those older identities intact. The corresponding risk these presidents run is that in trying to establish their third way, they may appear wholly lacking in political principles and come across as unscrupulous and cynically manipulative.

Observe further that third-way alternatives have never proven durable. Preemptive leaders tend to be politically successful during their terms in office, and reelection is the rule, but their "neo" parties with their hybrid agendas have characteristically held only a loose grip on the terms and conditions of national politics, and their influence over the future course of politics proves temporary. Historically, no "third way" has outlasted the president who articulated it. Those who try hardest to change things from this position in a durable way tend to foment a constitutional test of wills culminating in a showdown over presidential authority, as it did for John Tyler, Andrew Johnson, Woodrow Wilson, Richard Nixon, and Bill Clinton. Herein lies some important clues to the personality issues that come to surround these presidencies: more than at any other time, leadership in these circumstances becomes highly individualized, and the political contests it sets up become radically personalized.

Setting Clinton's experience against that of other preemptive presidents recasts understanding of both the typical and extraordinary aspects of his leadership. Although the convulsive character of the Clinton administration stands out among recent presidencies, it fits a recurrent pattern of extraordinary volatility in pursuit of a third way. Independence is the watchword of preemptive leadership, and in exercising this independence, preemptive leaders provoke intense political struggles in which their own personal codes of conduct take center stage. Other presidents may be judged incompetent or misguided; these presidents have been attacked as moral degenerates, congenitally incapable of rising above nihilism and manipulation.

When the attraction of third-way politics under Wilson and Nixon became evident, opponents labeled them "Shifty Tom" and "Tricky Dick."

When the same became evident under Clinton, his opponents saddled him with the label of "Slick Willy." These characterizations are all of a type, a political type, not a personality type. They are characteristic of the personalization of politics that occurs when an opposition leader seeks to preempt established conceptions of the political alternatives and to substitute a third way. Determined to sustain their contention that Clinton's "New Democratic Party" was really a ploy masking rearguard defense of liberalism, Republicans deftly transposed the question of ideology into a question of character. Character flaws offered an explanation for Clinton's repeated forays onto a conservative ground; they accounted for his use of the presidency to mask his party's true leanings and selectively incorporate his opponents' most attractive positions. As Clinton challenged received definitions of liberal and conservative, of Democrat and Republican, and of Left, Right, and Center, opponents compiled evidence from his personal life to suggest that he really had no standards at all, that he was wholly lacking in principles. By casting Clinton as a man who never cared much for the truth, who had proven incapable of standing by any commitment, and who had no higher purpose than his own self-indulgence, opponents found a way to preserve the truth that they wished to promote—namely, that Democrats remained a desperate party of discredited ideas and debased leadership while the Republicans remained the only legitimate exponents of national solutions.

The extraordinary convulsiveness and character-centeredness of preemptive politics are revealed most strikingly in the prominent use of impeachment threats against third-way presidents. John Tyler, Andrew Johnson, Richard Nixon, and Bill Clinton are not a random set of presidents whose personal quirks led them to blunder into impeachment crises. Rather, they were all third-way leaders who threatened received conceptions of the political alternatives, leaving desperate opponents to charge that they were abnormal, personally deranged, and dangerous to the republic. Their shared leadership stance suggests the primacy of political, rather than strictly legal, factors at work in these proceedings. The impulse has been to dislodge the threat to a more orthodox rendition of the governmental agenda by personalizing the political challenge it poses and stigmatizing it as an assault on constitutional government itself.

The Presidency as a Position of National Political Leadership

It turns out that every opposition leader elected to office in the first instance and surviving his first term was elected to a second term (14 presidents in all). In contrast, only 4 of the 24 presidents affiliated with dominant parties have been elected to second terms. Two of those four, Madison and Monroe, predate the rise of the two party system; a third, Grant, was reelected with much of his opposition under force of arms. More striking still is that the seven presidents in American history who voluntarily withdrew from second term bids were all affiliated leaders. Clearly, the opposition stance is more consistent with the political independence structured into the office by the constitutional separation of powers. The Constitution did not contemplate affiliated leadership, and it leaves affiliated leaders at cross purposes in the presidential office.

This is all to say that the presidency itself is deeply implicated in the fate of our presidents, and that presidential leadership in all its forms is inextricably bound up with larger operations of the American political system. When we explain the different outcomes we observe with reference to the personal attributes of the men in office, we miss their greater significance as a comment on the range and capacities of the office they inhabit and on how that office comes to bear over time on a changing political system. What we are observing over time is not *who* has made this system work, but *how* this system works under the different configurations of politics it characteristically spins out. Presidential leadership in all its political forms, and with its characteristic triumphs and failures, is the ultimate commentary on the peculiarities of constitutional government in the United States.

■ DISCUSSION QUESTIONS

1. Does Greenstein's emphasis on the individual or Skowronek's emphasis on the political structure provide the better understanding of presidential leadership?

2. How would Greenstein deal with the contention that even a president with strong character and skills would be unsuccessful in the face of unfavorable political circumstances?

3. How would Skowronek deal with the contention that even in the politics of reconstruction, the best opportunity structure a president can enjoy, the creation of a new regime requires vision and skill?

4. Why did Bill Clinton fail to achieve many of his aspirations in the presidency? Does the answer to this question lie in his character flaws or in the limited opportunities and unstable accomplishments of the politics of preemption?

5. How would Greenstein and Skowronek differ in their analyses of George W. Bush?

■ SUGGESTED READINGS AND INTERNET RESOURCES

The classic study of how presidents can gain—or lose—power in the White House is Richard E. Neustadt, *Presidential Power and the Modern Presidents* (New York: Free Press, 1990). The growing tendency of presidents to seek mass support is analyzed in Samuel Kernell, *Going Public: New Strategies of Presidential Leadership,* 3d ed. (Washington, D.C.: Congressional Quarterly Press, 1997). Stephen Skowronek demonstrates how presidential leadership is shaped by "political time" in *The Politics Presidents Make: Leadership from John Adams to Bill Clinton* (Cambridge, Mass.: Harvard University Press, 1997). For a lively anthology on presidential politics, see Michael Nelson, ed., *The Presidency and the Political System,* 7th ed. (Washington, D.C.: Congressional Quarterly Press, 2003). Portraits of both elite democratic and popular democratic leadership are found in Bruce Miroff, *Icons of Democracy: American Leaders as Heroes, Aristocrats, Dissenters, and Democrats* (Lawrence: University Press of Kansas, 2000).

The White House
www.whitehouse.gov
The president's web site, containing speeches, documents, press briefings, and assorted information on the administration, also offers email communication with the White House.

Center for the Study of the Presidency
www.cspresidency.org
This web site of a nonpartisan organization that holds student conferences and publishes a scholarly journal offers publications and provides links to research sites on the presidency.

The American Presidency.Net
www.theamericanpresidency.net
This web site contains information on many aspects of the presidency, ranging from the important to the trivial.

15

The Judiciary: What Should Its Role Be in a Democracy?

Americans like to think of the justices of the Supreme Court as grave and learned elders of the law engaged in a search for justice that has little to do with the selfish interests and ambitions that we so often associate with politics. The justices themselves encourage this view, holding court in a marble temple (the Supreme Court Building), wearing black robes, shrouding their decision-making processes in secrecy. Yet an institution that makes authoritative decisions about many of the most troublesome issues of our times—abortion, affirmative action, the rights of the accused, the relationship between church and state—cannot be kept aloof from politics. Thus, the Supreme Court's role in the political system has become one of the central issues in current debates about American democracy.

From one perspective, the Supreme Court is not really a democratic institution at all. The nine justices of the Supreme Court are not elected; they are nominated by the president and confirmed by the Senate. They serve during good behavior—that is, until they retire, die, or are impeached by the House and convicted by the Senate. Composed exclusively of one profession, lawyers, the Court can use its power of judicial review to strike down laws passed by legislatures that have been elected by the majority.

From another perspective, however, the Supreme Court is an essential component of American democracy. Its most important role is as a guardian of the Constitution, which is the fundamental expression of the people's will.

According to this view, the Court sometimes must oppose the wishes of a temporary majority in the name of the abiding principles and values contained in the Constitution.

During the last several decades, landmark decisions by the Supreme Court have often evoked democratic debates. Some decisions by the Court have been approved by a majority of Americans but have been fiercely resisted by intense minorities. Among these have been *Brown* v. *Board of Education* (1954), ordering school desegregation, and *Roe* v. *Wade* (1973), guaranteeing the right of a woman to choose to have an abortion. Other decisions have been opposed by a large majority. Among these have been *Engel* v. *Vitale* (1962), which forbade prayer in public schools, and *Miranda* v. *Arizona* (1966), which required police to inform criminal suspects of their rights before they could be interrogated.

Decisions such as these have led critics to charge the Court with overstepping its proper role in the political system. The most prominent critic has been Edwin Meese III, the attorney general of the United States during Ronald Reagan's presidency. In a series of speeches in 1985 (one of which is excerpted here), Meese accused the Court of substituting its own preferences and prejudices for the principles of the Constitution. Springing to the defense of the Court against Meese was Justice William Brennan Jr., who played an influential role in crafting many of the decisions that Meese was condemning. The debate between Meese and Brennan has been a profoundly important one because it cuts to the most basic issues concerning the judiciary's role in American democracy.

Meese insists that the justices of the Supreme Court should be strictly guided by the words of the Constitution and the laws and by the intentions of those who drafted them (he calls this a "Jurisprudence of Original Intention"). This emphasis on the original intention of the framers calls into question the Court's recent decisions on the rights of racial minorities, women, and persons accused of crimes. Meese wants the Supreme Court to play a more restrained role and to defer whenever possible to the elected branches of government.

Brennan rejects each of Meese's arguments. He suggests that the original intention of the framers cannot be known and that while justices must respect the past, they must ultimately be guided in their interpretations by what the words of the Constitution mean today. He believes that Meese's position is a cloak for a conservative political agenda, the aim of which is to reverse recent advances in our understanding of the constitutional rights of previously disadvantaged groups. Brennan denies that democracy requires a deferential judiciary: the Court, he argues, has a democratic responsibility to uphold the nation's founding "aspiration to social justice, brotherhood, and human dignity."

Among the three branches of the national government, the judiciary is clearly the most elite in its selection process, composition, and form of deliberation. Yet in the debate between Meese and Brennan, each tries to associate his view of the judiciary with a popular democratic position. You can decide for yourself whose position in this debate deserves to be identified with popular democracy by considering the following questions: Can we be guided in interpreting the Constitution by the original intention of its framers, or must we read the Constitution in a more adaptive and modern fashion? Should our understanding of constitutional rights be squarely rooted in the text of the Constitution, or should we apply constitutional values to the protection of rights for individuals and groups that the framers never thought to protect? Must the Court, as an unelected branch of government, avoid undemocratic action by acting with deference toward the elected branches, or must it actively pursue the democratic aspirations of the Constitution even when this brings the judiciary into conflict with the elected branches?

A Jurisprudence of Original Intention

EDWIN MEESE III

A large part of American history has been the history of Constitutional debate. From the Federalists and the Anti-Federalists, to Webster and Calhoun, to Lincoln and Douglas, we find many examples. Now, as we approach the bicentennial of the framing of the Constitution, we are witnessing another debate concerning our fundamental law. It is not simply a ceremonial debate, but one that promises to have a profound impact on the future of our Republic. . . .

Today I would like to discuss further the meaning of constitutional fidelity. In particular, I would like to describe in more detail this administration's approach.

Before doing so, I would like to make a few commonplace observations about the original document itself. It is easy to forget what a young country America really is. The bicentennial of our independence was just a few years ago, that of the Constitution still two years off. The period surrounding the creation of the Constitution is not a dark and mythical realm. The young America of the 1780's and 90's was a vibrant place, alive with pamphlets, newspapers and books chronicling and commenting upon the great issues of the day. We know how the Founding Fathers lived, and much of what they read, thought, and believed. The disputes and compromises of the Constitutional Convention were carefully recorded. The minutes of the Convention are a matter of public record. Several of the most important participants—including James Madison, the "father" of the Constitution—

wrote comprehensive accounts of the convention. Others, Federalists and Anti-Federalists alike, committed their arguments for and against ratification, as well as their understandings of the Constitution, to paper, so that their ideas and conclusions could be widely circulated, read, and understood.

In short, the Constitution is not buried in the mists of time. We know a tremendous amount of the history of its genesis. The Bicentennial is encouraging even more scholarship about its origins. We know who did what, when, and many times why. One can talk intelligently about a "founding generation." . . .

Our approach to constitutional interpretation begins with the document itself. The plain fact is, it exists. It is something that has been written down. Walter Berns of the American Enterprise Institute has noted that the central object of American constitutionalism was "the effort" of the Founders "to express fundamental governmental arrangements in a legal document—to 'get it in writing.'" Indeed, judicial review has been grounded in the fact that the Constitution is a written, as opposed to an unwritten, document. In *Marbury* v. *Madison*, [5 U.S. 137 (1803)] John Marshall rested his rationale for judicial review on the fact that we have a written constitution with meaning that is binding upon judges. "[I]t is apparent," he wrote, "that the framers of the Constitution contemplated that instrument as a rule for the government of *courts,* as well as of the legislature. Why otherwise does it direct the judges to take an oath to support it?"

The presumption of a written document is that it conveys meaning. As Thomas Grey of the Stanford Law School has said, it makes "relatively definite and explicit what otherwise would be relatively indefinite and tacit."

We know that those who framed the Constitution chose their words carefully. They debated at great length the most minute points. The language they chose meant something. They proposed, they substituted, they edited, and they carefully revised. Their words were studied with equal care by state ratifying conventions. This is not to suggest that there was unanimity among the framers and ratifiers on all points. The Constitution and the Bill of Rights, and some of the subsequent amendments, emerged after protracted debate. Nobody got everything they wanted. What's more, the Framers were not clairvoyants—they could not foresee every issue that would be submitted for judicial review. Nor could they predict how all foreseeable disputes would be resolved under the Constitution. But the point is, the meaning of the Constitution can be known.

What does this written Constitution mean? In places it is exactingly specific. Where it says that Presidents of the United States must be at least 35 years of age it means exactly that. (I have not heard of any claim that 35 means 30 or 25 or 20.) Where it specifies how the House and Senate are to be organized, it means what it says.

The Constitution also expresses particular principles. One is the right to be free of an unreasonable search or seizure. Another concerns religious liberty. Another is the right to equal protection of the laws.

Those who framed these principles meant something by them. And the meanings can be found. The Constitution itself is also an expression of certain general principles. These principles reflect the deepest purpose of the Constitution—that of establishing a political system through which Americans can best govern themselves consistent with the goal of securing liberty.

The text and structure of the Constitution is instructive. It contains very little in the way of specific political solutions. It speaks volumes on how problems should be approached, and by *whom*. For example, the first three articles set out clearly the scope and limits of three distinct branches of national government, the powers of each being carefully and specifically enumerated. In this scheme it is no accident to find the legislative branch described first, as the Framers had fought and sacrificed to secure the right of democratic self-governance. Naturally, this faith in republicanism was not unbounded, as the next two articles make clear.

Yet the Constitution remains a document of powers and principles. And its undergirding premise remains that democratic self-government is subject only to the limits of certain constitutional principles. This respect for the political process was made explicit early on. When John Marshall upheld the Act of Congress chartering a national bank in *McCulloch* v. *Maryland* [17 U.S. 316 (1819)], he wrote: "The Constitution [was] intended to endure for ages to come, and, consequently, to be adapted to the various crises of human affairs." But to use *McCulloch,* as some have tried, as support for the idea that the Constitution is a protean, changeable thing is to stand history on its head. Marshall was keeping faith with the original intention that Congress be free to elaborate and apply constitutional powers and principles. He was not saying that the Court must invent some new constitutional value in order to keep pace with the times. In Walter Berns' words: "Marshall's meaning is not that the Constitution may be adapted to the 'various crises of human affairs,' but that the legislative powers granted by the Constitution are adaptable to meet these crises."

The approach this administration advocates is rooted in the text of the Constitution as illuminated by those who drafted, proposed, and ratified it. In his famous Commentary on the Constitution of the United States, Justice Joseph Story explained that: "The first and fundamental rule in the interpretation of all instruments is, to construe them according to the sense of the terms, and the intention of the parties."

Our approach understands the significance of a written document and seeks to discern the particular and general principles it expresses. It recognizes that there may be debate at times over the application of these principles. But it does not mean these principles cannot be identified.

Constitutional adjudication is obviously not a mechanical process. It requires an appeal to reason and discretion. The text and intention of the Constitution must be understood to constitute the banks within which constitutional interpretation must flow. As James Madison said, if "the sense in which the Constitution was accepted and ratified by the nation . . .

be not the guide in expounding it, there can be no security for a consistent and stable government, more than for a faithful exercise of its powers."

Thomas Jefferson, so often cited incorrectly as a framer of the Constitution, in fact shared Madison's view: "Our peculiar security is in the possession of a written Constitution. Let us not make it a blank paper by construction." Jefferson was even more explicit in his personal correspondence:

> On every question of construction [we should] carry ourselves back to the time, when the constitution was adopted; recollect the spirit manifested in the debates; and instead of trying [to find], what meaning may be squeezed out of the text, or invented against it, conform to the probable one, in which it was passed.

In the main, jurisprudence that seeks to be faithful to our Constitution—a Jurisprudence of Original Intention, as I have called it—is not difficult to describe. Where the language of the Constitution is specific, it must be obeyed. Where there is a demonstrable consensus among the framers and ratifiers as to a principle stated or implied by the Constitution, it should be followed. Where there is ambiguity as to the precise meaning or reach of a constitutional provision, it should be interpreted and applied in a manner so as to at least not contradict the text of the Constitution itself.

Sadly, while almost every one participating in the current constitutional debate would give assent to these propositions, the techniques and conclusions of some of the debaters do violence to them. What is the source of this violence? In large part I believe that it is the misuse of history stemming from the neglect of the idea of a written constitution.

There is a frank proclamation by some judges and commentators that what matters most about the Constitution is not its words but its so-called "spirit." These individuals focus less on the language of specific provisions than on what they describe as the "vision" or "concepts of human dignity" they find embodied in the Constitution. This approach to jurisprudence has led to some remarkable and tragic conclusions.

In the 1850's, the Supreme Court under Chief Justice Roger B. Taney read blacks out of the Constitution in order to invalidate Congress' attempt to limit the spread of slavery. The *Dred Scott* decision, famously described as a judicial "self-inflicted wound," helped bring on the Civil War. There is a lesson in this history. There is danger in seeing the Constitution as an empty vessel into which each generation may pour its passion and prejudice.

Our own time has its own fashions and passions. In recent decades many have come to view the Constitution—more accurately, part of the Constitution, provisions of the Bill of Rights and the Fourteenth Amendment—as a charter for judicial activism on behalf of various constituencies. Those who hold this view often have lacked demonstrable textual or historical support for their conclusions. Instead they have "grounded" their rulings in appeals to social theories, to moral philosophies or personal notions of human dignity, or to "penumbras," somehow emanating ghostlike from various provisions—identified and not identified—in the Bill of Rights.[1] The problem with this approach, as John Hart Ely, Dean of the Stanford Law School has observed with respect to one such decision, is not that it is bad constitutional law, but that it is not constitutional law in any meaningful sense, at all.

Despite this fact, the perceived popularity of some results in particular cases has encouraged some observers to believe that any critique of the methodology of those decisions is an attack on the results. This perception is sufficiently widespread that it deserves an answer. My answer is to look at history.

When the Supreme Court, in *Brown* v. *Board of Education* [347 U.S. 483 (1954)], sounded the death knell for official segregation in the country, it earned all the plaudits it received. But the Supreme Court in that case was not giving new life to old words, or adapting a "living," "flexible" Constitution to new reality. It was restoring the original principle of the Constitution to constitutional law. The *Brown* Court was correcting the damage done 50 years earlier, when in *Plessy* v. *Ferguson* [163 U.S. 537 (1896)], an earlier Supreme Court had disregarded the clear intent of the Framers of the Civil War amendments to eliminate the legal degradation of blacks, and had contrived a theory of the Constitution to support the charade of "separate but equal" discrimination.

Similarly, the decisions of the New Deal and beyond that freed Congress to regulate commerce and enact a plethora of social legislation were not judicial adaptations of the Constitution to new realities. They were in fact removals of encrustations of earlier courts that had strayed from the original intent of the Framers regarding the power of the legislature to make policy.

It is amazing how so much of what passes for social and political progress is really the undoing of old judicial mistakes. Mistakes occur when the principles of specific constitutional provisions—such as those contained in the Bill of Rights—are taken by some as invitations to read into the Constitution values that contradict the clear language of other provisions.

Acceptances to this illusory invitation have proliferated in recent decades. One Supreme Court justice identified the proper judicial standard as asking "what's best for this country." Another said it is important to "keep the Court out in front" of the general society. Various academic commentators have poured rhetorical grease on this judicial fire, suggesting that constitutional interpretation appropriately be guided by such standards as whether a public policy "personifies justice" or "comports with the notion of moral evolution" or confers "an identity" upon our society or was consistent with "natural ethical law" or was consistent with some "right of equal citizenship."

---

1. Meese's use of *penumbras* refers to Justice William O. Douglas's opinion in *Griswold* v. *Connecticut* (1965), which established a constitutional right to privacy. Douglas argued that although this right was not explicitly stated in the Bill of Rights, it could be found in the penumbras of several of the first ten amendments.

Unfortunately, as I've noted, navigation by such lodestars has in the past given us questionable economics, governmental disorder, and racism—all in the guise of constitutional law. Recently one of the distinguished judges of one of our federal appeals courts got it about right when he wrote: "The truth is that the judge who looks outside the Constitution always looks inside himself and nowhere else" [Robert H. Bork, *Traditions and Morality in Constitutional Law* (1984)]. Or, as we recently put it before the Supreme Court in an important brief: "The further afield interpretation travels from its point of departure in the text, the greater the danger that constitutional adjudication will be like a picnic to which the framers bring the words and the judges the meaning" [Brief for the United States as *amicus curiae* at 24, *Thornburgh* v. *American College of Obstetricians and Gynecologists*, No. 844-95, June 11, 1986].[2]

In the *Osborne* v. *Bank of United States* [22 U.S. 738 (1824)], decision 21 years after *Marbury*, Chief Justice Marshall further elaborated his view of the relationship between the judge and the law, be it statutory or constitutional:

> Judicial power, as contradistinguished from the power of the laws, has no existence. Courts are the mere instruments of the law, and can will nothing. When they are said to exercise a discretion, it is a mere legal discretion, a discretion to be exercised in discerning the course prescribed by law; and, when that is discerned, it is the duty of the Court to follow it.

Any true approach to constitutional interpretation must respect the document in all its parts and be faithful to the Constitution in its entirety. What must be remembered in the current debate is that interpretation does not imply results. The Framers were not trying to anticipate every answer. They were trying to create a tripartite national government, within a federal system, that would have the flexibility to adapt to face new exigencies—as it did, for example, in chartering a national bank. Their great interest was in the distribution of power and responsibility in order to secure the great goal of liberty for all.

A jurisprudence that seeks fidelity to the Constitution—a Jurisprudence of Original Intention—is not a jurisprudence of political results. It is very much concerned with process, and it is a jurisprudence that in our day seeks to de-politicize the law. The great genius of the constitutional blueprint is found in its creation and respect for spheres of authority and the limits it places on governmental power. In this scheme the Framers did not see the courts as the exclusive custodians of the Constitution. Indeed, because the document posits so few conclusions it leaves to the more political branches the matter of adapting and vivifying its principles in each generation. It also leaves to the people of the states, in the 10th amendment,

---

2. *Amicus curiae* means friend of the court. Legal briefs of this kind are filed by those who are not the actual parties in a lawsuit.

those responsibilities and rights not committed to federal care. The power to declare acts of Congress and laws of the states null and void is truly awesome. This power must be used when the Constitution clearly speaks. It should not be used when the Constitution does not.

In *Marbury* v. *Madison,* at the same time he vindicated the concept of judicial review, Marshall wrote that the "principles" of the Constitution "are deemed fundamental and permanent," and, except for formal amendment, "unchangeable." If we want a change in our Constitution or in our laws we must seek it through the formal mechanisms presented in that organizing document of our government.

In summary, I would emphasize that what is at issue here is not an agenda of issues or a menu of results. At issue is a way of government. A jurisprudence based on first principles is neither conservative nor liberal, neither right nor left. It is a jurisprudence that cares about committing and limiting to each organ of government the proper ambit of its responsibilities. It is a jurisprudence faithful to our Constitution.

By the same token, an activist jurisprudence, one which anchors the Constitution only in the consciences of jurists, is a chameleon jurisprudence, changing color and form in each era. The same activism hailed today may threaten the capacity for decision through democratic consensus tomorrow, as it has in many yesterdays. Ultimately, as the early democrats wrote into the Massachusetts state constitution, the best defense of our liberties is a government of laws and not men.

Reading the Constitution as Twentieth-Century Americans

WILLIAM J. BRENNAN, JR.

I t will perhaps not surprise you that the text I have chosen for exploration is the amended Constitution of the United States, which, of course, entrenches the Bill of Rights and the Civil War amendments, and draws sustenance from the bedrock principles of another great text, the Magna Carta. So fashioned, the Constitution embodies the aspiration to social justice, brotherhood, and human dignity that brought this nation into being. The Declaration of Independence, the Constitution and the Bill of Rights solemnly committed the United States to be a country where the dignity and rights of all persons were equal before all authority. In all candor we must concede that part of this egalitarianism in America has been more pretension than realized fact. But we are an aspiring people, a people with faith in progress. Our amended Constitution is the lodestar for our aspirations. Like every text worth reading, it is not crystalline. The phrasing is broad and the limitations of its provisions are not clearly marked. Its majestic generalities and ennobling pronouncements are both luminous and obscure. This ambiguity of course calls forth interpretation, the interaction of reader and text. The encounter with the constitutional text has been, in many senses, my life's work. . . .

When Justices interpret the Constitution they speak for their community, not for themselves alone. The act of interpretation must be undertaken with full consciousness that it is, in a very real sense, the community's interpretation that is sought. Justices are not platonic guardians appointed to wield authority according to their personal moral predelictions. Precisely because coercive force must attend any judicial decision to countermand the will of a contemporary majority, the Justices must render constitutional interpretations that are received as legitimate. The source of legitimacy is, of course, a wellspring of controversy in legal and political circles. At the core of the debate is what the late Yale Law School professor Alexander Bickel labeled "the counter-majoritarian difficulty." Our commitment to self-governance in a representative democracy must be reconciled with vesting in electorally unaccountable Justices the power to invalidate the expressed desires of representative bodies on the ground of inconsistency with higher law. Because judicial power resides in the authority to give meaning to the Constitution, the debate is really a debate about how to read the text, about constraints on what is legitimate interpretation.

There are those who find legitimacy in fidelity to what they call "the intentions of the Framers." In its most doctrinaire incarnation, this view demands that Justices discern exactly what the Framers thought about the question under consideration and simply follow that intention in resolving the case before them. It is a view that feigns self-effacing deference to the specific judgments of those who forged our original social compact. But in truth it is little more than arrogance cloaked as humility. It is arrogant to pretend that from our vantage we can gauge accurately the intent of the Framers on application of principle to specific, contemporary questions. All too often, sources of potential enlightenment such as records of the ratification debates provide sparse or ambiguous evidence of the original intention. Typically, all that can be gleaned is that the Framers themselves did not agree about the application or meaning of particular constitutional provisions, and hid their differences in cloaks of generality. Indeed, it is far from clear whose intention is relevant—that of the drafters, the congressional disputants, or the ratifiers in the states?—or even whether the idea of an original intention is a coherent way of thinking about a jointly drafted document drawing its authority from a general assent of the states. And apart from the problematic nature of the sources, our distance of two centuries cannot but work as a prism refracting all we perceive. One cannot help but speculate that the chorus of lamentations calling for interpretation faithful to "original intention"—and proposing nullification of interpretations that fail this quick litmus test—must inevitably come from persons who have no familiarity with the historical record.

Perhaps most importantly, while proponents of this facile historicism justify it as a depoliticization of the judiciary, the political underpinnings of such a choice should not escape notice. A position that upholds constitutional claims only if they were within the specific contemplation of the Framers in effect establishes a presumption of resolving textual ambiguities against the claim of constitutional right. It is far from clear what justifies such a presumption against claims of right. Nothing intrinsic in the nature of interpretation—if there is such a thing as the "nature" of interpretation—commands such a passive approach to ambiguity. This is a choice no less political than any other; it expresses antipathy to claims of the minority rights against the majority. Those who would restrict claims of right to the values of 1789 specifically articulated in the Constitution turn a blind eye to social progress and eschew adaptation of overarching principles to changes of social circumstance.

Another, perhaps more sophisticated, response to the potential power of judicial interpretation stresses democratic theory: because ours is a government of the people's elected representatives, substantive value choices should by and large be left to them. This view emphasizes not the transcendent historical authority of the framers but the predominant contemporary authority of the elected branches of government. Yet it has similar consequences for the nature of proper judicial interpretation. Faith in the majoritarian process counsels restraint. Even under more expansive formulations of this approach, judicial review is appropriate only to the extent of ensuring that our democratic process functions smoothly. Thus, for example, we would protect freedom of speech merely to ensure that the people are heard by their representatives, rather than as a separate, substantive value. When, by contrast, society tosses up to the Supreme Court a dispute that would require invalidation of a legislature's substantive policy choice, the Court generally would stay its hand because the Constitution was meant as a plan of government and not as an embodiment of fundamental substantive values.

The view that all matters of substantive policy should be resolved through the majoritarian process has appeal under some circumstances, but I think it ultimately will not do. Unabashed enshrinement of majority would permit the imposition of a social caste system or wholesale confiscation of property so long as a majority of the authorized legislative body, fairly elected, approved. Our Constitution could not abide such a situation. It is the very purpose of a Constitution—and particularly of the Bill of Rights—to declare certain values transcendent, beyond the reach of temporary political majorities. The majoritarian process cannot be expected to rectify claims of minority right that arise as a response to the outcomes of that very majoritarian process. As James Madison put it:

> The prescriptions in favor of liberty ought to be levelled against that quarter where the greatest danger lies, namely, that which possesses the highest prerogative of power. But this is not found in either the Executive or Legislative departments of Government, but in the body of the people, operating by the majority against the minority (I Annals 437).

Faith in democracy is one thing, blind faith quite another. Those who drafted our Constitution understood the difference. One cannot read the text without admitting that it embodies substantive value choices; it places certain values beyond the power of any legislature. Obvious are the separation of powers; the privilege of the Writ of Habeas Corpus; prohibition of Bills of Attainder and *ex post facto* laws; prohibition of cruel and unusual punishments; the requirement of just compensation for official taking of property; the prohibition of laws tending to establish religion or enjoining the free exercise of religion; and, since the Civil War, the banishment of slavery and official race discrimination. With respect to at least such principles, we simply have not constituted ourselves as strict utilitarians. While the Constitution may be amended, such amendments require an immense effort by the People as a whole.

To remain faithful to the content of the Constitution, therefore, an approach to interpreting the text must account for the existence of these substantive value choices, and must accept the ambiguity inherent in the effort to apply them to modern circumstances. The Framers discerned fundamental principles through struggles against particular malefactions of the Crown; the struggle shapes the particular contours of the articulated principles. But our acceptance of the fundamental principles has not and should not bind us to those precise, at times anachronistic, contours. Successive generations of Americans have continued to respect these fundamental choices and adopt them as their own guide to evaluating quite different historical practices. Each generation has the choice to overrule or add to the fundamental principles enunciated by the Framers; the Constitution can be amended or it can be ignored. Yet with respect to its fundamental principles, the text has suffered neither fate. Thus, if I may borrow the words of an esteemed predecessor, Justice Robert Jackson, the burden of judicial interpretation is to translate "the majestic generalities of the Bill of Rights, conceived as part of the pattern of liberal government in the eighteenth century, into concrete restraints on officials dealing with the problems of the twentieth century" *Board of Education* v. *Barnette* [319 U.S. 624, 639 (1943)].

We current Justices read the Constitution in the only way that we can: as Twentieth Century Americans. We look to the history of the time of framing and to the intervening history of interpretation. But the ultimate question must be, what do the words of the text mean in our time? For the genius of the Constitution rests not in any static meaning it might have had in a world that is dead and gone, but in the adaptability of its great principles to cope with current problems and current needs. What the constitutional fundamentals meant to the wisdom of other times cannot be their measure to the vision of our time. Similarly, what those fundamentals mean for us, our descendants will learn, cannot be the measure to the vision of their time. This realization is not, I assure you, a novel one of my own creation. Permit me to quote from one of the opinions of our Court, *Weems* v. *United States* [217 U.S. 349], written nearly a century ago:

> Time works changes, brings into existence new conditions and purposes. Therefore, a principle to be vital must be capable of wider application than the mischief which gave it birth. This is peculiarly true of constitutions. They are not ephemeral enactments, designed to meet passing occasions. They are, to use the words of Chief Justice John Marshall, "designed to approach immortality as nearly as human institutions can approach it." The future is their care and provision for events of good and bad tendencies of which no prophecy can be made. In the application of a constitution, therefore, our contemplation cannot be only of what has been, but of what may be.

Interpretation must account for the transformative purpose of the text. Our Constitution was not intended to preserve a preexisting society but to make a new one, to put in place new principles that the prior political community had not sufficiently recognized. Thus, for example, when we interpret the Civil War Amendments to the charter—abolishing slavery, guaranteeing blacks equality under law, and guaranteeing blacks the right to vote—we must remember that those who put them in place had no desire to enshrine the status quo. Their goal was to make over their world, to eliminate all vestige of slave caste.

Having discussed at some length how I, as a Supreme Court Justice, interact with this text, I think it time to turn to the fruits of this discourse. For the Constitution is a sublime oration on the dignity of man, a bold commitment by a people to the ideal of libertarian dignity protected through law. Some reflection is perhaps required before this can be seen.

The Constitution on its face is, in large measure, a structuring text, a blueprint for government. And when the text is not prescribing the form of government it is limiting the powers of that government. The original document, before addition of any of the amendments, does not speak primarily of the rights of man, but of the abilities and disabilities of government. When one reflects upon the text's preoccupation with the scope of government as well as its shape, however, one comes to understand that what this text is about is the relationship of the individual and the state. The text marks the metes and bounds of official authority and individual autonomy. When one studies the boundary that the text marks out, one gets a sense of the vision of the individual embodied in the Constitution.

As augmented by the Bill of Rights and the Civil War Amendments, this text is a sparkling vision of the supremacy of the human dignity of every individual. This vision is reflected in the very choice of democratic self-governance: the supreme value of a democracy is the presumed worth of each individual. And this vision manifests itself most dramatically in the specific prohibitions of the Bill of Rights, a term which I henceforth will apply to describe not only the original first eight amendments, but the Civil War amendments as well. It is a vision that has guided us as a people throughout our history, although the precise rules by which we have protected fundamental human dignity have been transformed over time in response to both transformations of social condition and evolution of our concepts of human dignity. . . .

In general, problems of the relationship of the citizen with government have multiplied and thus have engendered some of the most important constitutional issues of the day. As government acts ever more deeply upon those areas of our lives once marked "private," there is an even greater need to see that individual rights are not curtailed or cheapened in the interest of what may temporarily appear to be the "public good." And as government continues in its role of provider for so many of our disadvantaged citizens, there is an even greater need to ensure that government act with integrity and consistency in its dealings with these citizens. To put this another way, the possibilities for collision between government activity and individual rights will increase as the power and authority of government itself expands, and this growth, in turn, heightens the need for constant vigilance at the collision points. If our free society is to endure, those who govern must recognize human dignity and accept the enforcement of constitutional limitations on their power conceived by the Framers to be necessary to preserve that dignity and the air of freedom which is our proudest heritage. Such recognition will not come from a technical understanding of the organs of government, or the new forms of wealth they administer. It requires something different, something deeper—a personal confrontation with the well-springs of our society. Solutions of constitutional questions from that perspective have become the great challenge of the modern era. All the talk in the last half-decade about shrinking the government does not alter this reality or the challenge it imposes. The modern activist state is a concomitant of the complexity of modern society; it is inevitably with us. We must meet the challenge rather than wish it were not before us.

The challenge is essentially, of course, one to the capacity of our constitutional structure to foster and protect the freedom, the dignity, and the rights of all persons within our borders, which it is the great design of the Constitution to secure. During the time of my public service this challenge has largely taken shape within the confines of the interpretive question whether the specific guarantees of the Bill of Rights operate as restraints on the power of State government. We recognize the Bill of Rights as the primary source of express information as to what is meant by constitutional liberty. The safeguards enshrined in it are deeply etched in the foundation of America's freedoms. Each is a protection with centuries of history behind it, often dearly bought with the blood and lives of people determined to prevent oppression by their rulers. The first eight Amendments, however, were added to the Constitution to operate solely against federal power. It was not until the Thirteenth and Fourteenth Amendments were added, in 1865 and 1868, in response to a demand for national protection against abuses of state power, that the Constitution could be interpreted to require application of the first eight amendments to the states.

It was in particular the Fourteenth Amendment's guarantee that no person be deprived of life, liberty or property without process of law that led us to apply many of the specific guarantees of the Bill of Rights to the States. In my judgment, Justice Cardozo best captured the reasoning that brought us to such decisions when he described what the Court has done as a process by which the guarantees "have been taken over from the earlier articles of the federal bill of rights and brought within the Fourteenth Amendment by a process of absorption . . . [that] has had its source in the belief that neither liberty nor justice would exist if [those guarantees] . . . were sacrificed" {*Palko* v. *Connecticut* [302 U.S. 319, 326 (1937)]}. But this process of absorption was neither swift nor steady. As late as 1922 only the Fifth Amendment guarantee of just compensation for official taking of property had been given force against the states. Between then and 1956 only the First Amendment guarantees of speech and conscience and the Fourth Amendment ban of unreasonable searches and seizures had been incorporated—the latter, however, without the exclusionary rule to give it force. As late as 1961, I could stand before a distinguished assemblage of the bar at New York University's James Madison Lecture and list the following as guarantees that had not been thought to be sufficiently fundamental to the protection of human dignity so as to be enforced against the states: the prohibition of cruel and unusual punishments, the right against self-incrimination, the right to assistance of counsel in a criminal trial, the right to confront witnesses, the right to compulsory process, the right not to be placed in jeopardy of life or limb more than once upon accusation of a crime, the right not to have illegally obtained evidence introduced at a criminal trial, and the right to a jury of one's peers.

The history of the quarter century following that Madison Lecture need not be told in great detail. Suffice it to say that each of the guarantees listed above has been recognized as a fundamental aspect of ordered liberty. Of course, the above catalogue encompasses only the rights of the criminally accused, those caught, rightly or wrongly, in the maw of the criminal justice system. But it has been well said that there is no better test of a society than how it treats those accused of transgressing against it. Indeed, it is because we recognize that incarceration strips a man of his dignity that we demand strict adherence to fair procedure and proof of guilt beyond a reasonable doubt before taking such a drastic step. These requirements are, as Justice Harlan once said, "bottomed on a fundamental value determination of our society that it is far worse to convict an innocent man than to let a guilty man go free" {*In re Winship* [397 U.S. 358, 372 (1970)] (concurring opinion)}. There is no worse injustice than wrongly to strip a man of his dignity. And our adherence to the constitutional vision of human dignity is so strict that even after convicting a person according to these stringent standards, we demand that his dignity be infringed only to the extent appropriate to the crime and never by means of wanton infliction of pain or deprivation. I interpret the Constitution plainly to embody these fundamental values.

Of course the constitutional vision of human dignity has, in this past quarter century, infused far more than our decisions about the criminal process. Recognition of the principle of "one person, one vote" as a constitutional one redeems the promise of self-governance by affirming the essential dignity of every citizen in the right to equal participation in the democratic process. Recognition of so-called "new property" rights in those receiving government entitlements affirms the essential dignity of the least fortunate among us by demanding that government treat with decency, integrity and consistency those dependent on its benefits for their very survival. After all, a legislative majority initially decides to create governmental entitlements; the Constitution's Due Process Clause merely provides protection for entitlements thought necessary by society as a whole. Such due process rights prohibit government from imposing the devil's bargain of bartering away human dignity in exchange for human sustenance. Likewise, recognition of full equality for women—equal protection of the laws—ensures that gender has no bearing on claims to human dignity.

Recognition of broad and deep rights of expression and of conscience reaffirm the vision of human dignity in many ways. They too redeem the promise of self-governance by facilitating—indeed demanding—robust, uninhibited and wide-open debate on issues of public importance. Such public debate is of course vital to the development and dissemination of political ideas. As importantly, robust public discussion is the crucible in which personal political convictions are forged. In our democracy, such discussion is a political duty, it is the essence of self-government. The constitutional vision of human dignity rejects the possibility of political orthodoxy imposed from above; it respects the right of each individual to form and to express political judgments, however far they may deviate from the mainstream and however unsettling they might be to the powerful or the elite. Recognition of these rights of expression and conscience also frees up the private space for both intellectual and spiritual development free of government dominance, either blatant or subtle. Justice Brandeis put it so well sixty years ago when he wrote: "Those who won our independence believed that the final end of the State was to make men free to develop their faculties; and that in its government the deliberative forces should prevail over the arbitrary. They valued liberty both as an end and as a means" {*Whitney* v. *California* [274 U.S. 357, 375 (1927)] (concurring opinion)}.

I do not mean to suggest that we have in the last quarter century achieved a comprehensive definition of the constitutional ideal of human dignity. We are still striving toward that goal, and doubtless it will be an eternal quest. For if the interaction of this Justice and the constitutional text over the years confirms any single proposition, it is that the demands of human dignity will never cease to evolve.

DISCUSSION QUESTIONS

1. Should justices of the Supreme Court be guided by the original intention of those who wrote the Constitution and the laws? What are the advantages of this approach to constitutional interpretation? What problems might justices face in trying to ascertain original intention?

2. If original intention is not to be the standard for constitutional interpretation, what can the standard be? How might Brennan respond to Meese's argument that if original intention is rejected, the door is opened to justices arbitrarily pouring their own values and goals into their decisions while claiming to base them on the Constitution?

3. Does the Constitution guarantee only those rights that are specified in its text? Can we derive such things as a right to privacy (the basis for Supreme Court decisions on contraception and abortion) from constitutional values even when the Constitution says nothing about such a right?

4. What is the place of the judiciary in American democracy? Does the Supreme Court's status as an unelected branch require that it play a limited and restrained role? Or does its claim to be the guardian of the Constitution warrant a more active role for the Court on behalf of democratic principles and values?

5. Is it possible to depoliticize the Supreme Court? Can the Supreme Court be removed from the central political controversies of American life?

SUGGESTED READINGS AND INTERNET RESOURCES

In *The Tempting of America: The Political Seduction of the Law* (New York: Free Press, 1990), Robert Bork develops a view of constitutional interpretation similar to Meese's and presents a scathing conservative critique of an activist judiciary. A skeptical argument that the judiciary cannot be the agent of social justice that Brennan envisions can be found in Gerald Rosenberg, *The Hollow Hope: Can Courts Bring About Social Change?* (Chicago: University of Chicago Press, 1991). The judiciary has been criticized from the left as well as from the right; for radical perspectives, see David Kairys, ed., *The Politics of Law: A Progressive Critique* (3d ed.; New York: Basic Books, 1998). An argument for a populist constitutional law that would deny the judicial branch the exclusive authority to interpret the Constitution is Mark Tushnet, *Taking the Constitution Away from the Courts* (Princeton, N.J.: Princeton University Press, 1999). For a popular democratic account of leading Supreme Court cases, see Peter Irons, *A People's History of the Supreme Court* (New York: Penguin Books, 2000).

Federalist Society
www.fed-soc.org
This web site of a prominent organization of conservative lawyers offers
perspectives on recent Supreme Court cases and other legal issues.

American Civil Liberties Union
www.aclu.org
This web site discusses legal issues and court cases viewed from the perspective
of the group who has argued many of the most prominent civil liberties issues
before the U.S. Supreme Court.

University of Pittsburgh School of Law
www.jurist.law.pitt.edu
This site provides Supreme Court opinions and stories on constitutional law.

Supreme Court of the United States
www.supremecourtus.gov
The Supreme Court's web site contains a searchable docket, the text of recent
decisions in PDF format, and information on Court rules and procedures.

16

Economic Inequality: A Threat to Democracy?

The United States has always prided itself on being a land of opportunity. Unlike the class-divided societies of Europe, American society is viewed as being more fluid and open to individual ambition. In the United States you can rise from "rags to riches," as the saying goes. The "American Dream," which is defined in many different ways but almost always involves economic success, is supposedly within everyone's grasp. Millions of immigrants have been drawn to our shores by the lure of the American Dream. Not only is the United States a land of opportunity and upward mobility, but it also is generally believed that we lack the extremes of wealth and poverty that characterize other societies. The United States is viewed as basically a middle-class society.

Almost everyone agrees that equal opportunity and a strong middle class are essential to the healthy functioning of American society and its political system. Throughout U.S. history, however, debates have periodically erupted about how to guarantee equal opportunity and how much economic inequality should be tolerated in a democracy before government needs to take action. One of the first such debates was between two giants of American political history, Thomas Jefferson and Alexander Hamilton. Jefferson argued that the stability of American democracy rested on the backs of small farmers, who, because they made a living through their own efforts on their own land, were free to speak out and participate fully in politics without any fears. Jefferson felt that manufacturing and large cities created wide inequalities and dangerous dependencies that corrupted democracy. His opponent, Alexander Hamilton, was much less fearful of economic inequalities. In his *Report on Manufactures,* Hamilton argued that the government should encourage manufacturing as a way to tie the wealthy classes to government, thus providing a check against the turbulence of the masses.

In the long run, Hamilton's vision of industrial expansion prevailed over Jefferson's agricultural ideal. After the Civil War (1861–1865), industry really began to take off. Entrepreneurs, such as Andrew Carnegie and John D. Rockefeller, amassed huge fortunes the likes of which had never been seen before in the New World. At the same time, millions of immigrants poured into U.S. cities to work in industry at low wages and long hours. Many observers believed that events were proving Jefferson's fears correct. Mark Twain called this "Gilded Age" a time of money lust. Muckraking journalists exposed the ways that Robber Barons corrupted the political process, sometimes buying off whole state legislatures. The Populist movement of the late nineteenth century fought to protect the small farmer and limit the power of corporations. It proposed legislation to break up the large corporations, expand the money supply to ease the debt burden on the small farmers, and impose a federal income tax to redistribute wealth.

The opponents of the Populists vigorously denied that industrialism was creating unfair inequalities that threatened American democracy. They did not deny that some people were very rich and others quite poor, but they argued that these inequalities were a natural result of economic competition that brought great benefits to all of society. Social Darwinists applied Charles Darwin's theory of human evolution to society, arguing that inequalities derived from economic competition, which resulted in the "survival of the fittest." Great wealth was the result of hard work and entrepreneurial genius. As the prominent Social Darwinist William Graham Sumner put it: "No man can acquire a million without helping a million men to increase their little fortunes all the way down all through the social grades." The United States was a land of opportunity where self-made men could rise up out of the working class to great riches. Indeed, there were many examples, besides Carnegie and Rockefeller, to point to. The principles of Social Darwinism were spread to the broad public by a "success" literature that told vivid stories of poor boys rising up out of poverty through hard work and moral uprightness. A Unitarian minister by the name of Horatio Alger published 106 such rags-to-riches books from 1868 to 1904, many of which became best-sellers.

A century later the democratic debate about economic inequality is once again heating up, albeit in very different economic circumstances. From World War II until the 1970s, according to most observers, economic inequalities remained the same or even shrank somewhat. Sometime in the 1970s, however, wages began to stagnate and even fall for most workers. Many reasons have been offered for this. Global competition has put downward pressure on U.S. industrial wages, which now must often compete with wages in Third World countries. It is not so much the decline in manufacturing wages as the shift from manufacturing to services that is hurting wages for many workers. Manufacturing employment has declined as jobs have migrated abroad and workers are replaced by machines, including industrial robots. Wages in the expanding service sector are generally lower than in manufacturing. Partly driven by the spread of computers into practically every workplace, education and skills have become even more important to earning a good wage. The wages of those with a high school education and less have fallen, while those with postgraduate degrees have seen their salaries soar. You can no longer earn a decent wage simply by having a strong back and being willing to work hard.

As in the Gilded Age, at the same time that many workers are struggling to get by, huge fortunes are being amassed at the top. The incredible bull market on Wall Street that lasted from in the late 1980s almost to 2000 brought fantastic returns for those who held stocks. Technological breakthroughs in computer technology have generated tremendous opportunities for daring entrepreneurs to accumulate vast wealth. Personal computers, software, and the development of the internet have created wealth more rapidly than at any time in American history. Bill Gates, the founder of Microsoft, which supplies the operating system for most personal computers, became the richest man in the world, worth well over $100 billion (that's billion, not million!). His fortune, even after it is corrected for inflation, is many times that of John D. Rockefeller. Reminiscent of the government's effort to break up Rockefeller's Standard Oil Trust, the federal government has prosecuted Microsoft for antitrust violations.

As with the inequalities generated by nineteenth-century industrialism, the inequalities of the so-called postindustrial economy have prompted a spirited political and policy debate. When deindustrialization hit with a vengeance in the 1980s, many people called for the United States to engage in industrial planning similar to that done by Japan. But national industrial planning never took off, however. Instead, led by President Ronald Reagan, the United States pursued a very different approach. Reagan argued that government regulation and high taxes were choking off economic growth. Reagan's supply-side economics recommended cutting taxes in order to increase incentives to work hard and invest. Inequalities were necessary as a goad to work hard, and in the long run everyone would benefit from a growing economy. "A rising tide would lift all boats."

Bill Clinton campaigned for the presidency in 1992 on promises to address inequalities, calling for a national health insurance program and greater investments in education and job training for American workers. Although Clinton lost on health insurance and largely jettisoned his proposals to invest in American workers in order to instead reduce the deficit, throughout his presidency he advocated government programs, such as increasing the minimum wage, to help those who were being left behind by the booming economy. Clinton strongly supported free trade, but many, most notably Pat Buchanan and Ross Perot, attacked free trade for exporting U.S. jobs (Perot's "giant sucking sound"). The inequality debate was renewed in 2001 when President George W. Bush succeeded in passing a $1.35 trillion tax cut spread over ten years. Opponents charged that 38 percent of the benefits would go to the wealthiest 1 percent of taxpayers. Supporters responded that it was only fair that those who paid the most in taxes would receive the most money back.

The two selections that follow address the contemporary inequality debate in our rapidly changing economy. The first excerpt is from a 1999 book entitled *Myths of Rich and Poor,* by W. Michael Cox, chief economist at the Federal Reserve Bank of Dallas, and Richard Alm. Acknowledging that some statistics show wide and widening income inequalities, they maintain that these inequalities are not threatening. According to Cox and Alm, we should not concentrate on the gap between the top and the bottom. Rather, we should focus on whether those at the bottom are better or worse off. In the book from which this excerpt is taken, the authors make a convincing case that those at the bottom generally are better off in terms of *consumption.* Breakthroughs in technology mean that we have more conveniences than ever, such as VCRs, color TVs, and telephone answering machines. In addition, these devices, which enhance the quality of our lives, are more efficient and powerful than ever (consider the improvement in home computers in recent years). In the section we have chosen, Cox and Alm make the point that snapshots of inequality at one point in time do not capture the movement of people out of poverty over their lifetimes. It is still a land of opportunity, they argue.

Paul Krugman, an iconoclastic MIT economist, argues in our other selection that it is precisely the gap between the rich and the poor that we should be focusing on. A middle-class nation, Krugman says, is a nation where "most people live more or less the same kind of life." Increasingly, however, those at the top are living very different lives from the rest of us; they are withdrawing into residential enclaves that make them feel little connection to the lives of ordinary people. For Krugman, rising inequalities are partly caused by economic factors such as global competition and new technologies. For the rest of the story, he says, we must look to changing corporate values and the power that corporations wield compared to the declining power of labor unions. The danger, Krugman suggests, is that growing inequalities reinforce themselves in a vicious cycle of spiraling inequality that could tear American society apart. What we need are new public policies, like those of Franklin Roosevelt's New Deal, that can reverse the process of widening inequalities.

Before reading the two selections, you may want to look back at the discussion of inequality in the Introduction to this book. Do the authors take a process orientation toward equality or a results orientation? Why do Cox and Alm think we should focus on what those at the bottom are able to consume, whereas Krugman says little about this and instead concentrates on the gap between the top and the bottom? Krugman clearly thinks that it is the political power of those at the top that is partly responsible for rising inequalities. What do Cox and Alm say is the cause of income differences?

Myths of Rich and Poor

W. MICHAEL COX
AND RICHARD ALM

"Land of Opportunity." Anywhere in the world, those three words bring to mind just one place: the United States of America.

Opportunity defines our heritage. The American saga entails waves of immigrant farmers, shopkeepers, laborers, and entrepreneurs, all coming to the United States for the promise of a better life. Some amassed enormous fortunes—the Rockefellers, the Carnegies, the DuPonts, the Fords, the Vanderbilts, to name just a few. Even today, America's opportunity is always on display. Bill Gates in computer software, Ross Perot in data processing, Bill Cosby and Oprah Winfrey in entertainment, Warren Buffett in investing, Sam Walton in retailing, Michael Jordan in sports, and Mary Kay Ash in cosmetics could head a list of the many thousands who catapulted from society's lower or middle ranks to the top. Many millions more, descendants of those who arrived with little more than the clothes on their backs and a few bucks in their pockets, took advantage of an open economic system to improve their lot in life through talent and hard work.

Even pessimists acknowledge that the Gateses, Perots, Cosbys, Winfreys, Buffetts, Waltons, Jordans, and Ashes are getting filthy rich, along with Wall Street's wheeler-dealers, Hollywood moguls, and big-league ballplayers. At the nation's 350 largest companies, top executives' median total compensation in 1996 was $3.1 million, or 90 times what a typical factory hand earns. We often hear that ordinary Americans aren't keeping up, that success isn't as easy, or at least not as democratic, as it once was. At the close of the twentieth century, one disturbing vision portrays the United States as a society pulling apart at the seams, divided into separate and unequal camps, an enclave of fat cats gorging themselves on the fruits of others' labor surrounded by a working class left with ever more meager opportunities.

The most-cited evidence of ebbing opportunity is the *distribution of income*—the slicing up of the American pie. Examining the data, analysts seize on two points. First, there's a marked inequality in earnings between society's haves and have-nots. Second, and perhaps more ominous, the gap between the richest and poorest households has widened over the past two decades. The Census Bureau provides the statistical ballast for these claims. In 1997, the top 20 percent of American households received almost half of the nation's income. Average earnings among this group are $122,764 a year. The distribution of income to the four other groups of 20 percent was as follows: The second fifth had 23.2 percent, with average earnings of $57,582; the third fifth had 15.0 percent, with average earnings of $37,177; the fourth fifth had 8.9 percent, with average earnings of $22,098. The bottom 20 percent earned 3.6 percent of the economic pie, or an average of $8,872 a year.

The case for the existence of a growing rift between rich and poor rests on longer-term trends in the same Census Bureau data. Since 1975, only the top 20 percent of Americans managed to expand their allotment of the nation's income—from 43.2 percent to 49.4 percent. Over the same period, the distribution to the middle three groups slipped slightly. The share going to the lowest 20 percent of income earners fell from 4.4 percent to 3.6 percent. The shift of income toward the upper end of the distribution becomes even more striking when it's put in dollars. After adjusting for inflation, the income of households in the bottom 20 percent increased by only $207 from 1975 to 1997. The top tier, meanwhile, jumped by $37,633.

Once again, the pessimists have it wrong. The income distribution only reveals how one group is doing relative to others at a particular moment. That kind of you-vs.-me score keeping has little to do with whether any American can get ahead. By its very nature, opportunity is individual rather than collective. Even for an individual, the concept can't be divorced from its time element, an assessment of how well someone is doing today relative to yesterday, or how he can expect to do tomorrow compared to today. How many of us worked our way up? How quickly did we move from one rung to the next? How many of us fell? Studies of income inequality cannot say whether individuals are doing better or worse. They lump together Americans who differ in age, educational level, work effort, family and marital status, gender and race. The sample never stays the same from one year to another, and researchers haven't a clue about what happened to any individual in the income distribution.

Annual snapshots of the income distribution might deserve attention if we lived in a caste society, with rigid class lines determining who gets what share of the national income—but we don't live in a caste society. It takes a heroic leap to look at the disparity between rich and poor and conclude that any one individual's chances of getting ahead aren't what they used to be. Even the most sophisticated income-distribution statistics fail to tell us what we really want to know: Are the majority of Americans losing their birthright—a chance at upward mobility? Static portraits, moreover, don't tell us whether low-income households tend to remain at the bottom year after year. By definition, a fifth of society will always inhabit the lowest 20 percent of the income distribution. We don't know, however, whether individuals and families stay there over long periods. It's no great tragedy if the bottom rung is where many Americans start to climb the ladder of success. To argue that upward mobility is being lost, we would have to show that the poorest remain stuck where they are, with little hope of making themselves better off. Nothing could be further from the truth. . . .

Making It from Bottom to Top

The Treasury Department affirms that most Americans still have a good shot at upward mobility. In a 1992 analysis covering nine years, researchers found that 86 percent of those in the lowest 20 percent of income earners in 1979 had moved to a higher grouping by 1988. Moreover, 66 percent reached the middle tier or above, with almost 15 percent making it all the way to the top fifth of income earners. Among Americans who started out above the bottom fifth in 1979, the Treasury found the same movement up the income ladder. Nearly 50 percent of those in the middle tier, for example, rose into the top two groupings, overwhelming whatever downward mobility that took place. . . .

In addition to confirming that most Americans are still getting ahead in life, the Treasury study verifies that the quickest rise occurs among the young, an antidote to the prevailing ennui among the so-called Generation X. It also found that wage and salary income was primarily responsible for pushing people upward in the distribution, indicating that work, not luck, is the widest path to opportunity. Ours is not a *Wheel of Fortune* economy, where a few lucky individuals win big, leaving paltry gains to the great mass of people. Most of us get ahead because we strive to make ourselves and our families better off.

By carefully tracking individuals' incomes over many years, . . . the Treasury study show[s] that our economic system is biased toward success. These results should go a long way toward quelling fears of an America polarized between privileged rich and permanently poor. The rich may indeed be getting richer. We ought to have little problem with that. The poor are also getting richer. We ought to celebrate that. Indeed, what's so encouraging is the ability of those who start out in the lowest income brackets to jump into the middle and upper echelons. There's evidence that most Americans are making their way up the income distribution through education, experience, and hard work.

That's what the American Dream, a dream of opportunity, is all about. . . .

The Common Thread: Lifetime Earnings

If so many Americans are rising through the income ranks, and if only a few of us stay stuck at the bottom, who makes up the lowest fifth of today's income earners? One group is the downwardly mobile, those who once took in enough money to be in a higher echelon. Descent can be voluntary, usually a result of retirement, or it can be involuntary, resulting from layoffs or other hard luck. Just changing jobs sometimes results in a dip in earnings.

We've already seen, though, that downward mobility happens to only a small segment of the population. By far the largest number of low-income earners are new entrants into the world of work, mostly young people. Many of us begin our working lives as part of the bottom 20 percent, either as students with part-time jobs or as relatively unskilled entrants to the labor force. Many immigrants, whatever their age, start off with low incomes.

Although they usually start at the bottom, the young tend to rise through the income distribution as they become better educated, develop skills, and gain experience. In fact, income tends to follow a familiar pattern over a person's lifetime: It rises rapidly in the early years of working, peaks during middle age, then falls toward retirement. When the average earnings at each age are placed side by side, it creates a lifetime earnings profile, shaped like a pyramid.

The changes in lifetime earnings over the past four decades tell us quite a bit about the evolution of our economy. In 1951, workers reached their peak earning years in ages 35 to 44, when their average annual earnings were 1.6 times the income of those in the 20-to-24 age group. By 1973, the ratio had risen to 2.4 to 1. By 1993, the peak earning years had shifted to ages 45 to 54, and workers in this highly paid group earned almost 3.2 times more than the 20-to-24-year-olds. . . .

A steeper lifetime earnings profile reflects greater opportunity. One way to see that is to imagine a perfectly flat pattern of lifetime income, with workers earning the same income every year. Paychecks for the middle years of life would match those for the early twenties. This would be a world devoid of upward mobility, offering workers no prospect of getting ahead during their lifetimes, no matter what their effort, no matter how much they improve their worth on the job.

What is behind the faster rise in Americans' lifetime earnings? Most likely, it's the by-product of broad changes in the way we work. When the economy was largely industrial, Americans worked with their hands and their backs. Today, more Americans than ever owe their paychecks to brainpower. The skills of the mind, unlike those of the body, are cumulative. Mental talents continue to sharpen long after muscles and dexterity begin to falter. These facts of physiology and economic development probably explain why the peak earning years have shifted to older age groups in the past two decades. As the United States retools itself for a more knowledge-intensive era, as the country moves from a blue-collar economy to a white-collar one, the rewards for education and experience are increasing.

The lifetime earnings profile is the thread that sews together recent trends in upward mobility and income inequality. As today's workers reap greater rewards for what they've learned on the job, earnings become sharply higher with experience. It's not that today's young workers are falling behind their counterparts of earlier generations. On the contrary, older workers are doing so much better than they used to. The result is an increase in the gap between youth and middle age. In the end, the steepening of lifetime earnings leads us to a surprising conclusion: Upward mobility may well be an important factor in the widening gap in income distribution.

All told, this isn't the harsh world seen by those who say the rich are getting richer and the poor are getting poorer. Both rich and poor are becoming better off. Are most of us going nowhere? Quite the contrary; the majority of Americans are busy climbing the income ladder. Greater returns to education and experience can skew income toward the upper end, but we would be foolhardy indeed to become so obsessed with the pecking order that we lose sight of what's really important—opportunity.

A steeper lifetime earnings profile also puts a different slant on the notion of a vanishing middle class. The center of the income distribution isn't a destination. It's just one step on the ladder of upward mobility. Forty years ago, with a flatter earnings profile, families spent most of their working lives in the middle income brackets. Today's more rapid rise in incomes means they move to the top faster, spending less time defined as "middle class." Worries about Generation X's future can be put to rest, too. Those entering the labor force in the 1900s may look at their parents' income and wonder how they will ever attain such heights. They should, however, find a steeper earnings profile encouraging. During their first two or three decades in the labor market, young workers are likely to see their incomes rise more quickly than their parents' did.

In the United States, getting ahead isn't a great mystery. The economy provides opportunity—more, in fact, than ever before—but it's up to each of us to grab it. Success isn't random. Luck and Daddy's money aren't the way most Americans get to the top. More often than not, the rewards go to education, experience, talent, ambition, vision, risk taking, readiness to change, and just plain hard work. Young people aren't guaranteed success any more than their parents were. Their chances will improve, though, if they make the right choices in life. Opportunity lies in the advice given by generations of parents and teachers: Study, work hard, and save. In short, the best advice for economic success is this: Listen to your elders. . . .

Inequality Is Not Inequity

Judging from the public debate, at least some Americans would prefer a more equal distribution of income to a less equal one, perhaps on moral grounds, perhaps as a part of an ideal of civic virtue. There's no *economic* reason, however, to prefer one pattern of income distribution over another. In fact, the income statistics do little but confirm what's obvious: America isn't an egalitarian society. It wasn't designed to be. Socialism, a failed and receding system, sought to impose an artificial equality. Capitalism, a successful and expanding system, doesn't fight a fundamental fact of human nature—we vary greatly in capabilities, motivation, interests, and preferences. Some of us are driven to get ahead. Some of us are just plain lazy. Some of us are willing to work hard so we can afford a lifestyle rich in material goods. Some of us work just hard enough to provide a roof overhead, food, clothes, and a few amenities. It shouldn't come as a surprise that our incomes vary greatly.

Income inequality isn't an aberration. Quite the opposite, it's perfectly consistent with the laws that govern a free-enterprise system. In the early 1970s, three groups of unemployed Canadians, all in their twenties, all with at least 12 years of schooling, volunteered to participate in a stylized economy where the only employment was making woolen belts on small hand looms. They could work as much or as little as they liked, earning $2.50 for each belt. After 98 days, the results were anything but equal: 37.2 percent of the economy's income went to the 20 percent with the highest earnings. The bottom 20 percent received only 6.6 percent. This economic microcosm tells us one thing: Even among similar people with identical work options, some workers will earn more than others.

In a modern economy, incomes vary for plenty of reasons having little to do with fairness or equity. Education and experience, for example, usually yield higher pay. As industry becomes more sophisticated, the rewards to skilled labor tend to rise, adding to the number of high-income earners. Location matters. New Yorkers earn more than Mississippians. Lifestyle choices play a part, too. Simply by having an additional paycheck, two-income families make more money than those with a single breadwinner. Longer retirements, however, will add to the number of households with low income, even if many senior citizens live well from their savings. Demographic changes can twist the distribution of income. As the Baby Boom enters its peak earning years, the number of high-income households ought to rise. Economic forces create ripples in what we earn. The ebb and flow of industries can shift workers to both ends of the income distribution. Layoffs put some Americans into low-income groups, at least temporarily. Companies with new products and new technologies create jobs and, in most cases, share the bounty by offering workers higher pay. In technology industries, bonuses and stock options are becoming more common. Higher rates of return on investments—with, for example, a stock-market boom—will create a windfall for households with money riding on financial markets.

In and of itself, moreover, income distribution doesn't say much about the performance of an economy or the opportunities it offers. A widening gap isn't necessarily a sign of failure, nor does a narrowing one guarantee that an economy is functioning well. As a matter of fact, it's quite common to find a widening of income distribution in boom times, when almost everyone's earnings are rising rapidly. All it takes is for one segment of the workforce to become better off faster than others. However, the distribution can narrow in hard times, as companies facing declining demand cut back on jobs, hours, raises, and bonuses. In fact, we often see a compression of incomes in areas where people are sinking into poverty.

There's no denying that our system allows some Americans to become much richer than others. We must accept that, even celebrate it.

Opportunity, not equality of income, is what made the U.S. economy grow and prosper. It's most important to provide equality of opportunity, not equality of results. There's ample evidence to refute any suggestion that the economy is no longer capable of providing opportunity for the vast majority of Americans. At the end of the twentieth century, upward mobility is alive and well. Even the lower-income households are sharing in the country's progress. What's more, data suggest that the populist view of America as a society torn between haves and have-nots, with rigid class lines, is just plain wrong. We are by no means a caste society.

The Spiral of Inequality

PAUL KRUGMAN

Ever since the election of Ronald Reagan, right-wing radicals have insisted that they started a revolution in America. They are half right. If by a revolution we mean a change in politics, economics, and society that is so large as to transform the character of the nation, then there is indeed a revolution in progress. The radical right did not make this revolution, although it has done its best to help it along. If anything, we might say that the revolution created the new right. But whatever the cause, it has become urgent that we appreciate the depth and significance of this new American revolution—and try to stop it before it becomes irreversible.

The consequences of the revolution are obvious in cities across the nation. Since I know the area well, let me take you on a walk down University Avenue in Palo Alto, California.

Palo Alto is the de facto village green of Silicon Valley, a tree-lined refuge from the valley's freeways and shopping malls. People want to live here despite the cost—rumor has it that a modest three-bedroom house sold recently for $1.6 million—and walking along University you can see why. Attractive, casually dressed people stroll past trendy boutiques and restaurants; you can see a cooking class in progress at the fancy new kitchenware store. It's a cheerful scene, even if you have to detour around the people sleeping in doorways and have to avoid eye contact with the beggars. (The town council plans to crack down on street people, so they probably won't be here next year, anyway.)

If you tire of the shopping district and want to wander further afield, you might continue down University Avenue, past the houses with their well-tended lawns and flower beds—usually there are a couple of pickup trucks full of Hispanic gardeners in sight. But don't wander too far. When University crosses Highway 101, it enters the grim environs of East Palo Alto. Though it has progressed in the past few years, as recently as 1992 East Palo Alto was the murder capital of the nation and had an unemployment rate hovering around 40 percent. Luckily, near the boundary, where there is a cluster of liquor stores and check-cashing outlets, you can find two or three police cruisers keeping an eye on the scene—and, not incidentally, serving as a thin blue line protecting the nice neighborhood behind them.

Nor do you want to head down 101 to the south, to "Dilbert Country" with its ranks of low-rise apartments, the tenements of the modern proletariat—the places from which hordes of lower-level white-collar workers drive to sit in their cubicles by day and to which they return to watch their VCRs by night.

No. Better to head up into the hills. The "estates" brochure at Coldwell Banker real estate describes the mid-Peninsula as "an area of intense equestrian character," and when you ascend to Woodside-Atherton, which the *New York Times* has recently called one of "America's born-again Newports," there are indeed plenty of horses, as well as some pretty imposing houses. If you look hard enough, you might catch a glimpse of one of the new $10 million-plus mansions that are going up in growing numbers.

What few people realize is that this vast gap between the affluent few and the bulk of ordinary Americans is a relatively new fixture on our social landscape. People believe these scenes are nothing new, even that it is utopian to imagine it could be otherwise.

But it has not always been thus—at least not to the same extent. I didn't see Palo Alto in 1970, but longtime residents report that it was a mixed town in which not only executives and speculators but schoolteachers, mailmen, and sheet-metal workers could afford to live. At the time, I lived on Long Island, not far from the old *Great Gatsby* area on the North Shore. Few of the great mansions were still private homes then (who could afford the servants?); they had been converted into junior colleges and nursing homes, or deeded to the state as historic monuments. Like Palo Alto, the towns contained a mix of occupations and education levels—no surprise, given that skilled blue-collar workers often made as much as, or more than, white-collar middle managers.

Now, of course, Gatsby is back. New mansions, grander than the old, are rising by the score; keeping servants, it seems, is no longer a problem. A couple of years ago I had dinner with a group of New York investment bankers. After the business was concluded, the talk turned to their weekend homes in the Hamptons. Naively, I asked whether that wasn't a long drive: after a moment of confused silence, the answer came back: "But the helicopter only takes half an hour."

You can confirm what your eyes see, in Palo Alto or in any American community, with dozens of statistics. The most straightforward are those on income shares supplied by the Bureau of the Census, whose statistics are among the most rigorously apolitical. In 1970, according to the bureau, the bottom 20 percent of U.S. families received only 5.4 percent of the income, while the top 5 percent received 15.6 percent. By 1994, the bottom fifth had only 4.2 percent, while the top 5 percent had increased its share to 20.1 percent. That means that in 1994, the average income among the top 5 percent of families was more than 19 times that of the bottom 20 percent of families. In 1970, it had been only about 11.5 times as much. (Incidentally, while the change in distribution is most visible at the top and bottom, families in the middle have also lost: The income share of the middle 20 percent of families has fallen from 17.6 to 15.7 percent.) These are not abstract numbers. They are the statistical signature of a seismic shift in the character of our society.

The American notion of what constitutes the middle class has always been a bit strange, because both people who are quite poor and those who are objectively way up the scale tend to think of themselves as being in the middle. But if calling America a middle-class nation means anything, it means that we are a society in which most people live more or less the same kind of life.

In 1970 we were that kind of society. Today we are not, and we become less like one with each passing year. As politicians compete over who really stands for middle-class values, what the public should be asking them is, *What* middle class? How can we have common "middle-class" values if whole segments of society live in vastly different economic universes?

If this election was really about what the candidates claim, it would be devoted to two questions: Why has America ceased to be a middle-class nation? And, more important, what can be done to make it a middle-class nation again?[1]

The Sources of Inequality

Most economists who study wages and income in the United States agree about the radical increase in inequality—only the hired guns of the right still try to claim it is a statistical illusion. But not all agree about why it has happened.

Imports from low-wage countries—a popular villain—are part of the story; but only a fraction of it. The numbers just aren't big enough. We invest billions in low-wage countries—but we invest trillions at home. What we spend on manufactured goods from the Third World represents just 2 percent of our income. Even if we shut out imports from low-wage countries (cutting off the only source of hope for the people who work in those factories), most estimates suggest it would raise the wages of low-skill workers here by only 1 or 2 percent.

---

1. This was written just before the 1996 presidential election between Bill Clinton and Bob Dole.

Information technology is a more plausible villain. Technological advance doesn't always favor elite workers, but since 1970 there has been clear evidence of a general "skill bias" toward technological change. Companies began to replace low-skill workers with smaller numbers of high-skill ones, and they continue to do so even though low-skill workers have gotten cheaper and high-skill workers more expensive.

These forces, while easily measurable, don't fully explain the disparity between the haves and the have-nots. Globalization and technology may explain why a college degree makes more difference now than it did 20 years ago. But schoolteachers and corporate CEOs typically have about the same amount of formal education. Why, then, have teachers' salaries remained flat while those of CEOs have increased fivefold? The impact of technology and of foreign trade do not answer why it is harder today for most people to make a living but easier for a few to make a killing. Something else is going on.

Values, Power, and Wages

In 1970 the CEO of a typical Fortune 500 corporation earned about 35 times as much as the average manufacturing employee. It would have been unthinkable to pay him 150 times the average, as is now common, and downright outrageous to do so while announcing mass layoffs and cutting the real earnings of many of the company's workers, especially those who were paid the least to start with. So how did the unthinkable become first thinkable, then doable, and finally—if we believe the CEOs—unavoidable?

The answer is that values changed—not the middle-class values politicians keep talking about, but the kind of values that helped to sustain the middle-class society we have lost.

Twenty-five years ago, prosperous companies could have paid their janitors minimum wage and still could have found people to do the work. They didn't, because it would have been bad for company morale. Then, as now, CEOs were in a position to arrange for very high salaries for themselves, whatever their performance, but corporate boards restrained such excesses, knowing that too great a disparity between the top man and the ordinary worker would cause problems. In short, though America was a society with large disparities between economic classes, it had an egalitarian ethic that limited those disparities. That ethic is gone.

One reason for the change is a sort of herd behavior: When most companies hesitated to pay huge salaries at the top and minimum wage at the bottom, any company that did so would have stood out as an example of greed; when everyone does it, the stigma disappears.

There is also the matter of power. In 1970 a company that appeared too greedy risked real trouble with other powerful forces in society. It would have had problems with its union if it had one, or faced the threat of union organizers if it didn't. And its actions would have created difficulties with the government in a way that is now unthinkable. (Can anyone imagine a current president confronting a major industry over price increases, the way John F. Kennedy did the steel industry?)

Those restraining forces have largely disappeared. The union movement is a shadow of its former self, lucky to hold its ground in a defensive battle now and then. The idea that a company would be punished by the government for paying its CEO too much and its workers too little is laughable today: since the election of Ronald Reagan the CEO would more likely be invited to a White House dinner.

In brief, much of the polarization of American society can be explained in terms of power and politics. But why has the tide run so strongly in favor of the rich that it continues regardless of who is in the White House and who controls the Congress?

The Decline of Labor

The decline of the labor movement in the United States is both a major cause of growing inequality and an illustration of the larger process under way in our society. Unions now represent less than 12 percent of the private workforce, and their power has declined dramatically. In 1970 some 2.5 million workers participated in some form of labor stoppage; in 1993, fewer than 200,000 did. Because unions are rarely able or willing to strike, being a union member no longer carries much of a payoff in higher wages.

There are a number of reasons for the decline of organized labor: the shift from manufacturing to services and from blue-collar to white-collar work, growing international competition, and deregulation. But these factors can't explain the extent or the suddenness of labor's decline.

The best explanation seems to be that the union movement fell below critical mass. Unions are good for unions: In a nation with a powerful labor movement, workers have a sense of solidarity, one union can support another during a strike, and politicians take union interests seriously. America's union movement just got too small, and it imploded.

We should not idealize the unions. When they played a powerful role in America, they often did so to bad effect. Occasionally they were corrupt, often they extracted higher wages at the consumer's expense, sometimes they opposed new technologies and enforced inefficient practices. But unions helped keep us a middle-class society—not only because they forced greater equality within companies, but because they provided a counterweight to the power of wealthy individuals and corporations. The loss of that counterweight is clearly bad for society.

The point is that a major force that kept America a more or less unified society went into a tailspin. Our whole society is now well into a similar downward spiral, in which growing inequality creates the political and economic conditions that lead to even more inequality.

The Polarizing Spiral

Textbook political science predicts that in a two-party democracy like the United States, the parties will compete to serve the interests of the median voter—the voter in the middle, richer than half the voters but poorer than the other half. And since ordinary workers are more likely to lose their jobs than strike it rich, the interests of the median voter should include protecting the poor. You might expect, then, the public to demand that government work against the growing divide by taxing the rich more heavily and by increasing benefits for lower-paid workers and the unemployed.

In fact, we have done just the opposite. Tax rates on the wealthy—even with Clinton's modest increase of 1993—are far lower now than in the 1960s. We have allowed public schools and other services that are crucial for middle-income families to deteriorate. Despite the recent increase, the minimum wage has fallen steadily compared with both average wages and the cost of living. And programs for the poor have been savaged: Even before the recent bipartisan gutting of welfare, AFDC payments for a typical family had fallen by a third in real terms since the 1960s.[2]

The reason why government policy has reinforced rather than opposed this growing inequality is obvious: Well-off people have disproportionate political weight. They are more likely to vote—the median voter has a much higher income than the median family—and far more likely to provide the campaign contributions that are so essential in a TV age.

The political center of gravity in this country is therefore not at the median family, with its annual income of $40,000, but way up the scale. With decreasing voter participation and with the decline both of unions and of traditional political machines, the focus of political attention is further up the income ladder than it has been for generations. So never mind what politicians say; political parties are competing to serve the interests of families near the 90th percentile or higher, families that mostly earn $100,000 or more per year.

Because the poles of our society have become so much more unequal, the interests of this political elite diverge increasingly from those of the typical family. A family at the 95th percentile pays a lot more in taxes than a family at the 50th, but it does not receive a correspondingly higher benefit from public services, such as education. The greater the income gap, the greater the disparity in interests. This translates, because of the clout of the elite, into a constant pressure for lower taxes and reduced public services.

Consider the issue of school vouchers. Many conservatives and even a few liberals are in favor of issuing educational vouchers and allowing parents to choose among competing schools. Let's leave aside the question of

---

2. The acronym AFDC stands for Aid to Families with Dependent Children, the main federal welfare program from 1935 to 1996.

what this might do to education and ask what its political implications might be.

Initially, we might imagine, the government would prohibit parents from "topping up" vouchers to buy higher-priced education. But once the program was established, conservatives would insist such a restriction is unfair, maybe even unconstitutional, arguing that parents should have the freedom to spend their money as they wish. Thus, a voucher would become a ticket you could supplement freely. Upper-income families would realize that a reduction in the voucher is to their benefit: They will save more in lowered taxes than they will lose in a decreased education subsidy. So they will press to reduce public spending on education, leading to ever-deteriorating quality for those who cannot afford to spend extra. In the end, the quintessential American tradition of public education for all could collapse.

School vouchers hold another potential that, doubtless, makes them attractive to the conservative elite: They offer a way to break the power of the American union movement in its last remaining stronghold, the public sector. . . . The leaders of the radical right want privatization of schools, of public sanitation—of anything else they can think of—because they know such privatization undermines what remaining opposition exists to their program.

If public schools and other services are left to deteriorate, so will the skills and prospects of those who depend on them, reinforcing the growing inequality of incomes and creating an even greater disparity between the interests of the elite and those of the majority.

Does this sound like America in the '90s? Of course it does. And it doesn't take much imagination to envision what our society will be like if this process continues for another 15 or 20 years. We know all about it from TV, movies, and best-selling novels. While politicians speak of recapturing the virtues of small-town America (which never really existed), the public—extrapolating from the trends it already sees—imagines a *Blade Runner*–style dystopia, in which a few people live in luxury while the majority grovel in Third World standards.

Strategies for the Future

There is no purely economic reason why we cannot reduce inequality in America. If we were willing to spend even a few percent of national income on an enlarged version of the Earned Income Tax Credit, which supplements the earnings of low-wage workers, we could make a dramatic impact on both incomes and job opportunities for the poor and near-poor—bringing a greater number of Americans into the middle class. Nor is the money for such policies lacking: America is by far the least heavily taxed of Western nations and could easily find the resources to pay for a major expansion of programs aimed at limiting inequality.

But of course neither party advanced such proposals during the electoral campaign. The Democrats sounded like Republicans, knowing that in a society with few counterweights to the power of money, any program that even hits at redistribution is political poison. It's no surprise that Bill Clinton's repudiation of his own tax increase took place in front of an audience of wealthy campaign contributors. In this political environment, what politicians would talk of taxing the well-off to help the low-wage worker?

And so, while the agenda of the GOP would surely accelerate the polarizing trend, even Democratic programs now amount only to a delaying action. To get back to the kind of society we had, we need to rebuild the institutions and values that made a middle-class nation possible.

The relatively decent society we had a generation ago was largely the creation of a brief, crucial period in American history: the presidency of Franklin Roosevelt (1933–1945), during the New Deal and especially during the war. That created what economic historian Claudia Goldin called the Great Compression—an era in which a powerful government, reinforced by and in turn reinforcing a newly powerful labor movement, drastically narrowed the gap in income levels through taxes, benefits, minimum wages, and collective bargaining. In effect, Roosevelt created a new, middle-class America, which lasted for more than a generation. We have lost that America, and it will take another Roosevelt, and perhaps the moral equivalent of another war, to get it back.

Until then, however, we can try to reverse some of the damage. To do so requires more than just supporting certain causes. It means thinking strategically—asking whether a policy is not only good in itself but how it will affect the political balance in the future. If a policy change promises to raise average income by a tenth of a percentage point, but will widen the wedge between the interests of the elite and those of the rest, it should be opposed. If a law reduces average income a bit but enhances the power of ordinary workers, it should be supported.

In particular, we also need to apply strategic thinking to the union movement. Union leaders and liberal intellectuals often don't like each other very much, and union victories are often of dubious value to the economy. Nonetheless, if you are worried about the cycle of polarization in this country, you should support policies that make unions stronger, and vociferously oppose those that weaken them. There are some stirrings of life in the union movement—a new, younger leadership with its roots in the service sector has replaced the manufacturing-based old guard, and has won a few political victories. They must be supported, almost regardless of the merits of their particular case. Unions are one of the few *political* counterweights to the power of wealth.

Of course, even to talk about such things causes the right to accuse us of fomenting "class warfare." They want us to believe we are all members of a broad, more or less homogeneous, middle class. But the notion of a middle-class nation was always a stretch. Unless we are prepared to fight the trend toward inequality, it will become a grim joke.

DISCUSSION QUESTIONS

1. Poll your class. Do most members of your class think they will be economically better off or worse off than their parents? Define *better off* and *worse off.*

2. Women (especially single mothers) and minorities are disproportionately poor. Part of the debate on inequality concerns whether existing inequalities reflect people's talents and work efforts or whether there is still significant racial and gender discrimination in job markets. What do you think, and how does your conclusion affect your attitude toward present inequalities?

3. No one favors a complete leveling of income and wealth, nor does anybody want all wealth to be concentrated in a few hands. But where do we draw the line? What level of inequality should be tolerated in our democracy before government is required to take action?

4. Do you think the present level of economic inequality is corrupting our political processes? Will the recently enacted campaign finance law protect the system from the unaccountable power of money, or do we need to reduce economic inequality itself?

5. In their book, Cox and Alm suggest that, because of technological advances, the average American is better off today than a millionaire was in the 1890s. Agree or disagree.

SUGGESTED READINGS AND INTERNET RESOURCES

For further elaboration of Cox and Alm's argument that nearly everyone is benefiting from our dynamic economy, see their *Myths of Rich and Poor: Why We're Better Off Than We Think* (New York: Basic Books, 1999), from which our excerpt was taken. The best compilation of data on the changing distribution of income and wealth (which can be viewed as a rejoinder to Cox and Alm) is *The State of Working America 2000–2001* (Ithaca, N.Y.: Cornell University Press, 2000), by Lawrence Mishel, Jared Bernstein, and John Schmitt. In one of the most controversial books in recent years, *The Bell Curve: Intelligence and Class Structure in American Life* (New York: Free Press, 1994), Richard J. Herrnstein and Charles Murray argue that economic inequalities in our technological society fairly reflect differences in people's intelligence, or IQ. In *Illusions of Opportunity: The American Dream in Question* (New York: Norton, 1997), John E. Schwarz argues that the American Dream is out of reach for many people because there is a shortage of 16 million jobs with decent enough wages to support a family ($7.60 an hour in 1994 dollars, plus health coverage).

United for a Fair Economy
www.stw.org
This web site spotlights the dangers of growing income and wealth inequality
in the United States and coordinates action to reduce the gap.

Economic Policy Institute
www.epinet.org
The Economic Policy Institute is a nonprofit, nonpartisan think tank that seeks
to broaden the public debate about strategies to achieve a strong economy.
Their web site stresses real-world analysis and a concern for the living standards
of working people.

Heritage Foundation
www.heritage.org/library/welfare.html
The Heritage Foundation web site stresses the principles of free enterprise,
limited government, individual freedom, traditional American values, and a
strong national defense.

Cato Institute
www.cato.org
The Cato Institute seeks to broaden the parameters of public policy debate to
allow consideration of more options that are consistent with the traditional
American principles of limited government. This web site reflects the liberterian
values of the Cato Institute and its commitment to limited government.

17

The United States and the Global Economy: Serving Citizens or Corporate Elites?

For nearly forty-five years after World War II, U.S. foreign policy concentrated on a cold war to contain communism. The costs were often great: massive casualties in two major wars in Korea and Vietnam, a militarization of U.S. society, and the fear spawned by the threat of nuclear holocaust. Through McCarthyism and other acts of government repression, the Cold War often distorted democracy at home. Fighting the Cold War required public support for massive military and intelligence expenditures. Americans largely supported both insofar as U.S. military power translated into American prosperity and economic power.

Yet by the 1970s and with defeat in Vietnam, the translation of military into economic prosperity was very much in doubt: the Vietnam War coincided with a reshaping of the global economic order. In the 1970s and early 1980s, energy crises, gas lines, and deindustrialization awakened the nation to a new and uncertain global economic order. Since the 1980s, the so-called new economy has emerged, with stock market surges and growing wealth rewarding many, while stagnation, downsizing, and uncertainty are the outcome for millions of others. By 1991, the Cold War had ended with the USSR's collapse. Ever since, and alongside September 11, the new global economy has emerged as the major focus of U.S. foreign policy and of widespread political debate. The war on terrorism may wax and wane in importance. What remains will be a consistent question: is the new global economic order good for democracy, or is it fundamentally undemocratic for Americans and for millions of others throughout the globe?

Perhaps more than ever in world history, the global economic order is dominated by two sets of institutions. The first comprises footloose global corporations and the volatile financial and equity markets that are able to move money and investments around the globe at lightning speed, with positive and negative effects. From the media empires of Rupert Murdoch's News Corporation, Disney, and AOL–Time Warner to the computer operating systems monopolized by Microsoft, transnational companies and their investors increasingly determine what we know, how we work, and what's fun. From banks to world stock exchanges and investment houses, giant private institutions have the power to make or break entire industries and countries—to employ or downsize, invest or withdraw.

The second new actor is a new set of transnational institutions that bring the world's governments together under a common financial and trade regime. Led by the International Monetary Fund (IMF), the World Bank, and the new-born World Trade Organization (WTO), these transnational institutions are accompanied by regional trade and monetary compacts such as the European Union (EU); the North American Free Trade Agreement (NAFTA) uniting Canada, the United States, and Mexico; and the proposed "Free Trade Area of the Americas" (FTAA).

To supporters, these new institutions and their practices have generated unprecedented growth, new wealth, and relative economic stability. To detractors in the United States and abroad—most visibly first in Seattle, then in Washington, D.C., Quebec City, and Davos, Switzerland, where corporate and government leaders mingle—the global economic order is a set of undemocratic elites who smooth the way for environmental degradation, destruction of local economies, and exploitation of workers. According to opponents, the power to invest or disinvest, employ or downsize, is delegated away from electorates and handed over to transnational investors and their agents.

In the new global economy, the United States remains the biggest and most powerful nation-state. The United States serves as the headquarters for the world's biggest stock and financial markets, is a worldwide innovator in many of the high-technology industries, and has dominant power in the IMF and World Bank. From the perspective of Wall Street, and from Capitol Hill and the White House as well, economic globalization is not only an inevitability, but also a boon to U.S. power. The point is to adjust to corporate-led economic globalization and its dictates, not avoid them.

Yet there are risks. The stock market and "dot.com" boom of the 1990s appears to be over. And even as the boom was going on, worldwide financial crises were hitting most East Asian countries and left entire continents and countries—Africa and most of West Asia—behind. In 2002, Latin America's richest economy—Argentina—simply melted down. Here in the United States, most wage-earners work more hours and for wages and benefits that are often less than in the 1970s. Universal health care, a secure retirement, quality public education, and job security are for many illusive dreams as government cuts taxes to encourage investment by corporations and the rich.

Does corporate globalization threaten democracy and prosperity, or does it enhance both? Can democratic politics control the forces that propel economic globalization, or must government succumb to them? Are there alternatives to corporate-led economic globalization? If so, what are they?

The two selections reprinted here present contrasting answers to these questions. The first is written by Thomas Friedman, a *New York Times* columnist and the author of the best-selling *The Lexus and the Olive Tree*. Friedman argues that economic globalization is inevitable and that modern governments should help people adjust to it rather than transform it. A benign but revolutionary process running at warp speed, globalization benefits the United States the most, argues Friedman, because America possesses the entrepreneurial culture and political and cultural institutions most appropriate to modern success. Globalization, Friedman admits, produces stresses, but its disadvantages are far outweighed by its production of new wealth, individual freedom, and U.S. world influence.

David Korten, the author of *When Corporations Rule the World* and a political activist, would certainly agree with Friedman about globalization's importance. Yet his perspective on its roots and implications couldn't be more different. Korten sees globalization not as a reversal of the Cold War, but an extension of the elite-centered, pro-corporate, and largely undemocratic policies established by the United States and its allies after World War II. Rather than a world of increased economic opportunity, Korten sees a planet lurching toward ecological suicide and authoritarian corporate rule over matters that affect all of the world's citizens. Echoing the case made by many anti-corporate globalization protestors at recent demonstrations, Korten envisions a people-centered reinvention of local and regional economies and governments, where workers, consumers, and citizens shape the decisions of corporate giants and such new transnational institutions as the WTO. Korten's essay is excerpted from a speech he gave in Bretton Woods, New Hampshire, site of the famous 1944 conference that established the international economic institutions of the post–World War II capitalist world.

As you read the two essays, consider the following questions: Do the authors define economic globalization and its features differently? What does each mean by "freedom" and "democracy"? Why is economic globalism inevitable for Friedman, but not for Korten? When each author speaks of U.S. power, which people and institutions are included and which excluded?

Revolution Is U.S.

THOMAS FRIEDMAN

T oday's era of globalization, which replaced the Cold War, is [an] international system with its own unique attributes.

To begin with, the globalization system, unlike the Cold War system, is not static, but a dynamic ongoing process. Globalization involves the inexorable integration of markets, nation-states and technologies to a degree never witnessed before—in a way that is enabling individuals, corporations and nation-states to reach around the world farther, faster, deeper and cheaper than ever before, and in a way that is also producing a powerful backlash from those brutalized or left behind by this new system.

The driving idea behind globalization is free-market capitalism—the more you let market forces rule and the more you open your economy to free trade and competition, the more efficient and flourishing your economy will be. Globalization means the spread of free-market capitalism to virtually every country in the world. Globalization also has its own set of economic rules—rules that revolve around opening, deregulating and privatizing your economy.

Unlike the Cold War system, globalization has its own dominant culture, which is why it tends to be homogenizing. In previous eras this sort of cultural homogenization happened on a regional scale. . . . Culturally speaking, globalization is largely, though not entirely, the spread of Americanization—from Big Macs to iMacs to Mickey Mouse—on a global scale.

Globalization has its own defining technologies: computerization, miniaturization, digitization, satellite communications, fiber optics and the Internet. And these technologies helped to create the defining perspective of globalization. If the defining perspective of the Cold War world was "division," the defining perspective of globalization is "integration." The symbol of the Cold War system was a wall, which divided everyone. The symbol of the globalization system is a World Wide Web, which unites everyone. The defining document of the Cold War system was "The Treaty." The defining document of the globalization system is "The Deal." . . .

While the defining measurement of the Cold War was weight—particularly the throw weight of missiles—the defining measurement of the globalization system is speed—speed of commerce, travel, communication and innovation. The Cold War was about Einstein's mass-energy equation, $e = mc^2$. Globalization is about Moore's law, which states that the computing power of silicon chips will double every eighteen to twenty-four months. In the Cold War, the most frequently asked question was: "How big is your missile?" In globalization, the most frequently asked question is: "How fast is your modem?" . . .

. . . If the Cold War were a sport, it would be sumo wrestling, says Johns Hopkins University foreign affairs professor Michael Mandelbaum. "It would be two big fat guys in a ring, with all sorts of posturing and rituals and stomping of feet, but actually very little contact, until the end of the match, when there is a brief moment of shoving and the loser gets pushed out of the ring, but nobody gets killed."

By contrast, if globalization were a sport, it would be the 100-meter dash, over and over and over. And no matter how many times you win, you have to race again the next day. And if you lose by just one-hundredth of a second it can be as if you lost by an hour. . . .

To paraphrase German political theorist Carl Schmitt, the Cold War was a world of "friends" and "enemies." The globalization world, by contrast, tends to turn all friends and enemies into "competitors." . . .

In the Cold War we reached for the hot line between the White House and the Kremlin—a symbol that we were all divided but at least someone, the two superpowers, was in charge. In the era of globalization we reach for the Internet—a symbol that we are all connected but nobody is in charge. The defining defense system of the Cold War was radar—to expose the threats coming from the other side of the wall. The defining defense system of the globalization era is the X-ray machine—to expose the threats coming from within.

Globalization also has its own demographic pattern—a rapid acceleration of the movement of people from rural areas and agricultural lifestyles to urban lifestyles more intimately linked with global fashion, food, markets and entertainment trends.

Last, and most important, globalization has its own defining structure of power, which is much more complex than the Cold War structure. The Cold War system was built exclusively around nation-states, and it was balanced at the center by two superpowers: the United States and the Soviet Union.

The globalization system, by contrast, is built around three balances. The first is the traditional balance between nation-states. In the globalization system, the United States is now the sole and dominant superpower and all other nations are subordinate to it to one degree or another. . . .

The second balance in the globalization system is between nation-states and global markets. These global markets are made up of millions of investors moving money around the world with the click of a mouse. I call them "the Electronic Herd," and this herd gathers in key global financial centers, such as Wall Street, Hong Kong, London and Frankfurt, which I call "the Supermarkets." The attitudes and actions of the Electronic Herd and the Supermarkets can have a huge impact on nation-states today, even to the point of triggering the downfall of governments. . . .

The third balance that you have to pay attention to in the globalization system—the one that is really the newest of all—is the balance between individuals and nation-states. Because globalization has brought down many of the walls that limited the movement and reach of people, and because it has simultaneously wired the world into networks, it gives more power to individuals to influence both markets and nation-states than at any time in history. . . .

Five Gas Stations

I believe in the five gas stations theory of the world.

That's right: I believe you can reduce the world's economies today to basically five different gas stations. First there is the Japanese gas station. Gas is $5 a gallon. Four men in uniforms and white gloves, with lifetime employment contracts, wait on you. They pump your gas. They change your oil. They wash your windows, and they wave at you with a friendly smile as you drive away in peace. Second is the American gas station. Gas costs only $1 a gallon, but you pump it yourself. You wash your own windows. You fill your own tires. And when you drive around the corner four homeless people try to steal your hubcaps. Third is the Western European gas station. Gas there also costs $5 a gallon. There is only one man on duty. He grudgingly pumps your gas and unsmilingly changes your oil, reminding you all the time that his union contract says he only has to pump gas and change oil. He doesn't do windows. He works only thirty-two hours a week, with ninety minutes off each day for lunch, during which time the gas station is closed. He also has six weeks' vacation every summer in the South of France. Across the street, his two brothers and uncle, who have not worked in ten years because their state unemployment insurance pays more than their last job, are playing boccie ball. Fourth is the developing-country gas station. Fifteen people work there and they are all cousins. When you drive in, no one pays any attention to you because they are all too busy talking to each other. Gas is only 35 cents a gallon because it is subsidized by the government, but only one of the six gas pumps actually works. The others are broken and they are waiting for the replacement parts to be flown in from Europe. The gas station is rather run-down because the owner lives in Zurich and takes all the profits out of the country. The owner doesn't know that half his employees actually sleep in the repair shop at night and use the car wash equipment to shower. Most of the customers at the developing-country gas station either drive the latest-model Mercedes or a motor scooter. The place is always busy, though, because so many people stop in to use the air pump to fill their bicycle tires. Lastly there is the communist gas station. Gas there is only 50 cents a gallon—but there is none, because the four guys working there have sold it all on the black market for $5 a gallon. Just one of the four guys who is employed at the communist gas station is actually there. The other three are working at second jobs in the underground economy and only come around once a week to collect their paychecks.

What is going on in the world today, in the very broadest sense, is that through the process of globalization everyone is being forced toward America's gas station. If you are not an American and don't know how to pump your own gas, I suggest you learn. With the end of the Cold War, globalization is globalizing Anglo-American-style capitalism. It is globalizing American culture and cultural icons. It is globalizing the best of America and the worst of America. It is globalizing the American Revolution and it is globalizing the American gas station. . . .

Rational Exuberance

. . . Since I spend a great deal of time overseas and away from Wall Street—looking at my country from the outside in—I am constantly exposed to the rational exuberance about America in the rest of the world. This rational exuberance is built on the following logic: If you look at globalization as the dominant international system today, and you look at the attributes that both companies and countries need to thrive in this system, you have to conclude that America has more assets, and fewer liabilities, in relation to this system than any other major country. This is what I call rational exuberance. It is the intuition among global investors that while many in Europe and Asia were still trying to adjust their societies to globalization, and some were barely up to the starting line, Uncle Sam was already around the first turn and in full sprint.

A useful way to analyze this rational exuberance is to ask the following question: If 100 years ago you had come to a visionary geo-architect and told him that in the year 2000 the world would be defined by a system called "globalization," what sort of country would he have designed to compete and win in that world? The answer is that he would have designed something that looks an awful lot like the United States of America. Here's what I mean:

First of all, he would have designed a country that was in an ideally competitive geographic position. That is, he would have designed a country that was both an Atlantic and a Pacific power, looking comfortably in both directions; and at the same time connected by landmass to both Canada and Latin America, so that it could easily interact with all three key markets of the world—Asia, Europe, and the Americas. That would come in handy.

He would have designed a country with a diverse, multicultural, multiethnic, multilingual population that had natural connections to all continents of the globe, but was, at the same time, bound together by a single language—English—which would also be the dominant language of the Internet. He would also have bestowed upon this country at least five different regional economies joined by a single currency, the dollar, which would also be the reserve currency for the rest of the world. Having a single country with different regional economies is a great asset because when one region might be slumping the other could be surging, helping to smooth out some of the peaks and valleys of the business cycle. All of that would be helpful.

He would have designed a country with extremely diverse, innovative and efficient capital markets, where venture capitalism was considered a noble and daring art, so that anyone with a reasonable (or even ridiculous) invention in his basement or garage could find a venture capitalist somewhere to back it. That would be nice. . . . If you compare a list of the twenty-five biggest companies in Europe twenty-five years ago with a list of the twenty-five biggest European companies today, the two lists are almost the same. But if you take a list of the twenty-five biggest companies in America twenty-five years ago and compare it with a list of the twenty-five biggest American companies today, most of the companies are different. Yes, America's financial markets, with their constant demands for short-term profits and quarterly earnings, often won't let corporations "waste money" by focusing on long-term growth. That's true. But these same markets will give someone with a half-baked idea $50,000 overnight to try to turn it into the next Apple computer. Massachusetts has a bigger venture capital industry than all of Europe combined. Venture capitalists are very important people in this day and age, and not just as a source of money. The best of them provide real expertise for start-up companies. They see a lot of them and they understand the stages through which companies have to go in order to develop, and they can help carry them through, which is often as important as seed money.

Our geo-architect would certainly have designed a country with the most honest legal and regulatory environment in the world. In this country, both domestic and foreign investors could always count on a reasonably level playing field, with relatively little corruption, plenty of legal safeguards for any foreigner who wants to make an investment and take out his profits at any time, and a rule of law that enables markets and contracts to work and protects and encourages innovation through patent protection. The U.S. capital markets today are not only more efficient than those of any other country, they are also the most transparent. The U.S. stock markets simply will not tolerate secrecy, so every listed company must file timely earnings reports, along with regularly audited financial statements, so that mismanagement and misallocation of resources is easily detected and punished.

He would have designed a country with a system of bankruptcy laws and courts that actually encourages people who fail in a business venture to declare bankruptcy and then try again, perhaps fail again, declare bankruptcy again, and then try again, before succeeding and starting the next Amazon.com—without having to carry the stigma of their initial bankruptcies for the rest of their lives. . . .

In Europe, bankruptcy carries a lifelong stigma. Whatever you do, do not declare bankruptcy in Germany: you, your children and your children's children will all carry a lasting mark of Cain in the eyes of German society.

If you must declare bankruptcy in Germany, you are better off leaving the country. (And you'll be welcomed with open arms in Palo Alto.)

On that subject, our geo-architect would certainly have designed a country that was hard-wired for accepting new immigrants, so that anyone could come to its shores and be treated as constitutionally equal to anyone else, thus enabling that country to be constantly siphoning off the best brains in the world and bringing them together in its companies, medical centers and universities. Roughly one-third of Silicon Valley's scientists and engineers today are foreign-born immigrants, who then turn around and project Silicon Valley values and products all over the world. According to University of California at Berkeley urban affairs expert AnnaLee Saxenian, research by the Public Policy Institute of California found that in 1996, 1,786 Silicon Valley technology companies, with $12.6 billion in sales and 46,000 employees, were run by Indian or Chinese immigrant executives alone. . . . To be a Japanese you pretty much have to be born a Japanese. To be a Swiss you pretty much have to be born a Swiss. To be an American you just have to want to be an American. That doesn't mean that we let everyone in who wants to be an American, but when citizenship is a legal question not an ethnic, racial or national one, it makes it much easier for a country to absorb new talent. . . .

The more knowledge workers you can attract to your shores, the more successful you will be. As far as America is concerned, I say bring 'em in, and not only the rich, educated entrepreneurs. I would never turn back a single Haitian boat person. Anyone who has the smarts and energy to build a raft out of milk cartons and then sail across the Atlantic to America's shores is someone I want as a new immigrant. . . .

Our geo-architect certainly would have designed a country with a democratic, flexible federal political system that allows for a high degree of decentralized political decision-making that enables different regions and localities to adjust themselves to world trends without waiting for the center to move. Indeed, a federal system—with fifty states all having an incentive to compete and experiment in finding solutions to the intertwined problems of education, welfare and health care—is an enormous asset in the era of globalization, when such problems can be highly complex and you rarely get the right answer without experimenting a few times.

Our geo-architect certainly would have designed a country with the most flexible labor market in the world—one that enables workers to move easily from one economic zone to another, and one that enables employers to hire and fire workers with relative ease. The easier it is to fire workers, the more incentive employers have to hire them. Compare the millions of jobs eliminated in America in the 1990s and the many millions more created in America in the 1990s with the virtually stagnant job turnover rate in Western Europe. In America, lose your job in Maine one day and, if one is available, you can get a new one in San Diego the next day. Lose your job in Tokyo one day and I wouldn't recommend looking for one in Seoul the next. Lose your job in Munich one day and, even with a common European currency market, it is not so easy to get one the next day in Milan.

Our geo-architect would have designed a country where government-protected cartels are abhorred, so every company and bank has to fight and stand on its own, and monopolies will not be tolerated. That would be important. Even when a U.S. firm becomes a much-envied, world-class gem, like Microsoft, it still has to answer to a Justice Department antitrust lawyer making $75,000 a year.

Our geo-architect would have designed a country that is tolerant of the oddball, the guy with the ponytail or the gal with the ring in her nose who is also a mathematical genius or software whiz. America is a country where the minute one person stands up and says, "That's impossible," someone else walks in the door and announces, "We just did it." Says Intel vice president Avram Miller: "The Japanese don't get it, because they are focused on homogeneity. When it was building a gazillion of all the same thing, they were the world experts and we mistook it for some special genius. But the world does not want a lot of the same thing today, and in a world where everyone wants something different—and the technology that will give them something perfectly tailored [to their own needs and specifications]—America has a real advantage."

Our geo-architect would have designed a country whose corporate sector, unlike Europe's or Japan's, had, by the mid-1990s, already gone through most of the downsizing, privatizing, networking, deregulation, reengineering, streamlining and restructuring required to fully adjust to, and exploit, the democratizations of finance, technology and information and to avoid Microchip Immune Deficiency. Just as America won the space race, it is now winning the cyberspace race. American companies spend more on information technology per capita than any others in the world.

He also would have designed a country with a deeply rooted entrepreneurial culture and a tax system that allows the successful investor or innovator to hold on to a large share of his or her capital gains, so there is a constant incentive to get enormously rich. In our ideal country, Horatio Alger is not a mythical character but sometimes your next-door neighbor, who just happened to get hired as an engineer at Intel or America Online when they were getting started and ended up being paid in stock options that are now worth $10 million.

Our geo-architect certainly would have designed a country that still had a lot of environmentally attractive, wide-open spaces and small towns, to attract knowledge workers. Because today, thanks to the Internet, fax machines and overnight package delivery, high-tech firms and knowledge workers can escape from urban centers and settle virtually anywhere they want. So having lots of lush green valleys not far from oceans or mountains can be a real asset. That's why states like Idaho, Washington, Oregon, Minnesota and North Carolina have booming high-tech sectors today.

He would have designed a country that values the free flow of information so much that it defends the rights of the worst pornographers and the most incendiary racists to do their things. That would be an asset. Because in a world in which information, knowledge, goods and services will flow with increasing speed across the Fast World or through cyberspace, those countries comfortable with such openness, and the cacophony and chaos that sometimes attend it, those countries comfortable competing on the basis of imagination, not behind walls of protection, will have a real advantage. America, with its Freedom of Information Act, which barely allows the government to keep secrets for long, has nurtured this culture of openness from its foundation.

And, most important, our geo-architect would have designed a country whose multinational companies and little entrepreneurs are increasingly comfortable thinking big and thinking globally, and excel now in virtually every fast, light, networked, knowledge-intensive field of endeavor. America today excels at software design, computing, Internet design, Internet marketing, commercial banking, E-mail, insurance, derivatives, genetic engineering, artificial intelligence, investment banking, high-end health care, higher education, overnight package delivery, consulting, fast food, advertising, biotechnology, media, entertainment, hotels, waste management, financial services, environmental industries and telecommunications. It's a postindustrial world, and America today is good at everything that is postindustrial.

. . . The publisher and editor of this book, Jonathan Galassi, called me one day and said, "I was telling some friends of mine that you're writing a book about globalization and they said, 'Oh, Friedman, he loves globalization.' What would you say to that?" I answered Jonathan that I feel about globalization a lot like I feel about the dawn. Generally speaking, I think it's a good thing that the sun comes up every morning. It does more good than harm. But even if I didn't much care for the dawn there isn't much I could do about it. I didn't start globalization, I can't stop it—except at a huge cost to human development—and I'm not going to waste time trying. All I want to think about is how I can get the best out of this new system, and cushion the worst, for the most people.

When Corporations
Rule the World

DAVID C. KORTEN

The fame of Bretton Woods and of this hotel dates from July 1944, when the United Nations Monetary and Financial Conference was held here. . . . The economic leaders who quietly gathered at this hotel were looking beyond the end of the war with hopes for a world united in peace through prosperity. Their specific goal was to create the institutions that would promote that vision.

By the end of this historic meeting, the World Bank and the International Monetary Fund (IMF) had been founded, and the groundwork had been laid for what later became GATT [General Agreement on Tariffs and Trade]. In the intervening years, these institutions have held faithfully to their mandate to promote economic growth and globalization. Through structural adjustment programs (SAPs),[1] the World Bank and the IMF have pressured countries of the South to open their borders and change their economies from self-sufficiency to *export* production. Trade agreements negotiated through GATT have reinforced these actions and opened economies . . . to the increasingly free importation of goods and money.

As we look back fifty years later, we can see that the Bretton Woods institutions have indeed met their goals. Economic growth has expanded fivefold. International trade has expanded by roughly twelve times, and foreign direct investment has been expanding at two to three times the rate of trade expansion. Yet, tragically, while these institutions have met their goals, they have failed in their purpose. The world has more poor people today than ever before. We have an accelerating gap between the rich and the poor. Widespread violence is tearing families and communities apart nearly everywhere. And the planet's ecosystems are deteriorating at an alarming rate.

Yet the prevailing wisdom continues to maintain that economic growth offers the answer to poverty, environmental security, and a strong social fabric, and that *economic globalization*—erasing economic borders to allow free flow of goods and money—is the key to such growth. Indeed, the more

---

1. SAPs, or structural adjustment programs, are the requirements the IMF imposes on nations in return for the fund's assistance. Usually, SAPs have required governments to cut social spending and consumption, open markets to foreign investors, and reduce wages in order to stimulate investor and banker confidence.

severe the economic, environmental, and social crises, the stronger the policy commitment to these same prescriptions, even as evidence mounts that they are not working. In fact, there is a growing consensus outside of official circles that they cannot work, for reasons I will explain.

Ecological Limit to Growth

. . . The human economy is embedded in and dependent on the natural ecosystems of our planet. Until the present moment in human history, however, the scale of our economic activity relative to the scale of the ecosystems has been small enough so that, in both economic theory and practice, we could, up to a point, afford to ignore this fundamental fact.

Now, however, we have crossed a monumental historical threshold. Because of the fivefold economic expansion since 1950 the environmental demands of our economic system have filled up the available environmental space of the planet. In other words, we live in a "full world.". . .

The first environmental limits that we have confronted and possibly exceeded are . . . the limits to renewable resources and to the environment's *sink functions*—its ability to absorb our wastes. These are limits related to the loss of soils, fisheries, forests, and water; to the absorption of CO_2 emissions; and to destruction of the ozone layer. We could argue whether a particular limit was hit at noon yesterday or will be passed at midnight tomorrow, but the details are far less important than the basic truth that we have no real option other than to adapt our economic institutions to the reality of a "full world."

The structure and ideology of the existing Bretton Woods system is geared to an ever-continuing expansion of economic output—*economic growth*—and to the integration of national economies into a seamless global economy. The consequence is to intensify competition for already overstressed environmental space. In a "full world," this intensified competition accelerates destruction of the regenerative capacities of the ecosystem on which we and future generations depend; it crowds out all forms of life not needed for immediate human consumption purposes; and it increases competition between rich and poor for control of ecological resources. In a free market—which responds only to money, not needs—the rich win this competition every time. We see it happening all over the world: Hundreds of millions of the financially disenfranchised are displaced as their lands, waters, and fisheries are converted to uses serving the wants of the more affluent.

As long as their resources remain, the demands of the rich can be met—which may explain why so many of the rich see no problem. The poor experience a very different reality, but in a market economy their experience doesn't count.

The market cannot deal with questions relating to the appropriate scale of economic activity. There are no price signals indicating that the poor are going hungry because they have been forced off their lands; nor is there any price signal to tell polluters that too much CO_2 is being released into the air, or that toxins should not be dumped into soils or waters. Steeped in market ideology and highly responsive to corporate interests, the Bretton Woods institutions have demonstrated little capacity to give more than lip service either to environmental concerns or to the needs of the poor. Rather, their efforts have . . . centered on ensuring that people with money have full access to whatever resources remain—with little regard for the broader consequences.

A new Bretton Woods meeting to update the international system would serve a significant and visionary need—if its participants were to accept that economic growth is no longer a valid public policy priority. Indeed, whether the global economy grows or shrinks is largely irrelevant. Having crossed the threshold to a full world, the appropriate concern is whether the available planetary resources are being used in ways that: (1) meet the basic needs of all people; (2) maintain biodiversity; and (3) ensure the sustained availability of comparable resource flows to future generations. Our present economic system fails on all three counts.

Economic Injustice

In *How Much Is Enough?* Alan Durning divided the world into three consumption classes: overconsumers, sustainers, and marginals. The overconsumers are the 20 percent of the world's people who consume roughly 80 percent of the world's resources—that is, those of us whose lives are organized around automobiles, airplanes, meat-based diets, and wastefully packaged disposable products. The marginals, also 20 percent of the world's people, live in absolute deprivation.

If we turn to measurements of *income* rather than *consumption,* the figures are even more stark. The United Nations Development Program (UNDP) *Human Development Report* for 1992 introduces the champagne glass as a graphic metaphor for a world of extreme economic injustice. The bowl of the champagne glass represents the abundance enjoyed by the 20 percent of people who live in the world's richest countries and receive 82.7 percent of the world's income. At the bottom of the stem, where the sediment settles, we find the poorest 20 percent of the world's people, who barely survive on 1.4 percent of the total income. The combined incomes of the top 20 percent are nearly sixty times larger than those of the bottom 20 percent. Furthermore, this gap has doubled since 1950, when the top 20 percent enjoyed only thirty times the income of the bottom 20 percent. And the gap continues to grow.

These figures actually understate the true inequality in the world, because they are based on national averages rather than actual individual incomes. If we take into account the very rich people who live in poor countries and the very poor people who live in rich countries, the incomes of the richest 20 percent of the world's people are approximately 150 times those of the poorest 20 percent. That gap is growing as well.

Robert Reich, the U.S. Secretary of Labor in the Clinton administration, explained in his book *The Work of Nations* (1991), that the economic globalization the Bretton Woods institutions have advanced so successfully has served to separate the interests of the wealthy classes from a sense of national interest and thereby from a sense of concern for and obligation to their less fortunate neighbors. A thin segment of the super rich at the very lip of the champagne glass has formed a stateless alliance that defines *global interest* as synonymous with the personal and corporate financial interests of its members.

This separation has been occurring in nearly every country in the world to such an extent that it is no longer meaningful to speak of a world divided into northern and southern nations. The meaningful divide is not geography—it is class.

Whether intended or not, the policies so successfully advanced by the Bretton Woods institutions have inexorably empowered the super rich to lay claim to the world's wealth at the expense of other people, other species, and the viability of the planet's ecosystem.

Freeing Corporations from Control

The issue is not the market per se. Trying to run an economy without markets is disastrous, as the experience of the Soviet Union demonstrated. However, there is a fundamentally important distinction between markets and free markets.

The struggle between two extremist ideologies has been a central feature of the twentieth century. Communism called for all power to the state. Market capitalism calls for all power to the market—a euphemism for giant corporations. Both ideologies lead to their own distinctive form of tyranny. The secret of Western success in World War II and the early postwar period was not a free market economy; it was the practice of democratic pluralism built on institutional arrangements that sought to maintain balance between the state and the market and to protect the right of an active citizenry to hold both accountable to the public interest.

Contrary to the claims of ideologues who preach a form of corporate libertarianism,[2] markets need governments to function efficiently. It is well established in economic theory and practice that markets allocate resources efficiently only when markets are competitive and when firms pay for the social and environmental impact of their activity—that is, when they *internalize* the costs of their production. This requires that governments set and enforce the rules that make cost internalization happen, and, since successful firms invariably grow larger and more monopolistic, governments regularly step in to break them up and restore competition.

---

2. Libertarianism is a doctrine that perceives government as the major threat to individual freedom.

For governments to play the necessary role of balancing market and community interests, governmental power must be equal to market power. If markets are national, then there must be a strong national government. By expanding the boundaries of the market beyond the boundaries of the nation-state through economic globalization, the concentration of market power moves inevitably beyond the reach of government. This has been a most important consequence of both the structural adjustment programs of the World Bank and IMF and the trade agreements negotiated under GATT. As a result, governance decisions are transferred from governments, which at least in theory represent the interests of all citizens, to transnational corporations, which by their nature serve the interests only of their dominant shareholders. Consequently, societies everywhere on the planet are no longer able to address environmental and other needs.

Enormous economic power is being concentrated in the hands of a very few global corporations relieved of constraints to their own growth. Antitrust action to restore market competition by breaking up the concentrations is one of the many casualties of globalization. Indeed, current policy encourages firms to merge into ever more powerful concentrations to strengthen their position in global markets.

The rapid rate at which large corporations are shedding employees has created an impression in some quarters that the firms are losing their power. It is a misleading impression. The Fortune 500 firms shed 4.4 million jobs between 1980 and 1993. During this same period, their sales increased 1.4 times, assets increased 2.3 times, and CEO compensation increased 6.1 times. Of the world's one hundred largest economies, fifty are now corporations, not including banking and financial institutions.

Any industry in which five firms control 50 percent or more of the market is considered by economists to be highly monopolistic. The *Economist* recently reported that five firms control more than 50 percent of the global market in the following industries: consumer durables, automotive, airlines, aerospace, electronic components, electricity and electronics, and steel. Five firms control over 40 percent of the global market in oil, personal computers, and—especially alarming in its consequences for public debate on these very issues—media.

Forums for Elite Domination

. . . The forums within which corporate and government elites shape the global policies of the Western world were not limited to Bretton Woods. . . .

. . . The Trilateral Commission was formed in 1973 by David Rockefeller, chair of Chase Manhattan Bank, and Zbigniew Brzezinski, who served as the commission's director/coordinator until 1977 when he became national security advisor to President Jimmy Carter.

The members of the Trilateral Commission include the heads of four of the world's five largest nonbanking transnational corporations; top officials of five of the world's six largest international banks; and heads of major media organizations. U.S. presidents Jimmy Carter, George Bush, and Bill Clinton were all members of the Trilateral Commission, as was Thomas Foley, former speaker of the House of Representatives. Many key members of the Carter administration were . . . Trilateral Commission members. Many of President Clinton's cabinet and other appointments are former members of the Trilateral Commission.

. . . The Trilateral Commission has provided forums in which top executives from the world's leading corporations meet regularly, informally, and privately with top national political figures and opinion leaders to seek consensus on immediate and longer-range problems facing the most powerful members of the Western Alliance.

To some extent, the meetings help maintain "stability" in global policies, but they also deprive the public of meaningful participation and choice—as some participants explicitly intend. Particularly significant about these groups is their bipartisan political membership. Certainly, the participation of both George Bush and Bill Clinton in the Trilateral Commission makes it easier to understand the seamless transition from the Republican Bush administration to the Democratic Clinton administration with regard to U.S. commitment to pass GATT and NAFTA. Clinton's leadership in advancing what many progressives saw as a Bush agenda won him high marks from his colleagues on the Trilateral Commission.

Instruments of Control

Corporations have enormous political power, and they are actively using it to reshape the rules of the market in their own favor. The GATT has now become one of the corporations' most powerful tools for reshaping the market. Under the new GATT agreement, a World Trade Organization, the WTO, has been created with far-reaching powers to provide corporations the legal protection they feel they need to continue expanding their far-flung operations without the responsibility to serve any interest other than their own bottom line. . . .

The WTO hears disputes brought against the national or local laws of any country that another member country considers to be a trade barrier. Secret panels made up of three unelected trade experts will hear the disputes, and their rulings can be overturned only by a unanimous vote of the member countries. In general, any health, safety, or environmental standard that exceeds international standards set by industry representatives is likely to be considered a trade barrier, unless the offending government can prove that the standard has a valid scientific basis.

As powerful as the large corporations are, they themselves function increasingly as agents of a global financial system that has become the world's most powerful governance institution. The power in this system lies within a small group of private financial institutions that have only one objective: to make money in massive quantities. A seamless electronic web allows anyone with proper access codes and a personal computer to conduct instantaneous trade involving billions of dollars on any of the world's financial markets. The world of finance itself has become a gigantic computer game. In this game the smart money does not waste itself on long-term, high-quality commitments to productive enterprises engaged in producing real wealth to meet real needs of real people. Rather, it seeks short-term returns from speculation in erratic markets and from simultaneous trades in multiple markets to profit from minute price variations. In this game the short-term is measured in microseconds, the long-term in days. The environmental, social, and even economic consequences of financial decisions involving more than a trillion dollars a day are invisible to those who make them.

Joel Kurtzman, former business editor of the *New York Times* and currently editor of the *Harvard Business Review,* estimates that for every $1 circulating in the productive economy today, $20 to $50 circulates in the world of pure finance. Since these transactions take place through unmonitored international computer networks, no one knows how much is really involved. The $1 trillion that changes hands each day in the world's international currency markets is itself twenty to thirty times the amount required to cover daily trade in actual goods and services. If the world's most powerful governments act in concert to stabilize exchange rates in these same markets, the best they can manage is a measly $14 billion a day—little more than pocket change compared to the amounts mobilized by speculators and arbitrageurs. . . .

The corporations that invest in *real* assets (as opposed to ephemeral financial assets) are forced by the resulting pressures to restructure their operations in order to maximize immediate short-term returns to shareholders. One way to do this is by downsizing, streamlining, and automating their operations, using the most advanced technologies to eliminate hundreds of thousands of jobs. The result is jobless economic growth. Contemporary economies simply cannot create jobs faster than technology and dysfunctional economic systems can shed them. In nearly every country in the world there is now a labor surplus, and those lucky enough to have jobs are increasingly members of a contingent work force without either security or benefits. The resulting fear and insecurity make the jobs-versus-environment issue a crippling barrier to essential environmental action.

Another way to increase corporate profits is to externalize the cost of the firm's operations on the community, pitting localities against one another in a standards-lowering competition to offer subsidies, tax holidays, and freedom from environmental and employment standards. Similarly, workers are pitted against one another in a struggle for survival that pushes wages down to the lowest common denominator. This is the true meaning of *global competitiveness*—competition among localities. Large corporations, by contrast, minimize their competition through mergers and strategic alliances.

Any corporation that does not play this game to its limit is likely to become a takeover target by a corporate raider who will buy out the company and profit by taking the actions that the previous management—perhaps in a fit of social conscience and loyalty to workers and community—failed to take. The reconstruction of the global economic system makes it almost impossible for even highly socially conscious and committed managers to operate a corporation responsibly in the public interest.

✱✱✱

We are caught in a terrible dilemma. We have reached a point in history where we must rethink the very nature and meaning of human progress; yet the vision and decisions that emerged some fifty years ago catalyzed events that have transformed the governance processes of societies everywhere such that the necessary changes in thought and structure seem very difficult to achieve. It has happened so quickly that few among us even realize what has happened. The real issues are seldom discussed in a media dependent on corporate advertising.

. . . What is the alternative? Among those of us who are devoting significant attention to this question, the answer is the opposite of economic globalization. It lies in promoting greater economic localization—breaking economic activities down into smaller, more manageable pieces that link the people who make decisions in ways both positive and negative. It means rooting capital to a place and distributing its control among as many people as possible.

Powerful interests stand resolutely in the way of achieving such a reversal of current trends. The biggest barrier, however, is the limited extent of public discussion on the subject. The starting point must be to get the issues on the table and bring them into the mainstream policy debates in a way that books like this may help to achieve.

■ DISCUSSION QUESTIONS

1. Despite big differences, both authors argue that nation-states and their governments are less powerful in the new globalized economic order than they used to be. Yet Friedman appears to welcome this development, while Korten is less sure. Is the decline of government power beneficial or detrimental to democracy?

2. Friedman argues that economic globalization creates vast new wealth, while Korten says that it creates new inequalities. How would Friedman justify these new inequalities? How would Korten deal with the issue of producing new wealth?

3. Friedman seems to argue that the U.S. national interest consists of encouraging free trade, technological innovation, and greater individual entrepreneurship. Korten argues that a democratic foreign policy would return power to the voters and communities. How might citizens better

control the movement of capital around the globe? If globalization is inevitable, is Korten's plea idealistic and impractical? Why or why not?

4. Recently, European and Japanese consumers have refused to buy genetically engineered food products, most of them concocted by U.S. companies like Monsanto. How would Friedman deal with such protests? How would Korten?

■ SUGGESTED READINGS AND INTERNET RESOURCES

Two prominent academic works about economic globalization are David Held, Anthony McGrew, David Goldblatt, and Jonathan Perraton, *Global Transformations: Politics, Economics, and Culture* (Stanford, Calif.: Stanford University Press, 1999); and Robert Gilpin, *Global Political Economy* (Princeton, N.J.: Princeton University Press, 2001). Perhaps the best critical account of corporate globalization's effects is William Greider, *One World, Ready or Not* (New York: Simon and Schuster, 1997). Should the United States erect trade barriers and encourage its citizens to buy U.S.-made goods? Answers via a historical examination are in Dana Frank, *Buy American: The Untold Story of Economic Nationalism* (Boston: Beacon Press, 1999).

United for a Fair Economy
www.ufenet.org
News, extensive data, and analysis from a labor-backed group committed to citizen education and mobilization for a global economic justice can be found on this web site.

World Trade Organization
www.wto.org
This is the official site of the WTO, with links to government and business sites interested in "free trade."

Global Exchange
www.globalexchange.org
This is the best site for labor, environmental, and other activists who seek links to international groups opposing corporate globalization.

International Bank for Reconstruction and Development (World Bank)
www.worldbank.org
This vast database of the World Bank, an organization established in 1944 and a major target of protestors, includes reports on world social and economic indicators such as the bank's often controversial loan priorities. The site has links to associated transnational organizations, including the IMF.

18

U.S. Foreign Policy: What Should It Be After September 11?

The terrorist attacks on the World Trade Center and the Pentagon on September 11, 2001, stunned and horrified an America that had largely lost interest in global politics after the end of the Cold War a decade earlier. The vast majority of Americans rallied behind the Bush administration in its swift, successful military campaign against the al Qaeda organization that had carried out the terror strike and the Taliban regime in Afghanistan that had harbored al Qaeda. But with victory in Afghanistan, President Bush has turned to a larger campaign against global terror, condemning an "axis of evil" that includes Iraq, Iran, and North Korea and calling for the largest American defense buildup in two decades. Although Americans are united on the need to combat terrorism, some foreign policy analysts in the United States (and most American allies abroad) question whether the administration's emphasis on aggressive military action is the best approach to the threat of terrorism. As international affairs regain the central place in American politics that they used to possess during the Cold War, the debate over what U.S. foreign policy should be after September 11 has become one of the most important facing the American people.

Conflicting perspectives in this new debate actually reflect a long-standing clash over the nature of American foreign policy. From the time of the American founding to the late nineteenth century, the keynote of American foreign policy was isolationism, coupled with an expansionism that drove the European powers off the North American continent and extended American power into Latin America. By the end of the nineteenth century, however, many American leaders began to advocate a larger global role for the United States. What this role should be generated an important debate that has been carried on for a century.

A useful, if oversimplified, way to characterize this debate is between *realists* and *idealists.* The original realists, whose most prominent spokesperson was Theodore Roosevelt, believed that the United States should behave like the other Great Powers in the conduct of its foreign policy, looking to its national interests and assuming that power and military might were what mattered in the lawless realm of international relations. The original idealists, whose most prominent spokesperson was Woodrow Wilson, believed that the United States should act differently from other Great Powers, following its democratic values and seeking a world where anarchy and conflict were replaced by international organization and cooperation. What makes the distinction between realists and idealists more complicated is that each side has traditionally claimed a share of the other's prized values: realists often depict the United States as more righteous than other Great Powers in its use of military might, while idealists often claim that the promotion of democracy and cooperation abroad will safeguard American security better than will a narrow preoccupation with military strength.

During the Cold War, American foreign policy reflected a shifting mix of realism and idealism. The realist side was best symbolized by the arms race, in which the United States spent enormous sums to deter the Soviet Union with nuclear weapons and to fight unconventional wars against communist forces in the Third World. The idealist side was best symbolized by the Peace Corps and other forms of humanitarian assistance, which aimed to show poorer nations that their economic and political development should follow the model of the western nations, not the communist ones. To American critics of the Cold War, a small cohort until the war in Vietnam swelled its ranks, both realism and idealism were suspect, ideological rationalizations for a foreign policy whose real concern was the protection and promotion of American corporate interests around the globe.

With the unexpected collapse of the Soviet Union and the sudden disappearance of the Cold War, makers of foreign policy struggled to find a new strategy for a more complicated and confusing world. Realists and idealists offered competing proposals in a bewildering variety of forms: an active projection of American military power in the name of national interests, a shift in focus from military to economic might, an assertive promotion of fledgling democracies and free markets abroad, a more limited foreign policy that cut back on crusading rhetoric and bloated defense budgets while redirecting resources to domestic needs. As the first post-Cold War president, Bill Clinton did not embrace any single strategy. His consistent campaign to promote global free trade seemed to reflect one form of the realist position. Military interventions in Haiti, Bosnia, and Kosovo that professed to seek humanitarian and peace-keeping objectives placed Clinton in the camp of the idealists. Critics disparaged Clinton's foreign policy as ad hoc, vacillating, and soft-minded. Clinton's defenders responded that the nation was prosperous and at peace during the Clinton years. By Clinton's second term, the public appeared to agree with his defenders, ranking him first in foreign policy among presidents since World War II in a 1998 Gallup Poll.

During the presidential campaign of 2000, candidate George W. Bush assailed Clinton's foreign policy as a way of attacking Vice President Al Gore. In traditional "realist" fashion, Bush charged that Clinton had enmeshed the United States in futile "nation-building" exercises in places like Kosovo while allowing American military strength to erode. Once in office, Bush abandoned many of Clinton's positions, such as support for the Kyoto Protocol to halt global warming, and pursued a more "unilateralist" foreign policy whereby America charted its own course regardless of the concerns of other countries. The terrorist attacks of September 11 initially propelled Bush to seek multilateral support, but after the American success in Afghanistan, the Bush administration again brushed aside the concerns of allied governments and played up the efficacy of America's armed might.

Charles Krauthammer, the conservative columnist who is the author of our first selection, presents a perspective on foreign policy close to the thinking of the Bush administration. Krauthammer pours scorn on President Clinton's foreign policy, depicting it as a "decade-long folly" that centered on a "policy of norms rather than of national interest" and was transfixed by such "transnational trendies" as global warming, the drug traffic, and AIDS. September 11, he suggests, opened our eyes and made us become serious (i.e., realist) again, as we had been during the Cold War. American foreign policy, Krauthammer argues, must be based on the recognition that we are the "hegemon," the dominant power in international relations, and that we should use our superior power actively and aggressively. Fortunately, he claims, no other major powers now resist our hegemony. According to Krauthammer, because nation-states are governed in their foreign policy calculations by "fear" and "respect," as long as the United States is militarily successful in the war on terrorism, the country's international leadership will be secure as it constructs "a New World Order."

The author of our second selection, Benjamin Barber, is a political theorist at the University of Maryland who was friendly with President Clinton. Barber draws different lessons from September 11. The theme of his essay is that the old realism has failed the United States and that "'idealistic' internationalism has become the new realism." From Barber's viewpoint, only if the United States steers clear of undemocratic regimes and addresses the economic injustices that feed terrorism, and only if it comes to understand the cultural conflicts inspiring a fanatical hatred of America among would-be martyrs, can it wage an effective campaign against terrorism. A particularly important stimulus to anti-American sentiment abroad, Barber contends, is the relentless, profit-driven export of American consumerism (he calls it "McWorld"), which threatens traditional religious and ethnic cultures with extinction. In his conclusion, Barber argues that America's strongest weapon in the fight against terror is not military force or free markets. Rather, it is democracy, which will best counter the appeal of fanaticism and reduce the threat of terror.

Realism, reflecting the assumptions of elite democracy, and idealism, reflecting the assumptions of popular democracy, have both been updated for the new debate over U.S. foreign policy after September 11. Which do you think should be the primary shaper of U.S. foreign policy in the struggle against terrorism? Should our foreign policy be based on the assertive use of superior military power in the service of an undisputed American hegemony? Or should military force be used selectively as one element of a foreign policy that promotes the spread of democracy and confronts the political and economic injustices that provoke the terrorists' rage?

The Real New World Order

CHARLES KRAUTHAMMER

I. The Anti-Hegemonic Alliance

On September 11, our holiday from history came to an abrupt end. Not just in the trivial sense that the United States finally learned the meaning of physical vulnerability. And not just in the sense that our illusions about the permanence of the post-Cold War peace were shattered.

We were living an even greater anomaly. With the collapse of the Soviet Union in the early 1990s, and the emergence of the United States as the undisputed world hegemon, the inevitable did not happen. Throughout the three and a half centuries of the modern state system, whenever a hegemonic power has emerged, a coalition of weaker powers has inevitably arisen to counter it. When Napoleonic France reached for European hegemony, an opposing coalition of Britain, Prussia, Russia, and Austria emerged to stop it. Similarly during Germany's two great reaches for empire in the 20th century. It is an iron law: History abhors hegemony. Yet for a decade, the decade of the unipolar moment, there was no challenge to the United States anywhere.

The expected anti-American Great Power coalition never materialized. Russia and China flirted with the idea repeatedly, but never consummated the deal. Their summits would issue communiqués denouncing hegemony, unipolarity, and other euphemisms for American dominance. But they were unlikely allies from the start. Each had more to gain from its relations with America than from the other. It was particularly hard to see why Russia would risk building up a more populous and prosperous next-door neighbor with regional ambitions that would ultimately threaten Russia itself.

The other candidate for anti-hegemonic opposition was a truncated Russia picking up pieces of the far-flung former Soviet empire. There were occasional feints in that direction, with trips by Russian leaders to former allies like Cuba, Iraq, even North Korea. But for the Russians this was even more a losing proposition than during their first go-round in the Cold War when both the Soviet Union and the satellites had more to offer each other than they do today.

With no countervailing coalition emerging, American hegemony had no serious challenge. That moment lasted precisely ten years, beginning with the dissolution of the Soviet Union in December 1991. It is now over. The challenge, long-awaited, finally declared itself on September 11 when the radical Islamic movement opened its worldwide war with a, literally, spectacular attack on the American homeland. Amazingly, however, this anti-hegemonic alliance includes not a single Great Power. It includes hardly any states at all, other than hostage-accomplice Afghanistan.

This is the good news. The bad news is that because it is a sub-state infiltrative entity, the al Qaeda network and its related terrorists around the world lack an address. And a fixed address—the locus of any retaliation—is necessary for effective deterrence. Moreover, with the covert support of some rogue regimes, this terrorist network commands unconventional weapons and unconventional tactics, and is fueled by a radicalism and a suicidal fanaticism that one does not normally associate with adversary states.

This radicalism and fanaticism anchored in religious ideology only increased our shocked surprise. We had given ourselves to believe that after the success of our classic encounters with fascism and Nazism, then communism, the great ideological struggles were finished. This was the meaning of Francis Fukuyama's End of History. There would, of course, be the usual depredations, invasions, aggressions, and simple land grabs of time immemorial. But the truly world-historical struggles were over. The West had won. Modernization was the way. No great idea would arise to challenge it.

Radical Islam is not yet a great idea, but it is a dangerous one. And on September 11, it arose.

II. The American Mind

It took only a few hours for elite thinking about U.S. foreign policy to totally reorient itself, waking with a jolt from a decade-long slumber. During the 1990s, American foreign policy became more utopian and divorced from reality than at any time since our last postwar holiday from history in the 1920s. The liberal internationalists of the Clinton era could not quite match the 1928 Kellogg-Briand Pact abolishing war forever for sheer cosmic stupidity. But they tried hard. And they came close.

Guided by the vision of an autonomous, active, and norm-driven "international community" that would relieve a unilateralist America from keeping order in the world, the Clinton administration spent eight years signing one treaty, convention, and international protocol after another. From this web of mutual obligations, a new and vital "international community" would ultimately regulate international relations and keep the peace. This would, of course, come at the expense of American power. But for those brought up to distrust, and at times detest, American power, this diminution of dominance was a bonus.

To understand the utter bankruptcy of this approach, one needs but a single word: anthrax. The 1972 Biological Weapons Convention sits, with the ABM treaty and the Chemical Weapons Convention, in the pantheon of arms control. We now know that its signing marks the acceleration of the Soviet bioweapons program, of which the 1979 anthrax accident at a secret laboratory at Sverdlovsk was massive evidence, largely ignored. It was not until the fall of the Soviet Union that the vast extent of that bioweapons program was acknowledged. But that—and the post-Gulf War evidence that Iraq, another treaty signatory in good standing, had been building huge stores of bioweapons—made little impression on the liberal-internationalist faithful. Just before September 11, a serious debate was actually about to break out in Congress about the Bush administration's decision to reject the biological weapons treaty's new, and particularly useless, "enforcement" protocol that the Clinton administration had embraced.

After the apocalypse, there are no believers. The Democrats who yesterday were touting international law as the tool to fight bioterrorism are today dodging anthrax spores in their own offices. The very idea of safety-in-parchment is risible. When war breaks out, even treaty advocates take to the foxholes. (The Bush administration is trying to get like-minded countries to sign onto an agreement to prevent individuals from getting easy access to the substrates of bioweapons. That is perfectly reasonable. And it is totally different from having some kind of universal enforcement bureaucracy going around the world checking biolabs, which would have zero effect on the bad guys. They hide everything.)

This decade-long folly—a foreign policy of norms rather than of national interest—is over. The exclamation mark came with our urgent post-September 11 scurrying to Pakistan and India to shore up relations for the fight with Afghanistan. Those relations needed shoring up because of U.S. treatment of India and Pakistan after their 1998 nuclear tests. Because they had violated the universal nonproliferation "norm," the United States automatically imposed sanctions, blocking international lending and aid, and banning military sales. The potential warming of relations with India after the death of its Cold War Soviet alliance was put on hold. And traditionally strong U.S.-Pakistani relations were cooled as a show of displeasure. After September 11, reality once again set in, and such refined nonsense was instantly put aside.

This foreign policy of norms turned out to be not just useless but profoundly damaging. During those eight Clinton years, while the United

States was engaged in (literally) paperwork, the enemy was planning and arming, burrowing deep into America, preparing for war.

When war broke out, eyes opened. You no longer hear that the real issue for American foreign policy is global warming, the internal combustion engine, drug traffic, AIDS, or any of the other transnational trendies of the '90s. On September 11, American foreign policy acquired seriousness. It also acquired a new organizing principle: We have an enemy, radical Islam; it is a global opponent of worldwide reach, armed with an idea, and with the tactics, weapons, and ruthlessness necessary to take on the world's hegemon; and its defeat is our supreme national objective, as overriding a necessity as were the defeats of fascism and Soviet communism.

That organizing principle was enunciated by President Bush in his historic address to Congress. From that day forth, American foreign policy would define itself—and define friend and foe—according to who was with us or against us in the war on terrorism. This is the self-proclaimed Bush doctrine—the Truman doctrine with radical Islam replacing Soviet communism.[1] The Bush doctrine marks the restoration of the intellectual and conceptual simplicity that many, including our last president, wistfully (and hypocritically) said they missed about the Cold War. Henry Kissinger's latest book, brilliant though it is, published shortly before September 11, is unfortunately titled *Does America Need a Foreign Policy*? Not only do we know that it does. We know what it is.

III. The New World Order

The post-September 11 realignments in the international system have been swift and tectonic. Within days, two Great Powers that had confusedly fumbled their way through the period of unchallenged American hegemony in the 1990s began to move dramatically. A third, while not altering its commitments, mollified its militancy. The movement was all in one direction: toward alignment with the United States. The three powers in question— India, Russia, and China—have one thing in common: They all border Islam, and all face their own radical Islamic challenges.

First to embrace the United States was India, a rising superpower, nuclear-armed, economically vibrant, democratic, and soon to be the world's most populous state. For half a century since Nehru's declaration of nonalignment, India had defined itself internationally in opposition to the United States. As one of the founders in 1955 of the nonaligned movement at Bandung, India helped define nonalignment as anti-American. Indeed, for reasons of regional politics (Pakistan's relations with China and with the United States) as well as ideology, India aligned itself firmly with the Soviet Union.

---

1. The Truman Doctrine of 1947 committed the United States to a global "containment" of communism.

That began to fade with the end of the Cold War, and over time relations with the United States might have come to full flower. Nonetheless, September 11 made the transition instantaneous. India, facing its own Taliban-related terrorism in Kashmir, immediately invited the United States to use not just its airspace but its military bases for the campaign in Afghanistan. The Nehru era had ended in a flash. Nonalignment was dead. India had openly declared itself ready to join Pax Americana.

The transformation of Russian foreign policy has been more subtle but, in the long run, perhaps even more far-reaching. It was symbolized by the announcement on October 17 that after 37 years Russia was closing its massive listening post at Lourdes, Cuba. Lourdes was one of the last remaining symbols both of Soviet global ambitions and of reflexive anti-Americanism.

Now, leaving Lourdes is no miracle. It would likely have happened anyway. It is a $200 million a year luxury at a time when the Russian military is starving. But taken together with the simultaneously reported Russian decision to leave Cam Ranh Bay (the former U.S. Naval base in South Vietnam, leased rent-free in 1979 for 25 years), it signaled a new orientation of Russian policy. On his trip to European Union headquarters in early October, President Vladimir Putin made clear that he sees Russia's future with the West—and that he wants the West to see its future including Russia.

This shift is tactical for now. America needs help in the Afghan war. Russia can provide it. It retains great influence over the "-stans," the former Soviet Central Asian republics. From their side, the Russians needs hands off their own Islamic problem in Chechnya. Putin came to deal. In Brussels, he not only relaxed his opposition to NATO's expansion to the borders of Russia, not only signaled his willingness to compromise with the United States on missile defense, but broadly hinted that Russia should in essence become part of NATO.

Were this movement to develop and deepen, to become strategic and permanent, it could become one of the great revolutions in world affairs. For 300 years since Peter the Great, Russia has been unable to decide whether it belongs east or west. But in a world realigned to face the challenge of radical Islam, it is hard to see why Russia could not, in principle, be part of the West. With the Soviet ideology abandoned, Russia's grievances against the West are reduced to the standard clash of geopolitical ambitions. But just as France and Germany and Britain have learned to harmonize their old geopolitical rivalries within a Western structure, there is no reason Russia could not.

Cam Ranh Bay and Lourdes signal Russia's renunciation of global ambitions. What remain are Russia's regional ambitions—to protect the integrity of the Russian state itself, and to command a sphere of influence including its heavily Islamic "near abroad." For the first decade of the post-Cold War era, we showed little sympathy for the first of these goals and none for the second. We looked with suspicion on Russia's reassertion of hegemony over once-Soviet space. The great fight over Caspian oil, for example, was intended to ensure that no pipeline went through Russia (or Iran), lest Russia end up wielding too much regional power.

That day may be over. Today we welcome Russia as a regional power, particularly in Islamic Central Asia. With the United States and Russia facing a similar enemy—the radical Islamic threat is more virulent towards America but more proximate to Russia—Russia finds us far more accommodating to its aspirations in the region. The United States would not mind if Moscow once again gained hegemony in Central Asia. Indeed, we would be delighted to give it back Afghanistan—except that Russia (and Afghanistan) would decline the honor. But American recognition of the legitimacy of Russian Great Power status in Central Asia is clearly part of the tacit bargain in the U.S.-Russian realignment. Russian accommodation to NATO expansion is the other part. The Afghan campaign marks the first stage of a new, and quite possibly historic, rapprochement between Russia and the West.

The third and most reluctant player in the realignment game is China. China is the least directly threatened by radical Islam. It has no Chechnya or Kashmir. But it does have simmering Islamic discontent in its western provinces. It is sympathetic to any attempt to tame radical Islam because of the long-term threat it poses to Chinese unity. At the just completed Shanghai Summit, China was noticeably more accommodating than usual to the United States. It is still no ally, and still sees us, correctly, as standing in the way of its aspirations to hegemony in the western Pacific. Nonetheless, the notion of China's becoming the nidus for a new anti-American coalition is dead. At least for now. There is no Russian junior partner to play. Pakistan, which has thrown in with the United States, will not play either. And there is no real point. For the foreseeable future, the energies of the West will be directed against a common enemy. China's posture of sympathetic neutrality is thus a passive plus: It means that not a single Great Power on the planet lies on the wrong side of the new divide. This is historically unprecedented. Call it hyper-unipolarity. And for the United States, it is potentially a great gain.

With Latin America and sub-Saharan Africa on the sidelines, the one region still in play—indeed the prize in the new Great Game—is the Islamic world. It is obviously divided on the question of jihad against the infidel. Bin Laden still speaks for a minority. The religious parties in Pakistan, for example, in the past decade never got more than 5 percent of the vote combined. But bin Ladenism clearly has support in the Islamic "street." True, the street has long been overrated. During the Gulf War, it was utterly silent and utterly passive. Nonetheless, after five years of ceaseless agitation through Al Jazeera, and after yet another decade of failed repressive governance, the street is more radicalized and more potentially mobilizable. For now, the corrupt ruling Arab elites have largely lined up with the United States, at least on paper. But their holding power against the radical Islamic challenge is not absolute. The war on terrorism, and in particular the Afghan war, will be decisive in determining in whose camp the Islamic

world will end up: ours—that of the United States, the West, Russia, India—
or Osama bin Laden's.

IV. The War

The asymmetry is almost comical. The whole world against one man. If in
the end the United States, backed by every Great Power, cannot succeed in
defeating some cave dwellers in the most backward country on earth, then
the entire structure of world stability, which rests ultimately on the pacify-
ing deterrent effect of American power, will be fatally threatened.[2]

Which is why so much hinges on the success of the war on terrorism.
Initially, success need not be defined globally. No one expects a quick victory over an entrenched and shadowy worldwide network. Success does,
however, mean demonstrating that the United States has the will and
power to enforce the Bush doctrine that governments will be held accountable for the terrorists they harbor. Success therefore requires making an example of the Taliban. Getting Osama is not the immediate goal. Everyone
understands that it is hard, even for a superpower, to go on a cave-to-cave
manhunt. Toppling regimes is another matter. For the Taliban to hold off
the United States is an astounding triumph. Every day that they remain in
place is a rebuke to American power. Indeed, as the war drags on, their
renown, particularly in the Islamic world, will only grow.

After September 11, the world awaited the show of American might. If
that show fails, then the list of countries lining up on the other side of the
new divide will grow. This is particularly true of the Arab world with its
small, fragile states. Weaker states invariably seek to join coalitions of the
strong. For obvious reasons of safety, they go with those who appear to be
the winners. (Great Powers, on the other hand, tend to support coalitions of
the weak as a way to create equilibrium. Thus Britain was forever balancing
power on the Continent by supporting coalitions of the weak against a suc-
cession of would-be hegemons.) Jordan is the classic example. Whenever
there is a conflict, it tries to decide who is going to win, and joins that side.
In the Gulf War, it first decided wrong, then switched to rejoin the American side. That was not out of affection for Washington. It was cold realpolitik. The improbable pro-American Gulf War coalition managed to include
such traditional American adversaries as Syria because of an accurate Syrian
calculation of who could overawe the region.

The Arab states played both sides against the middle during the Cold
War, often abruptly changing sides (e.g., Egypt during the '60s and '70s).
They lined up with the United States against Iraq at the peak of American
unipolarity at the beginning of the 1990s. But with subsequent American
weakness and irresolution, in the face both of post–Gulf War Iraqi defiance

---

2. Krauthammer's essay was published before the defeat of the Taliban regime.

and of repeated terrorist attacks that garnered the most feckless American military responses, respect for American power declined. Inevitably, the pro-American coalition fell apart.

The current pro-American coalition will fall apart even more quickly if the Taliban prove a match for the United States. Contrary to the current delusion that the Islamic states will respond to American demonstrations of solicitousness and sensitivity (such as a halt in the fighting during Ramadan), they are waiting to see the sources of American power before irrevocably committing themselves. The future of Islamic and Arab allegiance will depend on whether the Taliban are brought to grief.

The assumption after September 11 was that an aroused America will win. If we demonstrate that we cannot win, no coalition with moderate Arabs will long survive. But much more depends on our success than just the allegiance of that last piece of the geopolitical puzzle, the Islamic world. The entire new world alignment is at stake.

States line up with more powerful states not out of love but out of fear. And respect. The fear of radical Islam has created a new, almost unprecedented coalition of interests among the Great Powers. But that coalition of fear is held together also by respect for American power and its ability to provide safety under the American umbrella. Should we succeed in the war on terrorism, first in Afghanistan, we will be cementing the New World Order—the expansion of the American sphere of peace to include Russia and India (with a more neutral China)—just now beginning to take shape. Should we fail, it will be *sauve qui peut.*[3] Other countries—and not just our new allies but even our old allies in Europe—will seek their separate peace. If the guarantor of world peace for the last half century cannot succeed in a war of self-defense against Afghanistan(!), then the whole post-World War II structure—open borders, open trade, open seas, open societies—will begin to unravel.

The first President Bush sought to establish a New World Order. He failed, in part because he allowed himself to lose a war he had just won. The second President Bush never sought a New World Order. It was handed to him on Sept. 11. To maintain it, however, he has a war to win.

---

3. "Every man for himself."

On Terrorism
and the New
Democratic Realism

BENJAMIN R. BARBER

T
he terrorist attacks of September 11 did without a doubt change the world forever, but they failed to change the ideological viewpoint of either the left or the right in any significant way. The warriors and unilateralists of the right still insist war conducted by an ever-sovereign America is the only appropriate response to terrorism, while the left continues to talk about the need for internationalism, interdependency and an approach to global markets that redresses economic imbalances and thereby reduces the appeal of extremism—if, in the climate of war patriotism, it talks a little more quietly than heretofore. The internationalist lobby has a right to grow more vociferous, however, for what has changed in the wake of September 11 is the relationship between these arguments and political realism (and its contrary, political idealism). Prior to September 11, realpolitik (though it could speak with progressive accents, as it did with Ronald Steel and E. H. Carr before him) belonged primarily to the right—which spurned talk of human rights and democracy as hopelessly utopian, the blather of romantic left-wing idealists who preferred to see the world as they wished it to be rather than as it actually was

Following September 11, however, the realist tiger changed its stripes: "Idealistic" internationalism has become the new realism. We face not a paradigm shift but the occupation of an old paradigm by new tenants. Democratic globalists are quite abruptly the new realists while the old realism—especially in its embrace of markets—looks increasingly like a dangerous and utterly unrealistic dogma opaque to our new realities as brutally inscribed on the national consciousness by the demonic architects of September 11. The issue is not whether to pursue a military or a civic strategy, for both are clearly needed; the issue is how to pursue either one.

The historical realist doctrine was firmly grounded in an international politics of sovereign states pursuing their interests in a setting of shifting alliances where principles could only obstruct the achievement of sovereign ends that interests alone defined and served. Its mantras—the clichés of Lord Acton, Henry Morgenthau, George Kennan or, for that matter, Henry Kissinger—had it that nations have neither permanent friends nor permanent enemies but only permanent interests; that the enemies of our enemies are always our friends; that the pursuit of democratic ideals or human rights can often obfuscate our true interests; that coalitions and alliances in war or peace are tolerable only to the degree that we retain our sovereign independence in all critical decisions and policies; and that international institutions are to be embraced, ignored or discarded exclusively on the basis of how well they serve our sovereign national interests, which are entirely separable from the objectives of such institutions.

However appealing these mantras may seem, and though upon occasion they served to counter the hypocritical use of democratic arguments to disguise interests (as when true democrats attacked Woodrow Wilson's war to make the world "safe for democracy"), they can no longer be said to represent even a plausible, let along a realistic, strategy in our current circumstances. To understand why, we need to understand how September 11 put a period once and for all at the end of the old story of American independence.

Many would say the two great world wars of the past century, even as they proved American power and resilience, were already distinct if unheeded harbingers of the passing of our sovereignty; for, though fought on foreign soil, they represented conflicts from which America could not be protected by its two oceans, struggles whose outcomes would affect an America linked to the then-nascent global system. Did anyone imagine that America could be indifferent to the victory of fascism in Europe or Japanese imperialism in Asia (or, later, of Soviet Communism in Eurasia) as it might once have been indifferent to the triumph of the British or Belgian or French empires in Africa? By the end of the twentieth century, irresistible interdependence was a leitmotif of every ecological, technological and economic event. It could hardly escape even casual observers that global warming recognizes no sovereign territory, that AIDS carries no passport, that technology renders national boundaries increasingly meaningless, that the Internet defies national regulation, that oil and cocaine addiction circle the planet like twin plagues and that financial capital and labor resources, like their anarchic cousins crime and terror, move from country to country with "wilding" abandon without regard for formal or legal arrangements—acting informally and illegally whenever traditional institutions stand in their way.

Most nations understood the significance of these changes well enough, and well before the end of the past century Europe was already on the way to forging transnational forms of integration that rendered its member nations' sovereignty dubious. Not the United States. Wrapped in its national myths of splendid isolation and blessed innocence (chronicled insightfully by Herman Melville and Henry James), it held out. How easy it was, encircled by two oceans and reinforced lately in its belief in sovereign invincibility by the novel utopia of a missile shield—technology construed as a virtual ocean to protect us from the world's turmoil and dangers—to persist in the illusion of sovereignty. The good times of the 1990s facilitated an easy acquiescence in the founding myths, for in that (suddenly remote) era of prideful narcissism, other people's troubles and the depredations that were the collateral damage of America's prosperous and productive global markets seemed little more than diverting melodramas on CNN's evening "news" soap operas.

Then came September 11. Marauders from the sky, from above and abroad but also from within and below, sleepers in our midst who somehow were leveraging our own powers of technology to overcome our might, made a mockery of our sovereignty, demonstrating that there was no longer any difference between inside and outside, between domestic and international. We still don't know authoritatively who precisely sponsored the acts of September 11 or the bioterror that followed it: What alone has become clear is that we can no longer assign culpability in the neat nineteenth-century terms of domestic and foreign. And while we may still seek sovereign sponsors for acts of terror that have none, the myth of our independence can no longer be sustained. Nonstate actors, whether they are multinational corporations or loosely knit terrorist cells, are neither domestic nor foreign, neither national nor international, neither sovereign entities nor international organizations. Going on about states that harbor terrorists (our "allies" Egypt and Saudi Arabia? Our good friend Germany? Or how about Florida and New Jersey?) simply isn't helpful in catching the bad guys. The Taliban are gone, and bin Ladin will no doubt follow, but terrorism's network exists in anonymous cells we can neither identify nor capture. Declaring our independence in a world of perverse and malevolent interdependence foisted on us by people who despise us comes close to what political science roughnecks once would have called pissing into the wind. Pakistan and Saudi Arabia still foster schools that teach hate, and suicide bombers are still lining up in Palestine for martyrdom missions in numbers that suggest an open call for a Broadway show.

The American myth of independence is not the only casualty of September 11. Traditional realist paradigms fail us today also because our adversaries are no longer motivated by "interest" in any relevant sense, and this makes the appeal to interest in the fashion of realpolitik and rational-choice theory seem merely foolish. Markets may be transnational instruments of interest, and even bin Laden has a kind of "list of demands" (American troops out of Saudi Arabia, Palestine liberated from Israeli "occupation," down with the infidel empire), but terrorists are not stubborn negotiators pursuing rational agendas. Their souls yearn for other days when certainty was unencumbered, for other worlds where paradise offered other rewards. Their fanaticism has causes and their zeal has its reasons, but market conceptions of interest will not succeed in fathoming them. Bombing Hanoi never brought the Vietcong to their knees, and they were only passionate nationalists, not messianic fundamentalists; do we think we can bomb into submission the millions who resent, fear and sometimes detest what they think America means?

Or take the realist epigram about nations having neither permanent friends nor permanent enemies. It actually turns out that America's friends, defined not by interests but by principles, are its best allies and most reliable coalition partners in the war on terrorism. Even conservative realists have acknowledged that Israel—whatever one thinks of Sharon's policies—is a formidable ally in part because it is the sole democracy in the Middle East. By the same token, we have been consistently betrayed by an odd assortment of allies born of shifting alliances that have been forged and broken in pursuit of "friendship" with the enemies of our enemies: Iraq, Iran and those onetime allies of convenience in the war against the Soviets, the Taliban. Then there are the countless Islamic tyrannies that are on our side only because their enemies have in turn been the enemies of American economic interests or threats to the flow of oil. I will leave it to others to determine how prudent our realist logic is in embracing Egypt, Saudi Arabia, Yemen or Pakistan, whose official media and state-sponsored schools often promulgate the very propaganda and lies we have joined with them to combat.

On the other hand, the key principles at stake—democracy and pluralism, a space for religion safe from state and commercial interference, and a space for government safe from sectarianism and the ambitions of theocrats—actually turn out to be prudent and useful benchmarks for collecting allies who will stand with us in the war on terrorism. In the new post-September 11 realism, it is apparent that the only true friends we have are the democracies, and they are friends because they *are* democracies and share our values even when they contest our interests and are made anxious by our power. In the war against terror or the war for freedom, what true realist would trade a cantankerous, preternaturally anti-American France for a diplomatic and ostentatiously pro-American Saudi Arabia?

Yet the pursuit of democracy has been a sideline in an American realist foreign policy organized around oil and trade with despots pretending to be on our side—not just in Republican but in Democratic administrations as well, where democracy was proclaimed but (remember Larry Summers) market democracy construed as market fundamentalism was practiced.[1] In the old paradigm, democratic norms were very nice as emblems of abstract belief and utopian aspirations, or as rationalizations of conspicuous interests, but they were poor guides for a country seeking status and safety in the world. Not anymore. The cute cliché about democracies not making war on one another is suddenly a hard realist foundational principle for national security policy.

Except the truth today is not only that democracies do not make war on one another, but that democracies alone are secure from collective forms of violence and reactionary fundamentalism, whether religious or ethnic. Those Islamic nations (or nations with large Islamic populations) that have made progress toward democracy—Bangladesh, India or Turkey, for example—have been relatively free of systematic terrorism and reactionary

---

1. Lawrence Summers was President Clinton's third secretary of the treasury.

fundamentalism as well as the export of terrorism. They may still persecute minorities, harbor racists and reflect democratic aspirations only partially, but they do not teach hate in their schools or pipe propaganda through an official press or fund terrorist training camps. Like India recently, they are the victims rather than the perpetrators of international terrorism. Making allies of the enemies of democracy because they share putative interests with us is, in other words, not realism but foolish self-deception. We have learned from the military campaign against the Taliban and Al Qaeda how, when push comes to shove (push has come to shove!), the Egyptians and the Saudis can be unreliable in sharing intelligence, interdicting the funding of terrorism or standing firm against the terrorists at their own door. Pakistan still allows thousands of fundamentalist *madrassahs* to operate as holy-war training schools. Yet how can these "allies" possibly be tough when, in defense of their despotic regimes, they think that coddling the terrorists outside their doors may be the price they have to pay for keeping at bay the terrorists already in their front parlors? The issue is not religion, not even fundamentalism; the issue is democracy.

Unilateralism rooted in a keen sense of the integrity of sovereign autonomy has been another keynote of realism's American trajectory and is likely to become another casualty of September 11. From the Monroe Doctrine to our refusal to join the League of Nations, from the isolationism that preceded World War II, and from which we were jarred only by Pearl Harbor, to the isolationism that followed the war and that yielded only partially to the cold war and the arms race, and from our reluctance to pay our UN dues or sign on to international treaties to our refusal to place American troops under the command of friendly NATO foreigners, the United States has persisted in reducing foreign policy to a singular formula that preaches going it alone. Despite the humiliations of the 1970s, when oil shortages, emerging ecological movements and the Iranian hostage crisis should have warned us of the limitations of unilateralism, we went on playing the Lone Ranger, the banner of sovereign independence raised high.

We often seem nearly comatose when it comes to the many small injuries and larger incursions to which American sovereignty is subjected on a daily basis by those creeping forms of interdependence that characterize modernity—technology, ecology, trade, pop culture and consumer markets. Only the blunt assault of the suicide bombers awoke the nation to the new realities and the new demands on policy imposed by interdependence. Which is why, since September 11, there has been at least a wan feint in the direction of multilateralism and coalition-building. The long-unpaid UN bills were finally closed out, the Security Council was consulted and some Republican officials even whispered the dreaded Clinton-tainted name of nation-building as a possible requirement in a postwar strategy in Afghanistan.

Yet there is a long way to go. While the Colin Powell forces do battle with the Dick Cheney forces for the heart of the President, little is being done to open a civic and political front in the campaign against terrorism.[2] After what seemed a careful multilateral dance with President Putin on missile defense, President Bush has abruptly thrust his ballroom partner aside and waltzed off into the sunset by himself, leaving the Russians and Chinese (and our European allies) to sulk in the encroaching gloom. Even in Afghanistan, Nicholas Kristof, in his first contribution as the *New York Times's* new crisis-of-terrorism columnist, complained that even as other nations' diplomats poured into the capital after its fall, the United States posted not a single representative to Kabul to begin nurturing a postwar political and civil strategy—a reticence it has only just now begun to remedy.

Is there anything realistic about such reluctance? On the contrary, realism here in its new democratic form suggests that America must begin to engage in the slow and sovereignty-eroding business of constructing a cooperative and benevolent interdependence in which it joins the world rather than demanding that the world join it or be consigned to the camp of the terrorists ("You are with us or you are with the terrorists," intoned the President in those first fearful days after September 11). This work recognizes that while terrorism has no justification, it does have causes. The old realism went by the old adage *tout comprendre, c'est tout pardonner*[3] and eschewed deep explanations of the root causes of violence and terror. The new realism insists that to understand collective malice is not to pardon it but to assure that it can be addressed, interdicted and perhaps even preempted. "Bad seed" notions of original sin ("the evil ones") actually render perpetrators invulnerable—subject only to a manichean struggle in which the alternative to total victory is total defeat. Calling bin Laden and his associates "the evil ones" is not necessarily inaccurate, but it commits us to a dark world of *jihad* and counter*jihad* (what the President first called his crusade), in which issues of democracy, civil comity and social justice—let alone nuance, complexity and interdependence—simply vanish. It is possible to hate *jihad* without loving America. It is possible to condemn terror as absolutely wrong without thinking that those who are terror's targets possess absolute right.

This is the premise behind the thesis of interdependence. The context of jihadic resistance and its pathology of terrorism is a complex world in which there are causal interrelationships between the jihadic reaction to modernity and the American role in shaping it according to the peculiar logic of US technology, markets and branded pop culture (what I call McWorld). Determining connections and linkages is not the same thing as distributing blame. Power confers responsibility. The power enjoyed by the United States bestows on it obligations to address conditions it may not

---

2. Many observers of the Bush administration perceive a conflict over foreign policy between Secretary of State Colin Powell, a moderate, and Vice President Richard Cheney, a conservative.
3. "To understand all is to forgive all."

have itself brought into being. *Jihad* in this view may grow out of and reflect (among other things) a pathological metastasis of valid grievances about the effects of an arrogant secularist materialism that is the unfortunate concomitant of the spread of consumerism across the world. It may reflect a desperate and ultimately destructive concern for the integrity of indigenous cultural traditions that are ill equipped to defend themselves against aggressive markets in a free-trade world. It may reflect a struggle for justice in which Western markets appear as obstacles rather than facilitators of cultural identity.

Can Asian tea, with its religious and family "tea culture," survive the onslaught of the global merchandising of cola beverages? Can the family sit-down meal survive fast food, with its focus on individualized consumers, fuel-pit-stop eating habits and nourishment construed as snacking? Can national film cultures in Mexico, France or India survive Hollywood's juggernaut movies geared to universal teen tastes rooted in hard violence and easy sentiment? Where is the space for prayer, for common religious worship or for spiritual and cultural goods in a world in which the 24/7 merchandising of material commodities makes the global economy go round? Are the millions of American Christian families who home-school their children because they are so intimidated by the violent commercial culture awaiting the kids as soon as they leave home nothing but an American Taliban? Do even those secular cosmopolitans in America's coastal cities want nothing more than the screen diet fed them by the ubiquitous computers, TVs and multiplexes?

Terror obviously is not an answer, but the truly desperate may settle for terror as a response to our failure even to ask such questions. The issue for *jihad*'s warriors of annihilation is of course far beyond such anxieties: It entails absolute devotion to absolute values. Yet for many who are appalled by terrorism but unimpressed by America, there may seem to be an absolutist dimension to the materialist aspirations of our markets. Our global market culture appears to us as both voluntary and wholesome; but it can appear to others as both compelling (in the sense of compulsory) and corrupt—not exactly coercive, but capable of seducing children into a willed but corrosive secular materialism. What's wrong with Disneyland or Nikes or the Whopper? We just "give people what they want." But this merchandiser's dream is a form of romanticism, the idealism of neoliberal markets, the convenient idyll that material plenty can satisfy spiritual longing so that fishing for profits can be thought of as synonymous with trolling for liberty.

It is the new democratic realist who sees that if the only choice we have is between the mullahs and the mall, between the hegemony of religious absolutism and the hegemony of market determinism, neither liberty nor the human spirit is likely to flourish. As we face up to the costs both of fundamentalist terrorism and of fighting it, must we not ask ourselves how it is that when we see religion colonize every other realm of human life we call it theocracy and turn up our noses at the odor of tyranny; and when we see politics colonize every other realm of human life we call it absolutism and tremble at the prospect of totalitarianism; but when we see market relations and commercial consumerism try to colonize every other realm of human life we call it liberty and celebrate its triumph? There are too many John Walkers[4] who begin by seeking a refuge from the aggressive secularist materialism of their suburban lives and end up slipping into someone else's dark conspiracy to rid the earth of materialism's infidels. If such men are impoverished and without hope as well, they become prime recruits for *jihad.*

The war on terrorism must be fought, but not as the war of McWorld against *jihad.* The only war worth winning is the struggle for democracy. What the new realism teaches is that only such a struggle is likely to defeat the radical nihilists. That is good news for progressives. For there are real options for democratic realists in search of civic strategies that address the ills of globalization and the insecurities of the millions of fundamentalist believers who are neither willing consumers of Western commercial culture nor willing advocates of jihadic terror. Well before the calamities of September 11, a significant movement in the direction of constructive and realistic interdependence was discernible, beginning with the Green and human rights movements of the 1960s and '70s, and continuing into the NGO and "anti-globalization" movements of the past few years.[5] Jubilee 2000 managed to reduce Third World debt-service payments for some nations by up to 30 percent, while the Community of Democracies initiated by the State Department under Madeleine Albright has been embraced by the Bush Administration and will continue to sponsor meetings of democratic governments and democratic NGOs. International economic reform lobbies like the Millennium Summit's development goals project, established by the UN to provide responses to global poverty, illiteracy and disease; Inter Action, devoted to increasing foreign aid; Global Leadership, a start-up alliance of corporations and grassroots organizations; and the Zedillo Commission, which calls on the rich countries to devote 0.7 percent of their GNP to development assistance (as compared to an average of 0.2 percent today and under 0.1 percent for the United States), are making serious economic reform an issue for governments. Moreover, and more important, they are insisting with Amartya Sen and his new disciple Jeffrey Sachs that development requires democratization first if it is to succeed.[6]

George Soros's Open Society Institute and Civicus, the transnational umbrella organization for NGOs, continue to serve the global agenda of civil society. Even corporations are taking an interest: Hundreds are collabo-

---

4. John Walker Lindh is a young American captured while fighting for the Taliban forces in Afghanistan.
5. The acronym NGO stands for nongovernmental organization.
6. Amartya Sen and Jeffrey Sachs are prominent international economists.

rating in a Global Compact, under the aegis of UN Secretary General Kofi Annan, to seek a response to issues of global governance, while the World Economic Forum plans to include fifty religious leaders in a summit at its winter meeting in New York in late January.

This is only a start, and without the explicit support of a more multilateralist and civic-minded American government, such institutions are unlikely to change the shape of global relations. Nonetheless, in closing the door on the era of sovereign independence and American security, anarchic terrorism has opened a window for those who believe that social injustice, unregulated wild capitalism and an aggressive secularism that leaves no space for religion and civil society not only create conditions on which terrorism feeds but invite violence in the name of rectification. As a consequence, we are at a seminal moment in our history—one in which trauma opens up the possibility of new forms of action. Yesterday's utopia is today's realism; yesterday's realism, a recipe for catastrophe tomorrow. If ever there was one, this is democracy's moment. Whether our government seizes it will depend not just on George Bush but on us.

DISCUSSION QUESTIONS

1. Will the assertive projection of American global hegemony that Krauthammer proposes intimidate or crush American adversaries and remove the threat they pose to our security? Or will it foster fresh resentments and breed new terrorists who view the United States as the cause for their societies' problems?

2. Does Barber's emphasis on promoting the international spread of democracy offer an effective response to the terrorists? Will the reforms he favors take root too slowly to safeguard Americans from terrorist attacks?

3. Does U.S. security in the post-September 11 world lie more with the realists' recommendations for the assertive use of power and force or with the idealists' recommendations for addressing the undemocratic and unequal conditions that spawn hatred against Americans?

4. How might Krauthammer and Barber debate the impact of the war against terrorism on democracy, freedom, and equality in the United States?

SUGGESTED READINGS AND INTERNET RESOURCES

The interplay among rival American traditions in foreign policy is the subject of Walter Russell Mead, *Special Providence: American Foreign Policy and How It Reshaped the World* (New York: Knopf, 2001). An important new version of realist thinking is John J. Mearsheimer, *The Tragedy of Great Power Politics* (New York: Norton, 2001). International threats to democracy from both free market consumerism and its opposite, reactionary tribalism, are the concern of Benjamin R. Barber, *Jihad vs. McWorld: How Globalism and Tribalism Are Reshaping the World* (New York: Ballantine Books, 1996). For an iconoclastic account of the post–Cold War American military, see William Greider, *Fortress America: The American Military and the Consequences of Peace* (New York: Public Affairs, 1999). The origins of the Bush administration's drive for a national missile defense in the dreams of Ronald Reagan are described in revealing detail in Frances Fitzgerald, *Way Out There in the Blue: Reagan, Star Wars, and the End of the Cold War* (New York: Simon and Schuster, 2000).

Council on Foreign Relations
www.cfr.org
The web site for the premier mainstream organization of U.S. foreign policy offers information on numerous dimensions of international relations, including terrorism.

Center for Defense Information
www.cdi.org
This site offers detailed information and analyses on foreign policy issues and includes a frequently updated "terrorism project."

Federation of American Scientists
www.fas.org
This site offers numerous articles on terrorism, going back to the mid-1990s, and supplies links to government web sites that are focused on terrorist threats against Americans.

CREDITS

BARBER, BENJAMIN R.: Benjamin R. Barber, "On Terrorism and the New Democratic Realism," *The Nation,* January 21, 2002, pp. 11–18. Benjamin R. Barber is Kekst Professor of Civil Society at the University of Maryland, Director, New York office, *The Democratic Collaborative* and the author of many books including *Strong Democracy* (1984), *Jihad vs. McWorld* (Times Books, 1995), *The Truth of Power: Intellectual Affairs in the Clinton White House* (W.W. Norton & Company).

BOWLES, SAMUEL, AND RICHARD EDWARDS: Samuel Bowles and Richard Edwards, "The Market Erodes Democratic Government" from *Understanding Capitalism,* (pages 411, 413, 418–423, 430–439). © 1993 Addison Wesley Longman, Inc. Reprinted by permission of the authors.

BROOKS, DAVID: David Brooks, "The Age of Conflict: Politics and Culture after September 11," *The Weekly Standard,* Vol. 7, No. 8, p. 19, November 5, 2001. Reprinted by permission.

BROOKS, DAVID: David Brooks, "One Nation, Slightly Divisible," *The Atlantic Monthly,* December 2001, pp. 53–65. Reprinted by permission of the author.

COX, W. MICHAEL, AND RICHARD ALM: From *Myths of the Rich and Poor* by W. Michael Cox and Richard Alm. Copyright © 1999 by W. Michael Cox and Richard Alm. Reprinted by permission of Basic Books, a member of Perseus Books, L.L.C. This selection can be found on page 320 of this text.

DONAHUE, JOHN D.: From *Disunited States* by John D. Donahue. Copyright © 1997 by John D. Donahue. Reprinted by permission of Basic Books, a member of Perseus Books, L.L.C. This selection can be found on page 60 of this text.

EASTERBROOK, GREGG: Gregg Easterbrook, "Suburban Myth," is reprinted by permission of *The New Republic,* © 1999, The New Republic, L.L.C.

EGGERS, WILLIAM D., AND JOHN O'LEARY: Reprinted with the permission of The Free Press, an imprint of Simon & Schuster Adult Publishing Group, from *Revolution at the Roots: Making Our Government Smaller, Better, and Closer to Home* by William D. Eggers and John O'Leary. Copyright © 1995 by William D. Eggers and John O'Leary.

FIORINA, MORRIS P.: From *Congress: Keystone of the Washington Establishment* by Morris P. Fiorina. Copyright © 1989 by Yale University Press. Reprinted with permission.

FRANKEL, MARVIN E.: Excerpt from "Piety Versus 'Secular Humanism': A Phony War" from *On Faith and Freedom* by Marvin E. Frankel. Copyright © 1995 by Marvin

377

E. Frankel. Reprinted by permission of Hill and Wang, a division of Farrar, Straus and Giroux, L.L.C.

FRIEDMAN, MILTON: From *Capitalism and Freedom* by Milton Friedman. Copyright © 1982 by the University of Chicago Press. Reprinted by permission.

FRIEDMAN, THOMAS L.: Excerpts from Preface, Chapter 1 "Tourist with an Attitude," Chapter 15 "Rational Exuberance," and Chapter 16 "Revolution Is U.S." from *The Lexus and the Olive Tree: Understanding Globalization* by Thomas L. Friedman. Copyright 1999 by Thomas L. Friedman. Reprinted by permission of Farrar, Straus and Giroux, L.L.C.

GALSTON, WILLIAM A., AND PETER LEVINE: William A. Galston and Peter Levine, *America's Civic Condition: A Glance at the Evidence* from *The Brookings Review,* Fall 1997, Vol. 15, No. 4, pp. 23–26. Reprinted with permission by The Brookings Institution Press.

GUINIER, LANI: Lani Guinier, "What We Must Overcome," is reprinted with permission from *The American Prospect,* Volume 12, Number 5: March 12–26, 2001. The American Prospect, 5 Broad Steet, Boston, MA 02109. All rights reserved.

KORTEN, DAVID C.: From *The Case Against the Global Economy* by Jerry Mander and Edward Goldsmith. Copyright © 1996 by Sierra Club Books. Reprinted with permission.

KRAUTHAMMER, CHARLES: Charles Krauthammer, "The Real New World Order: The American and the Islamic Challenge." Charles Krauthammer is a contributing editor of *The Weekly Standard* magazine, where this article originally appeared (November 12, 2001). It is reprinted with Dr. Krauthammer's permission.

KRUGMAN, PAUL: Paul Krugman, "The Spiral of Inequality" from *Mother Jones* magazine (Nov.–Dec. 1996), © 1996, Foundation for National Progress. Reprinted by permission.

LOEB, PAUL ROGAT: Copyright © 1999 by Paul Rogat Loeb. From *Soul of a Citizen* by Paul Rogat Loeb. Reprinted by permission of St. Martin's Press, LLC.

MONSMA, STEPHEN V.: *Positive Neutrality: Letting Religious Freedom Ring,* Stephen V. Monsma. Copyright © 1993 by Stephen V. Monsma. Reproduced with permission of Greenwood Publishing Group, Inc., Westport, CT.

MOYERS, BILL: Bill Moyers, "Which America Will We Be Now?" Reprinted with permission from the November 19, 2001 issue of *The Nation.*

MUELLER, JOHN: John Mueller, *Capitalism, Democracy, and Ralph's Pretty Good Grocery.* Copyright © 1997 by Princeton University Press. Reprinted by permission of Princeton University Press.

PUTNAM, ROBERT D.: "The Collapse of American Community" is reprinted with permission of Simon & Schuster from *Bowling Alone: The Collapse and Revival of American Community* by Robert D. Putnam. Copyright © 2000 by Robert Putnam.

SHIPLER, DAVID K.: From *A Country of Strangers* by David K. Shipler. Copyright © 1997 by David K. Shipler. Reprinted by permission of Alfred A. Knopf, a division of Random House, Inc.

SKOWRONEK, STEPHEN: Reprinted by permission of Stephen Skowronek. Excerpts from "Notes on the Presidency in the Political Order" by Stephen Skowronek from *Studies in American Political Development,* Vol. 1 (1984). Reprinted with the permission of Cambridge University Press. Stephen Skowronek, "The Changing Political Structures of Presidential Leadership," adapted from the essay, "The Setting: Change and Continuity in the Politics of Leadership" from *The Elections of 2000,* Michael Nelson, Editor. Copyright © 2001 Congressional Quarterly, Inc.

SMITH, BRADLEY A.: Reprinted from *Commentary,* December 1997, by permission of the publisher and the author, all rights reserved. The author is an Associate Professor at Capital University Law School, Columbus, Ohio.

SUNSTEIN, CASS R.: Cass R. Sunstein, an edited version of "The Daily We" as originally published in the Summer of 2001 issue of *Boston Review.* Reprinted by permission of the author.

THERNSTROM, STEPHAN, AND ABIGAIL THERNSTROM: Reprinted with the permission of Simon & Schuster Adult Publishing Group from *America in Black and White: One Nation Indivisible* by Stephen Thernstrom and Abigail Thernstrom. Copyright © 1997 by Stephen Thernstrom and Abigail Thernstrom.